New Perspectives on

THE INTERNET

3rd Edition

Introductory

GARY P. SCHNEIDER
University of San Diego

JESSICA EVANS

**COURSE
TECHNOLOGY**
THOMSON LEARNING

Australia • Canada • Mexico • Singapore • Spain • United Kingdom • United States

COURSE TECHNOLOGY
™
THOMSON LEARNING

New Perspectives on The Internet—Introductory, 3rd Edition

is published by Course Technology.

Managing Editor:
Greg Donald

Senior Editor:
Donna Gridley

Senior Product Manager:
Kathy Finnegan

Product Manager:
Melissa Hathaway

Technology Project Manager:
Amanda Young

Editorial Assistant:
Jessica Engstrom

Marketing Manager:
Sean Teare

Developmental Editors:
Jane Pedicini
Lisa Ruffolo

Production Editor:
Daphne Barbas

Composition:
GEX Publishing Services

Text Designer:
Meral Dabcovich

Cover Designer:
Efrat Reis

Preface

Course Technology is the world leader in information technology education. The New Perspectives Series is an integral part of Course Technology's success. Visit our Web site to see a whole new perspective on teaching and learning solutions.

New Perspectives—Building Computer Skills Has Never Been This Real

Why New Perspectives will work for you.

Critical thinking and **problem solving**—without them, computer skills are learned but soon forgotten. With its **case-based** approach, the New Perspectives Series challenges students to apply what they've learned to real-life situations. Become a member of the New Perspectives community and watch your students not only **master** computer skills, but also **retain** and carry this **knowledge** into the world.

New Perspectives catalog
Our online catalog is never out of date! Go to the Catalog button on our Web site to check out our available titles, request a desk copy, download a book preview, or locate online files.

Complete system of offerings
Whether you're looking for a Brief book, an Advanced book, or something in between, we've got you covered. Go to the Catalog button on our Web site to find the level of coverage that's right for you.

Instructor materials
We have all the tools you need—data files, solution files, figure files, a sample syllabus, and ExamView, our powerful testing software package.

How well do your students know Microsoft Office?
Find out with performance-based testing software that measures your students' proficiency in the application. Click the Tech Center button to learn more.

Get certified
If you want to get certified, we have the titles for you. Find out more by clicking the Teacher's Lounge button.

Interested in online learning?
Enhance your course with any one of our online learning platforms. Go to the Teacher's Lounge to find the platform that's right for you.

Your link to the future is at
www.course.com/NewPerspectives

What you need to know about this book.

- Student Online Companion takes students to the Web for additional work.

- ExamView testing software gives you the option of generating a printed test, LAN-based test, or test over the Internet.

- New Perspectives Labs provide students with self-paced practice on computer-related topics.

- There are many NEW cases in this edition!

- Introduces latest Internet technologies such as satellite connectivity and Internet Protocol version 6.

- Coverage includes both major Web browsers in use today.

- New Session 3.4 covers Web-based e-mail clients and provides steps students can follow to create their own accounts.

- New Session 6.3 includes coverage of using online storage services to store and transfer files.

CASE	TROUBLE?	SESSION 1.1	QUICK CHECK	RW
Tutorial Case Each tutorial begins with a problem presented in a case that is meaningful to students. The case sets the scene to help students understand what they will do in the tutorial.	**TROUBLE? Paragraphs** These paragraphs anticipate the mistakes or problems that students may have and help them continue with the tutorial.	**Sessions** Each tutorial is divided into sessions designed to be completed in about 45 minutes each. Students should take as much time as they need and take a break between sessions.	**Quick Check Questions** Each session concludes with conceptual Quick Check questions that test students' understanding of what they learned in the session.	**Reference Windows** Reference Windows are succinct summaries of the most important tasks covered in a tutorial. They preview actions students will perform in the steps to follow.

BRIEF CONTENTS

TABLE OF CONTENTS

Tutorial 3   WEB 3.01

E-Mail Basics

Evaluating Integrated Browser E-Mail Programs and a Web-Based E-Mail Service

The Internet

Tutorial 4   WEB 4.03

Searching the Web

Using Search Engines and Directories Effectively

Tutorial 5 — WEB 5.01

Information Resources on the Web

Finding, Evaluating, and Using Web Information Resources

Tutorial 6 — WEB 6.01

FTP and Downloading and Storing Data

Using FTP and Other Services to Transfer and Store Data

Acknowledgments

Creating a textbook is a collaborative effort—authors and publisher work as a team to provide the highest quality book possible. The authors want to acknowledge the major contributions of the Course Technology editorial team members. We thank Mac Mendelsohn for his initial interest in and continual support of this book. It was Mac's vision for a book focused on the Internet, rather than on a specific software application, that motivated us to take on this project. We offer a special thank you to Martha Wagner, former Course Technology sales representative, for introducing us to Mac. We are grateful to Melissa Hathaway, Product Manager; Amanda Young, Associate Product Manager; Daphne Barbas, Production Editor; and John Bosco's team of Quality Assurance testers for being terrific, positive, and supportive members of a great publishing team. We also thank Jane Pedicini and Lisa Ruffolo, our Developmental Editors. Their sharp eyes caught many mistakes and they contributed excellent ideas for making the manuscript more readable. We offer our heartfelt thanks to the Course Technology organization as a whole. The people at Course Technology have been, by far, the best publishing team with which we have ever worked.

We want to thank the following reviewers for their insightful comments and suggestions at various stages of the book's development: Risa Blair, Champlain College; Donna Occhifinto, County College of Morris; Cathy Fothergill, Kilgore College; Don Lopez, The Clovis Center; Suzanne Nordhaus, Lee College; Sorel Reisman, California State University, Fullerton; T. Michael Smith, Austin Community College; and Bill Wagner, Villanova University. Margaret Beeler and Pamela Drotman provided helpful comments on early drafts of the outline for the first edition of this book.

Finally, we want to express our deep appreciation for the continuous support and encouragement of our spouses, Cathy Cosby and Richard Evans. They demonstrated remarkable patience as we worked to complete this book on a very tight schedule. We also thank our children for tolerating our absences while we were busy writing.

Gary P. Schneider

Jessica Evans

Dedication

To the memory of my brother, Bruce. — G.P.S.

To my little buddy, Hannah, who is "wise and talented." — J.E.

New Perspectives on

THE
INTERNET

3rd Edition

Read This Before You Begin

To the Student

Data Disks

To complete the Level I tutorials, Review Assignments, and Case Problems in this book, you need one Data Disk. Your instructor will either provide you with a Data Disk or ask you to make your own.

If you are making your own Data Disk, you will need **one** blank, formatted, high-density disk. You will need to copy a set of files and/or folders from a file server, a standalone computer, or the Web onto your disk. Your instructor will tell you which computer, drive letter, and folders contain the files you need. You could also download the files by going to **www.course.com** and following the instructions on the screen.

The information below shows you which folders go on your disk, so that you will have enough disk space to complete all the tutorials, Review Assignments, and Case Problems:

Data Disk 1

Write this on the disk label:
Data Disk 1: Tutorials 2 and 3

Put these folders on the disk:
Tutorial.02
Tutorial.03

When you begin each tutorial, be sure you are using the correct Data Disk. Refer to the "File Finder" chart at the back of this text for more detailed information on which files are used in the tutorials. See the inside front or inside back cover of this book for more information on Data Disk files, or ask your instructor or technical support person for assistance.

Course Labs

The tutorials in this book feature two interactive Course Labs to help you understand Internet and e-mail concepts. There are Lab Assignments at the end of Tutorials 2 and 3 that relate to these Labs.

To start a Lab, click the **Start** button on the Windows taskbar, point to **Programs**, point to **Course Labs**, point to **New Perspectives Course Labs**, and click the name of the Lab you want to use.

Using Your Own Computer

If you are going to work through this book using your own computer, you need:

■ **Computer System** Netscape Navigator 4.0 or higher or Microsoft Internet Explorer 4.0 or higher and Windows 95 or higher must be installed on your computer. This book assumes a complete installation of the Web browser software and its components, and that you have an existing e-mail account and an Internet connection. Because your Web browser may be different from the ones used in the figures or the book, your screens may differ slightly at times.

■ **Data Disk** You will not be able to complete the tutorials or exercises in this book using your own computer until you have a Data Disk.

■ **Course Labs** See your instructor or technical support person to obtain the Course Lab software for use on your own computer.

Visit Our World Wide Web Site

Additional materials designed especially for you are available on the World Wide Web.

Go to www.course.com/NewPerspectives.

To the Instructor

The Data Disk files and Course Labs are available on the Instructor's Resource Kit for this title. Follow the instructions in the Help file on the CD-ROM to install the programs to your network or standalone computer. For information on creating the Data Disk, see the "To the Student" section above. To complete the tutorials in this book, students must have a Web browser, an e-mail account, and an Internet connection.

You are granted a license to copy the Data Disk files and Course Labs to any computer or computer network used by students who have purchased this book.

In this tutorial you will:

- Obtain an overview of the tools and information that are available on the Internet

- Learn what computer networks are and how they work

- Find out how the Internet and World Wide Web began and grew

- Compare and evaluate different methods for connecting to the Internet

INTRODUCTION TO THE INTERNET AND THE WORLD WIDE WEB

History, Potential, and Getting Connected

CASE

Tropical Exotics Produce Company

Lorraine Tomassini, the owner of the Tropical Exotics Produce Company (TEPCo), is concerned about the firm's future. She started TEPCo 10 years ago to import organically grown exotic fruits and vegetables from South America, Africa, and Asia to the U.S. market. The TEPCo product line includes items such as Asian pear, cherimoya, feijoa, African horned melon, sapote, and tamarillo. The business has grown rapidly and thrived financially, but Lorraine is worried that TEPCo is failing to use technology effectively. She already knows that this weakness has caused TEPCo to lose customers and suppliers to competitors.

You started work as an intern at TEPCo six months ago to learn more about international business while you attend college. Justin Jansen has been with the firm for about five years and is Lorraine's key assistant. During this week's meeting with you and Justin, Lorraine expressed concern that TEPCo has become internally focused and might be missing major market trends that affect its worldwide suppliers. She worries that reading newspapers for market information and staying in touch with suppliers by telephone are time-consuming, ineffective strategies. She recalled this past year, when bad weather in Costa Rica destroyed most of their suppliers' sapote crop, TEPCo received the reports too late to change its customer price schedule, in effect, wiping out almost all of the company's second quarter profit.

Justin explained that people can follow weather reports from all over the world using the Internet. He then suggested that TEPCo might be able to attract new customers by creating a Web site on the Internet, but he also explained that first TEPCo's five computers would need to be connected to each other. Lorraine also knew that colleges and universities had been involved in the Internet for years. She asked you to research ways that TEPCo might use the Internet, and you agreed to begin the research immediately.

SESSION 1.1

In this session, you will learn about the Internet and World Wide Web. You will learn how they have grown from their beginnings in the military and research communities. You will learn about the vast array of resources they provide and how the Internet has become one of the most powerful communication tools the world has ever known.

Internet and World Wide Web: Amazing Developments

The **Internet**—a large collection of computers all over the world that are connected to one another in various ways—is one of the most amazing technological developments of the twentieth century. Using the Internet you can communicate with other people throughout the world through **electronic mail** (or **e-mail**); read online versions of newspapers, magazines, academic journals, and books; join discussion groups on almost any conceivable topic; participate in games and simulations; and obtain free computer software. In recent years, the Internet has allowed commercial enterprises to connect. Today, all kinds of businesses provide information about their products and services on the Internet. Many of these businesses use the Internet to market and sell their products and services. The part of the Internet known as the **World Wide Web** (or the **Web**), is a subset of the computers on the Internet that are connected to each other in a specific way that makes those computers and their contents easily accessible to all computers in that subset. The Web has helped to make Internet resources available to people who are not computer experts. Figure 1-1 shows some of the tools and resources available on the Internet today.

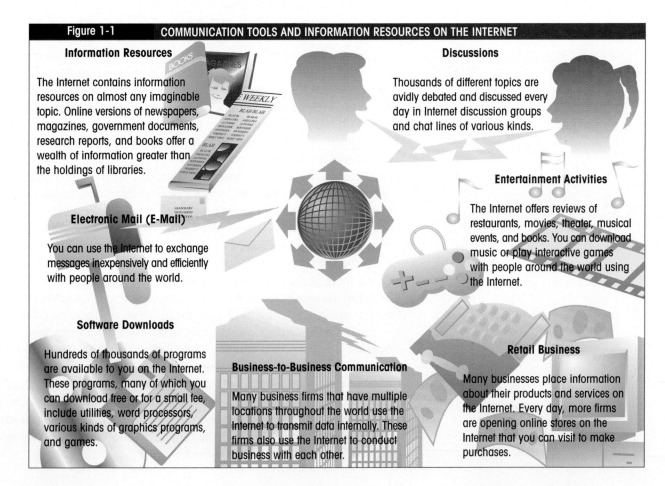

Figure 1-1   COMMUNICATION TOOLS AND INFORMATION RESOURCES ON THE INTERNET

Information Resources

The Internet contains information resources on almost any imaginable topic. Online versions of newspapers, magazines, government documents, research reports, and books offer a wealth of information greater than the holdings of libraries.

Discussions

Thousands of different topics are avidly debated and discussed every day in Internet discussion groups and chat lines of various kinds.

Entertainment Activities

The Internet offers reviews of restaurants, movies, theater, musical events, and books. You can download music or play interactive games with people around the world using the Internet.

Electronic Mail (E-Mail)

You can use the Internet to exchange messages inexpensively and efficiently with people around the world.

Software Downloads

Hundreds of thousands of programs are available to you on the Internet. These programs, many of which you can download free or for a small fee, include utilities, word processors, various kinds of graphics programs, and games.

Business-to-Business Communication

Many business firms that have multiple locations throughout the world use the Internet to transmit data internally. These firms also use the Internet to conduct business with each other.

Retail Business

Many businesses place information about their products and services on the Internet. Every day, more firms are opening online stores on the Internet that you can visit to make purchases.

As you begin Lorraine's research project, you remember her comment that TEPCo does not have its computers connected to each other. You decide to learn more about what computer networks are and how to connect computers to each other to form those networks.

Computer Networks

After talking with Adolfo Segura, the director of your school's computer lab, you realize that you will have some good news for Lorraine. Adolfo explained to you that he linked the lab computers to each other by inserting a network interface card into each computer and connecting cables from each card to the lab's main computer, called a server. Adolfo told you that a **network interface card** (often called a **NIC** or simply network card) is a card or other device used to connect a computer to a network of other computers. A **server** is a general term for any computer that accepts requests from other computers that are connected to it and shares some or all of its resources, such as printers, files, or programs, with those computers.

Client/Server Local Area Networks

The server runs software that coordinates the information flow among the other computers, which are called **clients**. The software that runs on the server computer is called a **network operating system**. Connecting computers this way, in which one server computer shares its resources with multiple client computers, is called a **client/server network**. Client/server networks commonly are used to connect computers that are located close together (for example, in the same room or building). Because the direct connection from one computer to another through network cards only works over relatively short distances (no more than a few thousand feet), this kind of network is called a **local area network** (**LAN**). Figure 1-2 shows a typical client/server LAN.

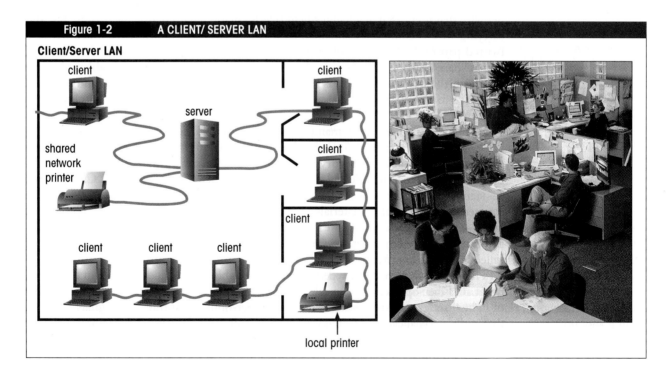

Figure 1-2   A CLIENT/ SERVER LAN

have voluntarily agreed to share resources and network connections with one another. You decide that your project is starting to become interesting and head toward the campus library to find out more about this huge interconnected network called the Internet.

How the Internet Began

In the early 1960s, the U.S. Department of Defense (DOD) undertook a major research project. Because this was a military project and was authorized as a part of national security, the true motivations are not known with certainty, but most people close to the project believe it arose from the government's concerns about the possible effects of nuclear attack on military computing facilities. The DOD realized that the weapons of the future would require powerful computers for coordination and control. The powerful computers of that time were all large mainframe computers, so the DOD began examining ways to connect these computers to each other and also to weapons installations that were distributed all over the world.

The agency charged with this task was the **Advanced Research Projects Agency (ARPA)**. (During its lifetime, this agency has used two acronyms, ARPA and DARPA; this book uses its current acronym, **DARPA**, for **Defense Advanced Research Projects Agency**.) DARPA hired many of the best communications technology researchers and for many years funded research at leading universities and institutes to explore the task of creating a worldwide network. DARPA researchers soon became concerned about computer networks' vulnerability to attack and worked hard to devise ways to eliminate the need for network communications to rely on a central control function.

Circuit Switching vs. Packet Switching

The first networks among computers were created in the 1950s. The models for those early networks were the telephone companies because most early WANs used leased telephone company lines to connect computers to each other. In telephone company systems of that time, a telephone call established a single connection between sender and receiver. Once the connection was established, all data then traveled along that single path. The telephone company's central switching system selected specific telephone lines, or circuits, that would be connected to create the single path. This centrally controlled, single-connection method is called **circuit switching**. Most local telephone traffic today is still handled using circuit switching technologies.

Although the circuit switching is efficient and economical, it relies on a central point of control and a series of connections that form a single path. This makes circuit-switched communications vulnerable to the destruction of the central control point or any link in the series of connections that make up the single path that carries the signal. DARPA researchers turned to a different method of sending information, packet switching. In a **packet switching** network, files and messages are broken down into packets that are labeled electronically with codes for their origin and destination. The packets travel from computer to computer along the network until they reach their destination. The destination computer collects the packets and reassembles the original data from the pieces in each packet. Each computer that an individual packet encounters on its trip through the network determines the best way to move the packet forward to its destination. Computers that perform this function on networks are often called **routers**, or routing computers, and the programs they use to determine the best path for packets are called **routing algorithms**. Thus, packet-switched networks are inherently more reliable than circuit-switched networks because they rely on multiple routers instead of a central point of control and because each router can send individual packets along different paths if parts of the network are not operating.

By 1967, DARPA researchers had published their plan for a packet switching network, and in 1969, they connected the first computer switches at the University of California at Los Angeles, SRI International, the University of California at Santa Barbara, and the University of Utah. This experimental WAN, called the **ARPANET**, grew over the next three years to include over 20 computers and used the **Network Control Protocol** (**NCP**). A **protocol** is a collection of rules for formatting, ordering, and error-checking data sent across a network.

Open Architecture Philosophy

As more researchers connected their computers and computer networks to the ARPANET, interest in the network grew in the academic community. The next several years saw many technological developments that increased the speed and efficiency with which the network operated. One reason for the project's success was its adherence to an **open architecture** philosophy; that is, each network could continue using its own protocols and data-transmission methods internally. Conversion to NCP occurred only when the data moved out of the local network and onto the ARPANET. The original purpose of the ARPANET was to connect computers in the field that were controlling a wide range of diverse weapons systems, so the ARPANET could not force its protocol or structure onto those individual component networks. This open approach was quite different from the closed architecture designs that companies such as IBM and Digital Equipment Corporation were using to build networks for their customers during this period. The open architecture philosophy included four key points:

- Independent networks should not require any internal changes to be connected to the Internet.
- Packets that do not arrive at their destinations must be retransmitted from their source network.
- The router computers do not retain information about the packets they handle.
- No global control will exist over the network.

One of the new developments of this time period that was rapidly adopted throughout the ARPANET was a set of new protocols developed by Vincent Cerf and Robert Kahn. These new protocols were the **Transmission Control Protocol** and the **Internet Protocol**, which usually are referred to by their combined acronym, **TCP/IP**. TCP includes rules that computers on a network use to establish and break connections; IP includes rules for routing of individual data packets. These two protocols were technically superior to the NCP that ARPANET had used since its inception and gradually replaced that protocol. TCP/IP continues to be used today in LANs and on the Internet. The term *Internet* was first used in a 1974 article about the TCP protocol written by Cerf and Kahn. The importance of the TCP/IP protocol in the history of the Internet is so great that many people consider Vincent Cerf to be the Father of the Internet.

ARPANET's successes were not lost on other network researchers. Many university and research institution computers used the UNIX operating system. When TCP/IP was included in a version of UNIX, these institutions found it easier to create networks and interconnect them. A number of TCP/IP-based networks—independent of the ARPANET—were created in the late 1970s and early 1980s. The National Science Foundation (NSF) funded the **Computer Science Network** (**CSNET**) for educational and research institutions that did not have access to the ARPANET. The City University of New York started a network of IBM mainframes at universities, called the **Because It's Time** (originally, "**There**") **Network** (**BITNET**).

Birth of E-Mail: A New Use for Networks

Although the goals of ARPANET were still to control weapons systems and transfer research files, other uses for this vast network began to appear in the early 1970s. In 1972, an ARPANET researcher named Ray Tomlinson wrote a program that could send and receive messages over the network. E-mail had been born and became widely used in 1976; the Queen of England sent an e-mail message over the ARPANET. By 1981, the ARPANET had expanded to include over 200 networks and was continuing to develop faster and more effective network technologies; for example, ARPANET began sending packets via satellite in 1976.

More New Uses for Networks Emerge

The number of network users in the military and education research communities continued to grow. Many of these new participants used the networking technology to transfer files and access computers remotely. The TCP/IP suite included two tools for performing these tasks. **File Transfer Protocol** (**FTP**) enabled users to transfer files between computers, and **Telnet** let users log in to their computer accounts from remote sites. Both FTP and Telnet still are widely used on the Internet today for file transfers and remote logins, even though more advanced techniques facilitate multimedia transmissions such as real-time audio and video clips. The first e-mail mailing lists also appeared on these networks. A **mailing list** is an e-mail address that takes any message it receives and forwards it to any user who has subscribed to the list.

Although file transfer and remote login were attractive features of these new TCP/IP networks, their improved e-mail and other communications facilities attracted many users in the education and research communities. For example, BITNET would run mailing list software (called **LISTSERV**) on its IBM mainframe computers that provided automatic control and maintenance for mailing lists. In 1979, a group of students and programmers at Duke University and the University of North Carolina started Usenet, an acronym for **User's News Network**. Usenet allows anyone that connects with the network to read and post articles on a variety of subjects.

Usenet survives on the Internet today, with more than a thousand different topic areas, called **newsgroups**. Going even farther from the initial purpose of TCP/IP networks, researchers at the University of Essex wrote a program that allowed users to assume character roles and play an adventure game. This adventure game let multiple users play at the same time and interact with each other. These text-based games are much more primitive than the video games that many people play today on their computers or gaming devices, however a surprising number of people continue to play them on the Internet. These games are called **MUDs**, which originally stood for **multiuser dungeon**, although many users now consider the term an acronym for **multiuser domain** or **multiuser dimension**.

Although the people using these networks were developing many creative applications, the number of persons who had access to the networks was relatively small and limited to members of the research and academic communities. The decade from 1979 to 1989 would be the time in which these new and interesting network applications were improved and tested with an increasing number of users. The TCP/IP set of protocols would become more widely used as academic and research institutions realized the benefits of having a common communications network. The explosion of PC use during that time also would help more people become comfortable with computing.

Interconnecting the Networks

The early 1980s saw continued growth in the ARPANET and other networks. The **Joint Academic Network** (**Janet**) was established in the United Kingdom to link universities there. Traffic increased on all of these networks, and in 1984, the Department of Defense

(DOD) split the ARPANET into two specialized networks: ARPANET would continue its advanced research activities, and **MILNET** (for **Military Network**) would be reserved for military uses that required greater security. That year also saw a new addition to CSNET, named the **National Science Foundation Network (NSFnet)**. By 1987, congestion on the ARPANET caused by a rapidly increasing number of users on the limited-capacity leased telephone lines was becoming severe. To reduce the government's traffic load on the ARPANET, the NSFnet merged with BITNET and CSNET to form one network. The resulting NSFnet awarded a contract to Merit Network, Inc., IBM, Sprint, and the State of Michigan to upgrade and operate the main NSFnet backbone. A **network backbone** includes the long-distance lines and supporting technology that transports large amounts of data between major network nodes. The NSFnet backbone connected 13 regional WANs and six supercomputer centers. By the late 1980s, many other TCP/IP networks had merged or established interconnections. Figure 1-4 summarizes how the individual networks described in this section combined to become the Internet as it is known today.

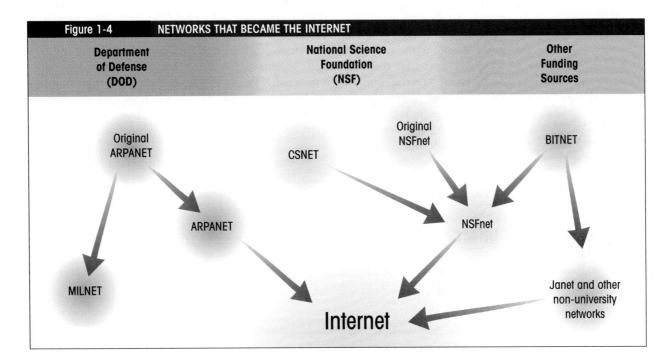

| Figure 1-4 | NETWORKS THAT BECAME THE INTERNET |

Commercial Interest Increases

As PCs became more powerful, affordable, and available during the 1980s, firms increasingly used them to construct LANs. Although these LANs included e-mail software that employees could use to send messages to each other, businesses wanted their employees to be able to communicate with people outside their corporate LANs. The National Science Foundation (NSF) prohibited commercial network traffic on the networks it funded, so businesses turned to commercial e-mail services. Larger firms built their own TCP/IP-based WANs that used leased telephone lines to connect field offices to corporate headquarters. Today, people use the term **intranet** to describe LANs or WANs that use the TCP/IP protocol but do not connect to sites outside the firm. Although most companies allow only their employees to use the company intranet, some companies give specific outsiders, such as customers, vendors, or business partners, access to their intranets. These outside parties agree to respect the confidentiality of the information on the network. An intranet that allows selected outside parties to connect is often called an **extranet**.

In 1989, the NSF permitted two commercial e-mail services, MCI Mail and CompuServe, to establish limited connections to the Internet that allowed their commercial subscribers to exchange e-mail messages with the members of the academic and research communities who were connected to the Internet. These connections allowed commercial enterprises to send e-mail directly to Internet addresses and allowed members of the research and education communities on the Internet to send e-mail directly to MCI Mail and CompuServe addresses. The NSF justified this limited commercial use of the Internet as a service that would primarily benefit the Internet's noncommercial users.

People from all walks of life—not just scientists or academic researchers—started thinking of these networks as a global resource that we now know as the Internet. Information systems professionals began to form volunteer groups such as the **Internet Engineering Task Force (IETF)**, which first met in 1986. The IETF is a self-organized group that makes technical contributions to the engineering of the Internet and its technologies. IETF is the main body that develops new Internet standards.

Just as the world was coming to realize the value of these interconnected networks, however, it also became aware of the threats to privacy and security posed by these networks. In 1988, Robert Morris launched a program called the **Internet Worm** that used weaknesses in e-mail programs and operating systems to distribute itself to over 6,000 of the 60,000 computers that were then connected to the Internet. The Worm program created multiple copies of itself on the computers it infected. The large number of program copies consumed the processing power of the infected computer and prevented it from running other programs. This event brought international attention and concern to the Internet. Unfortunately, worms and other programs still appear on the Internet from time to time today, and they still can do considerable damage.

Although the network of networks that is now known as the Internet had grown from four computers on the ARPANET in 1969 to over 300,000 computers on many interconnected networks by 1990, the greatest growth in the Internet was yet to come.

Growth of the Internet

A formal definition of Internet, which was adopted in 1995 by the Federal Networking Council (FNC), appears in Figure 1-5.

Figure 1-5	THE FNC'S OCTOBER 1995 RESOLUTION TO DEFINE THE TERM INTERNET

RESOLUTION: The Federal Networking Council (FNC) agrees that the following language reflects our definition of the term Internet. Internet refers to the global information system that

(i) is logically linked together by a globally unique address space based on the Internet Protocol (IP) or its subsequent extensions/follow-ons;

(ii) is able to support communications using the Transmission Control Protocol/Internet Protocol (TCP/IP) suite or its subsequent extensions/follow-ons, and/or other IP-compatible protocols; and

(iii) provides, uses or makes accessible, either publicly or privately, high level services layered on the communications and related infrastructure described herein.

Source: *http://www.fnc.gov/Internet_res.html*

Many people find it interesting that a formal definition of the term did not appear until 1995. The Internet was a phenomenon that surprised an unsuspecting world. The researchers who had been so involved in the creation and growth of the Internet accepted it as part of their working environment. People outside the research community were largely unaware of the potential offered by a large interconnected set of computer networks.

From Research Project to Information Infrastructure

By 1990, the Internet had become a well-functioning grid of useful technology. Much of the funding for these networks had come from the U.S. government, through the DOD and NSF. The NSFnet alone consumed over $200 million from 1986 to 1995 on research and development. Realizing that the Internet was no longer a research project, the DOD finally closed the research portion of its network, the ARPANET. The NSF also wanted to turn over the Internet to others so it could return its attention and funds to other research projects.

In 1991, the NSF further eased its restrictions on Internet commercial activity and began implementing plans to eventually privatize much of the Internet. The first parts of the NSFnet on which it encouraged commercial activity were the local and regional nodes, which allowed time for private firms to develop long-haul network capacity similar to that of the NSFnet national network backbone. Businesses and individuals connected to the Internet in ever-increasing numbers. Although nobody really knows how big the Internet is, one commonly used measure is the number of Internet hosts. An **Internet host** is a computer that connects a LAN or a WAN to the Internet. Each Internet host might have any number of computers connected to it. Figure 1-6 shows the rapid growth in the number of Internet host computers from 1991 through 2001. As you can see, the growth has been dramatic.

Figure 1-6	GROWTH IN THE NUMBER OF INTERNET HOSTS

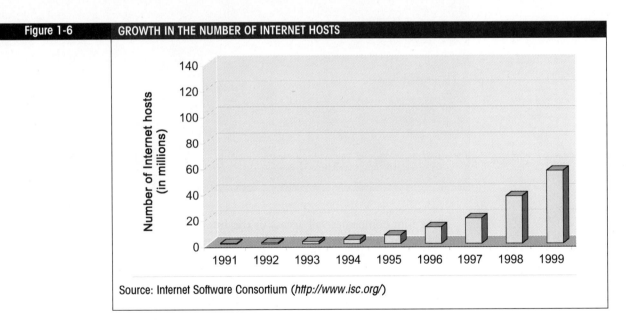

Source: Internet Software Consortium (*http://www.isc.org/*)

The numbers in Figure 1-6 probably understate the true growth of the Internet in recent years for two reasons. First, the number of hosts connected to the Internet includes only directly connected computers. In other words, if a LAN with 100 PCs is connected to the Internet through only one host computer, those 100 computers appear as one host in the count. Because the number and size of LANs has increased steadily in recent years, the host count probably is understated. Second, the number of computers is only one measure of growth. Internet traffic now carries more files that contain graphics, sound, and video, so Internet files have become larger. A given number of users sending video clips will use much more of the Internet's capacity than the same number of users will use by sending e-mail messages or text files. Many people are surprised to learn that no one knows how many users are on the Internet. The Internet has no central management or coordination, and the routing computers do not maintain records of the packets they handle. Although some companies and research organizations regularly estimate the Internet population, no one really knows how many individual e-mail messages or files travel on the Internet, and no one really knows how many people use the Internet today.

New Structure for the Internet

As NSFnet converted the main traffic-carrying backbone portion of its network to private firms, it organized the network around four network access points (NAPs). However, a different company now operates each of these NAPs, as shown in Figure 1-7.

Figure 1-7	NETWORK ACCESS POINTS ON THE INTERNET BACKBONE

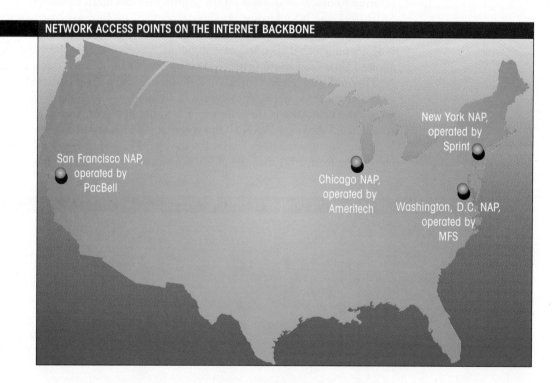

These four companies sell access to the Internet through their NAPs to organizations and businesses. The NSFnet still exists for government and research use, but it uses these same NAPs for long-range data transmission.

With more than 120 million connected Internet host computers and more than 500 million worldwide Internet users, the Internet faces some challenges. The firms that sell network access have enough incentive to keep investing in the network architecture because they can recoup their investments by attracting new Internet users. However, the existing TCP/IP numbering system that identifies users will run out of addresses in a few years if the Internet continues its current rate of growth. The version of the protocol that most router computers use today is IP version 4 (IPv4), which provides a maximum of about 4 billion addresses. In 1997, the IETF approved a new version of the protocol, IP version 6 (IPv6) that permits many more addresses (the actual number is 134 followed by 152 zeroes). The new addressing scheme will allow existing users to continue accessing the Internet while the new system is implemented. Although some organizations have rebuilt their networks to use IPv6, full adoption by all Internet users will take many years.

In just over 30 years, the Internet has become one of the most amazing technological and social accomplishments of the century. Millions of people use a complex, interconnected network of computers that run thousands of different software packages. The computers are located in almost every country of the world. Billions of dollars change hands every year over the Internet in exchange for all kinds of products and services. All of this activity occurs with no central coordination point or control. Even more interesting is that the Internet most likely began as a way for the military to maintain control while under attack.

The opening of the Internet to business enterprise helped increase its growth dramatically in recent years. However, another development worked hand-in-hand with the commercialization of the Internet to spur its growth. That development was the technological advance known as the World Wide Web.

World Wide Web

The World Wide Web (the Web) is more a way of thinking about information storage and retrieval than it is a technology. Because of this, its history goes back many years. Two important innovations played key roles in making the Internet easier to use and more accessible to people who were not research scientists: hypertext and graphical user interfaces (GUIs).

Origins of Hypertext

In 1945, Vannevar Bush, who was Director of the U.S. Office of Scientific Research and Development, wrote an *Atlantic Monthly* article about ways that scientists could apply the skills they learned during World War II to peacetime applications. The article included a number of visionary ideas about future uses of technology to organize and facilitate efficient access to information. He speculated that engineers eventually would build a machine that he called the **Memex**, a memory extension device that would store all of a person's books, records, letters, and research results on microfilm. Bush's Memex would include mechanical aids to help users consult their collected knowledge fast and in a wide variety of ways. In the 1960s, Ted Nelson described a similar system in which text on one page links to text on other pages. Nelson called his page-linking system **hypertext**. Douglas Englebart, who also invented the computer mouse, created the first experimental hypertext system on one of the large computers of the 1960s. Twenty years later, Nelson published *Literary Machines*, in which he outlined project Xanadu, a global system for online hypertext publishing and commerce.

Hypertext and Graphical User Interfaces Come to the Internet

In 1989, Tim Berners-Lee and Robert Calliau were working at CERN-The European Laboratory for Particle Physics and were trying to improve the laboratory's research document-handling procedures. CERN had been connected to the Internet for two years, but its scientists wanted to find better ways to circulate their scientific papers and data among the high-energy physics research community throughout the world. Independently, they each proposed a hypertext development project.

Over the next two years, Berners-Lee developed the code for a hypertext server program and made it available on the Internet. A **hypertext server** is a computer that stores files written in the hypertext markup language and lets other computers connect to it and read those files. **Hypertext Markup Language** (**HTML**) is a language that includes a set of codes (or tags) attached to text. These codes describe the relationships among text elements. For example, HTML includes tags that indicate which text is part of a header element, which text is part of a paragraph element, and which text is part of a numbered list element. One important type of tag is the hypertext link **tag**. A **hypertext link**, or **hyperlink**, points to another location in the same or another HTML document. You can use several different types of software to read HTML documents, but most people use a Web browser such as Netscape Navigator or Microsoft Internet Explorer. A **Web browser** is software that lets users read (or browse) HTML documents and move from one HTML document to another through the text formatted with hypertext link tags in each file. If the HTML documents are on computers connected to the Internet, you can use a Web browser to move from an HTML document on one computer to an HTML document on any other computer on the Internet. HTML is a subset of **Standard Generalized Markup Language** (**SGML**), which organizations have used for many years to manage large document-filing systems.

An HTML document differs from a word-processing document because it does not specify *how* a particular text element will appear. For example, you might use word-processing software to create a document heading by setting the heading text font to Arial, its font size to 14 points, and its position to centered. The document would display and print these exact settings whenever you opened the document in that word processor. In contrast, an HTML document would simply include a heading tag with the text. Many different programs can read an HTML document. Each program recognizes the heading tag and displays the text in whatever manner each program normally displays headers. Different programs might display the text differently.

A Web browser presents an HTML document in an easy-to-read format in its graphical user interface. A **graphical user interface** (**GUI,** pronounced "gooey") is a way of presenting program output using pictures, icons, and other graphical elements instead of just displaying text. Almost all PCs today use a GUI such as Microsoft Windows or the Macintosh user interface. Researchers have found that computer users—especially new users—learn new programs more quickly when they have a GUI interface instead of a text interface. Because each Web page has its own set of controls (hyperlinks, buttons to click, and blank text boxes in which to type text), every person who visits a Web site for the first time becomes a "new user" of that site. Thus, the GUI interface presented in Web browsers has been an important element in the rapid growth of the Web.

Berners-Lee and Calliau called their system of hyperlinked HTML documents the World Wide Web. The Web caught on rapidly in the scientific research community, but few people outside that community had software that could read the HTML documents. In 1993, a group of students led by Marc Andreessen at the University of Illinois wrote **Mosaic**, the first GUI program that could read HTML and use HTML documents' hyperlinks to navigate from page to page on computers anywhere on the Internet. Mosaic was the first Web browser that became widely available for PCs.

The Web and Commercialization of the Internet

Programmers quickly realized that a functional system of pages connected by hypertext links would provide many new Internet users with an easy way to locate information on the Internet. Businesses quickly recognized the profit-making potential offered by a worldwide network of easy-to-use computers. In 1994, Andreessen and other members of the University of Illinois Mosaic team joined with James Clark of Silicon Graphics to found Netscape Communications. Their first product, the Netscape Navigator Web browser program based on Mosaic, was an instant success. Netscape became one of the fastest growing software companies ever.

Microsoft created its Internet Explorer Web browser and entered the market soon after Netscape's success became apparent. Microsoft offered its browser at no cost to computer owners that used its Windows operating system. Within a few years, many users had switched to Internet Explorer, and Netscape was unable to earn enough money to continue in business. Microsoft was accused of wielding its monopoly power to drive Netscape out of business; these accusations led to the trial of Microsoft on charges that it violated the U.S. anti-trust laws. Parts of Netscape were sold to America Online, but the Netscape Navigator browser became open-source software. Open-source software is created and maintained by volunteer programmers, often hundreds of them, who work together using the Internet to build and refine a program. The program is made available to users at no charge. A few other Web browsers exist, but most people today use either Internet Explorer or Netscape Navigator.

The number of **Web sites**, which are computers connected to the Internet that store HTML documents, has grown even more rapidly than the Internet itself to include more than 30 million sites. Each Web site might have hundreds, or even thousands, of individual Web pages, so the amount of information on the Web is astounding. Figure 1-8 shows the phenomenal growth in the Web during its short lifetime.

Figure 1-8	GROWTH OF THE WORLD WIDE WEB

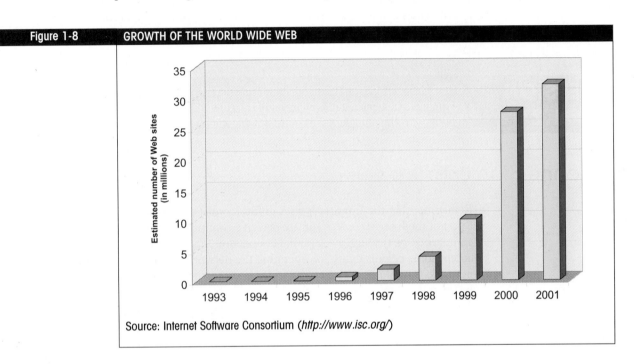

Source: Internet Software Consortium (*http://www.isc.org/*)

As more people obtain access to the Web, commercial uses of the Web and a variety of non-business uses will continue to increase. Although the Web has grown rapidly, many experts believe that it will grow at an increasing rate for the foreseeable future.

You have obtained a good background for your report on how TEPCo might use the Internet and the Web by learning about their histories. You are convinced that the Internet can help Lorraine and her staff manage the company better, identify new customers, and stay in contact with suppliers. You decide that the next logical step in your research is to identify ways that TEPCo can connect to the Internet. In the next session, you will learn how to evaluate Internet connection options.

Session 1.1 QUICK CHECK

1. Name three resources that computers connected to a client/server LAN can share.

2. The fastest and most expensive way to connect computers in a network is _____ *fiber optic* _____ cable.

3. Telephone companies use centrally controlled circuit switching to connect telephone callers and transmit data. The Internet uses the _____ *packet* _____ switching method.

4. The technical term for the collection of rules that computers follow when formatting, ordering, and error-checking data sent across a network is _____ *protocol* _____.

5. The networks that became the Internet were originally designed to transmit files; however, early in its history, people found other uses for the Internet. Name one of those uses.

6. A network that uses the TCP/IP protocol, but only connects computers within one company is called a(n) _____ *LAU* .

7. Two key factors that contributed to the Internet's rapid growth in the 1990s are _____ and _____ .

8. The software that network users can run on their computers to access HTML documents stored on other computers is called a(n) _____ .

SESSION 1.2

In this session, you will learn about how to connect your computer to the Internet. You will learn about the connection options that are available and their advantages and disadvantages. You will be able to then choose the one that is right for you.

Connection Options

Remember that the Internet is a set of interconnected networks. Thus, you cannot become a part of the Internet unless you are part of a communications network, whether it is a LAN, an intranet, or through a telephone connection. Each network that joins the Internet must accept some responsibility for operating the network by routing message packets that other networks pass along. As you consider your project for TEPCo, you become concerned that Justin and Lorraine are not going to want to become involved in something this complex. After all, they are exotic-produce experts—not computer wizards!

Business of Providing Internet Access

As you continue your research, you learn more about the NAPs (network access points) that maintain the core operations and long-haul backbone of the Internet. You find that they do not offer direct connections to individuals or small businesses. Instead, they offer connections to large organizations and businesses that, in turn, provide Internet access to other businesses and individuals. These firms are called **Internet access providers (IAPs)** or **Internet service providers (ISPs)**. Most of these firms call themselves ISPs because they offer more than just access to the Internet. ISPs usually provide their customers with the software they need to connect to the ISP, browse the Web, send and receive e-mail messages, and perform other Internet-related functions such as file transfer and remote login to other computers. ISPs often provide network consulting services to their customers and help them design Web pages. Some ISPs have developed a full range of services that include network management, training, and marketing advice. Some larger ISPs not only sell Internet access to end users, but also market Internet access to other ISPs, which then sell access and service to their own business and individual customers. This hierarchy of Internet access appears in Figure 1-9.

Figure 1-9	THE HIERARCHY OF INTERNET SERVICE OPTIONS

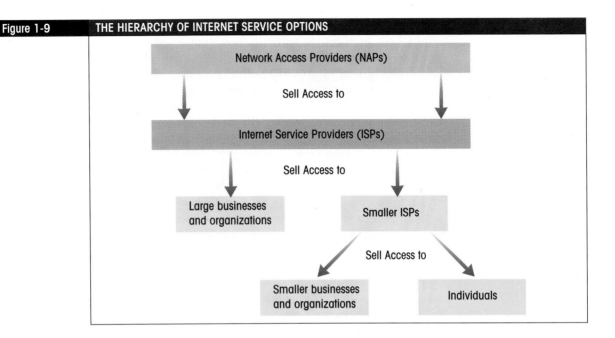

Connection Bandwidth

Of the differences that exist among service providers at different levels of the access hierarchy, one of the most important is the connection bandwidth that an ISP can offer. **Bandwidth** is the amount of data that can travel through a communications circuit in one second. The bandwidth that an ISP can offer you depends on the type of connection it has to the Internet and the kind of connection you have to the ISP.

The bandwidth for a network connection between two points is always limited to the narrowest bandwidth that exists in any part of the network. For example, if you connect to an ISP through a regular telephone line, your bandwidth is limited to the bandwidth of that telephone line, regardless of the bandwidth connection that the ISP has to the Internet. Bandwidth is measured in multiples of **bits per second (bps)**. Discussions of Internet bandwidth often use the terms **kilobits per second (Kbps)**, which is 1,024 bps; **megabits per second (Mbps)**, which is 1,048,576 bps; and **gigabits per second (Gbps)**, which is 1,073,741,824 bps. Most LANs run either an Ethernet network, which has a bandwidth of 10 Mbps, or Fast Ethernet, which operates at 100 Mbps. Some companies are starting to install the latest technology, Gigabit Ethernet, which operates at 1 Gbps. When you extend your network beyond a local area, the speed of the connection depends on what type of connection you use.

One way to connect computers or networks over longer distances is to use regular telephone service (sometimes referred to as **POTS**, or **plain old telephone service**). Regular telephone service to most U.S. residential and business customers provides a maximum bandwidth of between 28.8 Kbps and 56 Kbps. These numbers vary because the United States has a number of different telephone companies that do not all use the same technology. Some telephone companies offer a higher grade of service that uses one of a series of protocols called **Digital Subscriber Line** or **Digital Subscriber Loop (DSL)**. The first technology that was developed using a DSL protocol is called **Integrated Services Digital Network (ISDN)**. ISDN service has been available in various parts of the United States since 1984. Although considerably more expensive than regular telephone service, ISDN offers bandwidths of up to 256 Kbps. ISDN is much more widely available in Australia, France, Germany, Japan, and Singapore than in the United States because the regulatory structure of the telecommunications industries in those countries encouraged rapid deployment of this new technology. All technologies based on the DSL protocol require the implementing telephone company to install modems at its switching stations, which can be very expensive. New technologies that use the DSL protocol are currently being implemented around the world. One of those, **Asymmetric Digital Subscriber Line** (**ADSL**, also abbreviated **DSL**), offers transmission speeds ranging from 16 to 640 Kbps from the user to the telephone company and from 1.5 to 9 Mbps from the telephone company to the user.

Businesses and large organizations often connect to an ISP using higher-bandwidth telephone company connections called **T1** (1.544 Mbps) and **T3** (44.736 Mbps) connections (the names T1 and T3 were originally acronyms for Telephone 1 and Telephone 3, respectively, but very few people use these terms any longer). These connections are much more expensive than POTS or ISDN connections; however, organizations that must link hundreds or thousands of individual users to the Internet require the greater bandwidth of T1 and T3 connections. Smaller firms can share space on a T1 or T3 line. The NAPs currently operate the Internet backbone using a variety of connections. In addition to T1 and T3 lines, the NAPs use newer connections that have bandwidths of more than 1 Gbps—in some cases reaching 10 Gbps. These new connection options are numbered OC3, OC12, and so forth because when these technologies were developed they were the only connections that used optical fiber. The OC is short for optical carrier. NAPs also use high-bandwidth satellite and radio communications links to transfer data over long distances. The NAPs are working with a group of universities and the National Science Foundation (NSF) to develop a network called Internet 2 that will have backbone bandwidths that soon will exceed 10 Gbps.

A connection option that is available in parts of the United States and in some other countries is to connect to the Internet through a cable television company. The cable company transmits data in the same cables it uses to provide television service. Cable can deliver up to 10 Mbps to an individual user and can accept up to 768 Kbps from an individual user. These speeds far exceed those of existing POTS and ISDN connections and are comparable to speeds provided by the ADSL technologies currently being implemented by telephone companies and other companies that rent facilities from the telephone companies.

An option that is particularly appealing to users in remote areas is connecting via satellite. Using a satellite-dish receiver, you can download at a bandwidth of approximately 400 Kbps. Until recently, you could not send information to the Internet using a satellite dish antenna, so you needed to also have an ISP account to send files or e-mail. Very recently, two satellite companies began offering two-way satellite connections to the Internet. Figure 1-10 summarizes the bandwidths, costs, and typical uses for the various types of connections currently in use on the Internet.

Figure 1-10	BANDWIDTHS FOR VARIOUS TYPES OF INTERNET CONNECTIONS				
Service	Upstream Speed (Kbps)	Downstream Speed (Kbps)	Capacity (Number of Simultaneous Users)	One-time Startup Costs	Continuing Monthly Costs
Residential-Small Business Services					
Modem (POTS)	28–56	28–56	1	$0–$20	$12–$20
ISDN	128–256	128–256	1–3	$60–$300	$50–$90
ADSL	100–640	4,500–9,000	1–4	$50–$100	$40–$90
Cable modem	300–1,000	1,000–10,000	1–4	$0–$100	$40–$70
Satellite	125–150	400–500	1–3	$600–$1,200	$60–$70
Business Services					
Leased digital line (DS0)	64	64	1–10	$50–$200	$40–$150
Fractional T1 leased line	128–1,544	128–1,544	5–180	$50–$800	$100–$1,000
T1 leased line	1,544	1,544	100–200	$100–$2,000	$900–$1,600
T3 leased line	44,700	44,700	1,000–10,000	$1,000–$9,000	$5,000–$12,000
Large Business, ISP, NAP, and Internet 2 Services					
OC3 leased line	156,000	156,000	1,000–50,000	$3,000–$12,000	$9,000–$22,000
OC12 leased line	622,000	622,000	Backbone	Negotiated	$25,000–$100,000
OC48 leased line	2,500,000	2,500,000	Backbone	Negotiated	Negotiated
OC192 leased line	10,000,000	10,000,000	Backbone	Negotiated	Negotiated

As you evaluate the information you have gathered about ways Lorraine might connect TEPCo to the Internet, you realize that there are four ways that individuals or small businesses can link to the Internet. The first way, which is only for individuals, is a connection through your school or employer. The second option is to connect through an ISP. The third option is to connect through a cable television company. The fourth option is to use a satellite service provider. Next, you will learn about some of the advantages and disadvantages of each connection method that you have identified for your analysis and report to Lorraine.

Connecting **Through Your School or Employer**

One of the easiest ways to connect to the Internet is through your school or employer, if it already has an Internet connection. The connection is either free or very reasonably priced. If you do use your school or employer to connect to the Internet, you must comply with its rules. In some cases, this can outweigh the cost advantage.

Connecting Through Your School

Most universities and community colleges are connected to the Internet, and many offer Internet access to their students, faculty members, and other employees. In most schools, you can use computers in computing labs or in the library to access the Internet. Many schools provide a way to connect your own computer through the school's network to the Internet. The form of connection will depend on what your school offers. An increasing number of schools have dormitory rooms wired with LAN connections so students can connect using their own computers. Some schools even provide the computers as part of their tuition or housing charge.

Dialing In

Some schools and businesses still provide telephone numbers that students or employees can use to connect their computers to the Internet through a modem. **Modem** is short for **modulator-demodulator**. When you connect your computer, which communicates using digital signals, to another computer through a telephone line, which uses analog signals, you must perform a signal conversion. Converting a digital signal to an analog signal is **modulation**; converting that analog signal back into digital form is called **demodulation**. A modem performs both functions; that is, it acts as a modulator-demodulator. When you connect to the Internet through your school or employer, your computer's modem converts your computer's digital signals into analog signals that can travel on the telephone system's wires (POTS). A modem at your school or employer converts the analog signal back into a digital signal and sends it through a LAN and a router to the Internet for you.

Connecting Through Your Employer

Your employer might offer you a connection to the Internet through the computer you use in your job. This computer might be connected through a LAN to the Internet, or you might have to use a modem to connect it. Before you attempt to connect to the Internet this way, make sure that your employer permits personal use of company computing facilities. Remember, your employer owns the computers you use as an employee. In most of the world, this gives your employer the right to examine any e-mail or files that you transmit or store using those computers. A number of schools retain similar rights under the law or through policies they publish in their student handbooks.

Acceptable Use Policies

Most schools and employers have an **acceptable use policy (AUP)** that specifies the conditions under which you can use their Internet connections. Some organizations require you to sign a copy of the AUP before they permit you to use their computing facilities; others simply include it as part of your student or employee contract. AUPs often include provisions that require you to respect copyright laws, trade secrets, the privacy of other users, and standards of common decency. Many AUPs expressly prohibit you from engaging in commercial activities, criminal activities, or specific threat-making or equipment-endangering practices.

Many provisions in AUPs are open to honest misunderstanding or disagreement in interpretation. It is extremely important for you to read and understand any AUP with which you must comply when you use computing facilities at your school or employer. AUPs often include punitive provisions that include revocation of user accounts and all rights to use the network. Some AUPs state that a user can be expelled or fired for serious violations.

Advantages and Disadvantages

Although accessing the Internet through your school or employer might be the least expensive option, you might decide that the restrictions on your freedom of expression and actions are too great. For example, if you wanted to start a small business on the Web, you would not want to use your school account if its AUP has a commercial-activity exclusion. An important concern when using your employer's computing facilities to access the Internet is that the employer generally retains the right to examine any files or e-mail messages that you transmit through those facilities. You should carefully consider whether the limitations placed on your use of the Internet are greater than the benefits of the low cost of this access option. For example, you may not want to use your employer's Internet connection when you are sending your resume to another company in hopes of landing a different job.

Connecting Through an Internet Service Provider

Depending on where you live, you might find that an ISP is the best way for you to connect to the Internet. In major metropolitan areas, many ISPs compete for customers and, therefore connection fees often are reasonable. Smaller towns and rural areas have fewer ISPs and, thus might be less competitive. When you are shopping for an ISP, you will want to find information such as:

- The monthly base fee and number of hours it provides
- The hourly rate for time used over the monthly base amount
- Whether the telephone access number is local or long distance
- Which specific Internet services are included
- What software is included
- What user-support services are available

Advantages and Disadvantages

ISPs are the best option for many Internet users, in part, because they usually provide reliable connectivity at a reasonable price. The terms of their AUPs often are less restrictive than those imposed by schools on their students or employers on their employees. You should examine carefully the terms of the service agreement, and you always should obtain references from customers who use an ISP before signing any long-term contract.

Some ISPs limit the number of customers they serve, whereas others guarantee that you will not receive a busy signal when you dial in. These are significant factors in the quality of service you will experience. Remember, each ISP has a limited amount of bandwidth in its connection to the Internet. If your ISP allows more new customers to subscribe to its service than leave each month, each remaining user will have proportionally less bandwidth available. Be especially wary of ISPs that offer a large discount if you sign a long-term agreement. The quality of service might deteriorate significantly over time if the ISP adds many new customers without expanding its bandwidth.

You also should find out whether the ISP has an AUP and, if so, you should examine its terms carefully. Some ISPs have restrictive policies. For example, an ISP might have an entirely different fee structure for customers who use their Internet access for commercial purposes. Carefully outline how you plan to use your Internet connection, and decide what services you want before signing any long-term contract with an ISP.

Connecting Through Your Cable Television Company

One of the fastest growing means of Internet access is the cable modem. A **cable modem** performs a function similar to that of a regular modem; that is, it converts digital computer signals to analog signals. However, instead of converting the digital signals into telephone-line analog signals, a cable modem converts them into radio-frequency analog signals that are similar to television transmission signals. The converted signals travel to and from the cable company on the same lines that carry your cable television service. The cable company maintains a connection to the Internet and otherwise operates much like the ISPs discussed previously, which deliver an Internet connection through telephone lines.

To install a cable modem, the cable company first installs a **line-splitter**, a device that divides the combined cable signals into their television and data components, and then connects the television (or televisions) and the cable modem to the line-splitter. Most cable companies that offer this service rent the required line-splitter and cable modem to each customer.

Advantages and Disadvantages

The main advantage of a cable television connection to the Internet is its high bandwidth. A cable connection can provide very fast downloads to your computer from the Internet, as much as 170 times faster than a telephone line connection. Although upload speeds are not as fast, they are still about 14 times faster than a telephone line connection. The cost usually is higher than—and often more than double—what competing ISPs charge. However, if you consider that the cable connection might save you the cost of a second telephone line, the net benefit can be significant. The greatest disadvantage for most people right now is that the cable connection is simply not available in their area yet. Because cable companies must invest in expensive upgrades to offer this service, it might not become available in some parts of the U.S. for many years. Another problem arises from the shared nature of the cable connection. As more people in your neighborhood subscribe to cable modem service, they share the bandwidth of your connection. This can slow down your access speeds significantly. The cable company should monitor the traffic and, when needed, add more equipment to handle the increased load. Not all cable companies have been diligent in doing this. You should remember that, other than the nature of the connection, a cable company is the same as any other ISP. Therefore, all of the issues outlined in the previous section about contracting with ISPs apply equally to dealing with your cable company.

Connecting Through a DSL Provider

DSL connections (today, ADSL and other types of DSL connection are referred to as simply DSL) are increasingly available in the United States and a few other countries. These services are sold by telephone companies and in some locations by other companies. These other companies are called third-party DSL providers, and they are companies that lease lines from the local telephone company and resell Internet connection service through those lines to individuals and small businesses.

Advantages and Disadvantages

DSL providers often claim that their service is better than that offered by cable companies. Because the part of the DSL service that runs from the customer to the telephone company is not shared, the traffic loading problems that can occur with cable modem access cannot occur with DSL service. Of course, once the packets enter the DSL provider's network, the bandwidth is then shared and heavy traffic loads can slow down access for everyone using the service. DSL's speeds are similar to cable modems and the subscription rates are similar. The biggest drawback for most DSL users is that they are buying the service from either their local telephone company or a third-party provider that must work with the telephone company. Many people have experienced long delays in getting DSL service installed or in having repairs completed. Telephone companies have not done a very good job in training their employees to sell, install, and maintain DSL services. The third-party providers must depend on the telephone companies to install the service because it uses the telephone company's lines. A number of large DSL providers have gone out of business recently because they were unable to deliver the services they promised and make a profit. In many cases, their subscribers were left without an Internet connection for months before another company entered the market.

Connecting Via Satellite

Many rural areas in the United States do not have cable television service and may never have it because their low population density makes it too expensive—a cable company cannot afford to run miles of cable to reach one or two isolated customers. People in these areas often buy satellite receivers to obtain television signals. Recently, Internet connections via satellite became available. Some services provide a satellite connection for downlinks only, so you also must have another connection through an ISP that uses telephone lines to handle the uplink half of the connection. Recently, two companies have started offering satellite connections that are two-way. The satellite dish is a transmitting antenna as well as being a receiving antenna.

Advantages and Disadvantages

These services offer speeds and charge monthly fees that are similar to those of cable and DSL providers. The installation fee is usually considerably higher for a satellite connection because the dish must be installed and aimed at the satellite, tasks that often require the skills of a professional installer. Most satellite customers choose the option because they do not have cable or DSL service available and satellite is their only high-speed connection option.

You now have collected a great deal of information about the origins and history of the Internet and the Web. As you conducted your research project for TEPCo, you learned about some of the information and tools that exist on the Internet. You also gathered information about ways to connect to the Internet. Now you are ready to prepare your report for Lorraine and recommend a plan of action for connecting TEPCo to the Internet.

Session 1.2 QUICK CHECK

1. To connect to the Internet, your computer must be part of a(n) _____.

2. The acronym typically used when referring to a company that provides Internet access to individuals and small businesses is _____.

3. How much greater bandwidth does ISDN offer over plain old telephone service (POTS)?

4. A T3 leased line would be a good Internet connection option for a(n) _____.

5. The device that converts digital computer signals into analog signals that can travel over a standard telephone line is called a(n) _____.

6. A document that specifies the conditions under which you can use your school's or your employer's Internet connection is called a(n) _____.

7. Persons living in remote areas can have a fast connection to the Internet if they subscribe to a _____ service.

PROJECTS

1. *Diagramming School Networks* Your school probably has a number of computer networks. At most schools, you can find information about computing facilities from the department of academic computing or the school library. Identify what LANs and WANs you have on your campus, and determine whether any or all of them are interconnected. Draw a diagram that shows the networks, their connections to each other, and their connection to the Internet.

2. *DARPA Alternatives* The DARPA researchers that laid the foundation for the Internet were conducting research on ways to coordinate weapons control. They chose to develop a computer network that could operate without a central control mechanism. The DARPA researchers might have chosen to develop a centrally controlled system instead. Discuss whether you think that approach would have given birth to something similar to the Internet. Describe how you think the result would differ from the Internet and Web that exist today.

3. *School Cabling Choices* Select two or three buildings on your campus that have computers in offices, dormitory rooms, or computing labs. Find out from the appropriate office administrator, dormitory official, or lab supervisor what kind of computer cable the school uses to connect the computers. Evaluate the school's cabling choices. Would you make the same decisions? Why or why not?

4. *Using the Web and E-Mail* Describe three ways in which you might use the Web or e-mail to identify part-time job and internship opportunities that relate to your major.

5. *Acceptable Use Policy Evaluation* Obtain a copy of your school's or employer's acceptable use policy (AUP). Outline the main restrictions it places on student (or employee) activities. Compare those restrictions with the limits it places on faculty (or employer) activities. Analyze and evaluate any differences in treatment. If there are no differences, discuss whether the policy should be rewritten to include differences. If your school or employer has no policy, outline the key elements that you believe should be included in such a policy for your school or employer.

6. *Commercialization of the Internet* Many people who have been involved with the Internet for many years believe that the National Science Foundation (NSF) made a serious mistake when it opened the Internet to commercial traffic. Discuss the advantages and disadvantages of this policy decision. Do you think that the Internet would be as successful as it is today if no commercial activity had been allowed?

7. *The Web and the Memex Machine* Vannevar Bush died before the Web came into existence. Speculate on what he would have thought about the Web. Would he have seen it as the embodiment of his Memex machine? Why or why not?

8. *Evaluating ISPs* Contact three ISPs in your area and obtain information about their Internet access and related services. You can find ISPs in your local telephone directory (try headings such as "Internet Services," "Computer Networks," or "Computer On-Line Services"), or look for advertisements in your local or student newspaper. Summarize the services and the charges for each service by ISP. Which ISP would you recommend for an individual? Why? Which ISP would you recommend for a small business? Why?

QUICK | CHECK ANSWERS

Session 1.1

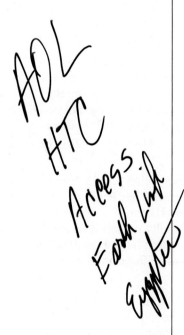

1. printers, scanners, digital cameras, data files, programs (or similar equipment or files)
2. fiber-optic
3. packet
4. protocol
5. e-mail, mailing lists, Usenet newsgroups, adventure gaming
6. intranet
7. commercialization, the development of the WWW
8. Web browser

Session 1.2

1. network
2. ISP
3. two to ten times
4. large company or other organization, an ISP, or a network backbone services provider
5. modem
6. acceptable use policy or AUP
7. satellite

OBJECTIVES

In this tutorial you will:

- Learn about Web browser software and Web pages

- Learn about Web addresses and URLs

- Save and organize Web addresses

- Navigate the Web

- Use the Web to find information

- Configure and use the Microsoft Internet Explorer Web browser

- Configure and use the Netscape Navigator Web browser

LAB

The Internet: World Wide Web

BROWSER BASICS

Introduction to Microsoft Internet Explorer and Netscape Navigator

CASE

Sunset Wind Quintet

The Sunset Wind Quintet is a group of five musicians who have played together for eight years. At first, the group began by playing free concerts for local charitable organizations, and as the group's reputation grew, the musicians were soon in demand at art gallery openings and other functions.

Each member of the quintet is an accomplished musician. The instruments in a wind quintet include flute, oboe, clarinet, bassoon, and French horn, which are all orchestral instruments. Each quintet member has experience as a player in a symphony orchestra as well. Three quintet members—the flutist, bassoonist, and the French horn player—currently hold positions with the local orchestra. The other two quintet members—the clarinetist and the oboist—teach classes in their respective instruments at the local university.

This past summer, a booking agent asked the quintet to do a short regional tour. Although the tour was successful, the quintet members realized that none of them had any business-management skills. Marianna Rabinovich, the clarinetist, handles most of the business details for the group. The quintet members realized that business matters related to the tour were overwhelming Marianna and that they wanted to do more touring, so they hired you as their business manager.

One of your tasks will be to help market the Sunset Wind Quintet. To do this, you must learn more about how other wind quintets operate and sell their services. At one of your early meetings with the group, you found that each member of the quintet had different priorities. In addition to marketing the quintet's performances, some members felt it would be a good idea to record and sell CDs, whereas others were concerned about finding instrument-repair facilities on the road when tours extended beyond the local area.

As you discussed these issues with the quintet members, you started thinking of ways to address their concerns. Your first idea was to find trade magazines and newspapers that might describe what other small classical musical ensembles were doing. As you considered the time and cost of this alternative, you realized that the Internet and World Wide Web might offer a better way to get started.

**SESSION
2.1**

In this session, you will learn how Web pages and Web sites make up the World Wide Web. You will learn what you should consider when selecting and using a specific software tool to find information on the Web. Finally, you will learn some basic browser concepts, which will help your browsing experience.

Web Browsers

The Internet: World Wide Web

As you start to consider how you might use the Web to gather information for the Sunset Wind Quintet, you remember that one of your college friends, Maggie Beeler, earned her degree in library science. You meet with Maggie at the local public library, where she is working at the reference desk. She is glad to assist you.

Maggie begins by explaining that the Web is a collection of files that reside on computers, called Web servers, that are located all over the world and are connected to each other through the Internet. Most files on computers, including computers that are connected to the Internet, are private; that is, only the computer's users can access those files. The owners of the computer files that make up the Web have made those files publicly available. Anyone who has a computer connected to the Internet can obtain access to those files.

Client/Server Structure of the World Wide Web

When you use your Internet connection to become part of the Web, your computer becomes a **Web client** in a worldwide client/server network. A **Web browser** is the software that you run on your computer to make it work as a Web client. The Internet connects many different types of computers running different operating system software. Web browser software lets your computer communicate with all of these different types of computers easily and effectively.

Computers that are connected to the Internet and that contain files that their owners have made available publicly through their Internet connections are called **Web servers**. Figure 2-1 shows how this client/server structure uses the Internet to provide multiple interconnections among the various kinds of client and server computers.

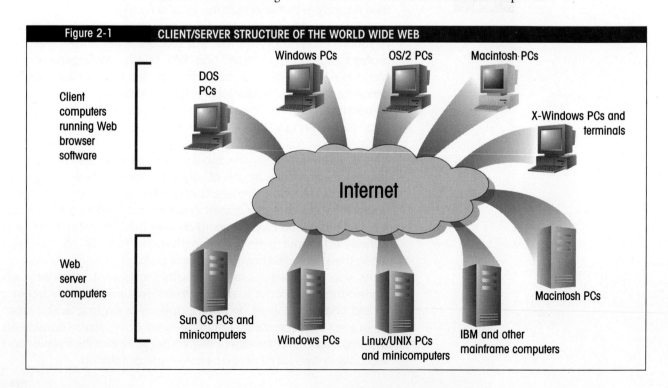

Figure 2-1   CLIENT/SERVER STRUCTURE OF THE WORLD WIDE WEB

Hypertext, Links, and Hypermedia

The public files on Web servers are ordinary text files, much like the files created and used by word-processing software. To enable Web browser software to read these files, however, the text must be formatted according to a generally accepted standard. The standard used on the Web is **Hypertext Markup Language** (**HTML**). HTML uses codes, or **tags**, that tell the Web browser software how to display the text contained in the text file. For example, a Web browser reading the following line of text

```
<B>A Review of the Book <I>Wind Instruments of the
18th Century</I></B>
```

recognizes the <B> and </B> tags as instructions to display the entire line of text in bold and the <I> and </I> tags as instructions to display the text enclosed by those tags in italics. Different Web clients that connect to this Web server might display the tagged text differently. For example, one Web browser might display text enclosed by bold tags in a blue color instead of displaying the text in bold. A text file that contains HTML tags is called an HTML document.

HTML provides a variety of text formatting tags that can be used to indicate headings, paragraphs, bulleted lists, numbered lists, and other text enhancements in an HTML document. The real power of HTML, however, lies in its anchor tag. The **HTML anchor tag** enables Web designers to link HTML documents to each other. Anchor tags in HTML documents create **hypertext links** to other HTML documents. Hypertext links can also connect one part of an HTML document to other sections of that document. Hypertext links also are called **hyperlinks** or **links**. Figure 2-2 shows how these hyperlinks can join multiple HTML documents to create a web of HTML documents across computers on the Internet. The HTML documents shown in the figure can be on the same computer or on different computers. The computers can be in the same room or an ocean away.

| Figure 2-2 | HYPERLINKS CREATE A WEB OF HTML TEXT ACROSS MULTIPLE FILES |

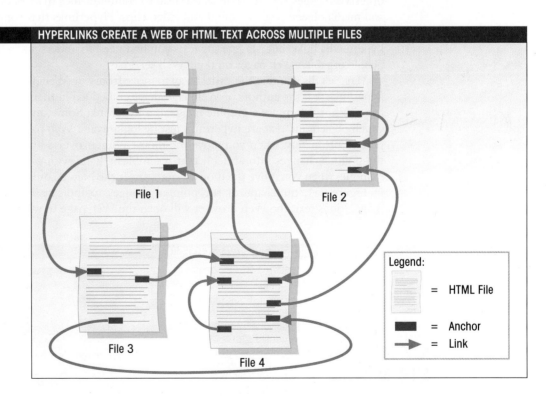

Most Web browsers display hyperlinks in a color that is different from other text in an HTML document and underline the hyperlinks so they are easy to distinguish. When a

Web browser displays an HTML document, it is often referred to as a Web page. Maggie shows you the Web page for the Lawrence Public Library (see Figure 2-3). The hyperlinks on this Web page are easy to identify because the Web browser software that displayed this page shows the hyperlinks as blue, underlined text.

| Figure 2-3 | LAWRENCE PUBLIC LIBRARY WEB PAGE |

Each of the hyperlinks on the Web page shown in Figure 2-3 enables the user to connect to another Web page. In turn, each of those Web pages contains hyperlinks to other pages, including one hyperlink that leads back to the first Web page. Hyperlinks often connect to other Web pages, and these links can lead to computer files that contain pictures, graphics, and media objects such as sound and video clips. Hyperlinks that connect to these types of files often are called **hypermedia links**. You are especially interested in learning more about hypermedia links, but Maggie suggests you first need to understand a little more about how people organize Web pages on their Web servers.

Maggie tells you that the easiest way to move from one Web page to another is to use the hyperlinks that the authors of Web pages have embedded in their HTML documents. Web page authors often use a graphic image as a hyperlink. Sometimes, it is difficult to identify which objects and text are hyperlinks just by looking at a Web page displayed on your computer. Fortunately, when you move the mouse pointer over a hyperlink in a Web browser, the pointer changes into an icon that resembles a hand with a pointing index finger. For example, when you move the mouse pointer over the New Acquisitions hyperlink, as shown in Figure 2-4, the shape of the pointer changes to indicate that if you click the New Acquisitions text, the Web browser will open the Web page to which that hyperlink points.

| Figure 2-4 | MOUSE POINTER HOVERING OVER A HYPERLINK |

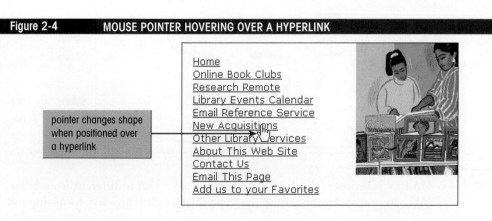

You might encounter an error message when you click on a hyperlink. Two common messages that you might see are "server busy" and "DNS entry not found". Either of these messages means that your browser was unable to communicate successfully with the Web server that stores the page you requested. The cause for this inability might be temporary—in which case, you might be able to use the hyperlink later—or the cause might be permanent. The browser has no way of determining the cause of the connection failure, so the browser provides the same types of error messages in either case. Another error message that you might receive appears as a Web page and includes the text "Error 404: File not Found." This error message usually means that the Web page's location has changed permanently or that the Web page no longer exists.

Web **Pages and Web Sites**

Maggie explains that people who create Web pages usually have a collection of pages on one computer that they use as their Web server. A collection of linked Web pages that has a common theme or focus is called a **Web site**. The main page that all of the pages on a particular Web site are organized around and link back to is called the site's **home page**.

Home Pages

Maggie warns you that the term *home page* is used at least three different ways on the Web and that it is sometimes difficult to tell which meaning people intend when they use the term. The first definition of home page indicates the main page for a particular site. This home page is the first page that opens when you visit a particular Web site. The second definition of home page is the first page that opens when you start your Web browser. This type of home page might be an HTML document on your own computer. Some people create such home pages and include hyperlinks to Web sites that they frequently visit. If you are using a computer on your school's or employer's network, its Web browser might be configured to open the main page for the school or firm. The third definition of home page is the Web page that a particular Web browser loads the first time you use it. This page usually is stored at the Web site of the firm or other organization that created the Web browser software. Home pages that meet the second or third definitions are sometimes called **start pages**.

Web Sites

Most Web sites store all of the site's pages in one location, either on one computer or on one LAN. Some large Web sites, however, are distributed over a number of locations. In fact, it is sometimes difficult to determine where one Web site ends and another begins. One common definition of a Web site is any group of Web pages that relates to one specific topic or organization, regardless of where the HTML documents are located.

Addresses **on the Web**

Maggie reminds you that there is no centralized control over the Internet. Therefore, no central starting point exists for the Web, which is a part of the Internet. However, each computer on the Internet does have a unique identification number, called an **IP (Internet Protocol) address**.

IP Addressing

The IP addressing system currently in use on the Internet is **IP version 4** (**IPv4**). IPv4 uses a 32-bit number to label each address on the Internet. The 32-bit IP address is usually written in four 8-bit parts. In most computer applications, an 8-bit number is called a **byte**; however, in networking applications, an 8-bit number is often called an **octet**. In the binary (base 2) numbering system, an octet can have values from 00000000 to 11111111; the decimal equivalents of these binary numbers are 0 and 255, respectively. Each part of a 32-bit IP address is separated from the previous part by a period, such as 106.29.242.17. You might hear a person pronounce this address as "one hundred six dot twenty-nine dot two four two dot seventeen." This notation is often called **dotted decimal** notation. The combination of these four parts provides 4.2 billion possible addresses ($256 \times 256 \times 256 \times 256$). Because each of the four parts of a dotted decimal number can range from 0 to 255, IP addresses range from 0.0.0.0 (which would be written in binary as 16 zeros) to 255.255.255.255 (which would be written in binary as 16 ones). Although many people find dotted decimal notation to be somewhat confusing at first, most do agree that writing, reading, and remembering a computer address as 216.115.108.245 is easier than 11010000111011000110100101011000 or its full decimal equivalent, which is 674,962,008.

In the mid-1990s, the accelerating growth of the Internet created concern that the world could run out of IP addresses within a few years. In the early days of the Internet, the 4 billion addresses provided by the IPv4 rules certainly seemed to be more addresses than an experimental research network would ever need. However, about 2 billion of those addresses today are either in use or unavailable for use because of the way blocks of addresses were assigned to organizations. The addition of new kinds of devices to the Internet's many networks, such as wireless personal digital assistants and cell phones that can access the Web, promises to keep the demand for IP addresses high.

Network engineers have devised a number of stop-gap techniques, such as **subnetting**, which is the use of reserved private IP addresses within LANs and WANs to provide additional address space. **Private IP addresses** are series of IP numbers that have been set aside for subnet use and are not permitted on packets that travel on the Internet. In subnetting, a computer called a **network address translation** (**NAT**) device converts those private IP addresses into normal IP addresses when the packets move from the LAN or WAN onto the Internet.

The **Internet Engineering Task Force** (**IETF**) worked on several new protocols that could solve the limited addressing capacity of IPv4 and, in 1997, approved **IP version 6** (**IPv6**) as the protocol that would replace IPv4. The new IP is being implemented gradually because the two protocols are not directly compatible. However, network engineers have devised ways to run both protocols together on interconnected networks. The major advantage of IPv6 is that it uses a 128-bit hexadecimal (base 16) number for addresses instead of the 32-bit binary (base 2) number used in IPv4. A **hexadecimal numbering system** uses 16 digits (0, 1, 2, 3, 4, 5, 6, 7, 8, 9, a, b, c, d, e, and f). For example, the dotted-decimal IP address 216.115.108.245 would be written as 283b1a58 in hexadecimal. The number of available addresses in IPv6 is 134 followed by 152 zeros—many billions of times larger than the address space of IPv4. The new IP also changes the format of the packet itself. Improvements in networking technologies over the past 20 years have made many of the fields in the IPv4 packet unnecessary. IPv6 eliminates those fields and adds news fields for security and other optional information.

Domain Name Addressing

Although each computer connected to the Internet has a unique IP address, most people do not use the IP address to locate Web sites and individual pages. Instead, the browsers use domain name addressing. A **domain name** is a unique name associated with a specific IP address by a program that runs on an Internet host computer. This program, which coordinates the IP addresses and domain names for all computers attached to it, is called

DNS (domain name system) software, and the host computer that runs this software is called a **domain name server**. Domain names can include any number of parts separated by periods; however, most domain names currently in use have only three or four parts. Domain names follow a hierarchical model that you can follow from top to bottom if you read the domain names from right to left. For example, the domain name gsb.uchicago.edu is the computer connected to the Internet at the Graduate School of Business (gsb), which is an academic unit of the University of Chicago (uchicago), which is an educational institution (edu). No other computer on the Internet has the same domain name.

The last part of a domain name is called its **top-level domain (TLD)**. For example, DNS software on the Internet host computer that is responsible for the "edu" domain keeps track of the IP address for all of the educational institutions in its domain, including "uchicago." Similar DNS software on the "uchicago" Internet host computer would keep track of the academic units' computers in its domain, including the "gsb" computer.

Since 1998, the **Internet Corporation for Assigned Names and Numbers (ICANN)** has had responsibility for managing domain names. In the United States, the six most common TLDs have been .com, .edu, .gov., mil, .net, and .org. Internet host computers outside the United States often use two-letter country domain names instead of, or in addition to, the six general TLDs. For example, the domain name uq.edu.au is the domain name for the University of Queensland (uq), which is an educational institution (edu) in Australia (au). State and local government organizations in the United States frequently use an additional domain name "us." The "us" domain is also used by U.S. primary and secondary schools because the "edu" domain is reserved for postsecondary educational institutions.

In 2000, ICANN added seven new TLDs to the general domain category. Although these new domain names were chosen after much deliberation and consideration of more than 100 possible new names, a number of people were highly critical of the selections. Figure 2-5 presents a list of the general TLDs, including the seven new additions, and some of the more popular country TLDs.

Figure 2-5	COMMON TOP-LEVEL DOMAINS (TLDS)				
Original General TLDs		**Country TLDs**		**General TLDs Approved in 2000**	
TLD	**Use**	**TLD**	**Country**	**TLD**	**Use**
.com	U.S. Commercial	.au	Australia	.aero	Air-transport industry
.edu	U.S. Four-year educational institution	.ca	Canada	.biz	Businesses
		.de	Germany	.coop	Cooperatives
.gov	U.S. Federal government	.fi	Finland	.info	General use
.mil	U.S. Military	.fr	France	.museum	Museums
.net	U.S. General use	.jp	Japan	.name	Individual persons
.org	U.S. Not-for-profit organization	.se	Sweden	.pro	Professionals (accountants, lawyers, physicians)
		.uk	United Kingdom		

Uniform Resource Locators

The IP address and the domain name each identify a particular computer on the Internet, but they do not indicate where a Web page's HTML document resides on that computer. To identify a Web page's exact location, Web browsers rely on Uniform Resource Locators. A **Uniform Resource Locator (URL)** is a four-part addressing scheme that tells the Web browser:

- The transfer protocol to use when transporting the file
- The domain name of the computer on which the file resides
- The pathname of the folder or directory on the computer on which the file resides
- The name of the file

The **transfer protocol** is the set of rules that the computers use to move files from one computer to another on an internet. The most common transfer protocol used on the Internet is the hypertext transfer protocol (HTTP). You can indicate the use of this protocol by typing http:// as the first part of the URL. People do use other protocols to transfer files on the Internet, but most of these protocols were used more frequently before the Web became part of the Internet. Two protocols that you still might see on the Internet are the file transfer protocol (FTP), which is indicated in a URL as ftp://, and the Telnet protocol, which is indicated in a URL as telnet://. FTP is just another way to transfer files, and Telnet is a set of rules for establishing a remote terminal connection to another computer.

The domain name is the Internet address of the computer described in the preceding section. The pathname describes the hierarchical directory or folder structure on the computer that stores the file. Most people are familiar with the structure used on Windows and DOS PCs, which uses the back slash character (\) to separate the structure levels. URLs follow the conventions established in the UNIX operating system that use the forward slash character (/) to separate the structure levels. The forward slash character works properly in a URL, even when it is pointing to a file on a Windows or DOS computer.

The filename is the name that the computer uses to identify the Web page's HTML document. On most computers, the filename extension of an HTML document is either .html or .htm. Although many PC operating systems are not case-sensitive, computers that use the UNIX operating system *are* case-sensitive. Therefore, if you are entering a URL that includes mixed-case and you do not know the type of computer on which the file resides, it is safer to retain the mixed-case format of the URL.

Not all URLs include a filename. If a URL does not include a filename, most Web browsers will load the file named index.html. The **index.html** filename is the default name for a Web site's home page on most computer systems. Figure 2-6 shows an example of a URL annotated to show its four parts.

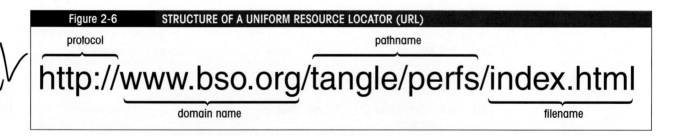

| Figure 2-6 | STRUCTURE OF A UNIFORM RESOURCE LOCATOR (URL) |

protocol ⌢   pathname ⌢

http://www.bso.org/tangle/perfs/index.html

domain name   filename

The URL shown in Figure 2-6 uses the HTTP protocol and points to a computer that is connected to the Web (www) at the Boston Symphony Orchestra (bso), which is a not-for-profit organization (org). The Boston Symphony's Web page contains many different kinds of information about the orchestra. The path shown in Figure 2-6 includes two levels. The first level indicates that the information is about the orchestra's summer home at Tanglewood (tangle), and the second level indicates that the page will contain information about the orchestra's performances (perfs) at Tanglewood. The filename (index.html) indicates that this page is the home page in the Tanglewood performances folder or directory.

You tell Maggie how much you appreciate all of the help she has given you by explaining how you can use Internet addresses to find information on the Web. Now you understand that the real secret to finding good information on the Web is to know the right URLs. Maggie tells you that you can find URLs in many places; for example, newspapers and magazines often publish URLs of Web sites that might interest their readers. Friends who know about the subject area in which you are interested also are good sources. The best source, however, is the Web itself.

You are eager to begin learning how to use a Web browser, so Maggie explains some elements common to all Web browsers. Most Web browsers have similar functions, which make it easy to use any Web browser after you have learned how to use one.

Main Elements of Web Browsers

Now that you know a little more about Web sites, you start to wonder how you can make your computer communicate with the Internet. Maggie tells you that there are a number of different Web browsers. Web browser software turns your computer into a Web client that can communicate through an Internet service provider (ISP) or a network connection with Web servers all over the world. Two popular browsers are **Microsoft Internet Explorer**, or simply **Internet Explorer**, and **Netscape Navigator**, or simply **Navigator**. Each browser has been released in different versions; however, the steps in this book are designed so they should work for most browsers.

Maggie reminds you that most Windows programs use a standard graphical user interface (GUI) design that includes a number of common screen elements. Figures 2-7 and 2-8 show the main elements of the Internet Explorer and Navigator program windows. These two Web browsers share many common Windows elements: a title bar at the top of the window, a scroll bar on the right side of the window, and a status bar at the bottom of the window.

Figure 2-7	MAIN ELEMENTS OF THE INTERNET EXPLORER PROGRAM WINDOW

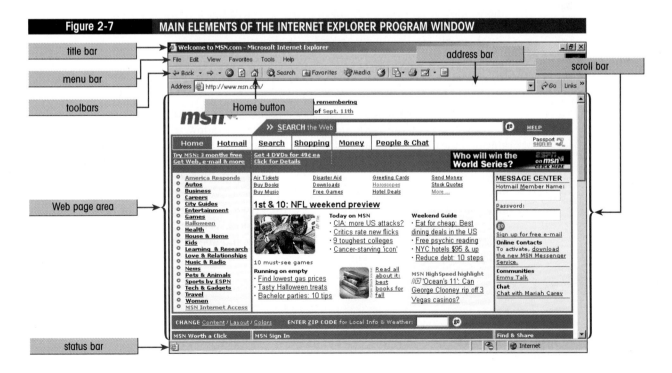

Figure 2-8   **MAIN ELEMENTS OF THE NAVIGATOR PROGRAM WINDOW**

In each program window, the menu bar appears below the title bar, and below the menu bar is a toolbar. Many of the toolbar button functions in Internet Explorer and Navigator are very similar. Next, Maggie describes each of these elements.

Title Bar

A Web browser's **title bar** shows the name of the open Web page and the Web browser's program name. As in all Windows programs, you can double-click the title bar to resize the window quickly. The title bar contains the **Minimize**, **Restore**, and **Close** buttons when the window is maximized to fill the screen. When the window is not maximized to fill the screen, the Restore button changes into a Maximize button. To expand such a browser window so it fills the screen, click the **Maximize** button.

Scroll Bars

A Web page can be much longer than a regular-sized document, so you often need to use the **scroll bar** at the right side of the program window to move the page up or down through the document window. You can use the mouse to click the **Up scroll button** or the **Down scroll button** to move the Web page up or down through the window's **Web page area**. You can also use the mouse to click and drag the **scroll box** up and down in the scroll bar to move the page accordingly. Although most Web pages are designed to resize automatically when loaded into different browser windows with different display areas, some Web pages can be wider than your browser window. When this happens, the browser places another scroll bar at the bottom of the window and above the status bar, so you can move the page horizontally through the browser.

Status Bar

The **status bar** at the bottom of the browser window includes information about the browser's operations. Each browser uses the status bar to deliver different information, but generally, the status bar indicates the name of the Web page that is loading, the load status (partial or complete), and important messages, such as "Document: Done." Some Web sites send messages as part of their Web pages that are displayed in the status bar as well. You will learn more about the specific functions of the status bar in Internet Explorer and Navigator in Sessions 2.2 and 2.3, respectively.

Menu Bar

The browser's **menu bar** provides a convenient way for you to execute typical File, Edit, View, and Help commands. In addition to these common Windows command sets, the menu bar also provides specialized commands for the browser that enable you to navigate the Web.

Home Button

Clicking the **Home** button in Internet Explorer or in Navigator displays the home (or start) page for the browser. Most Web browsers let you specify a page that loads automatically every time you start the program. You might not be able to do this if you are in your school's computer lab because schools often set the start page for all browsers on campus and then lock that setting. Some companies do the same thing on their employees' computers. If you are using your own computer, you can choose your own start page. Some people like to use a Web page that someone else has created and made available for others to use. One example of a start page that many people use as their start page is the refdesk.com Web page, shown in Figure 2-9.

Figure 2-9   REFDESK.COM WEB PAGE

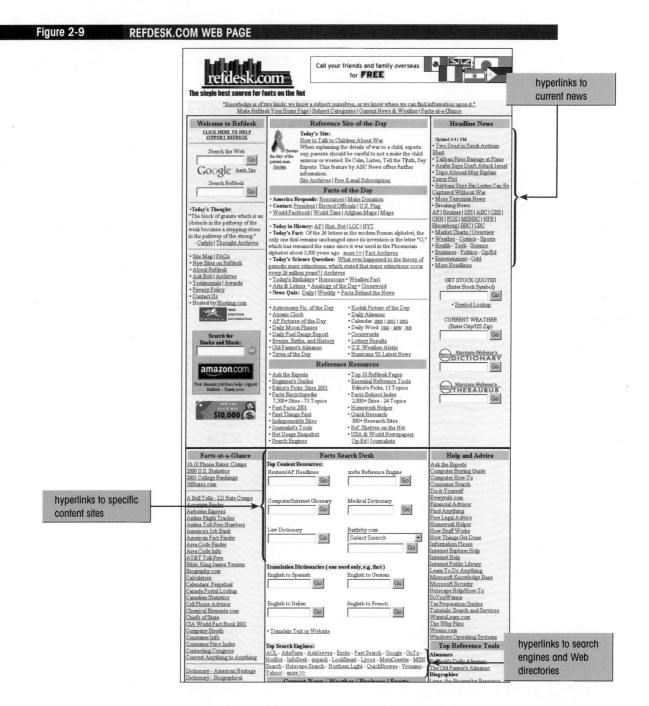

Pages such as the one shown in Figure 2-9 offer links to pages that many Web users frequently visit. The people and organizations that create these pages often sell advertising space on their pages to pay the cost of maintaining their sites.

Quick Access to Web Page Directories and Guides

You are starting to understand how to use the Internet to gather information. Maggie explains that a **Web directory** is a Web page that contains a list of Web page categories, such as education or recreation. The hyperlinks on a Web directory page lead to other pages that contain lists of subcategories that lead to other category lists and Web pages that relate to the category topics. **Web search engines** are Web pages that conduct searches of the Web to find the words or expressions that you enter. The result of such a search is a Web page that contains hyperlinks to Web pages that contain matching text or expressions. These pages can give new users an easy way to find information on the Web. Internet Explorer and Netscape each include a **Search** (the Internet) button. Clicking this button in either browser opens search engines and Web directories chosen by the companies that wrote the browser software. However, many people prefer to select their own tools for searching the Internet.

Web addresses can be long and hard to remember—even if you are using domain names instead of IP addresses. In Internet Explorer, you save the URL as a **favorite** in the Favorites folder. In Netscape, you use a **bookmark** to save the URL of a specific page so you can return to it. You realize that using the browser to remember important pages will be a terrific asset as you start collecting information for the quintet, so you ask Maggie to explain more about how to return to a Web page.

Using the History List

As you click the hyperlinks to go to new Web pages, the browser stores the locations of each page you visit during a single session in a **history list**. You click the **Back** button and the **Forward** button in both Internet Explorer and Navigator to move through the history list.

When you start your browser, both buttons are inactive (dimmed) because no history list for your new session exists yet. After you follow one or more hyperlinks, the Back button lets you retrace your path through the hyperlinks you have followed. Once you use the Back button, the Forward button becomes active and lets you move forward through the session's history list.

In most Web browsers, you can right-click either the Back or Forward button to display a portion of the history list. You can reload any page on the list by clicking its name in the list. The Back and Forward buttons duplicate the functions of commands on the browser's menu commands. You will learn more about the history list in Sessions 2.2 and 2.3.

Reloading a Web Page

Clicking the **Refresh** button in Internet Explorer or the **Reload** button in Navigator loads the same Web page that appears in the browser window again. The browser stores a copy of every Web page it displays on your computer's hard drive in a **cache** folder, which increases the speed at which the browser can display pages as you navigate through the history list. The cache folder lets the browser load the pages from the client instead of from the remote Web server.

When you click the Refresh or the Reload button, the browser contacts the Web server to see if the Web page has changed since it was stored in the cache folder. If it has changed, the browser gets the new page from the Web server; otherwise, the browser loads the cache folder copy. If you want to force the browser to load the page from the Web server, hold down the Shift key as you click the Refresh or Reload button.

Stopping a Web Page Transfer

Sometimes a Web page takes a long time to load. When this occurs, you can click the **Stop** button in Internet Explorer or Navigator to halt the Web page transfer from the server; you can then click the hyperlink again. A second attempt may connect and transfer the page more quickly. You also might want to use the Stop button to abort a transfer when you accidentally click a hyperlink that you do not want to follow.

Returning to a Web Page

You can use Internet Explorer's Favorites feature or a Navigator bookmark to store and organize a list of Web pages that you have visited so you can return to them easily without having to remember the URL or search for the page again. Internet Explorer favorites and Navigator bookmarks work very much like a paper bookmark that you might use in a printed book: They mark the page at which you stopped reading.

You can save as many Internet Explorer favorites or Navigator bookmarks as you want to mark all of your favorite Web pages, so you can return to pages that you frequently use or pages that are important to your research or tasks. You could bookmark every Web page you visit!

Keeping track of many favorites and bookmarks requires an organizing system. You store favorites or bookmarks in a system folder. Internet Explorer stores *each* favorite as a separate file on your computer, and Netscape stores bookmarks in one file on your computer. Storing each favorite separately, instead of storing all bookmarks together, offers somewhat more flexibility but uses more disk space. You can organize your favorites or bookmarks in many different ways to meet your needs. For example, you might store all of the favorites or bookmarks for Web pages that include information about wind quintets in a folder named "Wind Quintet Information."

Printing and Saving Web Pages

As you use your browser to view Web pages, you will find some pages that you want to print or store for future use. Web browsers include both the print and save capabilities. Web browsers allow you to save entire Web pages or just parts of the Web page, such as selections of text or graphics.

Printing a Web Page

The easiest way to print a Web page in Internet Explorer or Navigator is to click the browser's **Print** button. In either case, the current page (or part of a page, called a **frame**) that appears in the Web page area of the browser is sent to the printer. If the page contains light colors or many graphics, you might consider changing the printing options so the page prints without the background or with all black text. You will learn how to change the print settings for Internet Explorer and Navigator in Sessions 2.2 and 2.3, respectively.

Although printing an entire Web page is often useful, there are times when you will want to save all or part of the page to disk.

Saving a Web Page

When you save the HTML code of a Web page to disk, you save only the text portion. If the Web page contains graphics, such as photos, drawings, or icons, they will not be saved with the HTML document. To save a graphic separately, right-click the graphic in the browser window, click Save Picture As (in Internet Explorer) or Save Image (in Navigator) on the shortcut menu, and then save the graphic to the same location to which you saved the Web's HTML document. The graphics file is referenced in the HTML document as a hyperlink. Depending on how the Web page designer created the reference, you might have to edit the HTML code in the Web page to identify the new location of the graphic. Copying the graphics files to the same disk (or the same folder on a hard disk) as the HTML document will *usually* work. You will learn more about saving a Web page and its graphics in Sessions 2.2 and 2.3.

Reproducing Web Pages and Copyright Law

Maggie explains that there can be significant restrictions on the way that you can use information or images that you copy from another entity's Web site. Because of the way a Web browser works, it copies all of the HTML code and most of the graphics and media files to your computer before it can display them in the browser. Just because copies of these files are stored temporarily on your computer does not mean that you have the right to use them in any way other than having your computer display them in the browser window. The United States and other countries have copyright laws that govern the use of photocopies, audio or video recordings, and other reproductions of authors' original work. A **copyright** is the legal right of the author or other owner of an original work to control the reproduction, distribution, and sale of that work. A copyright comes into existence as soon as the work is placed into a tangible form, such as a printed copy, an electronic file, or a Web page. The copyright exists even if the work does not contain a copyright notice. If you do not know whether material that you find on the Web is copyrighted, the safest course of action is to assume that it is.

You can use limited amounts of copyrighted information in term papers and other reports that you prepare in an academic setting, but you must cite the source. Commercial use of copyrighted material is much more restricted. You should obtain permission from the copyright holder before using anything you copy from a Web page. It can be difficult to determine the owner of a source's copyright if no notice appears on the Web page; however, most Web pages provide a hyperlink to the e-mail address of the person responsible for maintaining the page. That person, often called a **webmaster**, usually can provide information about the copyright status of materials on the page.

Now that you understand the basic function of a browser and how to find information on the Web, you are ready to start using your browser to find information for the quintet. If you are using Internet Explorer, your instructor will assign Session 2.2; if you are using Navigator, your instructor will assign Session 2.3. The authors recommend, however, that you read both sessions because you might encounter a different browser on a public or employer's computer in the future.

Session 2.1 QUICK CHECK

1. True or False: Web browser software runs on a Web server computer.

2. True or False: You can format text using HTML tags.

3. The Web page that opens when you start your browser is called a(n) _____ or a(n) _____ .

4. The general term for graphic images, sound clips, or video clips that appear in a Web page is _____ .

5. A local political candidate is creating a Web site to help in her campaign for office. Describe three things she might want to include in her Web site.

6. What is the difference between IP addressing and domain name addressing?

7. Identify and interpret the meaning of each part of the following URL: http://www.savethetrees.org/main.html.

8. What is the difference between a Web directory and a Web search engine?

SESSION 2.2

In this session, you will learn how to configure the Microsoft Internet Explorer Web browser and use it to display Web pages. You will learn how to use Internet Explorer to follow hyperlinks from one Web page to another and how to record the URLs of sites to which you would like to return. Finally, you will print and save Web pages.

Starting Microsoft Internet Explorer

Microsoft Internet Explorer is Microsoft's Web browser that installs with Windows 95, Windows 98, Windows 2000, or Windows XP. This introduction assumes that you have Internet Explorer installed on your computer. You should have your computer turned on so the Windows desktop is displayed.

To start Internet Explorer:

1. Click the **Start** button on the taskbar, point to **Programs**, point to **Internet Explorer**, and then click **Internet Explorer**. After a moment, Internet Explorer opens.

   TROUBLE? If you cannot find Internet Explorer on the Programs menu, check to see if an Internet Explorer shortcut icon appears on the desktop, and then double-click it. If you do not see the shortcut icon, ask your instructor or technical support person for help. The program might be installed in a different folder on your computer.

2. If the program does not fill the screen entirely, click the **Maximize** button on the Internet Explorer program's title bar. Your screen should look like Figure 2-10.

Figure 2-10	INTERNET EXPLORER MAIN PROGRAM WINDOW

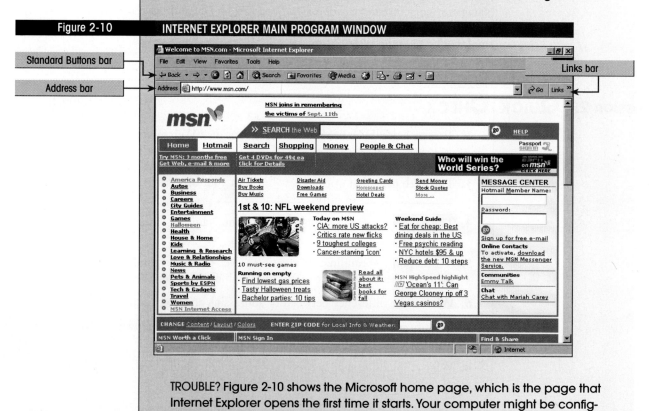

Standard Buttons bar

Address bar

Links bar

TROUBLE? Figure 2-10 shows the Microsoft home page, which is the page that Internet Explorer opens the first time it starts. Your computer might be configured to open to a different Web page or no page at all.

TROUBLE? If you do not see the bars shown in Figure 2-10, click View on the menu bar, point to Toolbars, and then click the name of the bar that is not displayed on the screen. A toolbar that is displayed has a check mark to the left of its name.

Internet Explorer includes a **Standard Buttons toolbar** with 13 buttons. Many of these buttons execute frequently used commands for browsing the Web. Figure 2-11 shows these buttons and describes the functions of the most commonly used buttons.

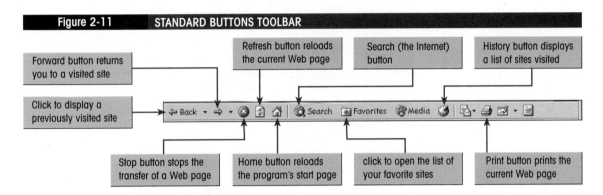

Figure 2-11   STANDARD BUTTONS TOOLBAR

Now that you understand how to start Internet Explorer, you want to learn more about components of the Internet Explorer program window.

Status Bar

The **status bar** at the bottom of the window includes several panels that give you information about Internet Explorer's operations. The first panel—the **transfer progress report**— presents status messages that show, for example, the URL of a page while it is loading. When a page is completely loaded, this panel displays the text "Done" until you move the mouse over a hyperlink. This panel displays the URL of any hyperlink on the page when you move the mouse pointer over it. A second panel that opens when a Web page is loading displays a blue **graphical transfer progress indicator** that moves from left to right in the right side of the panel to indicate how much of a Web page has loaded while Internet Explorer is loading it from a Web server. This indicator is especially useful for monitoring progress when you are loading large Web pages.

Another status bar panel displays a locked padlock icon when the browser loads a Web page that has a security certificate. You can double-click on the padlock icon to open a dialog box that contains information about the security certificate for a Web page.

The last (rightmost) status bar panel displays the **security zone** to which the page you are viewing has been assigned. As part of its security features, Internet Explorer lets you classify Web pages by the security risk you believe they present. You can open the Internet Security Properties dialog box shown in Figure 2-12 by double-clicking the last (rightmost) status bar panel. This window lets you set four levels of security-enforcing procedures: High, Medium, Medium-Low, and Low. In general, the higher level of security you set for your browser, the slower it will operate. Higher security settings also disable some of the browser features. You can click the Custom Level button to configure the way each security level operates on your computer.

Figure 2-12	INTERNET SECURITY PROPERTIES DIALOG BOX

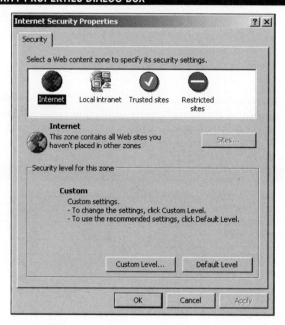

Menu Bar

In addition to the standard Windows commands, the menu bar also provides access to Favorites. The Favorites menu command lets you store and organize URLs of sites that you have visited and want or need to return to on regular basis.

Hiding and Showing the Internet Explorer Toolbars

Internet Explorer lets you hide its menu bar and toolbars to show more of the Web page area. To hide the menu bar, you can select the Full Screen option on the View menu. When the window is in **Full Screen**, the menu bar is no longer visible, and a smaller version of the Standard Buttons toolbar appears at the top of the screen. To hide the small Standard Buttons toolbar, right-click the toolbar and click Auto-Hide to give you some room for displaying the Web page. To restore the screen so both the menu bar and Standard Buttons toolbar are visible, press the F11 key.

REFERENCE WINDOW RW

<u>Hiding and Restoring the Toolbars in Internet Explorer</u>
- To hide a toolbar, click View on the menu bar, point to Toolbars, and deselect the toolbar you want to hide; or right-click a toolbar, and deselect the toolbar listed in the shortcut menu that you want to hide.
- To hide a toolbar in Full Screen, right-click the small Standard Buttons toolbar that appears at the top of the screen, and then click Auto-Hide on the shortcut menu.
- To restore a toolbar, click View on the menu bar, point to Toolbars, and click to select the toolbar you want to restore; or right-click a toolbar, and click the toolbar listed in the shortcut menu that you want to restore.
- To temporarily restore the small Standard Buttons toolbar in Full Screen, move the mouse to the top of the screen until the toolbar displays.
- To restore the small Standard Buttons toolbar in Full Screen, move the mouse to the top of the screen until the toolbar displays, and then click the Restore button at the far right of the toolbar.

You will switch to Full Screen and try hiding and then restoring the small Standard Buttons toolbar.

To use the Full Screen and Auto Hide commands:

1. Click **View** on the menu bar, then click **Full Screen**.

2. Right-click the small Standard Buttons toolbar that appears at the top of the screen to open the shortcut menu, and then click **Auto-Hide** on the shortcut menu if it is not already checked.

3. Move the mouse pointer away from the top of the screen for a moment. Now, you can see more of the Web page area. When the toolbar disappears, return the mouse pointer to the top of the screen to display it again.

4. With the toolbar displayed, right-click the toolbar and then click **Auto-Hide** on the shortcut menu. This removes the check mark from the Auto-Hide entry on the menu and turns the toolbar on again.

5. Click the **Restore** button to return to the normal Internet Explorer window.

You can use the Customize command on the View Toolbars menu to change the appearance of the toolbars. For example, you can choose to show the Standard Buttons toolbar buttons with large icons or small icons.

You may have noticed that there is another option on the shortcut menu that opens when you right-click a toolbar—Lock the Toolbars. If there is a check mark next to the Lock the Toolbars option, then you cannot move the toolbars. To unlock the toolbars, click Lock the Toolbars again to clear the check mark.

Entering a URL in the Address Bar

Maggie explains that you can use the **Address bar** to enter URLs directly into Internet Explorer. As you learned in Session 2.1, you must enter the URL to identify a Web page's exact location. Although a complete URL includes the name of a file, entering just the IP address and the domain name should be enough information to find the home page of the site.

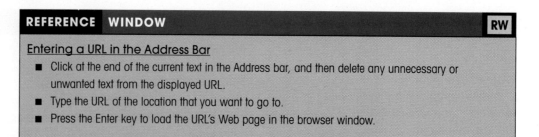

REFERENCE WINDOW   **RW**

Entering a URL in the Address Bar
- Click at the end of the current text in the Address bar, and then delete any unnecessary or unwanted text from the displayed URL.
- Type the URL of the location that you want to go to.
- Press the Enter key to load the URL's Web page in the browser window.

Marianna has asked you to start your research by examining the Web page for the Miami Wind Quintet. She has given you the URL so that you can find its Web page.

To load the Miami Wind Quintet's Web page:

1. Click at the end of the text in the Address bar, and then delete any unnecessary or unwanted text by pressing the **Backspace** key.

   TROUBLE? Make sure that you delete all of the text in the Address bar so the text you type in Step 2 will be correct.

2. Type **www.course.com/newperspectives/internet3** in the Address bar. This URL will take you to the Student Online Companion page on the Course Technology Web site, and then you can click the hyperlinks provided in the steps in this tutorial to go to individual Web pages.

3. Press the **Enter** key. The Student Online Companion Web page loads, as shown in Figure 2-13. When the entire page has loaded, the graphical transfer progress indicator in the status bar will stop moving and the transfer progress report panel will display the text "Done."

Figure 2-13   **STUDENT ONLINE COMPANION PAGE AT COURSE.COM**

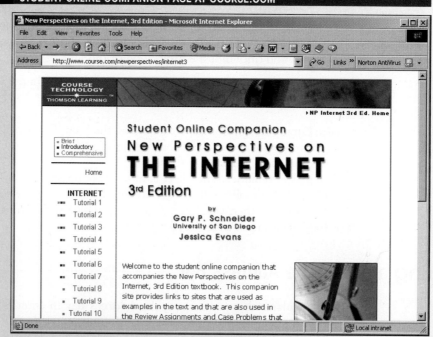

4. Click the hyperlink for your book, click the **Tutorial 2** link, and then click the **Session 2.3** link.

5. Click the link to the **Miami Wind Quintet** in the right frame. The Web page opens, as shown in Figure 2-14.

| Figure 2-14 | MIAMI WIND QUINTET WEB PAGE |

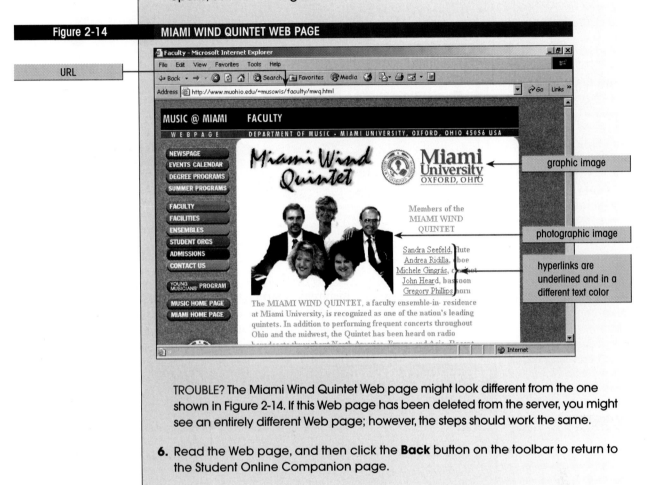

TROUBLE? The Miami Wind Quintet Web page might look different from the one shown in Figure 2-14. If this Web page has been deleted from the server, you might see an entirely different Web page; however, the steps should work the same.

6. Read the Web page, and then click the **Back** button on the toolbar to return to the Student Online Companion page.

You like the format of the Miami Wind Quintet's home page, so you want to make sure that you can go back to that page later if you need to review its contents. Maggie explains that you can write down the URL so you can refer to it later, but an easier way is to store the URL in the Favorites list for future use.

Using the Favorites List

Internet Explorer's **Favorites** feature lets you store and organize a list of Web pages that you have visited so you can return to them easily. The Favorites button on the Standard Buttons toolbar opens the Favorites bar shown in Figure 2-15. You can use the Favorites bar to open URLs you have stored as Favorites.

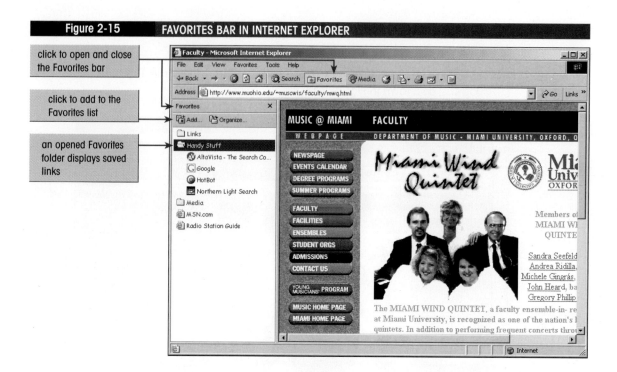

| Figure 2-15 | **FAVORITES BAR IN INTERNET EXPLORER** |

click to open and close the Favorites bar

click to add to the Favorites list

an opened Favorites folder displays saved links

Figure 2-15 shows the hierarchical structure of the Favorites feature. There are four search engine Web pages stored in a folder named "Handy Stuff." You can organize your favorites in the way that best suits your needs and working style.

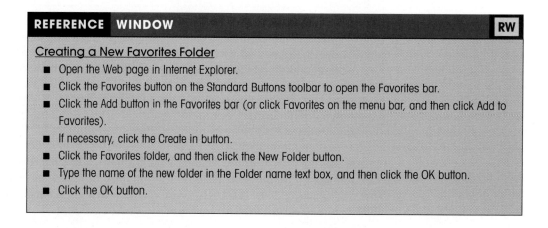

REFERENCE WINDOW   **RW**

Creating a New Favorites Folder

- Open the Web page in Internet Explorer.
- Click the Favorites button on the Standard Buttons toolbar to open the Favorites bar.
- Click the Add button in the Favorites bar (or click Favorites on the menu bar, and then click Add to Favorites).
- If necessary, click the Create in button.
- Click the Favorites folder, and then click the New Folder button.
- Type the name of the new folder in the Folder name text box, and then click the OK button.
- Click the OK button.

You will save the URL for the Miami Wind Quintet Web page as a favorite in a Wind Quintet Information folder.

To create a new Favorites folder:

1. Click the **Forward** button on the Standard Buttons toolbar to return to the Miami Wind Quintet Web page.

2. Click the **Favorites** button on the Standard Buttons toolbar to open the Favorites bar.

3. Click the **Add** button at the top of the Favorites bar. The Add Favorite dialog box opens.

4. Delete the text in the Name field, and then type **Miami Wind Quintet**.

    If the symbols on the Create in button appear as >>, you will need to expand the dialog box so you can select the Favorites folder in which you will create a new folder.

5. If necessary, click the **Create in** button. Note that the dialog box expands to display a list of Favorites folders and that the symbols now appear as <<.

6. Click the **Favorites** folder in the Create in box, and then click the **New Folder** button. The new folder will be stored as a subfolder in the Favorites folder.

7. Type **Wind Quintet Information** in the Folder name text box, and then click the **OK** button. See Figure 2-16. Notice that the page name appears automatically in the Name text box in the Add Favorite dialog box. You can edit the suggested page name.

Figure 2-16	CREATING A NEW FAVORITES FOLDER

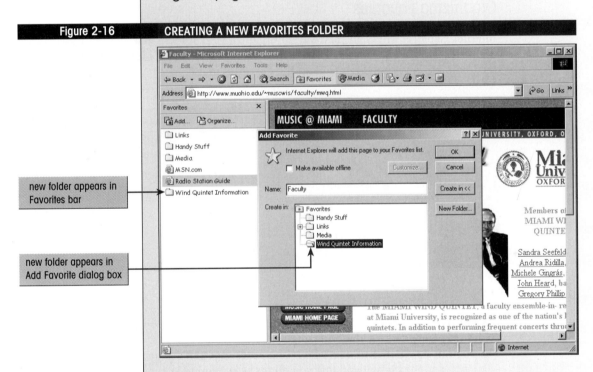

new folder appears in Favorites bar

new folder appears in Add Favorite dialog box

8. Click the **OK** button to close the Add Favorite dialog box. Now, the favorite is saved in Internet Explorer. You can test the favorite by opening it from the Favorites bar.

9. Click the **Back** button on the Standard Buttons toolbar to return to the previous page, click the **Wind Quintet Information** folder in the Favorites bar to open the folder, and then click **Miami Wind Quintet**. The Miami Wind Quintet page opens in the browser.

TROUBLE? If the Miami Wind Quintet page does not open, click Favorites on the menu bar, click the Wind Quintet Information folder, right-click the Miami Wind Quintet favorite, and then click Properties. Click the Internet Shortcut tab, and make sure that a URL appears in the Target URL text box; if there is no URL, then click the OK button to close the dialog box. Click Favorites on the menu bar, click the Wind Quintet Information folder, right-click the Miami Wind Quintet folder, and then click Delete. Repeat the steps to re-create the favorite, and then try again. If you still have trouble, ask your instructor or technical support person for help.

As you use the Web to find information about wind quintets and other sites of interest for the group, you might find yourself creating many favorites so you can return to sites of interest. When you start accumulating favorites, it is important to keep them organized. Internet Explorer helps you keep your favorites organized.

Organizing Favorites

Internet Explorer offers an easy way to organize your folders in a hierarchical structure—even after you have stored them. To rearrange URLs or even folders within folders, you use the Organize Favorites command on the Favorites menu.

REFERENCE WINDOW   **RW**

Moving an Existing Favorite into a New Folder
- Click Favorites on the menu bar, and then click Organize Favorites.
- Click the folder under which you want to add the new folder.
- Click the Create Folder button.
- Type the name of the new folder, and then press the Enter key.
- Drag the favorite that you want to move into the new folder.
- Click the Close button.

You explain to Maggie that you have created a new folder for Wind Quintet Information in the Internet Explorer Favorites bar and stored the Miami Wind Quintet's URL in that folder. Maggie suggests that you might not want to keep all of the wind quintet-related information you gather in one folder. She notes that you are just beginning your work for Marianna and the quintet and that you might be collecting all types of information for them. Maggie suggests that you might want to put information about the Miami Wind Quintet in a separate folder named Midwestern Ensembles under the Wind Quintet Information folder. As you collect information about other performers, you might add folders for categories such as East Coast and West Coast ensembles, too.

To move an existing favorite into a new folder:

1. Click **Favorites** on the menu bar, and then click **Organize Favorites**.

2. Click the **Wind Quintet Information** folder in the Organize Favorites dialog box.

3. Click the **Create Folder** button. The default "New Folder" text is automatically selected.

4. Type **Midwestern Ensembles** to replace the text, and then press the **Enter** key to rename the folder.

5. Click and drag the **Miami Wind Quintet** favorite to the new Midwestern Ensembles folder, and then release the mouse button. Now, the Midwestern Ensembles folder contains the favorite, as shown in Figure 2-17.

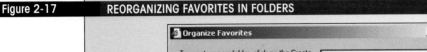

Figure 2-17   REORGANIZING FAVORITES IN FOLDERS

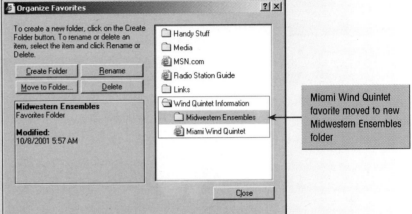

6. Click the **Close** button. The Favorites bar is updated automatically to reflect your changes.

7. Click the **Favorites** button on the Standard Buttons toolbar to close the Favorites bar.

Hyperlink Navigation Using the Mouse

Now you know how to use the Internet to find information that will help you with the Sunset Wind Quintet. Maggie tells you that the easiest way to move from one Web page to another is to use the mouse to click hyperlinks that the authors of Web pages embed in their HTML documents. You can also right-click the mouse on the background of a Web page to open a shortcut menu that includes navigation options.

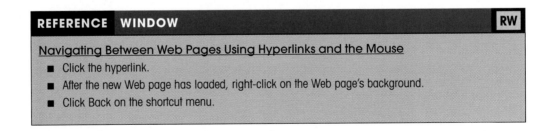

REFERENCE   WINDOW   RW

Navigating Between Web Pages Using Hyperlinks and the Mouse
- Click the hyperlink.
- After the new Web page has loaded, right-click on the Web page's background.
- Click Back on the shortcut menu.

To follow a hyperlink to a Web page and return using the mouse:

1. Click the **Back** button on the Standard Buttons toolbar to return to the Student Online Companion page, click the **Lewis Music** link, and then point to the **Instrument Accessories** hyperlink shown in Figure 2-18. Note that your pointer changes to the shape of a hand with a pointing index finger.

Figure 2-18	LEWIS MUSIC HOME PAGE

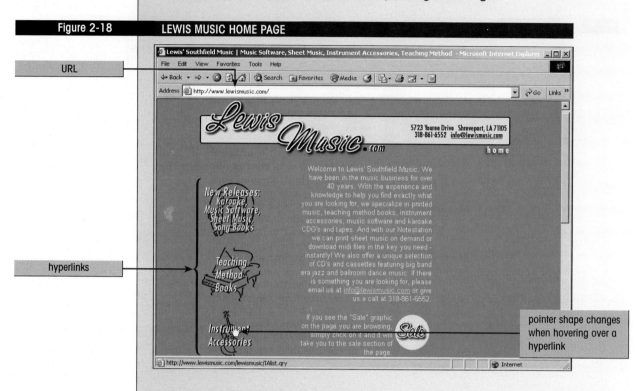

URL

hyperlinks

pointer shape changes when hovering over a hyperlink

2. Click the **Instrument Accessories** hyperlink. Watch the first panel in the status bar—when it displays the text "Done," you know that Internet Explorer has loaded the full page.

3. Right-click anywhere in the Web page area that is not a hyperlink to display the shortcut menu, as shown in Figure 2-19.

| Figure 2-19 | USING THE SHORTCUT MENU TO GO BACK TO THE PREVIOUS PAGE |

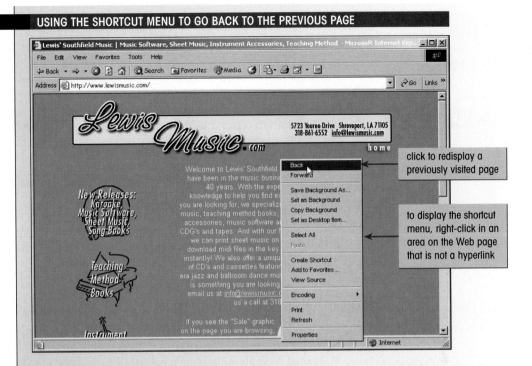

TROUBLE? If you right-click a hyperlink, your shortcut menu will display a list that differs from the one shown in Figure 2-19; therefore the Back item might not appear in the same position on the menu or not appear at all. If you do not see the shortcut menu shown in Figure 2-19, click anywhere outside of the short-cut menu to close it, and then repeat Step 3.

TROUBLE? Web pages change frequently, so the Instrument Accessories page you see might look different from the one shown in Figure 2-19, but right-clicking anywhere on the Web page area that is not a hyperlink will still work.

4. Click **Back** on the shortcut menu to return to the Lewis Music home page.

5. Repeat Step 4 to return to the Student Online Companion page.

Using the History List

The Back and Forward buttons on the Standard Buttons toolbar enable you to move to and from previously visited pages. As you move back and forth between pages, Internet Explorer records these visited sites in the history list. To see where you have been during a session, you also can open the history list by clicking the **History** button on the Standard Buttons toolbar.

To view the history list for this session:

1. Click the **History** button on the Standard Buttons toolbar. The history list opens in a hierarchical structure in a separate window on the left side of the screen. The history list stores each URL you visited during the past week or during a specified time period. It also maintains the hierarchy of each Web site; that is, pages you visit at a particular Web site are stored in a separate folder for that site. To return to a particular page, click that page's entry in the list. You can see the full URL of any item in the History bar by moving the mouse pointer over the history list item.

2. Click the **Close** button on the History bar title bar to close it.

You can right-click any entry in the history list and then copy the URL or delete it from the list. Internet Explorer stores each history entry as a shortcut in a History folder, which is in the Windows folder.

Refreshing a Web Page

The Refresh button on the Standard Buttons toolbar loads a new copy of the current Web page that currently appears in the browser window. Internet Explorer stores a copy of every Web page it displays on your computer's hard drive in a **Temporary Internet Files** folder in the Windows folder. Storing this information increases the speed at which Internet Explorer can display pages as you move back and forth through the history list because the browser can load the pages from a local disk drive instead of reloading the page from the remote Web server. When you click the Refresh button, Internet Explorer contacts the Web server to see if the Web page has changed since it was stored in the cache folder. If it has changed, Internet Explorer gets the new page from the Web server; otherwise, it loads the cache folder copy.

Returning to the Home Page

The Home button on the Standard Buttons toolbar displays the home (or start) page for your copy of Internet Explorer. You can change the setting for the Home toolbar button to display the page you want to use as the default home page.

REFERENCE WINDOW	RW

Changing the Default Home Page in Internet Explorer
- Click Tools on the menu bar, and then click Internet Options.
- Click the General tab.
- Select whether you want Internet Explorer to open with the current page, its default page, or a blank page by clicking the corresponding button in the Home page section of the Internet Options dialog box.
- To specify a home page, type the URL of that Web page in the Address text box.
- Click the OK button.

To view the settings for the default home page:

1. Click **Tools** on the menu bar, and then click **Internet Options**. The Internet Options dialog box opens, as shown in Figure 2-20. To use the currently loaded Web page as your home page, click the Use Current button. To use the default home page that was installed with your copy of Internet Explorer, click the Use Default button. If you don't want a page to open when you start your browser, click the Use Blank button. If you want to specify a home page other than the current, default, or blank page, type the URL for that page in the Address box.

| Figure 2-20 | CHANGING THE DEFAULT HOME PAGE |

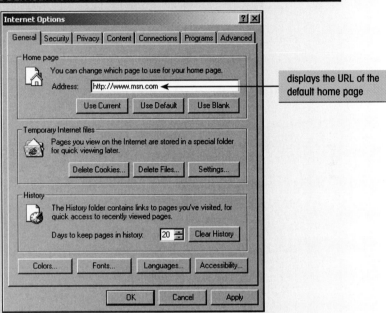

displays the URL of the default home page

TROUBLE? Do not change any settings unless you are instructed to do so by your instructor. Many organizations set the home page defaults on all of their computers and then lock those settings.

2. Click the **Cancel** button to close the dialog box without making any changes.

Printing a Web Page

The Print button on the Standard Buttons toolbar lets you print the current Web frame or page. You can use the Print command to make a printed copy of most Web pages (some Web pages disable the Print command).

REFERENCE WINDOW   **RW**

Printing the Current Web Page
- Click the Print button on the Standard Buttons toolbar to print the current Web page with the default print settings.

or

- Click File on the menu bar, and then click Print.
- Select the printer you want to use, and indicate the pages you want to print and the number of copies you want to make of each page.
- To print a range of pages, click the Pages option button, and then type the first page of the range in the from box and the last page of the range in the to box.
- Click the OK button.

To print a Web page:

1. Click in the main (right) frame of the Student Online Companion page to select it.

2. Click **File** on the menu bar, and then click **Print** to open the Print dialog box.

3. Make sure that the printer in the Name list box display the printer you want to use; if not, click the Name list arrow to change the selection.

4. Click the **Pages** option button in the Print range section of the Print dialog box, type **1** in the from text box, press the **Tab** key, and then type **1** in the to text box to specify that you only want to print the first page.

5. Make sure that the Number of copies text box displays **1**.

6. Click the **OK** button to print the Web page and close the Print dialog box.

Changing the Settings for the Page Setup

You have seen how to print a Web page using the basic options available in the Print dialog box. Usually, the default settings in the Print dialog box are fine for printing a Web page, but you can use the Page Setup dialog box to change the way a Web page prints. Figure 2-21 shows the Page Setup dialog box, and Figure 2-22 describes its settings.

Figure 2-21	PAGE SETUP DIALOG BOX

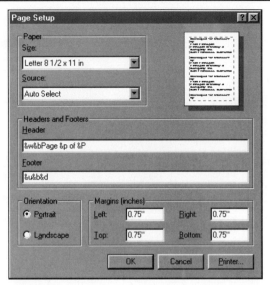

Figure 2-22	PAGE SETUP DIALOG BOX OPTIONS	
OPTION	**DESCRIPTION**	**USE**
Paper Size	Changes the size of the printed page.	Use the Letter size default unless you are printing to different paper stock, such as Legal.
Paper Source	Changes the printer's paper source.	Use the default Auto Select unless you want to specify a different tray or manual feed for printing on heavy paper.
Header	Prints the Web page's title, URL, date/time printed, and page numbers at the top of each page.	To obtain details on how to specify exact header printing options, click the Header text box to select it, and then press the F1 key.
Footer	Prints the Web page's title, URL, date/time printed, and page numbers at the bottom of each page.	To obtain details on how to specify exact footer printing options, click the Footer text box to select it, and then press the F1 key.
Orientation	Selects the orientation of the printed output.	Portrait works best for most Web pages, but you can use landscape orientation to print the wide tables of numbers included on some Web pages.
Margins	Changes the margin of the printed page.	Normally, you should leave the default settings, but you can change the right, left, top, or bottom margins as needed.

When printing long Web pages, another print option that is extremely useful for saving paper is to reduce the font size of the Web pages before you print them. To do this, click View on the menu bar, point to Text Size, and then click Smaller or Smallest on the menu.

Checking **Web Page Security**

You can check some of the security elements of a Web page by clicking File on the menu bar, clicking Properties, and then clicking the Certificates button. Internet Explorer will display security information for the page, if it is available, to advise you of the overall security of the page that appears in the browser window. An example of this type of security information appears in Figure 2-23.

Figure 2-23   WEB PAGE SECURITY INFORMATION

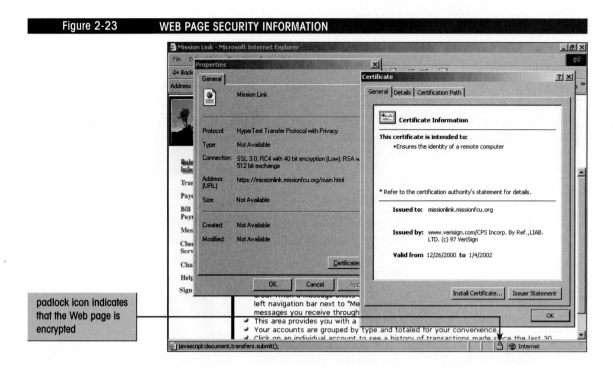

padlock icon indicates that the Web page is encrypted

Encryption is a way of scrambling and encoding data transmissions that reduces the risk that a person who intercepts the Web page as it travels across the Internet will be able to decode and read the page's contents. Web sites use encrypted transmission to send and receive information, such as credit card numbers, to ensure privacy. When Internet Explorer loads an encrypted Web page, a padlock symbol appears in the fourth pane (second from the right) of the status bar at the bottom of the Internet Explorer window.

Getting **Help in Internet Explorer**

Internet Explorer includes a comprehensive online Help system. You can open the Help Contents window to learn more about the Help options that are available.

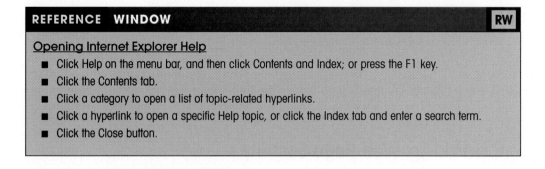

REFERENCE WINDOW   RW

Opening Internet Explorer Help

- Click Help on the menu bar, and then click Contents and Index; or press the F1 key.
- Click the Contents tab.
- Click a category to open a list of topic-related hyperlinks.
- Click a hyperlink to open a specific Help topic, or click the Index tab and enter a search term.
- Click the Close button.

To open the Internet Explorer Help:

1. Click **Help** on the menu bar, and then click **Contents and Index** to open the Internet Explorer Help window.

2. If necessary, click the **Maximize** button on the Internet Explorer Help window so it fills the desktop.

3. Click the **Contents** tab, click **Finding the Web Pages You Want**, and then click **Listing your favorite pages for quick viewing** to open that help topic in the Help window. Notice that the page that opens in a Help window contains links to related categories that you can explore, as shown in Figure 2-24.

Figure 2-24	INTERNET EXPLORER HELP WINDOW

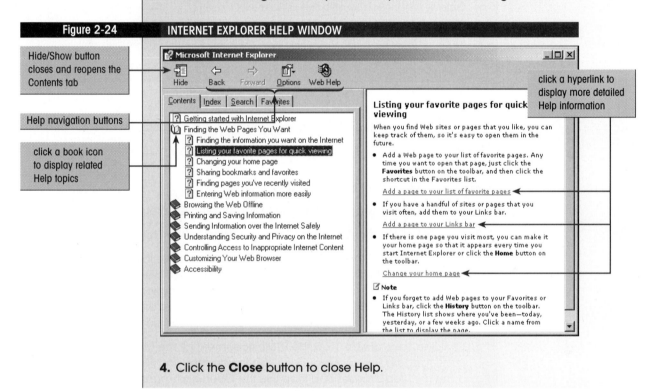

4. Click the **Close** button to close Help.

You feel confident that you have the tools you need to successfully find information on the Web. Marianna probably will be interested in seeing the Miami Wind Quintet Web page, but you are not sure if she will have Internet access while she is touring. Maggie says that you can save the Web page on disk, so Marianna can open the page locally in her Web browser using the files you save on that disk.

Using **Internet Explorer to Save a Web Page**

There will be times when you will want to refer to the information that you have found on a Web page without having to search the site. In Internet Explorer you can store entire Web pages, selected portions of Web page text, or particular graphics from a Web page to a disk.

Saving a Web Page

You like the Miami Wind Quintet's Web site and want to save a copy of the page to a disk so you can show the Web page to Marianna. That way, she can review it without having an Internet connection. To save a Web page, you must have the page open in Internet Explorer.

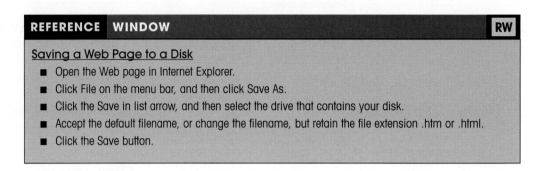

REFERENCE WINDOW   RW

Saving a Web Page to a Disk
- Open the Web page in Internet Explorer.
- Click File on the menu bar, and then click Save As.
- Click the Save in list arrow, and then select the drive that contains your disk.
- Accept the default filename, or change the filename, but retain the file extension .htm or .html.
- Click the Save button.

You will save the Miami Wind Quintet page to a disk so you can send it to Marianna for her review.

To save the Web page to a disk:

1. Use your Favorites list to return to the Miami Wind Quintet page.

2. Click **File** on the menu bar, and then click **Save As**. The Save As dialog box opens.

3. If necessary, click the **Save in** list arrow, select the drive that contains your disk, select the **Tutorial.02** folder, and then type **MiamiWindQuintet.htm** in the File name box. Note that you can select the Web Page option in the Save as type list and type the name of the file without typing the file extension; with the Web Page option selected the program will automatically add the file extension.

4. Click the **Save** button. Now the HTML document for the Miami Wind Quintet's home page is saved on your disk. When you send it to Marianna, she can open her Web browser and then use the Open command on the File menu to open the Web page.

If the Web page contains graphics, such as photos, drawings, or icons, they might not be saved with the HTML document. To save a graphic, right-click it in the browser window, click Save Picture As on the shortcut menu, and then save the graphic to the same location as the Web's HTML document. The graphics file will appear on the HTML document as a hyperlink; therefore, you might have to change the HTML code in the Web page to identify the location of the graphic. Copying the graphics files to the same disk as the HTML document will *usually* work. In Internet Explorer, you can make sure that a graphic is stored with the text file by selecting Web Page as the Save as type field. With this setting, Internet Explorer will create a separate folder for all of the graphic page elements and will rewrite the HTML of the Web page to ensure that its links to the graphics files are rewritten if necessary. If the page has many graphics elements, however, it is possible that the files containing those elements will not all fit on a standard 3 ½-inch disk.

Saving Web Page Text to a File

You can save portions of Web page text to a file, so that you can use the file in other programs. You will use WordPad to save text that you will copy from a Web page; however, any word processor or text editor will work.

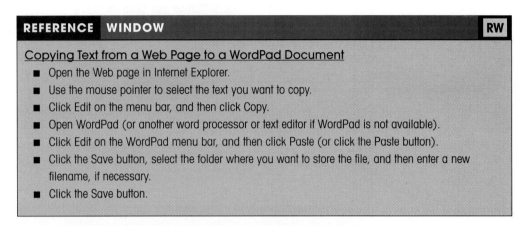

REFERENCE WINDOW   **RW**

Copying Text from a Web Page to a WordPad Document
- Open the Web page in Internet Explorer.
- Use the mouse pointer to select the text you want to copy.
- Click Edit on the menu bar, and then click Copy.
- Open WordPad (or another word processor or text editor if WordPad is not available).
- Click Edit on the WordPad menu bar, and then click Paste (or click the Paste button).
- Click the Save button, select the folder where you want to store the file, and then enter a new filename, if necessary.
- Click the Save button.

Marianna just called to let you know that the quintet will play a concert in Grand Rapids on a Friday night, and she asks you to identify other opportunities for scheduling local concerts during the following weekend. Often, museums are willing to book small ensembles for weekend afternoon programs, and Marianna has given you the URL for the Grand Rapids Art Museum. You will visit the site and then get the museum's address and telephone number so you can contact it about scheduling a concert.

To copy text from a Web page and save it as a WordPad document:

1. Use the **Back** button to return to the Student Online Companion page, and then click the **Grand Rapids Art Museum** link to open that Web page in the browser window.

2. Click the **address** hyperlink in the left frame on the Web page to open the museum information page in the main (right) frame.

3. Drag the mouse pointer over the address and telephone number to select it, as shown in Figure 2-25.

Figure 2-25   SELECTING TEXT ON A WEB PAGE

selected text is
highlighted

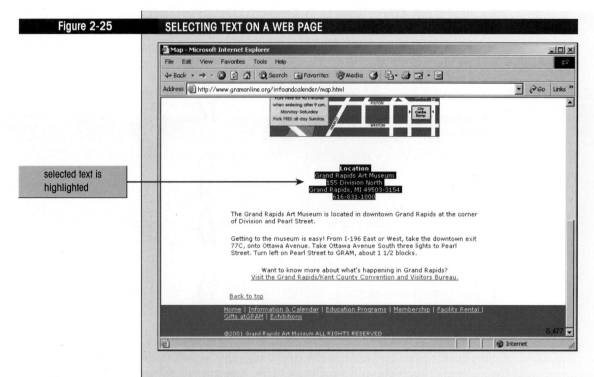

4. Click **Edit** on the menu bar, and then click **Copy** to copy the selected text to the Clipboard.

   Now, you will start WordPad and then paste the copied text into a new document.

5. Click the **Start** button on the taskbar, point to **Programs**, point to **Accessories**, and then click **WordPad** to start the program and open a new document.

6. Click the **Paste** button on the WordPad toolbar to paste the text into the WordPad document, as shown in Figure 2-26.

   TROUBLE? If the WordPad toolbar does not appear, click View on the menu bar, click Toolbar to turn it on, and then repeat Step 2. Your WordPad program window might be a different size from the one shown in Figure 2-26, which does not affect the steps.

Figure 2-26   **PASTING TEXT FROM A WEB PAGE INTO A WORDPAD DOCUMENT**

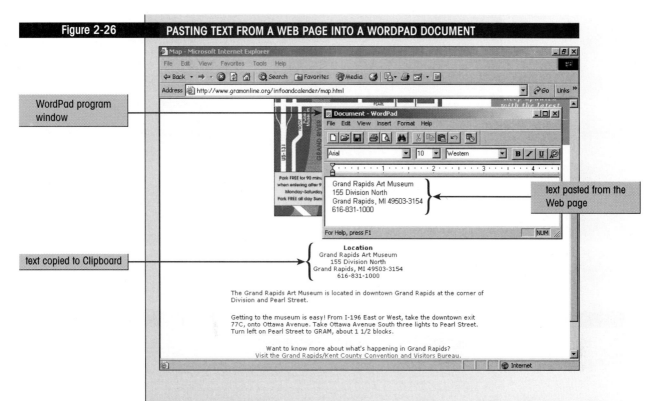

7. Click the **Save** button on the WordPad toolbar to open the Save As dialog box.

8. Click the **Save in** list arrow, select the drive that contains your disk, and then select the **Tutorial.02** folder.

9. Delete the text in the File name text box, type **GRAM-Address.txt**, and then click the **Save** button. Now, the address and phone number of the museum are saved in a file on your disk for future reference.

   TROUBLE? If a dialog box opens, asking if you want to replace the existing GRAM-Address.txt file on your disk, click the Yes button.

10. Click the **Close** button on the WordPad title bar to close it.

You will use this information to contact the museum at a later time. As you examine the Web page, you notice a street map of the area surrounding the museum, which Marianna might like to have.

Saving a Web Page Graphic to a Disk

The Web page with directions and transportation information will be helpful to Marianna, so you decide to save the map graphic to your disk. You can then send the file to Marianna so she has a resource for getting to the museum.

REFERENCE   WINDOW   RW

Saving an Image from a Web Page to a Disk
- Open the Web page in Internet Explorer.
- Right-click the image you want to copy, and then click Save Picture As.
- Select the drive and the folder that you want to save the image in, and change the default file-name, if necessary.
- Click the Save button.

Now you will save the image of the street map to your disk, which you will later send to Marianna.

To save the street map image to a disk:

1. Right-click the map image to open its shortcut menu, as shown in Figure 2-27.

Figure 2-27   SAVING THE MAP IMAGE TO A DISK

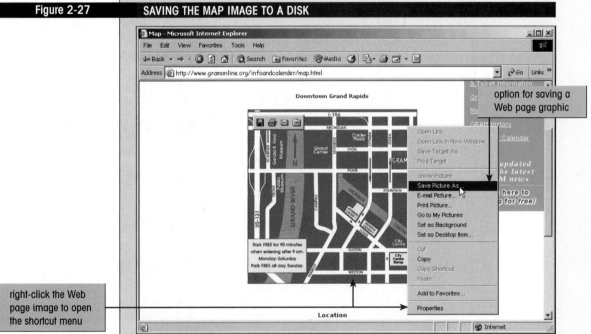

2. Click **Save Picture As** on the shortcut menu to open the Save As dialog box. Internet Explorer also opens a shortcut bar whenever you move the mouse pointer over a downloadable graphic on a Web page. This shortcut bar includes three buttons that you can click to save the image to a disk, print the image, or e-mail the image. A fourth button opens the My Pictures folder on your computer.

3. Click the **Save in** list arrow, select the drive that contains your disk, and then select the **Tutorial.02** folder.

4. Delete the text in the File name text box, type **GRAM-Map.jpg**, and then click the **Save** button to save the file.

5. Close your Web browser, and if necessary, log off your Internet connection.

Now, you can send a disk to Marianna so she will have the Miami Wind Quintet Web page and a map to show how to get to the museum. She will be able to use her Web browser to open the files and print them.

Session 2.2 QUICK CHECK

1. Describe two ways to increase the Web page area in Internet Explorer.

2. You can use the _____ button in Internet Explorer to visit previously visited sites during your Web session.

3. Clicking the _____ button on the Standard Buttons toolbar opens a search frame that contains a number of different searching options.

4. List the names of two additional Favorites folders you might want to add to the Wind Quintet Information folder as you continue to gather information for the Sunset Wind Quintet.

5. To ensure that Internet Explorer loads a Web page from the server rather than from its cache, you can hold down the _____ key as you click the Refresh button.

6. True or False: You can identify encrypted Web pages when viewing them in Internet Explorer.

7. Describe two ways to obtain help on a specific topic in Internet Explorer.

If your instructor assigns Session 2.3, continue reading. Otherwise complete the Review Assignments at the end of this tutorial.

SESSION 2.3

In this session, you will learn how to configure the Netscape Navigator Web browser and use it to display Web pages and follow hyperlinks to other Web pages. You will learn how to copy text and images from Web pages and how to mark pages so you can return to them easily.

Starting Netscape Navigator

To effectively search the Web for the Sunset Wind Quintet, you need to become familiar with Netscape Navigator. The other programs in Netscape provide e-mail, instant messaging, Web page creation tools, and other functions. This introduction assumes that you have Navigator installed on your computer. You should have your computer turned on so the Windows desktop is displayed.

To start Navigator:

1. Click the **Start** button on the taskbar, point to **Programs**, point to **Netscape Navigator** or **Netscape**, and then click **Netscape 6**. After a moment, Netscape opens.

TROUBLE? If you cannot find Netscape on the Programs menu, check to see if a Netscape Navigator shortcut icon appears on the desktop, and then double-click it. If you do not see the shortcut icon, ask your instructor or technical support person for help. The program might be installed in a different folder on the computer you are using.

2. If the program does not fill the screen entirely, click the **Maximize** button on the Navigator program's title bar. Your screen should look like Figure 2-28.

Figure 2-28	NETSCAPE NETCENTER HOME PAGE

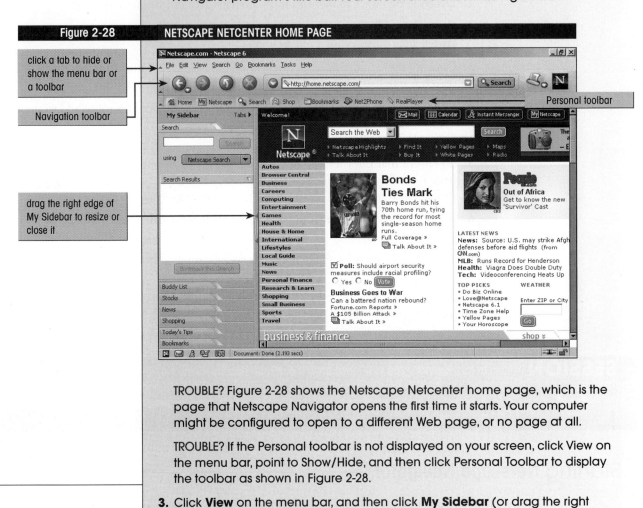

click a tab to hide or show the menu bar or a toolbar

Navigation toolbar

Personal toolbar

drag the right edge of My Sidebar to resize or close it

TROUBLE? Figure 2-28 shows the Netscape Netcenter home page, which is the page that Netscape Navigator opens the first time it starts. Your computer might be configured to open to a different Web page, or no page at all.

TROUBLE? If the Personal toolbar is not displayed on your screen, click View on the menu bar, point to Show/Hide, and then click Personal Toolbar to display the toolbar as shown in Figure 2-28.

3. Click **View** on the menu bar, and then click **My Sidebar** (or drag the right edge of the My Sidebar frame to the left side of the browser window to close My Sidebar). This will give you more room to view Web pages when using the Navigator browser. You can reopen My Sidebar at any time using the View menu or by clicking and dragging the left edge of the browser window to the right.

Now that you understand how to start Navigator, you want to learn more about the components of the Navigator program window.

Using **the Navigation and Personal Toolbars**

The **Navigation toolbar** includes six buttons that execute frequently used commands for browsing the Web. Figure 2-29 shows the Navigation toolbar buttons and describes their functions. (Depending on which version of Navigator you are using, you might see different toolbar buttons. Use online Help to get more information about buttons not pictured in Figure 2-29.)

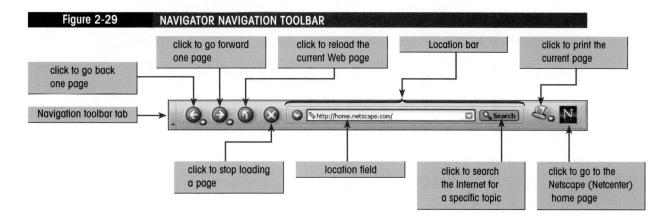

Figure 2-29   NAVIGATOR NAVIGATION TOOLBAR

click to go forward one page

click to reload the current Web page

Location bar

click to print the current page

click to go back one page

Navigation toolbar tab

http://home.netscape.com/

Search

click to stop loading a page

location field

click to search the Internet for a specific topic

click to go to the Netscape (Netcenter) home page

In addition to the toolbar buttons, the Navigation toolbar contains a Location bar. The Location bar is in the center of the Navigation toolbar and includes a location field and a Search (the Internet) button. You can type a URL in the location bar and then click the Search button to load a Web page. The Navigation toolbar also has a toolbar tab that you can click to hide the toolbar so there is more room to display a Web page in the Web page area. You can hide the Navigation toolbar so that the toolbar tab folds up and remains visible, or you can hide the toolbar completely by using the options on the View menu, as you will see next.

REFERENCE WINDOW   **RW**

Hiding or Showing a Toolbar In Navigator
- To hide the toolbar, click the toolbar tab for the toolbar that you want to hide; or click View on the menu bar, point to Show/Hide, and then click the name of the toolbar that you want to hide.
- To show a hidden toolbar, click the toolbar tab for the toolbar you want to show; or click View on the menu bar, click Show/Hide, and then click the name of the toolbar that you want to show.

To hide the Navigation toolbar and then show it again:

1. Click the **Navigation toolbar** tab. The toolbar disappears, but its tab redisplays under the Personal toolbar, which moves up under the menu bar.

2. Move the pointer to the Navigation toolbar tab below the Personal toolbar.

3. Click the **Navigation toolbar** tab. The Navigation toolbar appears above the Personal toolbar.

You can use the toolbar tabs to hide or show the toolbars quickly. However, if you want to hide the toolbars and their tabs, you must use the View menu. The View menu commands are toggles. A **toggle** is like a pushbutton switch on a television set; you press the button once to turn on the television and press it a second time to turn it off.

To hide the Navigation toolbar using the View menu:

1. Click **View** on the menu bar, point to **Show/Hide**, and then click **Navigation Toolbar**. Both the Navigation toolbar and its toolbar tab are no longer visible on the screen. To redisplay the Navigation toolbar and its tab, you repeat the same steps.

   TROUBLE? If the Navigation Toolbar does not have a check mark next to it, then the Navigation toolbar already is hidden.

2. Click **View** on the menu bar, point to **Show/Hide**, and then click **Navigation Toolbar**. The toolbar and its tab are displayed again.

Using the Location Bar

You can use the **Location bar** to enter URLs directly into Navigator. As you learned in Session 2.1, you must enter the URL to identify a Web page's exact location. Although a complete URL includes the name of a file, entering just the IP address or the domain name will usually be sufficient to take you to the home page of the site.

REFERENCE WINDOW	RW

Entering a URL in the Location Bar
- Click at the end of the current text in the location field, and then delete any unnecessary or unwanted text from the displayed URL.
- Type the URL to which you want to go.
- Press the Enter key to load the URL's Web page in the browser window.

Marianna has asked you to start your research by examining the Web page for the Miami Wind Quintet. She has given you the URL so that you can find its Web page.

To load the Miami Wind Quintet's Web page:

1. Click at the end of the text in the location field, and then delete any unnecessary or unwanted text by pressing the **Backspace** key.

   TROUBLE? Make sure that you delete all of the text in the location field so the text you type in Step 2 will be correct.

2. Type **www.course.com/newperspectives/internet3** in the location field. This URL will take you to the Student Online Companion page on the Course Technology Web site, and then you can click the hyperlinks provided in the steps in this tutorial to go to individual Web pages.

3. Press the **Enter** key. The Student Online Companion Web page loads, as shown in Figure 2-30.

Figure 2-30 STUDENT ONLINE COMPANION PAGE AT COURSE.COM

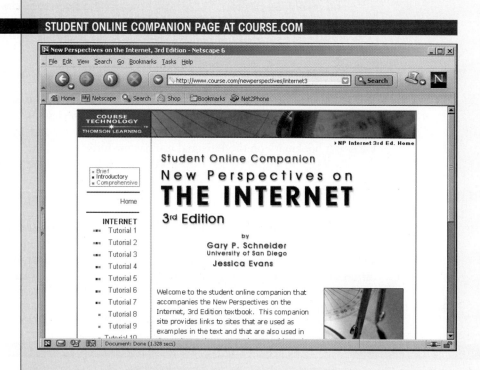

4. Click the hyperlink for your book, click the **Tutorial 2** link, and then click the **Session 2.2** link.

5. Click the **Miami Wind Quintet** link. The Web page opens, as shown in Figure 2-31.

Figure 2-31 MIAMI WIND QUINTET WEB PAGE

URL

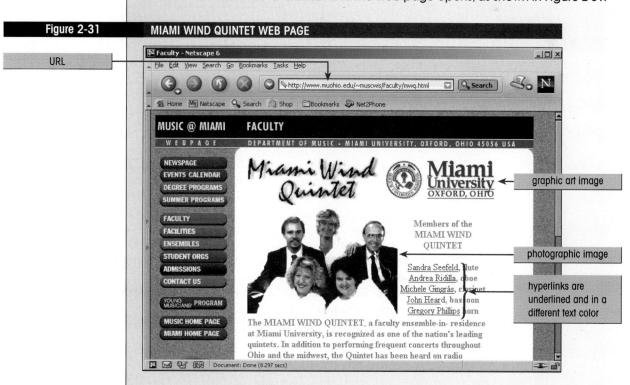

> TROUBLE? The Miami Wind Quintet Web page might look different from the one shown in Figure 2-31. If this Web page has been deleted from the server, you might see an entirely different Web page; however, the steps should work the same.
>
> **6.** Read the Web page, and then click the **Back** button on the toolbar to return to the Student Online Companion page.

You like the format of the Miami Wind Quintet's home page, so you want to make sure that you can go back to that page later if you need to review its contents. Maggie explains that you can write down the URL so you can refer to it later, but an easier way is to store the URL as a bookmark on the Personal toolbar for future use.

Using the Personal Toolbar

The **Personal toolbar** works very much like the Navigation toolbar, but with one significant difference. You can customize the Personal toolbar to meet your needs by adding and removing toolbar buttons. Because each person who installs Navigator can place a different set of buttons on the Personal toolbar, yours may look somewhat different from the one shown in Figure 2-32, depending on who installed the program on the computer you are using.

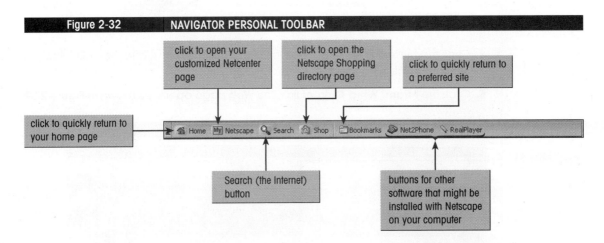

Figure 2-32   NAVIGATOR PERSONAL TOOLBAR

The Home button loads the program's defined start page. The **My Netscape** button opens a version of the Netscape's Netcenter page that you can customize. The **Search** button opens a Web page that has hyperlinks to Web search engines and directories. The **Shop** button opens the Netscape Shopping directory page, which contains links to featured products. The **Bookmarks** button opens a list of Web sites whose URLs you have saved. You will learn how to save bookmarks later in this session. Your Personal toolbar may have other buttons that lead to specific Web pages or that open other programs. For example, the Personal toolbar shown in Figure 2-32 is the default toolbar that results from a Navigator installation, which also includes the Net2Phone program (which allows the user to place telephone calls through the browser) and the RealPlayer program (which enables Navigator to play sound and video clips that have been stored on Web servers in the Real format).

Hiding and Showing the Personal Toolbar

You can click the Personal toolbar tab or use the View menu to hide and show the tool-bar, just as you did to hide and show the Navigation toolbar and its tab. Clicking the Personal toolbar tab hides the toolbar, but keeps the tab visible so you can redisplay the toolbar quickly.

Creating a Bookmark for a Web Site

You use a **bookmark** to store and organize a list of Web pages that you have visited so you can return to them easily. Figure 2-33 shows an open Bookmarks window, which contains bookmarks sorted into categories according to the user's needs.

Figure 2-33	BOOKMARKS SORTED INTO CATEGORIES

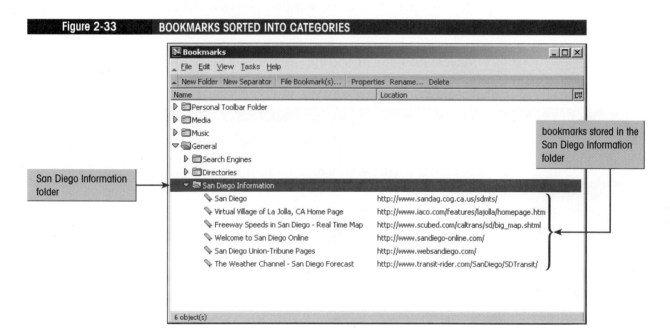

The hierarchical structure of the bookmark file is easy to see in Figure 2-33. For exam-ple, the six Web pages shown in the San Diego Information folder provide information about San Diego.

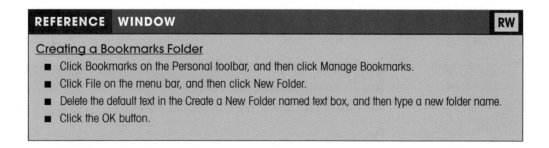

REFERENCE WINDOW   **RW**

Creating a Bookmarks Folder

- Click Bookmarks on the Personal toolbar, and then click Manage Bookmarks.
- Click File on the menu bar, and then click New Folder.
- Delete the default text in the Create a New Folder named text box, and then type a new folder name.
- Click the OK button.

You will create a bookmark for the Miami Wind Quintet Web page, but first, you need to create a folder in which to store your bookmarks. You will then save your bookmark in that folder. You might not work on the same computer again, so you will save a copy of the bookmark file to a floppy disk for future use.

To create a new Bookmarks folder:

1. Click the **Bookmarks** button on the Personal toolbar, and then click **Manage Bookmarks**. The Bookmarks window opens. Note that the title bar of the Bookmarks window indicates that this window is "for" a specific user. The title bar of the Bookmarks window on your computer might display your name or the name provided by the system administrator or technical support person.

2. Click **File** on the menu bar, and then click **New Folder**. The Create New Folder dialog box opens.

3. Delete the default text in the Create a New Folder named text box, type **Wind Quintet Information**, and then click the **OK** button. The Wind Quintet Information folder appears in the Bookmarks window, as shown in Figure 2-34.

Figure 2-34	WIND QUINTET INFORMATION FOLDER

the folders in the Bookmarks window on your screen might differ

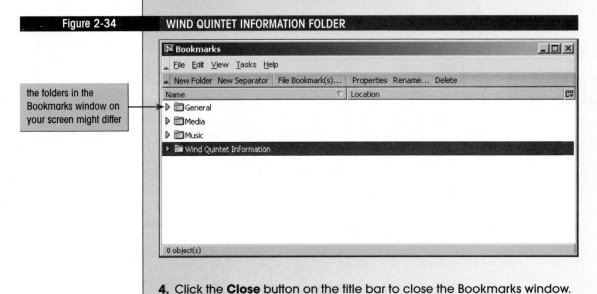

4. Click the **Close** button on the title bar to close the Bookmarks window.

Now that you have created a folder, you can save your bookmark for the Miami Wind Quintet Web page in the new folder.

REFERENCE WINDOW   RW

Saving a Bookmark in a Bookmarks Folder
- Open the page that you want to bookmark in Navigator.
- Click Bookmarks on the menu bar, and then click File Bookmark.
- Type a descriptive name in the box.
- Select the folder in which you want to save the bookmark.
- Click the OK button.

Before you save the bookmark, first you must return to the Web page that you want to bookmark.

> ### *To save a bookmark for the Miami Wind Quintet Web page in the Bookmarks folder:*
>
> 1. Click the **Forward** button on the Navigation toolbar to return to the Miami Wind Quintet Web page.
>
> 2. Click **Bookmarks** on the menu bar, and then click **File Bookmark**. The Add Bookmark dialog box opens.
>
> 3. Type **Miami Wind Quintet** in the Name text box.
>
>   TROUBLE? If necessary, delete any unnecessary text that appears in the Name text box before you begin typing the name for the bookmark.
>
> 4. Click the **Wind Quintet Information** folder in the Create in box, and then click the **OK** button. Now, the bookmark is saved in the correct folder. You can test your bookmark by using the bookmark to visit the site.
>
> 5. Click the **Back** button on the Navigation toolbar to go to the previous Web page.
>
> 6. Click **Bookmarks** on the menu bar, point to **Wind Quintet Information**, and then click **Miami Wind Quintet**. The Miami Wind Quintet page opens in the browser.
>
>   TROUBLE? If the Miami Wind Quintet page does not open, click Edit Bookmarks on the menu bar, make sure that you have the correct URL for the page, and then repeat Steps 6. If you still have trouble, ask your instructor or technical support person for help.

Because you might need to visit a Web page when you are working at another computer, you can save your bookmark file on a disk.

REFERENCE WINDOW   **RW**

Saving a Bookmark File to a Disk
- Click Bookmarks on the menu bar, and then click Manage Bookmarks.
- Click File on the menu bar, and then click Export Bookmarks.
- Click the Save in list arrow, and then select the drive that contains your disk.
- Type a name for the bookmark file.
- Click the Save button.

Because you might need to visit the Miami Wind Quintet page when you are working at another computer, you will save your bookmark file on a disk.

To store the Miami Wind Quintet bookmark file to a disk:

1. Click **Bookmarks** on the menu bar, and then click **Manage Bookmarks**. When you save a bookmark, you save all of the bookmarks, not just the one that you need.

2. Click **File** on the menu bar in the Bookmarks window, and then click Export Bookmarks. The Export bookmark file dialog box opens.

   TROUBLE? If prompted to, insert a disk in the appropriate drive on your computer.

3. If necessary, click the **Save in** list arrow, select the drive that contains your disk, and then select the **Tutorial.02** folder.

   TROUBLE? If you were prompted to insert a disk in Step 2, then the correct drive and disk should automatically appear in the Save in list box.

   The filename that you give the bookmark file should indicate the Web page you have marked. The file extension must be .htm or .html so the browser into which you load this file will recognize it as an HTML file. Most browsers will recognize either file extension; however, some do not. Also note that the filename cannot contain spaces.

4. Type **WindQuintetBookmarks.html** in the File name text box. Note that you can select the Web Page option in the Save as type list and type the name of the file without typing the file extension; with the Web Page option selected, the program will automatically add the file extension.

5. Click the **Save** button, and then close the Bookmarks window.

When you use another computer, you can open the bookmark file from your disk by starting Navigator, clicking Bookmarks on the menu bar, clicking Manage Bookmarks, clicking File on the menu bar, and then clicking Import Bookmarks. Change to the drive that contains your disk, and then open the HTML file. Your bookmark file will open in the Bookmarks window.

Hyperlink **Navigation Using the Mouse**

Now you know how to use Navigator to find information that will help you with the Sunset Wind Quintet. Maggie tells you that the easiest way to move from one Web page to another is to use the mouse to click hyperlinks that the authors of Web pages embed in their HTML documents. You can also right-click the mouse on the background of a Web page to open a shortcut menu that includes navigation options.

REFERENCE   WINDOW   **RW**

Navigating Between Web Pages Using Hyperlinks and the Mouse
- Click the hyperlink.
- After the new Web page has loaded, right-click on the Web page's background.
- Click Back on the shortcut menu.

To follow a hyperlink to a Web page and return using the mouse:

1. Click the **Back** button on the Navigation toolbar to return to the Student Online Companion page, click the **Lewis Music** link to open that page, and then point to the **Instrument Accessories** hyperlink shown in Figure 2-35 so your pointer changes to an icon of a hand with a pointing index finger.

Figure 2-35	LEWIS MUSIC WEB PAGE

URL

hyperlinks

pointer shape changes when hovering over a hyperlink

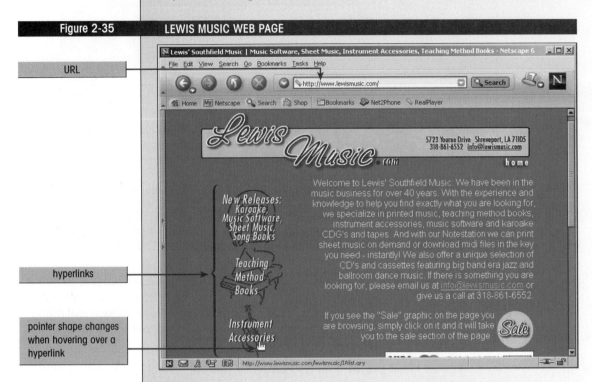

2. Click the **Instrument Accessories** link to load the page. Watch the second panel in the status bar. When the shadow disappears, you know that Navigator has loaded the full page.

3. Right-click anywhere in the Web page area to open the shortcut menu, as shown in Figure 2-36.

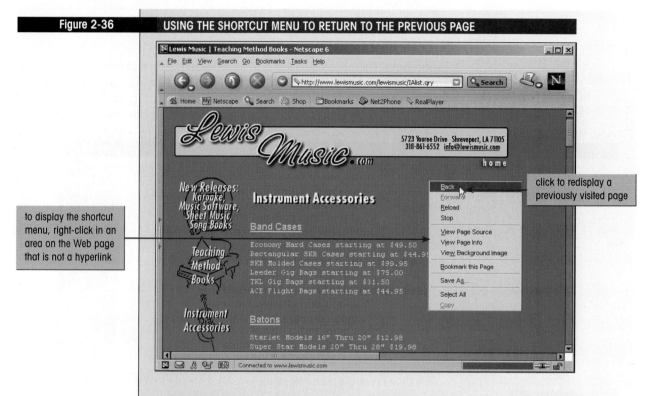

Figure 2-36   USING THE SHORTCUT MENU TO RETURN TO THE PREVIOUS PAGE

to display the shortcut menu, right-click in an area on the Web page that is not a hyperlink

click to redisplay a previously visited page

TROUBLE? If you right-click a hyperlink, your shortcut menu displays a list that differs from the one shown in Figure 2-36; therefore, the Back option might not appear in the same position on the menu. If you don't see the shortcut menu shown in Figure 2-36, click anywhere outside of the shortcut menu to close it, and then repeat Step 3.

TROUBLE? Web pages change frequently. The Instrument Accessories page you see might look different from the one shown in Figure 2-36, however, right-clicking anywhere on the Web page area will still work.

4. Click **Back** on the shortcut menu to go back to the Lewis Music home page.

5. Repeat Step 4 to return to the Student Online Companion page.

Using the History List

The Back and Forward buttons on the Navigation toolbar enable you to move to and from recently visited pages. These buttons duplicate the functions of the commands on the Go menu. The options on the Go menu enable you to move back and forward through a portion of the history list and allow you to choose a specific Web page from that list. To see where you have been during a session, you also can open the history list for your current session.

To view the history list for this session:

1. Click **Tasks** on the menu bar, click **Tools**, and then click **History** to open the history list in its own window.

2. Click the small arrow next to the **Today** folder to open the list of Web sites visited today, as shown in Figure 2-37.

| Figure 2-37 | VIEWING THE HISTORY LIST |

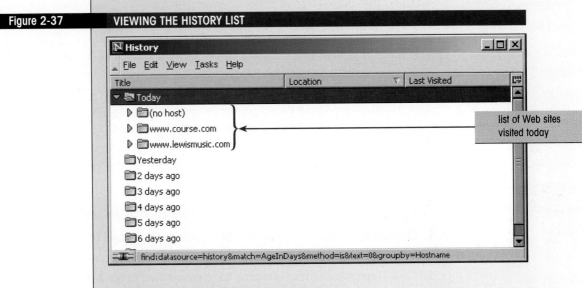

TROUBLE? The History window that appears on your computer might be a different size and contain different entries from the one that appears in Figure 2-37. You can resize the History window as you would any window by dragging its edges, and you can resize the columns in the window by dragging on the edges of the column headers.

To return to a previously visited Web page, double-click the page in the list.

3. Click the **Close** button on the History window title bar to close it.

You can change the way that pages are listed in the History window by using the commands on the View menu; for example, you can list the pages by title or in the order in which you visited them.

Reloading a Web Page

The Reload button on the Navigator toolbar loads again the Web page that currently appears in the browser window. You can force Navigator to load the page from the Web server instead of your computer's temporary storage cache by pressing the Shift key when you click the Reload button.

Returning to the Home Page

The Home button on the Personal toolbar displays the home (or start) page for your copy of Navigator. You can go to the Netscape Netcenter page, which is the software's default installation home page, by clicking the **Netscape** button on the Navigator toolbar. You cannot change the page that loads when you click the Netscape button, but you can change the default URL that opens when you click the Home button by using the Preferences dialog box.

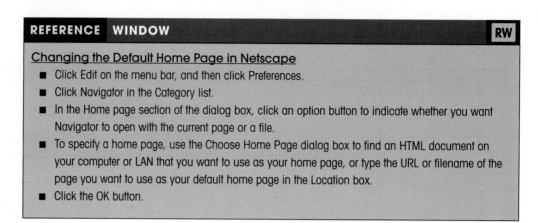

REFERENCE WINDOW   **RW**

<u>Changing the Default Home Page in Netscape</u>
- Click Edit on the menu bar, and then click Preferences.
- Click Navigator in the Category list.
- In the Home page section of the dialog box, click an option button to indicate whether you want Navigator to open with the current page or a file.
- To specify a home page, use the Choose Home Page dialog box to find an HTML document on your computer or LAN that you want to use as your home page, or type the URL or filename of the page you want to use as your default home page in the Location box.
- Click the OK button.

To view the settings for the default home page:

1. Click **Edit** on the menu bar, and then click **Preferences**. The Preferences dialog box opens.

2. Click **Navigator** in the Category list, as shown in Figure 2-38.

| Figure 2-38 | PREFERENCES DIALOG BOX |

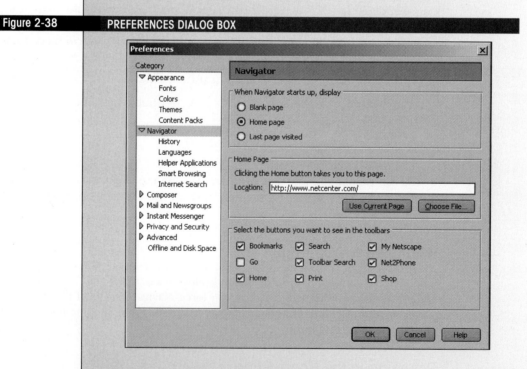

3. To open with the current page or a home page you specify, click the corresponding option button in the Home Page section of the Preferences dialog box.

TROUBLE? Do not change any settings unless you are instructed to do so by your instructor. Many organizations set the home page defaults on all of their computers and lock those settings.

To specify a home page, you would select the text in the Location box and then enter the URL of the Web page you want to use. If you load the Web page that you want as your new home page before beginning these steps, you can click the Use Current Page button to place the page's URL in the Location box. You also can specify an HTML document on your computer or LAN by clicking the Choose File button and selecting the disk drive and folder location of that HTML document.

4. Click the **Cancel** button to close the dialog box without making any changes.

Printing a Web Page

The Print button on the Navigation toolbar lets you print the current Web frame or page. You can use this button to make a printed copy of most Web pages (some Web pages disable the Print command). Navigator uses a default layout for printing Web pages that cannot be changed. The default print layout includes information about the Web page you are printing. The name of the Web page, which is the text that the Web page designer has included within the page's TITLE tags, appears at the top left of the printed page (not all Web designers give their pages such titles). The URL of the Web page appears at the top right of the printed page. A page number appears at the lower left of the page and the date and time the page was printed appear at the lower right of the page.

REFERENCE WINDOW　　　　　　　　　　　　　　　　　　　　　　　**RW**

Printing the Current Web Page
- Click the Print button on the Navigation toolbar (or click File on the menu bar, and then click Print).
- Select the printer you want to use and indicate the pages you want to print and the number of copies you want to make of each page.
- Click the OK button.

To print a Web page:

1. Click in the main (right) frame of the Student Online Companion page to select it.

2. Click the **Print** button on the Navigation toolbar to open the Print dialog box, as shown in Figure 2-39.

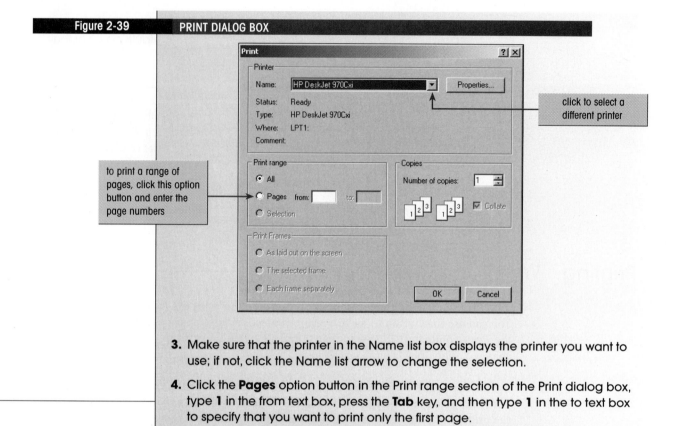

Figure 2-39   PRINT DIALOG BOX

click to select a different printer

to print a range of pages, click this option button and enter the page numbers

3. Make sure that the printer in the Name list box displays the printer you want to use; if not, click the Name list arrow to change the selection.

4. Click the **Pages** option button in the Print range section of the Print dialog box, type **1** in the from text box, press the **Tab** key, and then type **1** in the to text box to specify that you want to print only the first page.

5. Make sure that the Number of copies text box displays **1**.

6. Click the **OK** button to print the Web page and close the Print dialog box.

Checking **Web Page Security**

The **Security indicator button** is a small picture of a padlock that appears at the right edge of the status bar at the bottom of the Navigator browser window. This button lets you check some of the security elements of a Web page. The button will display as either an open padlock icon or a closed padlock icon to indicate whether the Web page was encrypted during transmission from the Web server. The closed padlock icon indicates that the page was encrypted.

Encryption is a way of scrambling and encoding data transmissions that reduces the risk that a person who intercepts the Web page as it travels across the Internet will be able to decode and read the page's contents. Web sites use encrypted transmission to send and receive information, such as credit card numbers, to ensure privacy. You can obtain more information about the details of the encryption used on a Web page by examining the Page Info dialog box that opens when you click the Security indicator button. Figure 2-40 shows the Page Info dialog box for an encrypted Web page after the user clicked the Security indicator button.

Figure 2-40   **PAGE INFO DIALOG BOX FOR AN ENCRYPTED WEB PAGE**

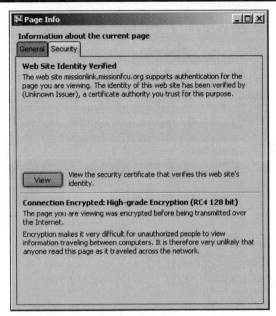

Managing Cookies

Another issue that concerns many Web users is the use of cookies. A **cookie** is a small file that a Web server writes to the disk drive of the client computer (the computer on which the Web browser is running). The cookie can contain information about the user such as login names and passwords. By storing this information on the user's computer, the Web server can perform functions such as automatic login. Often, the user is unaware that these files are being written to their computer's disk drive. Navigator stores all of these cookies in one file and gives the user a tool to manage that file called the **Cookie Manager**.

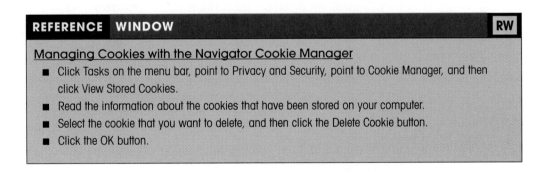

REFERENCE WINDOW   RW

Managing Cookies with the Navigator Cookie Manager
- Click Tasks on the menu bar, point to Privacy and Security, point to Cookie Manager, and then click View Stored Cookies.
- Read the information about the cookies that have been stored on your computer.
- Select the cookie that you want to delete, and then click the Delete Cookie button.
- Click the OK button.

You will delete a cookie stored on your computer using the Cookie Manager.

To manage cookies with the Cookie Manager:

1. Click **Tasks** on the menu bar, point to **Privacy and Security**, point to **Cookie Manager**, and then click **View Stored Cookies**.

2. Examine the cookies in the list that appears in the Cookie Manager dialog box. If your computer has many cookies stored on it, you can use the scroll bar to move up and down in the list. An example of a Cookie Manager dialog box with five cookies appears in Figure 2-41.

Figure 2-41   **COOKIE MANAGER DIALOG BOX**

cookie left by the
Lewis Music Web site

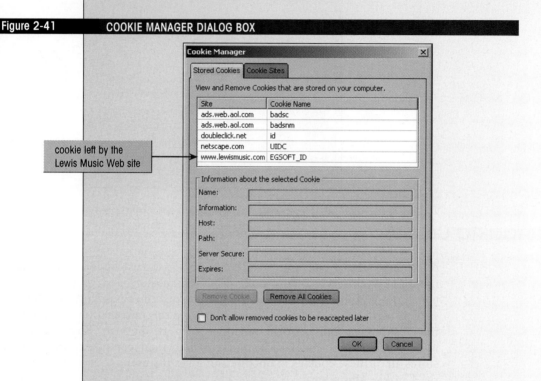

3. Click any cookie in the list to select it. Note the Remove Cookie button near the bottom of the dialog box becomes available.

4. Find a cookie that you want to delete, click to select it, and then click the **Remove Cookie** button. You may notice that many of the cookies on your computer are placed there by companies that sell banner advertising on Web pages (such as doubleclick.net). These companies use cookies to record which ads have appeared on pages you have viewed so that they can present different ads the next time you open a Web page. In Figure 2-41, you can see that the Lewis Music Web site left a cookie on this computer.

   TROUBLE? You may be instructed to delete specific cookies or no cookies at all. Ask you instructor or technical support person for assistance if you are unsure which cookies can be deleted.

5. When you are finished exploring and deleting cookies, click the **OK** button to close the Cookie Manager dialog box.

If you want to delete all the cookies that have been stored on your computer, click the Remove All Cookies button. You can also indicate whether or not you want cookies that you have removed to be stored again.

Getting **Help in Navigator**

Navigator includes a limited Help system. You can open the Help Contents window to learn more about the Help options that are available.

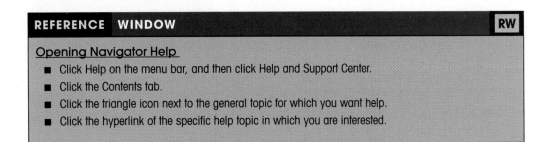

REFERENCE WINDOW   RW

Opening Navigator Help
- Click Help on the menu bar, and then click Help and Support Center.
- Click the Contents tab.
- Click the triangle icon next to the general topic for which you want help.
- Click the hyperlink of the specific help topic in which you are interested.

You will use Navigator Help to read about browsing the Web.

To use Navigator Help:

1. Click **Help** on the menu bar, and then click **Help and Support Center**.

2. If necessary, click the **Contents** tab to display the Contents window.

3. Click the triangle icon next to the **Browsing the Web** category to open a list of specific help topics in that category. Examine the page, which should be similar to the one shown in Figure 2-42, and use the scroll box or scroll down button to move down the page.

Figure 2-42   NETSCAPE HELP WINDOW

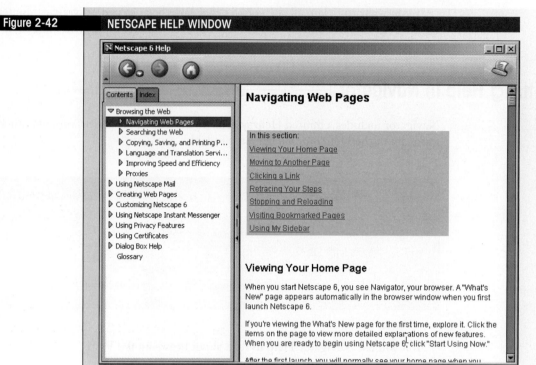

You can click any of the hyperlinks to obtain help on the specific topics listed. You can also click the Index tab to obtain an alphabetized list of hyperlinks to specific terms used in the Help pages.

4. Click the **Close** button to close Help.

You feel confident that you have the tools you need to successfully find information on the Web. Marianna probably will be interested in seeing the Miami Wind Quintet Web page, but you are not sure if she will have Internet access while she is touring. Maggie says that you can save the Web page to a disk, so Marianna can open the page locally in her Web browser using the files you saved on that disk.

Using **Navigator to Save a Web Page**

There will be times when you will want to refer to the information that you have found on a Web page without having to search the site. In Netscape, you can store entire Web pages, selected portions of Web page text, or particular graphics from a Web page to a disk.

Saving a Web Page

You like the Miami Wind Quintet's Web site and want to save a copy of the page to a disk so you can show the Web page to Marianna. That way, she can review it without having an Internet connection. To save a Web page, you must have the page open in Navigator.

REFERENCE WINDOW   **RW**

<u>Saving a Web Page to a Disk</u>
- Open the Web page in Navigator.
- Click File on the menu bar, and then click Save As.
- Click the Save in list arrow, and then select the drive that contains your disk.
- Accept the default filename, or change the filename, but retain the file extension .htm or .html.
- Click the Save button.

You will save the Miami Wind Quintet page to a disk so you can send it to Marianna for her review.

To save the Web page to a disk:

1. Use your bookmark to return to the Miami Wind Quintet page.

2. Click **File** on the menu bar, and then click **Save As**. The Save As dialog box opens.

3. Click the **Save in** list arrow, click the drive that contains your disk, select the **Tutorial.02** folder, and then type the name **MiamiWindQuintet.htm** in the File name box.

4. Click the **Save** button. Now the HTML document for the Miami Wind Quintet's home page is saved on your disk. When you send it to Marianna, she can open her Web browser and then use the Open command on the File menu to open the Web page.

If the Web page contains graphics, such as photos, drawings, or icons, they will not be saved with the HTML document. To save a graphic, right-click it in the browser window, click Save Image on the shortcut menu, and then save the graphic to the same location as the Web's HTML document. The graphics file will appear on the HTML document as a hyperlink; therefore, you might have to change the HTML code in the Web page to identify the location of the graphic. Copying the graphics files to the same disk as the HTML document will *usually* work.

Saving Web Page Text to a File

You can save portions of Web page text to a file, so that you can use the file in other programs. You will use WordPad to save text that you will copy from a Web page; however, any word processor or text editor will work.

REFERENCE WINDOW   **RW**

<u>Copying Text from a Web Page to a WordPad Document</u>
- Open the Web page in Navigator.
- Use the mouse pointer to select the text you want to copy.
- Click Edit on the menu bar, and then click Copy.
- Start WordPad (or another word processor or text editor if WordPad is not available).
- Click Edit on the WordPad menu bar, and then click Paste (or click the Paste button).
- Click the Save button, select the folder where you want to store the file, and then enter a new filename, if necessary.
- Click the Save button.

Marianna just called to let you know that the quintet will play a concert in Grand Rapids on a Friday night, and she asks you to identify other opportunities for scheduling local concerts during the following weekend. Often museums are willing to book small ensembles for weekend afternoon programs, and Marianna has given you the URL for the Grand Rapids Art Museum. You will visit the site and then get the museum's address and telephone number so you can contact it about scheduling a concert.

To copy text from a Web page and save the text as a WordPad document:

1. Use the **Back** button to return to the Student Online Companion page, and then click the **Grand Rapids Art Museum** link to open that Web page in the browser window.

2. Click the **Information & Calendar** hyperlink to open the museum information page, and then click the **Map** hyperlink.

3. Scroll down to display the text below the map image, and then drag the mouse pointer over the address and telephone number to select it, as shown in Figure 2-43.

| Figure 2-43 | SELECTING TEXT ON A WEB PAGE |

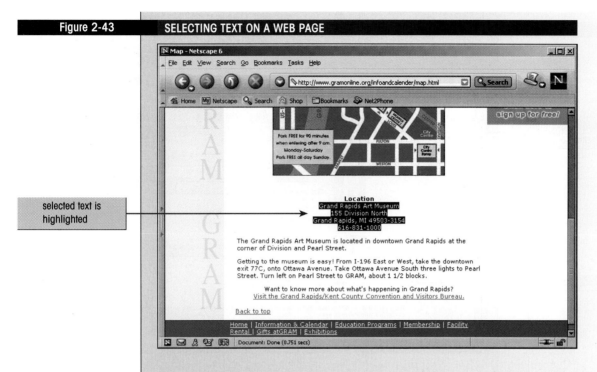

selected text is highlighted

4. Click **Edit** on the menu bar, and then click **Copy** to copy the selected text to the Clipboard.

Now, you will start WordPad and then paste the copied text into a new document.

5. Click the **Start** button on the taskbar, point to **Programs**, point to **Accessories**, and then click **WordPad** to start the program and open a new document.

6. Click the **Paste** button on the WordPad toolbar to paste the text into the WordPad document, as shown in Figure 2-44

TROUBLE? If the WordPad toolbar does not appear, click View on the menu bar, click Toolbar, and then repeat Step 2. Your WordPad program window might be a different size from the one shown in Figure 2-44, which does not affect the steps.

| Figure 2-44 | PASTING TEXT FROM A WEB PAGE INTO A WORDPAD DOCUMENT |

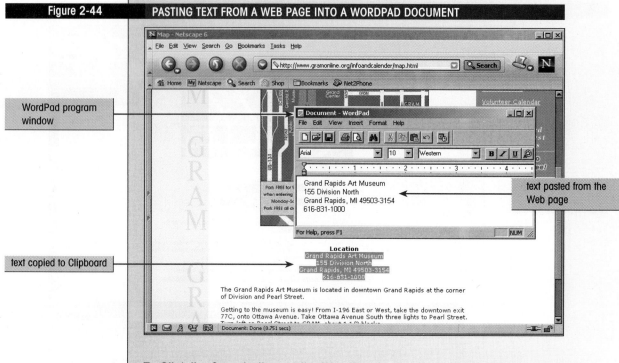

WordPad program window

text pasted from the Web page

text copied to Clipboard

7. Click the **Save** button on the WordPad toolbar to open the Save As dialog box.

8. Click the **Save in** list arrow, select the drive that contains your disk, and then select the Tutorial.02 folder.

9. Delete the text in the File name text box, type **GRAM-Address.txt**, and then click the **Save** button to save the file. Now, the address and phone number of the museum is saved in a file on your disk for future reference.

10. Click the **Close** button on the WordPad title bar to close it.

You will use this information to contact the museum at a later time. As you examine the Web page, you notice a street map of the area surrounding the museum, which Marianna might like to have.

Saving a Web Page Graphic to a Disk

The Web page with directions and transportation information will be helpful to Marianna, so you decide to save the map graphic to your disk. You can then send the file to Marianna so she has a resource for getting to the museum.

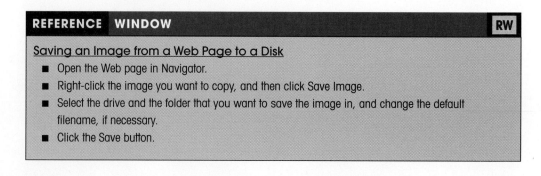

| REFERENCE | WINDOW | RW |

Saving an Image from a Web Page to a Disk
- Open the Web page in Navigator.
- Right-click the image you want to copy, and then click Save Image.
- Select the drive and the folder that you want to save the image in, and change the default filename, if necessary.
- Click the Save button.

Now you will save the image of the street map to your disk, which you will later send to Marianna.

To save the street map image to a disk:

1. Right-click the map image to open its shortcut menu, as shown in Figure 2-45.

| Figure 2-45 | SAVING THE MAP IMAGE TO A DISK |

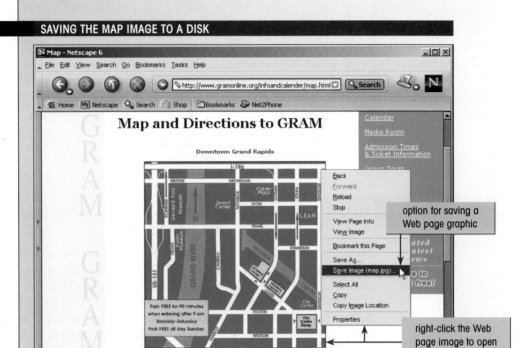

2. Click **Save Image** on the shortcut menu to open the Save As dialog box.

3. Click the **Save in** list arrow, select the drive that contains your disk, and then select the Tutorial.02 folder.

4. Delete the text in the File name text box, type **GRAM-Map.jpg**, and then click the **Save** button to save the file.

5. Close your Web browser, and if necessary, log off your Internet connection.

Now, you can send a disk to Marianna so she will have the Miami Wind Quintet Web page and a map to show how to get to the museum. She will be able to use her Web browser to open the files and print them.

Session 2.3 QUICK CHECK

1. Describe three ways to load a Web page in the Navigator browser.

2. You can use the _____ in Navigator to visit previously visited sites during your Web session.

3. When would you use the Reload command?

4. What happens when you click the Home button on the Navigation toolbar?

5. Some Web servers _____ Web pages before returning them to the client to prevent unauthorized access.

6. True or False: You can identify an encrypted Web page when viewing it in Navigator.

7. What is a Netscape Navigator bookmark?

REVIEW ASSIGNMENTS

Marianna is pleased with the information you gathered thus far about other wind quintet Web pages and potential recital sites. In fact, she is thinking about hiring someone to create a Web page for the Sunset Wind Quintet. Because Marianna wants to be prepared for her meetings with potential Web designers, she has asked you to compile some information about the Web pages that other small musical ensembles have created. Although you have searched for information about wind quintets, you will search for additional background information, which will include a large number of string quartets (two violinists, a violist, and a cellist) that play similar venues by completing the following steps.

1. Start your Web browser, open the Student Online Companion page at www.course.com/newperspectives/internet3, click the hyperlink for your book, click the Tutorial 2 link, and then click the Review Assignments link.

2. Click the hyperlinks listed under the category heading Small Musical Ensembles to explore the Web pages for these types of organizations.

3. Choose three interesting home pages, and print the first page of each. Create a bookmark or favorite for each of these sites, and then answer the following questions for these three sites:

   a. Which sites include a photograph of the ensemble?
   b. Which photographs are in color and black and white?
   c. Which sites show the ensemble members dressed in formal concert dress?

4. Choose your favorite ensemble photograph and save it to a floppy disk.

5. Do any of the three sites you have chosen provide information about the ensemble's CDs? If so, which ones? Is this information on the home page, or did you click a hyperlink to find it?

6. Do any of the sites offer CDs or other products for sale? If so, which ones? Is this information on the home page, or did you click a hyperlink to find it?

7. Write a one-page report that summarizes your findings for Marianna. Include a recommendation regarding what the Sunset Wind Quintet should consider including in its Web site.

8. Close your Web browser and, if necessary, log off your Internet connection.

CASE PROBLEMS

Case 1. Businesses on the Web Business Web sites range from very simple informational sites to comprehensive sites that offer information about the firm's products or services, history, current employment openings, and financial information. An increasing number of business sites offer products or services for sale using their Web sites. You just started a position on the public relations staff of Value City Central, a large retail chain of television and appliance stores. Your first assignment is to research and report on the types of information that other large firms offer on their Web sites, which you will do by completing the following steps.

1. Start your Web browser, open the Student Online Companion page at www.course.com/ newperspectives/internet3, click the hyperlink for your book, click the Tutorial 2 link, and then click the Case Problems link.

2. Use the Case Problem 1 hyperlinks to open the business sites on that page.

3. Choose three of those business sites that you believe would be most relevant to your assignment.

4. Print the home page for each Web site that you have chosen.

5. Select one site that you feel does the best job in each of the following five categories:
   a. overall presentation of the corporate image   *Site Name   why*
   b. description of products or services offered
   c. presentation of the firm's history
   d. description of employment opportunities
   e. presentation of financial statements or other financial information about the company.

6. Prepare a report that includes one paragraph describing why you believe each of the sites you identified in the preceding step did the best job.

7. Close your Web browser, and log off the Internet, if necessary.

Case 2. Browser Wars Your employer, Bristol Mills, is a medium-sized manufacturer of specialty steel products. The firm has increased its use of computers in all of its office operations and in many of its manufacturing operations. Many of Bristol's computers currently run either Microsoft Internet Explorer or Netscape Navigator; however, the chief financial officer (CFO) has decided the firm can support only one of these products. The CFO has also heard some good things about another browser named Opera and is wondering if that might be the right product for the company. As the CFO's special assistant, you have been asked to recommend which of these three Web browsers the company should choose to support. You will research the browsers for your report by completing the following steps.

1. Start your Web browser, open the Student Online Companion page at www.course.com/ newperspectives/internet3, click the hyperlink for your book, click the Tutorial 2 link, and then click the Case Problems link.

2. Use the Case Problem 2 hyperlinks to learn more about these three Web browser software packages.

3. Write a one-page memo to the CFO (your instructor) that outlines the strengths and weaknesses of each product. Recommend one program and support your decision using the information you collected.

4. Prepare a list of features that you would like to see in a new Web browser software package that would overcome important limitations in Opera, Internet Explorer, or Navigator. Do you think it would be feasible for a firm to develop and use such a product? Why or why not?

5. Close your Web browser, and log off the Internet, if necessary.

Case 3. Citizens Fidelity Bank You are a new staff auditor at the Citizens Fidelity Bank. You have had more recent computer training than other audit staff members at Citizens, so Sally DeYoung, the audit manager, asks you to review the bank's policy on Web browser cookie settings. Some of the bank's board members expressed concerns to Sally about the security of the bank's computers. They understand that the bank has PCs on its networks that are connected to the Internet. One of the board members learned about browser cookies and was afraid that a naive bank employee might open a Web site that would write a dangerous cookie file on the bank's computer network. Not all Web servers write cookies, but those that do can read the cookie file the next time the Web browser on that computer connects to the Web server. The Web server can then retrieve information about the Web browser's last connection to the server. None of the bank's board members knows very much about computers, but all of them became concerned that a virus-laden cookie could significantly damage the bank's computer system. Sally asks you to help inform the board of directors about cookies and to establish a policy on using them. You will accomplish these tasks by completing the following steps.

1. Start your Web browser, open the Student Online Companion page at www.course.com/ newperspectives/internet3, click the hyperlink for your book, click the Tutorial 2 link, and then click the Case Problems hyperlink.

2. Use the Case Problem 3 hyperlinks to Cookie Information Resources to learn more about cookie files.

3. Prepare a brief outline of the content on each Web page you visit.

4. List the risks that Citizens Fidelity Bank might face by allowing cookie files to be written to their computers.

5. List the benefits that individual users obtain by allowing Web servers to write cookies to the computers that they are using at the bank to access the Web.

6. Close your Web browser, and log off the Internet, if necessary.

Case 4. Columbus Suburban Area Council The Columbus Suburban Area Council is a charitable organization devoted to maintaining and improving the general welfare of people living in Columbus suburbs. As the director of the council, you are interested in encouraging donations and other support from area citizens and would like to stay informed of grant opportunities that might benefit the council. You are especially interested in developing an informative and attractive presence on the Web and will pursue that goal by completing the following steps.

1. Start your Web browser, open the Student Online Companion page at www.course.com/ newperspectives/internet3, click the hyperlink for your book, click the Tutorial 2 link, and then click the Case Problems link.

2. Follow the Case Problem 4 hyperlinks to charitable organizations to find out more about what other organizations are doing with their Web sites.

3. Select three of the Web sites you visited and, for each, prepare a list of the site's contents. Note whether each site included financial information and whether the site disclosed how much the organization spent on administrative or nonprogram-related activities.

4. Identify which site you believe would be a good model for the Council's new Web site. Explain why you think your chosen site would be the best example to follow.

5. Close your Web browser, and log off the Internet, if necessary.

Case 5. Emma's Start Page Your neighbor, Emma Inkster, was an elementary school teacher for many years. She is now retired and has just purchased her first personal computer. Emma is excited about getting on the Web and exploring its resources. She has asked for your help. After you introduce her to what you have learned in this tutorial about Web browsers, she is eager to spend more time gathering information on the Web. Although she is retired, Emma has continued to be very active. She is an avid bridge player, enjoys golf, and is one of the neighborhood's best gardeners. Although she is somewhat limited by her schoolteacher's pension, Emma loves to travel to foreign countries and especially likes to learn the languages of her destinations. She would like to have a start page for her computer that would include hyperlinks that would help her easily visit and return regularly to Web pages related to her interests. Her nephew knows HTML and can create the page, but Emma would like you to help her design the layout of her start page. You know that Web directory sites are designed to help people find interesting Web sites, so you begin your search with them by completing the following steps.

1. Start your Web browser, open the Student Online Companion page at www.course.com/newperspectives/internet3, click the hyperlink for your book, click the Tutorial 2 link, and then click the Case Problems link.

2. Use the Case Problem 5 hyperlinks to Web directories to learn what kind of organization they use for their hyperlinks.

3. You note that many of the Web directories use a similar organization structure for their hyperlinks and categories; however, you are not sure if that organization structure would be ideal for Emma. You decide to create categories that suit Emma's specific interests. List five general categories around which you would organize Emma's start page. For each of those five general categories, list three subcategories that would help Emma find and return to Web sites she would find interesting.

4. Write a report of 100 words in which you explain why the start page you designed for Emma would be more useful to her than a publicly available Web directory.

5. Close your Web browser, and log off the Internet, if necessary.

LAB ASSIGNMENTS

The Internet:
World Wide
Web

One of the most popular services on the Internet is the World Wide Web. This Lab is a Web simulator that teaches you how to use Web browser software to find information. You can use this Lab whether or not your school provides you with Internet access.

1. Click the Steps button to learn how to use Web browser software. As you proceed through the Steps, answer all of the Quick Check questions that appear. After you complete the Steps, you will see a Quick Check Summary Report. Follow the instructions on the screen to print this report.

2. Click the Explore button on the Welcome screen. Use the Web browser to locate a weather map of the Caribbean Virgin Islands. What is its URL?

3. A SCUBA diver named Wadson Lachouffe has been searching for the fabled treasure of Greybeard the pirate. A link from the Adventure Travel Web site, www.atour.com, leads to Wadson's Web page called "Hidden Treasure." In Explore, locate the Hidden Treasure page and answer the following questions:

   a. What was the name of Greybeard's ship?
   b. What was Greybeard's favorite food?
   c. What does Wadson think happened to Greybeard's ship?

4. In the steps, you found a graphic of Jupiter from the photo archives of the Jet Propulsion Laboratory. In the Explore section of the Lab, you can also find a graphic of Saturn. Suppose one of your friends wanted a picture of Saturn for an astronomy report. Make a list of the blue, underlined links your friend must click in the correct order to find the Saturn graphic. Assume that your friend will begin at the Web Trainer home page.

5. Enter the URL http://www.atour.com to jump to the Adventure Travel Web site. Write a one-page description of this site. In your paper include a description of the information at the site, the number of pages the site contains, and a diagram of the links it contains.

6. Chris Thomson is a student at UVI and has his own Web pages. In Explore, look at the information Chris has included on his pages. Suppose you could create your own Web page. What would you include? Use word-processing software to design your own Web pages. Make sure you indicate the graphics and links you would use.

QUICK | CHECK ANSWERS

Session 2.1

   1. False

   2. True

   3. home page; start page

   4. hypermedia or media

   5. Any three of these: Candidate's name and party affiliation; list of qualifications; biography; position statements on campaign issues; list of endorsements with hyperlinks to the Web pages of individuals and organizations that support her candidacy; audio or video clips of speeches and interviews; address and telephone number of the campaign office

   6. A computer's IP address is a unique identifying number; its domain name is a unique name associated with the IP address on the Internet host computer responsible for that computer's domain.

   7. "http://" indicates use of the hypertext transfer protocol; "www.savethetrees.org" is the domain name and suggests a charitable or not-for-profit organization that is probably devoted to forest ecology; "main.html" is the name of the HTML file on the Web server

   8. A Web directory contains a hierarchical list of Web page categories; each category contains hyperlinks to individual Web pages. A Web search engine is a Web site that accepts words or expressions you enter and finds Web pages that include those words or expressions.

Session 2.2

1. You can hide its toolbars or click the Full Screen command on the View menu.
2. History
3. Search
4. East Coast Ensembles, West Coast Ensembles
5. Shift
6. True
7. press F1, click Help on the menu bar

Session 2.3

1. Any three of these: Type the URL in the location field; click a hyperlink on a Web page; click the Back button; click the Forward button; click the Bookmarks button and select a page; click Task on the menu bar, point to Tools, click History, and then click the entry for the site you want to visit
2. history list (or the Back or Forward button)
3. When you want the browser to check to see if the Web page has changed since you last visited it
4. Navigator loads the page that is specified in the Home page section of the Preferences dialog box (which you can open from the Edit menu).
5. encrypt
6. True
7. Navigator feature that enables you to store and organize a list of Web pages that you have visited

In this tutorial you will:

- Learn about e-mail and how it works

- Configure and use two popular e-mail programs and a popular Web-based e-mail service

- Send and receive e-mail messages

- Print an e-mail message

- Forward and reply to e-mail messages

- Create folders for saving e-mail messages

- File and delete e-mail messages and folders

- Create and maintain an electronic address book

E-MAIL BASICS

Evaluating Integrated Browser E-Mail Programs and a Web-Based E-Mail Service

CASE

Kikukawa Air

Since 1994, Sharon and Don Kikukawa have operated an air charter service in Maui, Hawaii. At first, Kikukawa Air employed only Sharon, who managed the office, reservations, and the company's financial details; and her husband Don, who flew their twin-engine, six-passenger plane between Maui and Oahu. After many successful years in business, Sharon and Don expanded their business to include scenic tours and charter service to all of the Hawaiian Islands. As a result of their expansion, Kikukawa Air now boasts six twin-engine planes, two turbo prop planes, and a growing staff of over 30 people.

Because Kikukawa Air has a ticket counter at airports on all of the Hawaiian Islands, many miles now separate the company's employees. Originally employees used the telephone and conference calling to coordinate the business's day-to-day operations, such as schedule and reservation changes, new airport procedures, and maintenance requests. Sharon soon realized that the long-distance rates and the fees associated with conference calling services made these forms of communication too expensive to continue using. In addition to these expenses, Sharon was overwhelmed by the effort required to manage the busy schedules of many ground-service agents and pilots and to find convenient times to meet. Sharon believes that Kikukawa Air could benefit from an alternate form of communication. Sharon has hired you to investigate the use of e-mail for the different Kikukawa Air offices and ticket counter facilities. Your job includes evaluating available e-mail systems and overseeing the software's installation. Eventually you will train the staff so they can use the new e-mail system efficiently and effectively.

SESSION 3.1

In this session, you will learn what e-mail is, how it travels to its destination, and what are the parts of a typical e-mail message. You will learn about signature files and how to use them. You will learn how to use an e-mail program to send, receive, print, delete, file, forward, reply to, and respond to e-mail messages. Finally, you will learn how to use an electronic address book to store and manage e-mail addresses.

What Is E-Mail and How Does It Work?

Electronic mail, or **e-mail**, is one of the most popular forms of business communication, and for many people it is their primary use of the Internet. In fact, many people view the Internet as an electronic highway that transports e-mail messages, without realizing that the Internet provides a wide variety of services. E-mail travels across the Internet to its destination and is deposited in the recipient's electronic mailbox. Although similar to other forms of correspondence, including letters and memos, e-mail has the added advantage of being fast and inexpensive. Instead of traveling through a complicated, expensive, and often slow mail delivery service such as a postal system, e-mail travels quickly, efficiently, and inexpensively to its destination down the hall or around the world. You can send a message any time you want, without worrying about when the mail is collected and delivered or adding any postage. For many personal and business reasons, people rely on e-mail as an indispensable form of communication.

E-mail travels across the Internet like other forms of information—that is, in small packets that are reassembled at the destination and delivered to the recipient, whose address you specify in the message. When you send an e-mail message, the message is sent to a **mail server**, which is a hardware and software system that determines from the recipient's address one of several electronic routes on which to send the message. The message is routed from one computer to another and is passed through several mail servers. Each mail server determines the next leg of the message's journey until it finally arrives at the recipient's electronic mailbox.

Sending e-mail uses one of many Internet technologies. Special **protocols**, or rules that determine how the Internet handles message packets flowing on it, are used to interpret and transmit e-mail. **SMTP (Simple Mail Transfer Protocol)** decides which paths your e-mail message takes on the Internet. SMTP handles outgoing messages; another protocol called **POP (Post Office Protocol)** handles incoming messages. POP is a standard, extensively used protocol that is part of the Internet suite of recognized protocols. Other protocols used to deliver mail include **IMAP (Internet Message Access Protocol)** and **MIME (Multipurpose Internet Mail Extensions)**. IMAP is a protocol for retrieving mail messages from a server, and the MIME protocol specifies how to encode nontext data, such as graphics and sound, so they can travel over the Internet.

When an e-mail message arrives at its destination mail server, the mail server's software handles the details of distributing the message locally, in the same way that a mailroom worker unbundles a mailbag and places letters and packages into individual mail slots. When the server receives a new message, it is not saved directly on the recipient's computer, but rather, the message is held on the mail server. When you check for new e-mail messages, you use a program stored on your personal computer (PC) to request the mail server to deliver any stored mail to your PC. The software that requests mail delivery from the mail server to your PC is known as **mail client software**, or an **e-mail program**. You will learn about two popular e-mail programs—Microsoft Outlook Express and Netscape Mail—in Sessions 3.2 and 3.3, respectively.

Common **Features of an E-Mail Message**

An e-mail message consists of two major parts: the message header and the message body. The **message header** contains all the information about the message, and the **message body** contains the actual message. A message header contains the recipient's e-mail address (To), the sender's e-mail address (From), and a subject line (Subject) indicating the message's topic. In addition, the message header can contain a carbon copy (or courtesy copy) address (Cc), a blind carbon copy (or blind courtesy copy) address (Bcc), and optional attachment filename(s). Your name automatically appears on the From line when you send a message. When you receive an e-mail message, the date and time it was sent and other information is added to the message header automatically.

Figure 3-1 shows a message that Sharon Kikukawa wrote to Bob Merrell, the company's ground service agent at the Honolulu, Oahu airport. The message contains an attached file named MaintenanceSchedule.xls. Sharon created this file using a spreadsheet program, saved it, and then attached it to the message. Notice that Bob's e-mail address appears on the To line. When Bob receives Sharon's message, Sharon's name and e-mail address will appear on the From line. Following good e-mail etiquette, Sharon included a short subject so Bob can quickly determine the content of the message. The Cc line includes an abbreviated address for the maintenance department; each member of this department will receive a copy of the message. Don Kikukawa will also receive a copy of the message, but Sharon entered Don's e-mail address on the Bcc line, so neither Bob nor the maintenance department will know that Don also received a copy of the message. Each of the message parts is described in the next sections.

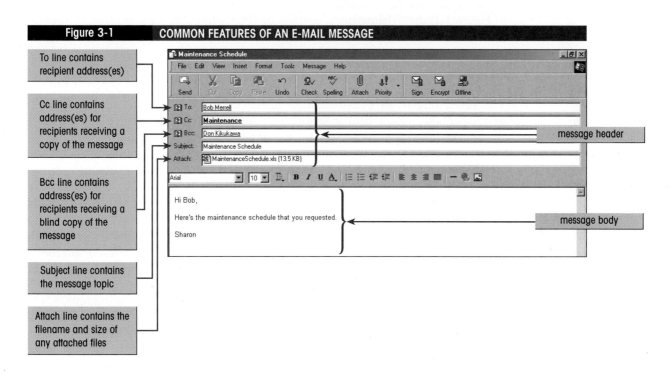

Figure 3-1   **COMMON FEATURES OF AN E-MAIL MESSAGE**

To

You type the recipient's full e-mail address in the **To line** of an e-mail header. Make sure that you type the e-mail addresses correctly because mistakes can lead to undeliverable messages or messages sent to the wrong recipients. You can send the same message to multiple recipients by typing a comma or semicolon between the recipients' e-mail addresses in the To line. There is no real limit on the number of addresses you can type in the To line or in the other parts of the message header that require an address. Figure 3-2 shows the message header for a message that Sharon is sending to three people.

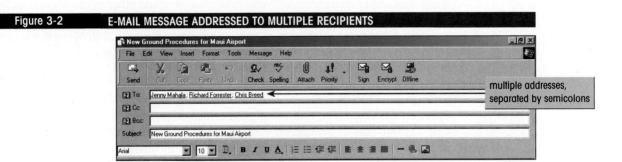

Figure 3-2   **E-MAIL MESSAGE ADDRESSED TO MULTIPLE RECIPIENTS**

Sometimes the To address contains one physical mailing address that is not one person's address, but rather, a message to a special address called a mailing list. In a mailing list, a single e-mail address can contain several or even thousands of individual e-mail addresses. In Figure 3-1, the "Maintenance" address on the Cc line actually sends the message to the three e-mail addresses contained within it, and not to a "Maintenance" address.

From

The **From line** of an e-mail message includes the sender's name, the sender's e-mail address, or both. Most e-mail programs automatically insert the sender's e-mail address into all messages. Even if you don't insert your e-mail address in an outgoing message, the recipient should *always* be able to see the sender's e-mail address in the message—in other words, you should not send anonymous e-mail.

Subject

The content of the **Subject line** is very important. Often the recipient will scan an abbreviated display of incoming messages, looking for the most interesting or important messages based on the content of the Subject line. If the Subject line is blank, then the recipient might not read the associated message immediately. It is always best to include a message subject so the reader can determine the message's content and importance. For example, a Subject line such as "Just checking" is far less informative and certainly less interesting than "Urgent: new staff meeting time." The e-mail message shown in Figure 3-1, for example, contains the subject "Maintenance Schedule" and thus indicates that the message concerns maintenance.

Cc and Bcc

You can use the optional **carbon copy (Cc)** and the **blind carbon copy (Bcc)** header lines to send mail to people who should be aware of the e-mail message, but who are not the message's main addressees. When an e-mail message is delivered, every recipient can see the addresses of other recipients, except for those recipients who receive a blind carbon copy. Neither the primary recipient (in the To line) nor Cc recipients can view the list of Bcc recipients because Bcc addresses are excluded from messages sent to addresses on the To and Cc lines. Bcc recipients are unaware of other Bcc recipients. For example, if you send a thank-you message to a salesperson for performing a task especially well, you might consider sending a blind carbon copy to that person's supervisor. That way, the supervisor knows a customer is happy and that the praise was unsolicited.

Attachments

Because of the way the messaging system is set up, you can send only text messages using SMTP—the protocol that handles outgoing e-mail. When you need to send a more complex document, such as a Word document or an Excel worksheet, you send it along as an attachment. An **attachment** is encoded so that it can be carried safely over the Internet, to "tag along" with the message. Frequently, the attached file is the most important part of the e-mail message, and the message body contains only a brief statement, such as "Here's the maintenance schedule that you requested." Sharon's e-mail message (see Figure 3-1) contains an attached file, whose filename and size in kilobytes (a **kilobyte** is approximately 1,000 characters and abbreviated as KB) appear in the Attach line in the message header. You can attach more than one file to an e-mail message; if you include multiple recipients in the To, Cc, and Bcc lines of the message header, each recipient will receive the message and the attached files. E-mail attachments provide a simple and convenient way of transmitting electronic documents to one or more people.

When you receive an e-mail message with an attached file, you can view and save the file. E-mail programs differ in how they handle and display attachments. Several e-mail programs identify an attached file with an icon that represents the program associated with the attachment's file type. In addition to an icon, several programs also display an attached file's size in kilobytes and indicate the attached file's name. Other e-mail programs display an attached file in a preview window when they recognize the attached file's format and can start a program to open the file.

Some people refer to the process of saving an e-mail attachment as **detaching** the file. An icon representing an attached file usually accompanies the file. If a worksheet is attached to an e-mail message, for example, a spreadsheet program on your computer starts and opens the worksheet. Similarly, a Word document opens in the Word program window when you double-click the icon representing the Word document inside your e-mail message. When you detach a file, you indicate the disk and folder in which to save it. You won't always need to save an e-mail attachment; sometimes you can view it and then delete it.

Message Body and Signature Files

Most often, people use e-mail to write short, quick messages. However, e-mail messages can be dozens or hundreds of pages long, although the term "pages" has little meaning in the e-mail world. Few people using e-mail think of a message in terms of page-sized chunks; e-mail is more like an unbroken scroll with no physical page boundaries.

Frequently, an e-mail message includes an optional signature that identifies the sender. You can sign a message by typing your name and other information at the end of each message you send, or you can create a signature file. A **signature**, or **signature file**, contains the standard information you routinely type at the end of your e-mail messages. You can set your e-mail program to insert a signature file into every message automatically so you don't have to type it. A signature usually contains the sender's name, title, and company name. Signature files often contain a complete nonelectronic address, facsimile telephone number, a voice phone number, and a Web site address. Some signature files might also include graphics, such as a company logo. Including a signature file in an e-mail message ensures that e-mail recipients can contact you in a variety of ways.

Signatures can be formal, informal, or a combination of both. A **formal signature** usually includes the sender's name, title, company name, company address, telephone and fax numbers, and e-mail address. **Informal signatures** can include nicknames and graphics or quotations that express a more casual style found in correspondence between friends and acquaintances. Most e-mail programs have an option that lets you automatically include a signature at the end of each e-mail message you send. You can easily modify your signature or choose not to include it in selected messages. Most e-mail programs allow you to create multiple signature files so you can choose which one to include when sending a message.

When you create a signature, don't overdo it. A signature that is extremely long is in bad taste—especially if it is much longer than the message. It is best to keep a signature to a few lines that identify ways to contact you. Figure 3-3 shows two examples of signatures. The first signature is informal and typical of one Sharon might send with her internal business correspondence. The second signature is formal and one that Sharon uses for all external business correspondence to identify herself, her title, and her contact information.

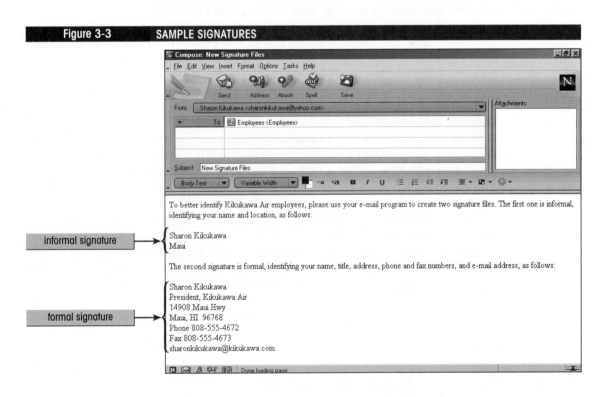

Figure 3-3   SAMPLE SIGNATURES

informal signature

formal signature

E-Mail **Addresses**

E-mail addresses, also called Internet addresses, uniquely identify an individual or organization that is connected to the Internet. They are like telephone numbers—when you want to call a friend or business, you dial a series of numbers that route your call through a series of switchboards until your call reaches its destination. For example, calling a friend in San Diego from another country requires you to dial the country code for the United States (the country code varies according to the country from which you are calling). Next, you must dial the three-digit area code for the part of San Diego in which your friend lives. Finally, you must dial your friend's seven-digit local number. Like telephone numbers, e-mail addresses consist of a series of numbers. An address can consist of three or four groups of numbers that are separated by periods. For instance, the number 127.0.0.1 is an **Internet Protocol address**, or more commonly an **IP address**, which corresponds to a single computer connected to the Internet. The IP address uniquely identifies the computer at the organization you want to contact. To route an e-mail message to an *individual* whose mail is stored on a particular computer, you must identify that person by his or her account name, or **user name**, and also by the computer on which mail is stored. The two parts of an e-mail address—the user name and the computer name—are separated by an "at" sign (@). Sharon Kikukawa, for example, uses the user name *sharonkikukawa* for her e-mail. If her account were stored on a computer whose address is 127.0.0.1, then one form of her e-mail address would be sharonkikukawa@127.0.0.1.

Fortunately, you will rarely have to use IP addresses when addressing e-mail messages. Instead, you can purchase and use a **host name**, which is a unique name that is equivalent to an IP address from an Internet Web site that registers and sells them. Sharon Kikukawa's address using a host name is simply sharonkikukawa@kikukawa.com, which is much easier to remember and type. A full e-mail address consists of a user name, followed by @ and the host name (or address). A user name usually specifies a person within an organization, although a user name can also refer to an entire group. In some instances you can select your own user name, but usually an organization through which you obtain an e-mail account has rules about acceptable user names. Some organizations set standards so user names consist of a person's first initial followed by up to seven characters of the person's last name. Other institutions prefer that user names contain a person's first and last names separated by an underscore character (for example, Sharon_Kikukawa). Occasionally, you can pick a nickname such as "ziggy" as your user name. Most e-mail addresses aren't case-sensitive; in other words, the addresses sharonkikukawa@kikukawa.com and SharonKikukawa@Kikukawa.com are the same. It is important for you to enter a recipient's address carefully; if you omit or mistype even one character, your message could be undeliverable or sent to the wrong recipient. When mail cannot be delivered, the electronic postmaster sends the mail back to you and indicates the addressee is unknown—just like conventional mail.

The host name is the second part of an e-mail address. The host name specifies the computer to which the mail is to be delivered on the Internet. Host names contain periods, which are usually pronounced "dot," to divide the host name. The most specific part of the host name appears first in the host address followed by more general destination names. Sharon's host name, kikukawa.com (and pronounced "kikukawa dot com"), contains only two names separated by a period. The *com* in the address indicates that this company falls into the large, general class of commercial locations.

E-Mail **Programs**

Because no single program works on all computers, there are many choices for receiving, sending, and managing e-mail messages. The good news is that you can use any e-mail program to send mail to people using the same or different e-mail programs. Regardless of which e-mail program you use to send e-mail, recipients can read your messages. If you have an Internet service provider (ISP) with a PPP or SLIP connection, then you can select one of many e-mail programs to use to manage your mail. On the other hand, you might have to use the e-mail program provided by your college or university if you have a dial-up connection that does not provide access to the Internet. Some e-mail programs—called **shareware**—are free or very inexpensive, and others are not. Some e-mail programs are software clients that run on your personal computer (PC) and receive mail from the mail server. Other e-mail programs run strictly on a server that you access from your PC, which acts as a dumb terminal. A **dumb terminal** is an otherwise "smart" computer that passes all your keystrokes to another computer to which you are connected and does not attempt to do anything else during the e-mail session. Examples of popular e-mail programs operating in the Windows environment are Microsoft Outlook Express, Netscape Mail, and Eudora. A widely used e-mail program running on larger, multiuser computers is Pine. Especially popular on university campuses, Pine is a simple system that accepts and displays only plain-text messages. In your future personal and professional life, chances are good that you will encounter a different e-mail program from the one you are currently using, so learning about different e-mail programs is a good idea.

Web-Based **E-Mail Services**

Many Internet Web sites provide free e-mail addresses and accounts for registered users along with the capability to use any Web browser with Internet access to send and receive e-mail messages. Many people rely on Web-based e-mail as their primary e-mail address; others use Web-based e-mail accounts to set up a separate, personal address when their employer or other owner of their primary e-mail address restricts use of personal e-mail. Some popular choices for free Web-based e-mail services are Yahoo! Mail, ExciteMail, and Hotmail. Figure 3-4 shows how a user views an e-mail message using Yahoo! Mail.

Figure 3-4   **WEB-BASED E-MAIL MESSAGE**

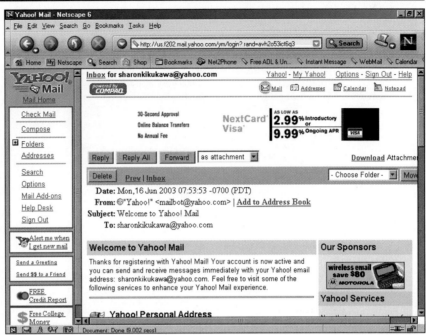

To get your free e-mail address, use your Web browser to visit the sponsor's Web site. After locating the link to the site's e-mail service, you'll need to provide some basic information about yourself, such as your name, address, and phone number. Then you choose a user name and password. If e-mail service verifies that your user name is not in use, you are immediately enrolled in the e-mail service. However, if the user name you selected is in use, the service will ask you to submit a new user name or to change the one you chose slightly by adding digits to the end of it. Web-based e-mail provides a means for people who do not have their own ISP accounts to use e-mail. You can use your Web-based e-mail service from anywhere in the world where there's an Internet connection. None of the messages that you send and receive are stored on the computer that you use; everything happens on the Web-based mail servers. The e-mail messages you send and receive are protected by your password and function just like e-mail messages sent from an e-mail program running on a PC.

You might wonder how these companies can provide free e-mail—after all, nothing is free. The answer is advertising. When you use a Web-based mail service, you will see advertising, such as the **banner** at the top of the page shown in Figure 3-5. You'll also see links to other services offered by the Web-based mail service—in Figure 3-5, you can link to sites that sell airline tickets or let you shop online.

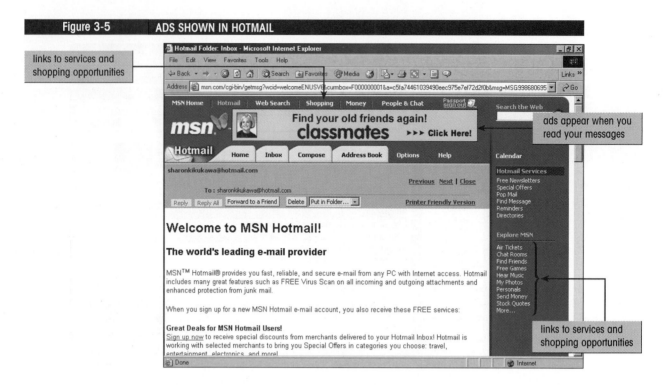

Figure 3-5   ADS SHOWN IN HOTMAIL

In addition to showing its account holders advertising messages and providing links to additional services, e-mail messages sent from Web-based mail accounts might also contain some sort of advertisement, such as a promotional message or a link to the Web-based mail service. Advertising revenues pay for free e-mail, so you must decide whether you are willing to endure a little advertising in exchange for use of the free e-mail service. Most users of these free services agree that seeing some ads is a small price to pay for the great convenience e-mail provides.

The only real drawback of Web-based e-mail services, other than the advertising messages that pay for it, is that your mailbox size might be limited to a specified amount of file space in which to store your messages. Yahoo! Mail limits the free mailbox to six megabytes; Hotmail limits it to three megabytes. Some Web-based e-mail services offer an option to purchase additional space for a fee. As long as you delete old messages and messages with large file attachments, you shouldn't encounter any space problems in your free mailbox. Most e-mail messages are small in file size.

Setting Up and Using An E-Mail Program

Many ISPs support POP or SMTP, whereby the mail server receives mail and stores it until you use your e-mail program to request delivery of your mail from the mail server to your computer. Similarly, when you send e-mail from your computer, that mail is forwarded across the Internet until the message reaches its destination. Once e-mail reaches the mail server at the recipient's location, the message is stored. Subsequently, e-mail is downloaded from the server to a user on request. In either case—sending or receiving—an e-mail program must notify the mail server to deliver the outgoing mail or accept incoming mail.

Your message might not be sent to the mail server immediately, depending on how the e-mail program is configured on your computer. A message can be **queued**, or temporarily held with other messages, and then sent when you either exit the program or check to see if you received any new e-mail.

Remember, e-mail correspondence can be formal or informal, but you should still follow the rules of good writing and grammar. After typing the content of your message—even a short message—you should check your spelling and grammar. Most mail systems do not allow you to retract mail after you send it, so you should examine your messages carefully before sending them. Always exercise politeness and courtesy in your messages. Don't write anything in an e-mail message that you wouldn't want someone else to post on a public bulletin board.

Receiving Mail

The mail server is always ready to process mail; in theory, the mail server never sleeps. That means that when you receive e-mail, it is held on the mail server until you start an e-mail program on your PC and ask the server to retrieve your mail. Most clients allow you to save delivered mail in any of several standard or custom mailboxes or folders on your PC. However, the mail server is a completely different story. Once the mail is delivered to your PC, one of two things can happen to it on the server: either the server's copy of your mail is deleted, or it is preserved and marked as delivered or read. Marking mail as delivered or read is the server's way of identifying new mail from mail that you have read. For example, when Sharon receives mail on the Kikukawa mail server, she might decide to save her accumulated mail—even after she reads it—so she has an archive of e-mail messages she has received. On the other hand, Sharon might want to delete old mail to save space on the mail server. Both methods have advantages. Saving old mail on the server lets you access your mail from any PC that can connect to your mail server. On the other hand, if you automatically delete mail after reading it, you don't have to worry about storing and organizing messages that you don't need, which requires less effort. In a Web-based mail service, the service might impose limits on the amount of material you can store, so that you must occasionally delete mail from your account to avoid interruption of service. In fact, with most Web-based e-mail services, once you exceed your storage space limit, you cannot receive any messages until you delete existing messages from the server.

Printing a Message

Reading mail on the computer is fine, but there are times when you'll need to print some or all of your messages. Other times, you need to file a message in an appropriate folder and deal with it later or simply file it for safekeeping. You also might find that you don't need to keep or file certain messages, so you can read and immediately delete them. Most e-mail programs provide these capabilities to help you manage your electronic correspondence.

The majority of e-mail programs let you print a message you are composing or that you have received at any time. The Print command usually appears on the File menu, or as a Print button on the toolbar. In a character-based program, the Print command is usually a key combination, such as Ctrl + P.

Filing a Message

Most clients let you create separate mailboxes or folders in which to store related messages. You can create new mailboxes or folders when needed, rename existing mailboxes and folders, or delete mailboxes and folders and their contents when you no longer need them. You can move mail from the incoming mailbox or folder to any other mailbox or folder to file it. Some programs let you use a **filter** to move incoming mail into one or several mailboxes or folders automatically based on the content of the message. Filters are especially useful for moving messages from certain senders into designated folders, and for moving junk mail to a trash folder. If your e-mail program does not provide filters, you can filter the messages manually by reading them and filing them in the appropriate folders.

Forwarding a Message

You can forward any message that you receive to one or more recipients. When you **forward** a message to another recipient, a copy of the original message is sent to the new recipient you specify, without the original sender's knowledge. You might forward a misdirected message to another recipient or to someone who was not included in the original message routing list.

For example, suppose you receive a message intended for someone else, or the message requests information that you do not have but you know a colleague who can provide it. In either case, you can forward the message you received to the person who can best deal with the request. When you forward a message, your e-mail address and name appear automatically on the From line; most e-mail programs amend the Subject line with the text "Fwd," "Forward," or something similar to indicate that the message has been forwarded. You simply fill in the To line and then send the message. Sometimes a forwarded message is sent as an attached file; sometimes it is sent as quoted text. A **quoted** message is a copy of the sender's original message with your inserted comments. A special mark (usually the greater than symbol, >) or a solid, colored vertical line, sometimes precedes each line of the quoted message. Figure 3-6 shows a quoted message; notice the > symbol to the left of each line of the original message and the "Fwd:" text in the Subject line, indicating a forwarded message.

Figure 3-6	SAMPLE FORWARDED MESSAGE

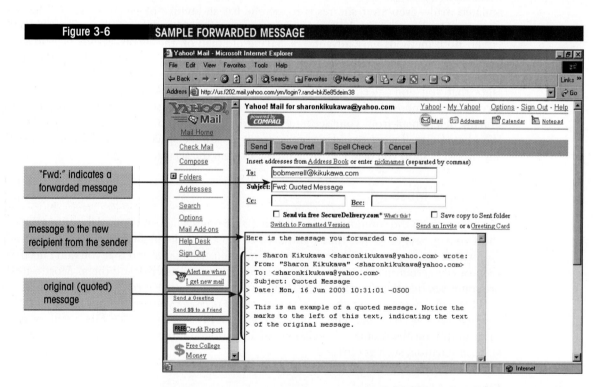

Replying to a Message

When you **reply** to a message, the e-mail program creates a new message and automatically addresses it to the sender. Replying to a message is a quick way of sending a response to someone who sent a message to you. Most e-mail programs will copy the contents of the original message and place it in the message body. Usually, a special mark appears at the beginning of each line to indicate the text of the original message. When you are responding to more than one question, you might type your responses below the original questions. That way, the recipient can better understand the context of your responses. When you respond to a message that has been sent to several people—perhaps some people received the message as a carbon copy—be careful about responding. You can choose to respond to all the original recipients or only to the sender.

Deleting a Message

In most e-mail programs, deleting a message is a two-step process to prevent accidentally deleting important messages. First, you temporarily delete a message by placing it in a "trash" folder or by marking it for deletion. Then you permanently delete the trash or marked messages by emptying the trash or by indicating to the client to delete the messages. It is a good idea to delete mail you no longer need because it takes a lot of space on the drive or server on which your e-mail messages are stored.

Maintaining **an Address Book**

E-mail addresses are sometimes difficult to remember and type, especially when you send many e-mail messages to the same recipients. You use an **address book** to save e-mail addresses and to associate those addresses with nicknames that are easy to remember.

The features of an e-mail address book vary by e-mail program. Usually, you can organize information about individuals and groups. Each entry in the address book can contain an individual's full e-mail address (or a group e-mail address that represents several individual addresses), full name, and complete contact information. In addition, some e-mail programs allow you to include notes for each contact. You can assign a unique nickname to each entry so it is easier to remember and use e-mail addresses.

After saving entries in your address book, you can refer to them at any point while you are composing, replying to, or forwarding a message. You can review your address book and sort the entries in alphabetical order by nickname, or you can view them in last name order.

Creating a Group Mailing List

What happens if you frequently need to send the same messages to different recipients? You could send the message to all recipients by typing their nicknames in the To line and separating them with a comma. But what if you need to send a message to an entire department or the entire sales staff? You can create a handy address entry called a distribution list. A **distribution list**, or a **group mailing list**, is a single nickname that represents two or more individual e-mail address. For example, you might use the nickname "Web Site" to save the e-mail addresses of your partners on a Web site project. When you need to send a message to your partners, you just type "Web Site" in the To line, and then the client will send the same message to each individual's e-mail address.

Session 3.1 QUICK CHECK

1. True or False: E-mail travels across the Internet in small packets that are reassembled at the destination and delivered to the recipient.

2. The special rules governing how information is handled on the Internet are collectively called _____.

3. An e-mail message consists of two parts: the message _____ and the message _____.

4. When sending the same message to more than one recipient, how do you separate the recipients' addresses on the To line?

5. True or False: Bcc recipients of an e-mail message are aware of other Bcc recipients of the same e-mail message.

6. Can you send a Word document over the Internet? If so, how?

7. What are the two parts of an e-mail address and what information do they provide?

8. Why is it important to delete mail messages that you no longer need?

9. What is a group mailing list?

Now that you understand some basic information about e-mail and e-mail program software, you are ready to start using your e-mail program. If you are using Microsoft Outlook Express, your instructor will assign Session 3.2; if you are using Netscape Mail, your instructor will assign Session 3.3. If you are using Hotmail, your instructor will assign Session 3.4. The authors recommend, however, that you read all sessions to familiarize yourself with the different e-mail programs. In the future, you might encounter a different e-mail program on a public or employer's computer, so it is important to be familiar with many e-mail programs. Fortunately, most e-mail programs work the same, so it is easy to use other programs once you master the basics.

SESSION 3.2

In this session, you will learn how to use Microsoft Outlook Express to send and receive e-mail. You will use this e-mail program to print, file, save, delete, respond to, and forward e-mail messages. Finally, you will organize e-mail addresses in an address book.

Microsoft Outlook Express

Microsoft Outlook Express, or simply **Outlook Express**, is an e-mail program that you use to send and receive e-mail. Outlook Express is installed with Internet Explorer. Outlook Express starts when you click a hyperlink in a Web page to an e-mail address or when you start it using the Start menu.

You are eager to begin your evaluation of e-mail software for Sharon. You start Outlook Express by clicking its icon on the Quick Launch toolbar or by using the Start menu. Figure 3-7 shows the Outlook Express Inbox window.

| Figure 3-7 | OUTLOOK EXPRESS INBOX WINDOW |

The Inbox window contains four panes: the Folders list, the Contacts list, the message list, and the preview pane. The **Folders list** displays a list of folders for receiving, saving, and deleting mail messages. You might see different folders from those shown in Figure 3-7, but you should see five default folders. The **Inbox folder** stores messages you have received, the **Outbox folder** stores outgoing messages that have not been sent, the **Sent Items folder** stores copies of messages you have sent, and the **Deleted Items folder** stores messages you have deleted. The **Drafts folder** stores messages that you have written but have not sent. Your copy of Outlook Express may also contain folders you've created, such as a folder in which you store all messages from a certain recipient.

The **Contacts list**, which may be hidden, contains information about the information stored in your address book. You can click a contact in the Contacts list to quickly address a new message to an individual or group.

The **message list** contains summary information for each message that you have received. The first three columns on the left might display none or all of three e-mail message icons for each message. The first column indicates the message's priority; you might see an exclamation point to indicate a message with high priority, a blue down arrow icon to indicate a message with low priority, or nothing, which indicates normal priority. The sender indicates a message's priority before sending it; most messages have no specified priority. The second column displays a paperclip icon when a message contains an attachment. Finally, if you click the third column of a message you have received, a red flag will appear. Usually you use the flags to remind yourself to follow up on the message later.

The message list also displays the sender's name in the From column, the message's subject in the Subject column, and the date and time the message was received in the Received column. You can sort messages by clicking any column in the message list.

The message that is selected in the message list appears in the preview pane. The preview pane appears below the message list and displays the content of the selected message in the message list. You can use the horizontal scroll bar to scroll the message, if necessary. You can customize Outlook Express in many ways by resizing, hiding, and displaying different windows and their individual elements, so your screen might look different from Figure 3-7.

Setting Up E-Mail

You are eager to get started using Outlook Express. Cost is not a consideration because the Outlook Express program is free when you download it as part of the Internet Explorer program from Microsoft's Web site. These steps assume that Outlook Express 6 is already installed on your computer. First, you need to configure Outlook Express so it will retrieve your mail from your ISP.

To configure Outlook Express to manage your e-mail:

1. Click the **Start** button on the Windows taskbar, point to **Programs**, and then click **Outlook Express** to start the program. You normally do not need to be connected to the Internet to configure Outlook Express; however, your system might be configured differently. If necessary, connect to the Internet.

TROUBLE? If you cannot find the Outlook Express program on your computer, ask your instructor or technical support person for assistance.

TROUBLE? If the Internet Connection Wizard starts, click the Cancel button.

2. If necessary, click the **Inbox** folder in the Folders list to open it. (See Figure 3-7.)

3. Click **Tools** on the menu bar, click **Accounts**, and then if necessary, click the **Mail** tab so you can set up your mail account settings.

TROUBLE? If you have already set up your mail account (or if someone has set up another for you), click the Close button in the Internet Accounts dialog box and skip the remaining steps. If you are unsure about any existing account, ask your instructor or technical support person for help.

4. Click the **Add** button in the Internet Accounts dialog box, and then click **Mail**. The Internet Connection Wizard starts. You use this wizard to identify yourself, your user name, and the settings for your mail server. See Figure 3-8.

| Figure 3-8 | INTERNET CONNECTION WIZARD DIALOG BOX |

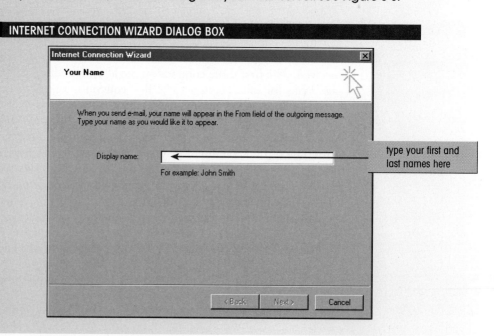

5. Type your first and last names in the Display name text box, and then click the **Next** button to open the next dialog box, where you enter your e-mail address.

6. Type your full e-mail address (such as student@university.edu) in the E-mail address text box, and then click the **Next** button. The next dialog box asks you for your incoming and outgoing mail server names.

7. Enter the name of your incoming and outgoing mail servers in the text boxes where indicated. Your instructor or technical support person will provide this information for you. Usually, your incoming mail server name is POP, POP3, or IMAP followed by a host name. Your outgoing mail server name is either SMTP or MAIL followed by a host name. When you are finished, click the **Next** button to continue.

8. In the Account name text box, type your Internet mail user name, as supplied by your instructor or technical support person. Make sure that you type only your user name and not your host name.

9. Press the **Tab** key, and then type your password in the Password text box. To protect your password's identity, Outlook Express displays asterisks instead of the characters you type. To prevent other users from being able to access your mail account, you will clear the Remember password check box. When you access your mail account, Outlook Express will prompt you for your password. If you are working on a computer on which you have sole access, you might want to set Outlook Express to remember your password, so you don't have to type it every time you access your e-mail.

10. Click the **Remember password** check box to clear it, and then click the **Next** button.

11. Click the **Finish** button to save the mail account information and close the Internet Connection Wizard. The Internet Accounts dialog box reappears, and your account is listed on the Mail tab. Figure 3-9 shows Sharon Kikukawa's information.

| Figure 3-9 | MAIL ACCOUNT CREATED FOR SHARON KIKUKAWA |

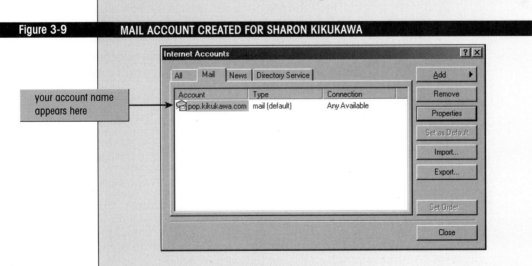

your account name appears here

12. Click the **Close** button in the Internet Accounts dialog box to close it.

Now Outlook Express is set up to send and receive messages, so you are ready to send a message to Sharon. *Note:* In this tutorial, you will send messages to a real mailbox with the address sharonkikukawa@yahoo.com. Follow the instructions carefully and use the correct address. Messages sent to this mailbox are deleted without being opened or read.

Sending a Message Using Outlook Express

You are ready to use Outlook Express to send a message with an attached file to Sharon. You will send a carbon copy of the message to your own e-mail address to make sure that the message and attached file are sent correctly.

REFERENCE WINDOW   **RW**

Sending a Message Using Outlook Express
- Click the Create Mail button on the toolbar to open the New Message window.
- In the To box, type the recipient's e-mail address. To send the message to more than one recipient, separate additional e-mail addresses with commas. If necessary, click View on the menu bar, and then click All Headers to display the Bcc box.
- Type the e-mail address of any Cc or Bcc recipients in the appropriate boxes. Separate multiple recipients' e-mail addresses with commas.
- If necessary, click the Attach button on the toolbar, and then browse to and select a file to attach to the message.
- In the message body, type your message.
- Check your message for spelling and grammatical errors.
- Click the Send button on the toolbar.

To send a message with an attachment:

1. Make sure that the **Inbox** folder is selected in the Folders list, and then click the **Create Mail** button on the toolbar to open the New Message window. If necessary, click the **Maximize** button on the New Message window. See Figure 3-10. The New Message window contains its own menu bar, toolbar, message display area, and boxes in which you enter address and subject information. The insertion point is positioned in the To box when you open a new message.

| Figure 3-10 | NEW MESSAGE WINDOW |

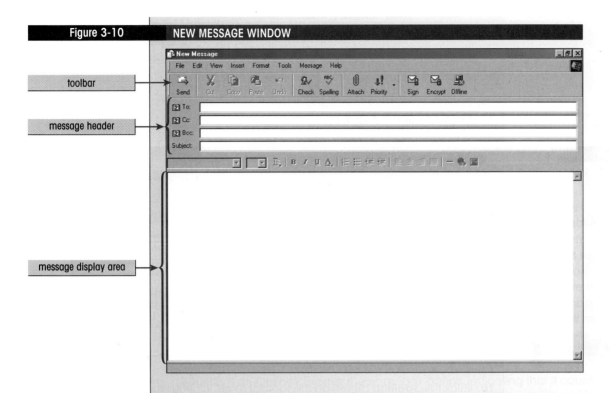

toolbar

message header

message display area

TROUBLE? If you do not see the Bcc box, click View on the menu bar, and then click All Headers.

2. In the To box, type **sharonkikukawa@yahoo.com**, and then press the **Tab** key to move to the Cc box.

TROUBLE? Make sure that you use the address sharonkikukawa@yahoo.com, instead of sharonkikukawa@kikukawa.com. If you type Sharon's e-mail address incorrectly, your message will be returned as undeliverable.

3. Type your full e-mail address in the Cc box. When you send this message, you and Sharon will both receive copies.

TROUBLE? If you make a typing mistake on a previous line, use the arrow keys or click the insertion point to return to a previous line so you can correct your mistake. If the arrow keys do not move the insertion point backward or forward in the message header, press Shift + Tab or the Tab key to move backward or forward, respectively.

4. Press the **Tab** key twice to move the insertion point to the Subject box, and then type **Test**. Notice that the title bar now displays "Test" as the window title.

5. Click the **Attach** button on the toolbar. The Insert Attachment dialog box opens.

6. Make sure your Data Disk is in the appropriate drive, click the **Look in** list arrow, and then click the appropriate drive to display the contents of your Data Disk.

7. Double-click the **Tutorial.03** folder, and then double-click **Physicals**. The Insert Attachment dialog box closes, and the attached file's icon, filename, and file size appear in the Attach box.

7. Scrolling as necessary, open the drive that contains your Data Disk, click the **Tutorial.03** folder to select it, and then click the **OK** button. The Save Attachments dialog box appears again. The Save To location indicates that you will save the attached file to the Tutorial.03 folder. See Figure 3-14.

Figure 3-14	SAVE ATTACHMENTS DIALOG BOX

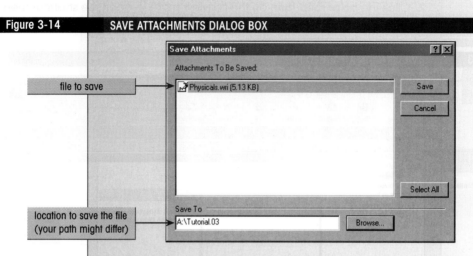

file to save

location to save the file
(your path might differ)

8. Click the **Save** button to save the attached file, and then click the **Yes** button to overwrite the file with the same name on your Data Disk.

When you receive a message with an attached file, you can view and save the attachment for as long as you store the message. When you delete the message, you will delete the file attached to the message. However, because you saved the attachment on your Data Disk, the file exists there for as long as you need it.

Replying to and Forwarding Messages

You can forward any message you receive to one or more e-mail addresses. Similarly, you can respond to the sender of a message quickly and efficiently by replying to a message. Replying to and forwarding messages are common tasks for e-mail users.

Replying to an E-Mail Message

To reply to a message, select the message in the message list, and then click the Reply button on the toolbar to reply only to the sender, or click the Reply All button to reply to the sender and other people who received the original message (those e-mail addresses listed in the To and Cc boxes). Outlook Express will open a new "Re:" message window and place the original sender's address in the To box; other e-mail addresses that received the original message will appear in the To and Cc boxes as appropriate. You can leave the Subject box as is or modify it. Most programs, including Outlook Express, will copy the original message and place it in the response window. Usually, a special mark to the left of the response indicates the text of the original message. Figure 3-15 shows a reply to the Test message.

Figure 3-15	REPLYING TO A MESSAGE

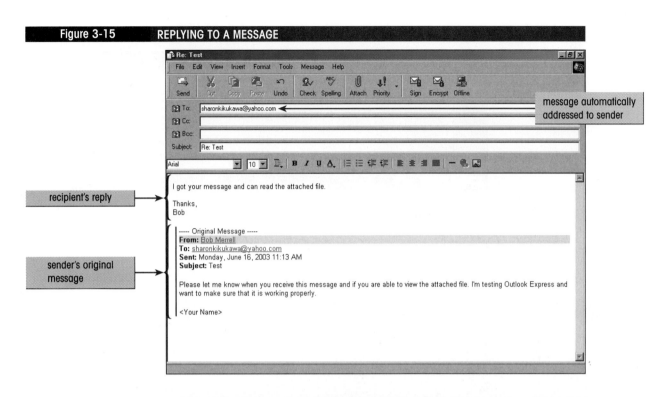

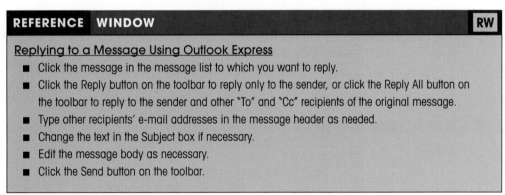

REFERENCE WINDOW   **RW**

Replying to a Message Using Outlook Express

- Click the message in the message list to which you want to reply.
- Click the Reply button on the toolbar to reply only to the sender, or click the Reply All button on the toolbar to reply to the sender and other "To" and "Cc" recipients of the original message.
- Type other recipients' e-mail addresses in the message header as needed.
- Change the text in the Subject box if necessary.
- Edit the message body as necessary.
- Click the Send button on the toolbar.

Forwarding an E-Mail Message

When you forward a message, you are sending a copy of your message to one or more recipients who were not included in the original message. To forward an existing mail message to another user, open the folder containing the message you want to forward, select it in the message list, and then click the Forward button on the toolbar. The "Fw:" window opens, where you can type the address of the recipient in the To box. If you want to forward the message to several people, type their addresses, separated by commas (or semicolons), in the To box (or Cc or Bcc boxes). Outlook Express inserts a copy of the original message in the message display area (as it does when you reply to a message). However, no special mark appears in the left margin to indicate the original message. Figure 3-16 shows a forwarded copy of the Test message.

Figure 3-16	FORWARDING A MESSAGE

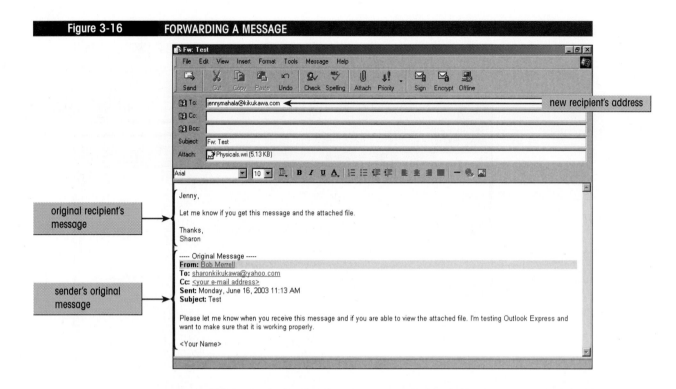

new recipient's address

original recipient's message

sender's original message

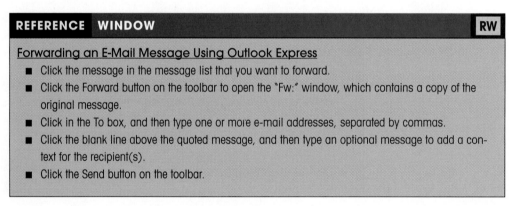

REFERENCE WINDOW   **RW**

Forwarding an E-Mail Message Using Outlook Express
- Click the message in the message list that you want to forward.
- Click the Forward button on the toolbar to open the "Fw:" window, which contains a copy of the original message.
- Click in the To box, and then type one or more e-mail addresses, separated by commas.
- Click the blank line above the quoted message, and then type an optional message to add a context for the recipient(s).
- Click the Send button on the toolbar.

Occasionally, you will receive important messages, so you want to make sure that you can print and file them as needed.

Filing and Printing an E-Mail Message

You can use the Outlook Express mail folders to file your e-mail messages by category. When you file a message, you move it from the Inbox to another folder. You can also make a *copy* of a message in the Inbox and save it in another folder by right-clicking the message in the message list, clicking Copy to Folder on the shortcut menu, and then selecting the folder to store the copy. You will file Sharon's message in a new folder named "FAA" for safekeeping. Later, you can create other folders to suit your style and working situation.

To create a new folder:

1. Right-click the **Inbox** folder in the Folders list to open the shortcut menu, and then click **New Folder**. The Create Folder dialog box opens. When you create a new folder, you first must select the folder at the level above which to create the new folder. Because the Inbox folder is selected, the new folder that you will create will be a subfolder of the Inbox folder.

2. Type **FAA** in the Folder name text box. See Figure 3-17.

Figure 3-17	CREATING A NEW FOLDER

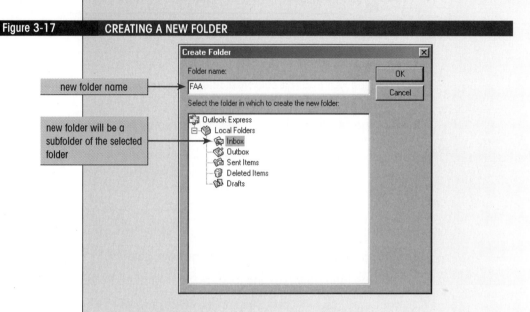

new folder name

new folder will be a subfolder of the selected folder

3. Click the **OK** button to create the new folder and to close the Create Folder dialog box. The new FAA folder appears in the Folders list below the Inbox folder.

After you create the FAA folder, you can transfer messages to it. Besides copying or transferring mail from the Inbox folder, you can select messages in any other folder and then transfer them to another folder.

To file the Test message:

1. Click the **Test** message in the message list to select it.

2. Drag the **Test** message from the message list to the FAA folder in the Folders list. See Figure 3-18.

Figure 3-18	FILING A MESSAGE

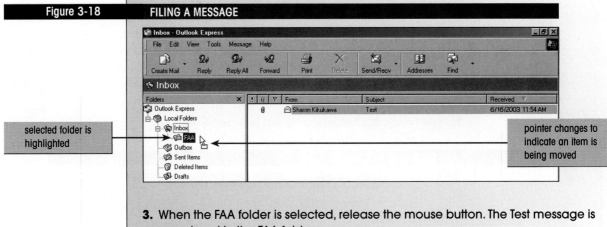

selected folder is
highlighted

pointer changes to
indicate an item is
being moved

3. When the FAA folder is selected, release the mouse button. The Test message is now stored in the FAA folder.

4. Click the **FAA** folder in the Folders list to display its contents. The Test message appears in the FAA folder.

You will print the message before deleting it.

To print the e-mail message:

1. Click the **Test** message in the message list to select it.

2. Click the **Print** button on the toolbar. The Print dialog box opens.

3. If necessary, select your printer in the list of printers.

4. Click the **Print** button. The message is printed.

You can print a message at any time—when you receive it, before you send it, or after you file it.

Deleting an E-Mail Message and Folder

When you don't need a message any longer, select the message in the message list, and then click the Delete button on the toolbar. You can select multiple messages by pressing and holding the Ctrl key, clicking each message in the message list, and then releasing the Ctrl key. When you click the Delete button on the toolbar, each selected message is deleted. You can select folders and delete them using these same steps. When you delete a message, you are simply moving it to the Deleted Items folder; when you delete a folder you send the folder and its contents to the Deleted Items folder. To remove items permanently, use the same steps to delete the items from the Deleted Items folder. If you are using a public PC in a university computer lab, it is always a good idea to delete all of your messages from the Inbox and then to delete them again from the Deleted Items folder when you finish your session. Otherwise, the next person who uses Outlook Express will be able to access and read your messages.

Deleting an E-Mail Message or a Folder in Outlook Express
- Click the message in the message list you want to delete. If you are deleting a folder, click the folder to be deleted in the Folders list.
- Click the Delete button on the toolbar.
- To delete items permanently, click the Deleted Items folder to open it, click the message or folder that you want to delete permanently, click the Delete button on the toolbar, and then click the Yes button.

or

- Right-click the Deleted Items folder to open the shortcut menu, click Empty 'Deleted Items' Folder, and then click the Yes button.

To delete the message:

1. If necessary, select the **Test** message in the message list.

2. Click the **Delete** button on the toolbar. The message is deleted from the FAA folder and is moved to the Deleted Items folder.

3. Click the **Deleted Items** folder in the Folder list to display the contents of the folder.

4. Click the **Test** message to select it, and then click the **Delete** button on the toolbar. A dialog box opens and asks you to confirm the deletion. See Figure 3-19.

Figure 3-19   DELETING A MESSAGE

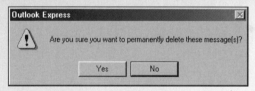

5. Click the **Yes** button. The Test message is deleted from the Deleted Items folder.

To delete the FAA folder, you follow the same steps.

To delete the FAA folder:

1. Click the **FAA** folder in the Folders list to select it. Because this folder doesn't contain any messages, the message list is empty.

2. Click the **Delete** button on the toolbar. A dialog box opens and asks you to confirm moving the folder to the Deleted Items folder.

3. Click the **Yes** button. The FAA folder moves to the Deleted Items folder. The Deleted Items folder contains a plus box to its left, indicating that this folder contains another folder.

4. Click the **plus box** to the left of the Deleted Items folder to display its contents, and then click the **FAA** folder to select it.

5. Click the **Delete** button on the toolbar, and then click the **Yes** button to permanently delete the FAA folder.

6. Click the **Inbox** folder in the Folders list.

Maintaining **an Address Book**

As you use e-mail to communicate with business associates and friends, you will want to save their addresses in an address book to make it easier to address your messages.

Adding a Contact to the Address Book

You can open the Outlook Express address book by clicking the Addresses button on the toolbar. To create a new address, you open the address book, click the New button on the toolbar, click New Contact from the drop-down list, and then enter information into the Properties dialog box for that contact. On the Name tab, you can enter a contact's names and e-mail address; you use the other tabs to enter optional address, business, personal, and other information about that contact. If you enter a short name in the Nickname text box, then you can type the nickname instead of a person's full name when you address a new message.

REFERENCE WINDOW   `RW`

Adding a Contact to the Outlook Express Address Book
- Click the Addresses button on the toolbar.
- In the Address Book window, click the New button on the toolbar, and then click New Contact.
- On the Name tab, enter the contact's name and e-mail address. Use the other tabs in the Properties dialog box as necessary to enter other information about the contact.
- Click the OK button to add the contact to the address book.
- Click the Close button.

You are eager to add information to your address book. You'll begin by adding Sharon Kikukawa's contact information to your address book.

To add a contact to your address book:

1. Click the **Addresses** button on the toolbar. The Address Book window opens. If necessary, maximize the Address Book window.

2. Click the **New** button on the toolbar, and then click **New Contact**. The Properties dialog box opens with the insertion point positioned in the First text box.

3. Type **Sharon** in the First text box. As you type the contact's first name (and eventually the last name), the name of the Properties dialog box changes to indicate that the properties set in this dialog box belong to the specified contact.

4. Press the **Tab** key twice to move the insertion point to the Last text box, type **Kikukawa** in the Last text box, and then press the **Tab** key three times to move the insertion point to the Nickname text box.

| Figure 3-21 | CREATING A GROUP OF CONTACTS |

individual contacts in the address book (your contacts might differ)

contacts added to the "Maintenance" group of contacts

7. Click the **OK** button to close the Select Group Members dialog box. The Properties dialog box for the Maintenance group now displays three group members.

8. Click the **OK** button to close the Maintenance Properties dialog box. The nickname of the new group, Maintenance, appears in the address book on the left side of the window and the members of the group are listed in the window on the right.

9. Close the Address Book window by clicking the **Close** button on its title bar. The Maintenance group appears in the Contacts list.

Now, test the new group of contacts by creating a new message.

To address a message to a group of contacts and close Outlook Express:

1. Click the **Create Mail** button on the toolbar. The New Message window opens.

2. Type **Maintenance** in the To box. As you type the first two or three letters, Outlook Express might complete your entry for you by selecting the Maintenance group.

3. Press the **Tab** key.

4. Click the **Check** button on the toolbar, right-click **Maintenance** in the To box to open the shortcut menu, and then click **Properties**. The Properties dialog box shows the three group members who will receive messages sent to the Maintenance group. Now, when Sharon sends mail to the maintenance department members, she can type the group name "Maintenance" in any of a message's boxes (To, Cc, or Bcc) instead of typing each address individually.

5. Click the **OK** button to close the Properties dialog box, click the **Close** button on the New Message window title bar, and then click the **No** button to close the message without saving it.

6. Click **File** on the menu bar, and then click **Exit**. Outlook Express closes.

7. If necessary, log off your Internet connection.

When you need to modify a group's members, you can delete one or more members from the group by opening the address book, double-clicking the group name, and then deleting a selected member's name by clicking the Remove button. Similarly, you can add members using the group's Properties dialog box.

Session 3.2 QUICK CHECK

1. The folder that stores messages you have written but have not yet sent is the _____ folder.

2. True or False: You can set Outlook Express so it remembers your e-mail account password.

3. What happens when Outlook Express queues a message?

4. When you receive a message with an attachment, what two options are available for the attached file?

5. When you delete a message from the Inbox folder, can you recover that message? Why or why not?

6. What information can you store about a person in a contact?

If your instructor assigned Session 3.3, continue reading. If your instructor assigned Session 3.4, proceed to that session. Otherwise, complete the Review Assignments at the end of this tutorial.

SESSION 3.3

In this session, you will learn how to use Netscape Mail to send and receive e-mail. You will use this e-mail program to print, file, save, delete, respond to, and forward e-mail messages. Finally, you will organize e-mail addresses in an address book.

Netscape Mail

Netscape Mail, or simply **Mail**, is the e-mail program that you use to send and receive e-mail. Mail is installed with Netscape Communicator. Mail starts when you click a hyperlink in a Web page to an e-mail address or when you start it using the Start menu.

You are eager to begin your evaluation of e-mail software for Sharon. You start Mail using the Start menu. Figure 3-22 shows the Mail window.

Figure 3-22   MAIL WINDOW

Mail Folders pane (your folders and mailboxes might differ)

toolbar

Local Folders mail account selected

Message pane

Thread button

message list

The Mail window contains three panes: the Mail Folders pane, the message list, and the Message pane. The **Mail Folders pane** displays a list of mailboxes and folders for receiving, saving, and storing mail messages. You might see different folders from those shown in Figure 3-22, but you should see six default mailboxes and folders. The **Inbox** is a mailbox that receives your downloaded messages (this mailbox isn't shown in Figure 3-22 because Mail hasn't been configured for any user yet). The **Unsent Messages mailbox** stores out-going messages that have not been sent. The **Drafts folder** stores messages that you are composing, but are not yet ready to send. The **Templates folder** contains any template files that you have created for your messages. The **Sent folder** stores copies of each message that you send (note that you can disable this feature). Finally, the **Trash folder** stores messages you have deleted. Your copy of Mail may also contain folders and mailboxes you've created, such as a folder in which you store all messages from a certain recipient.

The **message list** contains summary information for each message that you have received. Clicking the Thread button in the message list groups messages by their threads, or common topics, so you can quickly find all messages you have received based on a specific subject. Messages appearing in bold type are ones that you haven't opened or read yet; other messages appear without bold formatting to indicate that you have reviewed them. To change a message's status from read to unread, click the green dot in the fourth column. The Date column indicates when you received the message, and the Priority column indicates a priority from highest to lowest. If this column's entry is blank, then the sender did not choose a priority. The sender indicates a message's priority before sending it; most messages have no priority specified. Figure 3-22 shows the default configuration for Mail's message list; you might also see other columns if you or another user has used the arrows on the column headings row to display or hide additional columns. You can sort messages by clicking any column in the message list.

The message that is selected in the message list appears in the **Message pane**. The Message pane appears below the message list and displays the message's contents. You use the horizontal scroll bar to scroll the message, if necessary. You can customize Mail in many ways by resizing, hiding, and displaying different panes and their individual elements, so your screen might look different from Figure 3-22.

Setting Up E-Mail

You are eager to get started using Mail. Cost is not a consideration because the Mail program is free when you download it as part of the Netscape Communicator suite from Netscape's Web site. These steps assume that Mail 6.1 is already installed on your computer. First, you need to configure Mail so it will retrieve your mail from your ISP.

To configure Mail to manage your e-mail:

1. Click the **Start** button on the Windows taskbar, point to **Programs**, point to **Netscape 6**, and then click **Mail** to start the program.

TROUBLE? If you cannot find the Mail program on your computer, ask your instructor or technical support person for assistance.

TROUBLE? You can configure Mail to open in different ways and to display a Web page in the Message pane when it starts. These screen differences should cause no problems.

2. Click **Edit** on the menu bar, and then click **Mail/News Account Settings**. The Account Settings window opens. You use this window to set up your mail account and to change settings in Mail.

TROUBLE? If you have already set up your mail account (or if someone else has set up your mail account), click the OK button in the Account Settings window and skip to the next set of steps. If you are unsure about any existing account, ask your instructor or technical support person for help.

3. In the text box on the left, click **Local Folders**, and then click the **New Account** button. The Account Wizard starts so you can set up a new mail account. See Figure 3-23.

| Figure 3-23 | ACCOUNT WIZARD |

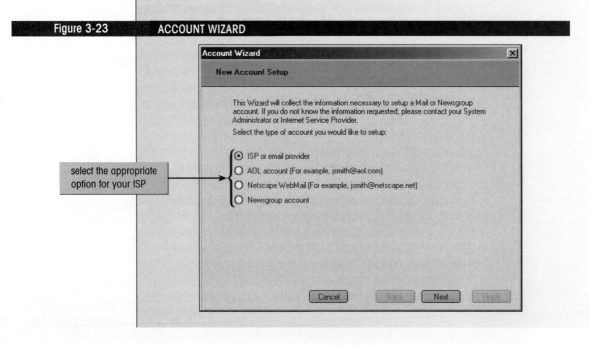

select the appropriate option for your ISP

4. Click the option button for the type of service that you have, and then click the **Next** button. The Account Wizard opens the Identity page, which asks for your full name and e-mail address. Mail will insert this information in the From field when you send messages.

   TROUBLE? If you are unsure of which option to choose, ask your instructor or technical support person for help.

5. Click in the **Your Name** text box, type your first and last names, click in the **Email Address** text box, type your full e-mail address, and then click the **Next** button. The Account Wizard opens the Server Information page, which requests the name of your incoming and outgoing mail servers.

6. Click the POP or IMAP option button to indicate your ISP's incoming server type.

7. In the Server Name text box, type the name of your incoming mail server. Your instructor or technical support person will provide this information for you. Usually, your incoming mail server name is POP, POP3, or IMAP followed by a host name.

8. Press the **Tab** key, type the name of your ISP's outgoing mail server in the Server Name text box, and then click the **Next** button. The Account Wizard opens the User Name page, where you enter the user name given to you by your ISP.

9. Click in the **User Name** text box, and then type your user name, as specified by your instructor or technical support person. Make sure that you type only your user name and not your host name.

10. Click the **Next** button, click the **Next** button again to accept the default account name, confirm the information in the Congratulations! page, and then click the **Finish** button when you are sure that your settings are correct. If you need to make any changes, use the Back button to return to a previous page.

11. Click the **OK** button to close the Account Settings window, and then click **Inbox** for your account in the Mail Folders pane.

Now Mail is set up to send and receive messages, so you are ready to send a message to Sharon. *Note:* In this tutorial, you will send messages to a real mailbox with the address sharonkikukawa@yahoo.com. Follow the instructions carefully and use the correct address. Messages sent to this mailbox are deleted without being opened or read.

Sending a Message Using Mail

You are ready to use Mail to send a message with an attached file to Sharon. You will send a carbon copy of the message to your own e-mail address to make sure that the message and attached file are sent correctly.

REFERENCE   WINDOW   **RW**

Sending a Message Using Mail

- Click the New Msg button on the toolbar to open the Compose window.
- In the To field, type the recipient's e-mail address. To send the message to more than one recipient, separate additional e-mail addresses with commas.
- If necessary, click the box below the To button, click the list arrow on the To button that appears in the second row of the message header, click Cc: or Bcc: as needed to add a Cc or Bcc button to the message header, and then type the recipient's e-mail address. Separate multiple recipients' e-mail addresses with commas.
- Type a subject in the Subject field.
- If necessary, click the Attach button on the toolbar, and then browse to and select a file to attach to the message.
- Click in the message display area, and then type your message.
- Check your message for spelling and grammatical errors.
- Click the Send button on the toolbar.

To send a message with an attachment:

1. Click the **New Msg** button on the toolbar. The Compose window opens. If necessary, click the **Maximize** button on the Compose window to maximize it. See Figure 3-24. The Compose window contains a menu bar, toolbar, message display area, and fields in which to enter addresses and subject information. The insertion point is positioned in the To field when you create a new message.

Figure 3-24	COMPOSE WINDOW

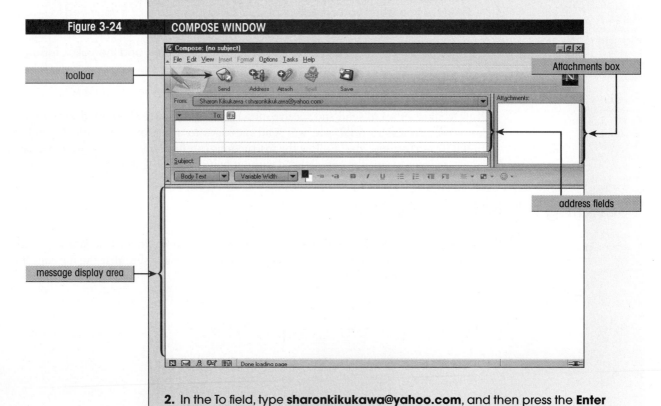

toolbar

Attachments box

message display area

address fields

2. In the To field, type **sharonkikukawa@yahoo.com**, and then press the **Enter** key. A To button is added to the second row of the message header.

TROUBLE? Make sure that you use the address sharonkikukawa@yahoo.com, instead of sharonkikukawa@kikukawa.com. If you type Sharon's e-mail address incorrectly, your message will be returned as undeliverable.

3. Click the **list arrow** on the second To button in the message header, and then click **Cc:** in the list. A Cc button replaces the To button on the second row of the message header and the insertion point is positioned in the message header.

4. Type your e-mail address in the Cc field. When you send this message, you and Sharon will both receive copies.

   TROUBLE? If you make a typing mistake on a previous line, use the arrow keys or click the insertion point to return to a previous line so you can correct your mistake. If the arrow keys do not move the insertion point backward or forward in the address fields, then press Shift + Tab or press the Tab key to move backward or forward, respectively.

5. Click in the **Subject** field, and then type **Test**.

6. Click the **Attach** button on the toolbar. The Enter file to attach dialog box opens.

7. Make sure your Data Disk is in the appropriate drive, click the **Look in** list arrow, and then click the appropriate drive to display the contents of your Data Disk.

8. Double-click the **Tutorial.03** folder, and then double-click **Physicals**. The Enter file to attach dialog box closes, and the Attachments box now displays the Physicals.wri file.

9. Click the insertion point in the message body, and then type **Please let me know when you receive this message and if you are able to view the attached file. I'm testing Netscape Mail and want to make sure that it is working properly.**

10. Press the **Enter** key twice, and then type your first and last names to sign your message. See Figure 3-25.

| Figure 3-25 | SENDING AN E-MAIL MESSAGE |

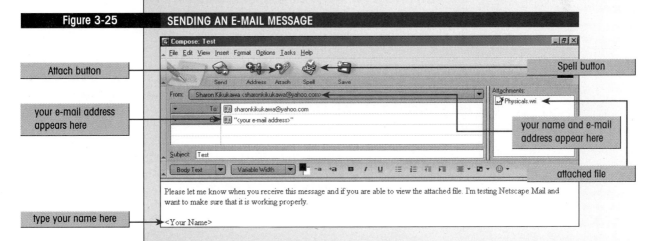

11. Click the **Spell** button on the toolbar to check your spelling before sending the message. If necessary, correct any typing errors. When you are finished, click the **Close** button to close the Check Spelling dialog box.

12. Click the **Send** button on the toolbar to send the message. The Compose window closes, and the message is sent to the mail server for delivery to Sharon.

TROUBLE? If a dialog box opens and tells you that Netscape cannot locate your mail server, click the OK button, connect to your ISP or log on to the network, and then repeat Step 12.

Receiving and Reading a Message

When you receive new mail, messages that you have not opened have closed envelope icons in the message list, and messages that you have opened have open envelope icons. You will check for new mail next.

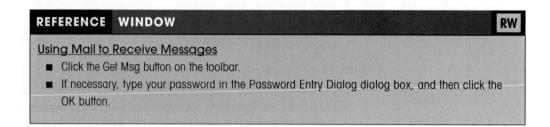

REFERENCE WINDOW   **RW**

Using Mail to Receive Messages
- Click the Get Msg button on the toolbar.
- If necessary, type your password in the Password Entry Dialog dialog box, and then click the OK button.

To check for incoming mail:

1. Click the **Get Msg** button on the toolbar. The Password Entry Dialog dialog box opens.

2. Type your password in the text box, and then click the **OK** button. Within a few moments, your mail server transfers all new mail to your Inbox. You should see the Test message in the Inbox. The Inbox in the Mail Folders pane is bold, but other folders and mailboxes are not. A bold folder or mailbox indicates that it contains unread mail; the "(1)" next to the mailbox name indicates the number of new messages.

TROUBLE? If you do not see any messages in your Inbox, then you either did not receive any new mail or you might be looking in the wrong mailbox. If necessary, click the Inbox in the Mail Folders pane. If you still don't have any mail messages, wait a few moments, and then click the Get Msg button again.

3. Click the **Test** message in the message list to open the message in the Message pane. The Attachments box in the Message pane indicates that the message contains an attached file. See Figure 3-26.

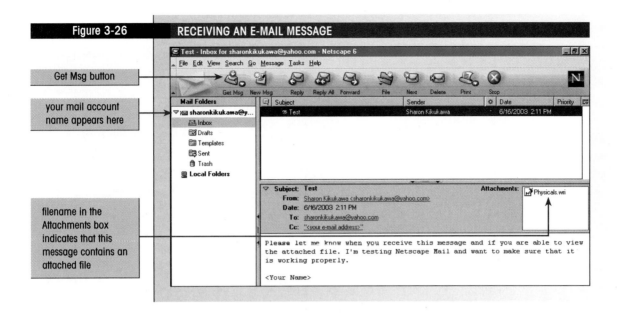

Figure 3-26 RECEIVING AN E-MAIL MESSAGE

- Get Msg button
- your mail account name appears here
- filename in the Attachments box indicates that this message contains an attached file

You received a copy of the test message that you sent to Sharon. The Attachments box shows the name of the attached file that you received with the message. When you receive a message with one or more attachments, you can open the attachment or save it.

Viewing and Saving an Attached File

You want to make sure that your attached file was sent properly, so you decide to open it. After you are finished viewing the contents of an attached file, you can save or delete it.

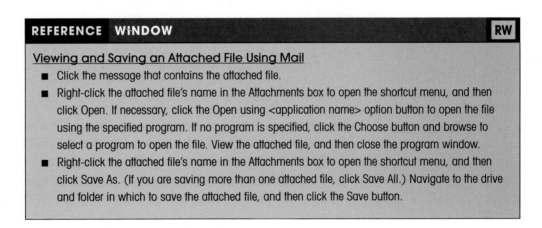

REFERENCE WINDOW RW

Viewing and Saving an Attached File Using Mail
- Click the message that contains the attached file.
- Right-click the attached file's name in the Attachments box to open the shortcut menu, and then click Open. If necessary, click the Open using <application name> option button to open the file using the specified program. If no program is specified, click the Choose button and browse to select a program to open the file. View the attached file, and then close the program window.
- Right-click the attached file's name in the Attachments box to open the shortcut menu, and then click Save As. (If you are saving more than one attached file, click Save All.) Navigate to the drive and folder in which to save the attached file, and then click the Save button.

To view and save the attached file:

1. Right-click **Physicals.wri** to open the shortcut menu. See Figure 3-27.

Figure 3-27   VIEWING AN ATTACHED FILE

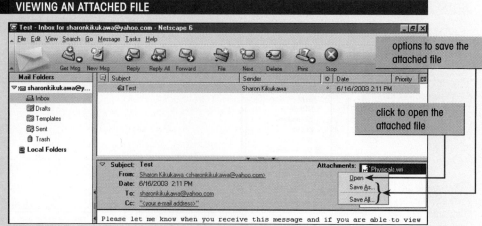

The shortcut menu contains three options: Open, Save As, and Save All. Clicking Open starts a program on your computer that can open the file. Clicking Save As lets you save the file to the drive and folder that you specify. Clicking Save All lets you simultaneously save more than one attachment to the drive and folder that you specify.

2. Click **Open** on the shortcut menu. The Downloading dialog box opens and displays the option of opening the file using a specified program (or one that you choose) or saving the file to disk. The default editor for a file with the .wri extension is WordPad, so the Open using option button is "Open using wordpad.exe."

TROUBLE? If you can't see the entire Downloading dialog box, drag it to another location.

TROUBLE? If the Open using option button is set to Word, Notepad, or another text editor, no special action is necessary. If the Open using option button is set to Open using <no application specified>, click the Open using option button, click the Choose button, navigate to the wordpad.exe file on your computer (the default directory is C:\Program Files\Windows\Accessories\), click the wordpad.exe file, and then click the Open button. Continue with Step 3.

3. Click the **Open using** option button if necessary, and then click the **OK** button. WordPad or another text editor starts and opens the file. If necessary, maximize the program window.

4. Click the **Close** button on the program window. Now that you have viewed the attachment, you can save it on your Data Disk.

TROUBLE? If the Saving File dialog box opens, click the Close button.

5. Right-click **Physicals.wri** in the Attachments box, and then click **Save As** on the shortcut menu. The Save Attachment dialog box opens. The Physicals file is already selected for you in the File name text box.

6. If necessary, click the **Save in** list arrow, browse to and select the drive that contains your Data Disk, and then double-click the **Tutorial.03** folder to open it.

7. Click the **Save** button, and then click the **Yes** button to overwrite the file with the same name on your Data Disk.

When you receive a message with an attached file, you can view and save the attachment for as long as you store the message. When you delete the message, you will delete the file attached to the message. However, because you saved the attachment on your Data Disk, the file exists there for as long as you need it.

Replying to and Forwarding Messages

You can forward any message you receive to one or more e-mail addresses. Similarly, you can respond to the sender of a message quickly and efficiently by replying to a message. Replying to and forwarding messages are common tasks for e-mail users.

Replying to an E-Mail Message

To reply to a message, select the message in the message list, and then click the Reply button on the toolbar to reply only to the sender, or click the Reply All button on the toolbar to reply to the sender and to other people who received the original message (those e-mail addresses listed in the To and Cc fields). Mail will open a new Compose window and place the original sender's address in the To field; other e-mail addresses that received the original message will appear in the To and Cc fields as appropriate. You can leave the Subject field as is or modify it. In Mail, when you reply to a message the original message has a blue line to the left of its content to indicate the original message text. Figure 3-28 shows a reply to the Test message.

Figure 3-28   REPLYING TO A MESSAGE

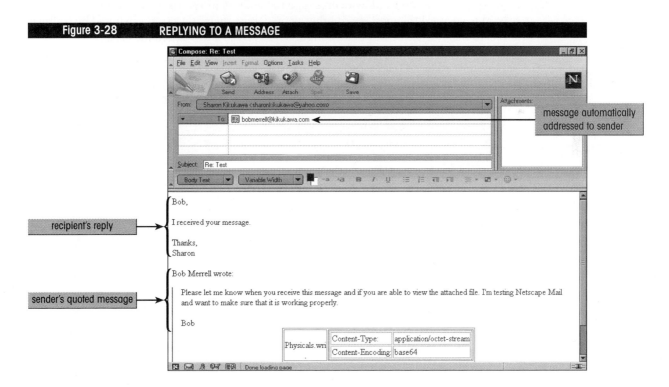

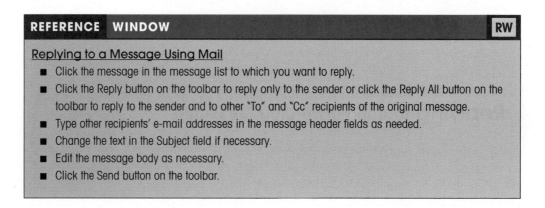

Forwarding an E-Mail Message

When you forward a message, you are sending a copy of the message to one or more recipients who were not included in the original message. To forward an existing mail message to another user, open the folder or mailbox containing the message you want to forward, select it in the message list, and then click the Forward button on the toolbar. In Mail, the default setting is to send a forwarded message as inline text, where an "Original Message" separator separates the current and forwarded messages. You can also send a forwarded message as an attachment, where the forwarded message is sent as an attached file, by clicking Message on the menu bar of the Inbox window, pointing to Forward As, and then clicking Attachment. After the Compose window opens, type the address of the recipient in the To field. If you want to forward the message to other people, type their addresses, separated by commas, in the To field (or Cc or Bcc fields). Figure 3-29 shows a forwarded message.

Figure 3-29   FORWARDING A MESSAGE

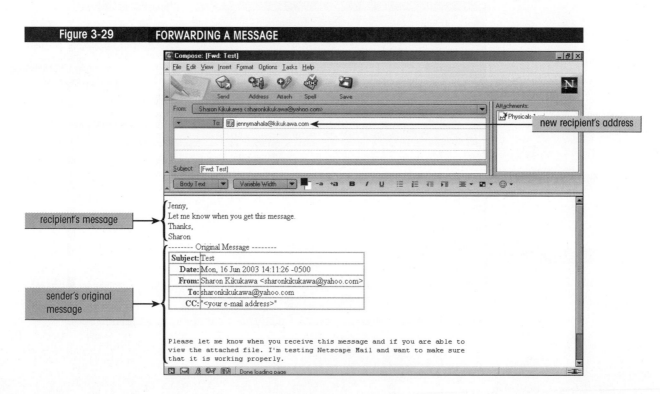

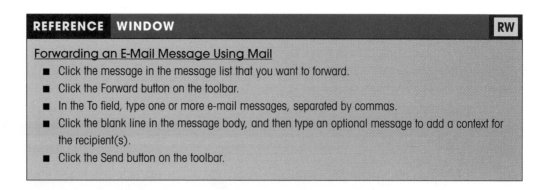

REFERENCE WINDOW RW

Forwarding an E-Mail Message Using Mail
■ Click the message in the message list that you want to forward.
■ Click the Forward button on the toolbar.
■ In the To field, type one or more e-mail messages, separated by commas.
■ Click the blank line in the message body, and then type an optional message to add a context for the recipient(s).
■ Click the Send button on the toolbar.

Occasionally, you will receive important messages, so you want to make sure that you print them and then file them in a safe place.

Filing and Printing an E-Mail Message

You can use the folders and mailboxes in Mail to file your e-mail messages by category. When you file a message, you move it from the Inbox to another folder. You can also make a *copy* of a message in the Inbox and save it in another folder by right-clicking the message in the message list, pointing to Copy To on the shortcut menu, and then clicking the mailbox or folder in which to store the copy. You will file Sharon's message in a new folder named "FAA" for safekeeping. Later you can create other folders to suit your style and working situation.

To create the new folder:

1. Right-click **Inbox** in the Mail Folders pane to open the shortcut menu, and then click **New Folder**. The New Folder dialog box opens.

2. In the Name text box, type **FAA**. See Figure 3-30.

Figure 3-30 CREATING A NEW FOLDER

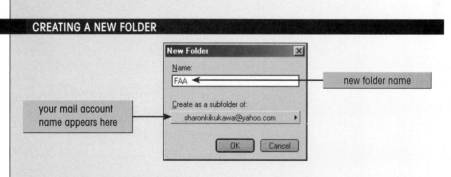

3. Click the **OK** button. The new FAA folder appears in the Mail Folders pane.

After you create the FAA folder, you can transfer messages to it. Besides copying or transferring mail from the Inbox, you can select messages in any other folder and then transfer them to another folder.

To file the message:

1. Click the **Test** message in the message list to select it.

2. Drag the **Test** message from the message list to the FAA folder in the Mail Folders pane. See Figure 3-31.

Figure 3-31	FILING A MESSAGE

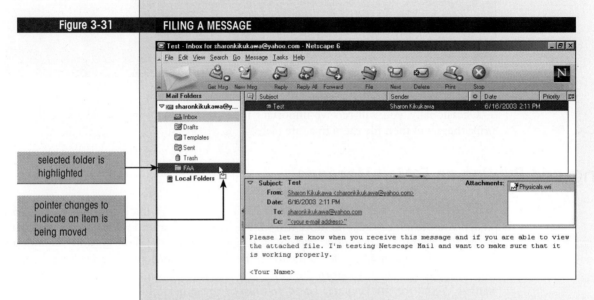

selected folder is highlighted

pointer changes to indicate an item is being moved

3. When the FAA folder is selected, release the mouse button. The Test message is now stored in the FAA folder.

4. Click the **FAA** folder in the Mail Folders pane to display its contents. The Test message appears in the FAA folder.

You might need to print important messages in the future, so you want to make sure that you can print and file messages in a safe place.

To print an e-mail message:

1. Click the **Test** message in the message list to select it.

2. Click the **Print** button on the toolbar. The Print dialog box opens.

3. If necessary, select your printer in the Printer section.

4. Click the **OK** button. The message is printed.

You can print a message at any time—when you receive it, before you send it, or after you file it.

Deleting an E-Mail Message and Folder

When you don't need a message any longer, select the message in the message list, and then click the Delete button on the toolbar. You can select multiple messages by pressing and holding the Ctrl key, clicking each message in the message list, and then releasing the Ctrl key.

When you click the Delete button on the toolbar, each selected message is deleted. You can select folders and delete them using these same steps. When you delete a message, you are really moving it to the Trash folder; when you delete a folder you send the folder and its contents to the Trash folder. To remove items permanently, you need to empty the Trash folder. If you are using a public PC in a university computer lab, it is always a good idea to delete all of your messages from the Inbox and then empty the Trash folder when you finish your session. Otherwise, the next person who uses Mail will be able to access and read your messages.

REFERENCE WINDOW **RW**

Deleting an E-Mail Message or a Folder Using Mail
- Click the message in the message list to delete. If you are deleting a folder, click the folder to delete in the Mail Folders pane.
- Click the Delete button on the toolbar.
- To delete items permanently, click the Trash folder in the Mail Folders pane to open it, click the message or folder that you want to delete permanently, and then click the Delete button on the toolbar.

or

- Right-click the Trash folder in the Mail Folders pane to open the shortcut menu, and then click Empty Trash Can.

To delete the message:

1. If necessary, click the **Test** message in the message list.

2. Click the **Delete** button on the toolbar. The message is deleted from the FAA folder and is moved to the Trash folder.

3. Click the **Trash** folder in the Mail Folders pane to open it.

4. Click the **Test** message to select it, and then click the **Delete** button on the toolbar. The message is deleted from the Trash folder.

To delete a folder, you follow the same steps.

To delete a folder:

1. Click the **FAA** folder in the Mail Folders pane to select it. Because this folder doesn't contain any messages, the message list is empty.

2. Click the **Delete** button on the toolbar. A dialog box opens and asks you to confirm moving the folder to the Trash folder. See Figure 3-32.

Figure 3-32 | DELETING A MESSAGE

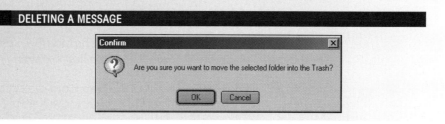

3. Click the **OK** button. The FAA folder moves to the Trash folder. The Trash folder contains an arrow to its left, indicating that this folder contains another folder.

4. Right-click the **Trash** folder in the Mail Folders pane to open the shortcut menu, and then click the **Empty Trash Can**. Mail deletes all items in the Trash folder, which permanently deletes the items from your computer.

Maintaining **an Address Book**

As you use e-mail to communicate with business associates and friends, you will want to save their addresses in an address book to make it easier to address your messages.

Adding a Card to the Address Book

You can open the address book in Mail by clicking Tasks on the menu bar, and then clicking Address Book. To create a new address, you open the address book, click the New Card button on the toolbar, and then enter information into the New Card dialog box that opens. On the Name tab, you can enter a person's name, e-mail address, and various phone numbers. If you enter a short name in the Nickname text box, then you can type the nickname instead of a person's full name when you address a new message.

REFERENCE WINDOW   **RW**

Adding a Card to the Mail Address Book
- Click Tasks on the menu bar, and then click Address Book.
- In the Address Book window, click the New Card button on the toolbar.
- Use the New Card dialog box to enter the person's name, e-mail address, nickname, and phone numbers as necessary. Use the other tabs in the New Card dialog box as necessary to enter other information about the contact.
- Click the OK button to add the card to the address book.
- Click the OK button, and then close the Address Book window.

You are eager to add information to your address book. You'll begin by adding Sharon Kikukawa's contact information to your address book.

To add a card to the address book:

1. Click **Tasks** on the menu bar, and then click **Address Book**. The Address Book window opens. If necessary, maximize the Address Book window.

TROUBLE? If an Instant Messenger Setup dialog box opens, click the Cancel button.

2. Click the **New Card** button on the toolbar. The New Card dialog box opens with the insertion point positioned in the First text box.

TROUBLE? If you cannot see all of the New Card dialog box, move it so the entire dialog box is visible on the screen.

3. Type **Sharon** in the First text box, and then press the **Tab** key to move the insertion point to the Last text box.

4. Type **Kikukawa** and then press the **Tab** key twice to move the insertion point to the Nickname text box.

5. Type **Sharon** in the Nickname text box, press the **Tab** key to move the insertion point to the Email text box, and then type **sharonkikukawa@yahoo.com**. Your New Card dialog box looks like Figure 3-33.

Figure 3-33	ADDING A CARD TO THE ADDRESS BOOK

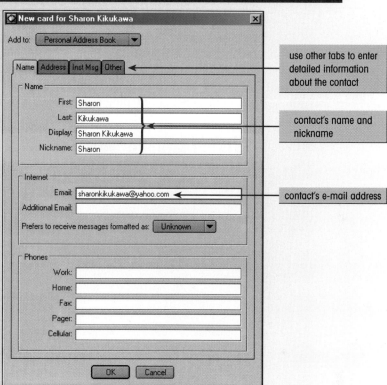

6. Click the **OK** button. The New Card dialog box closes and you return to the Address Book window. Sharon's card information now appears in the Address Book window.

7. Repeat Steps 2 through 6 to create new cards for the following Kikukawa Air employees:

First	Last	Nickname	E-mail
Chris	**Breed**	**Chris**	**chrisbreed@kikukawa.com**
Jenny	**Mahala**	**Jen**	**jennymahala@kikukawa.com**
Richard	**Forrester**	**Rich**	**richardforrester@kikukawa.com**

8. When you are finished adding the addresses, click the **Close** button on the Address Book window title bar to close it.

Now that these e-mail addresses are stored in the address book, when you start entering the first few letters of a nickname or first name, Mail will complete the entries for you. Clicking the Address button on the toolbar in the Compose window lets you select names from the address book instead of typing them. If you need to delete an address, click it to select it, and then click the Remove button.

When you receive mail from someone who is not in your address book, double-click the message in the message list to open it, right-click the "From" name to open the shortcut menu, and then click Add to Address Book. This process adds the sender's name and e-mail address to your address book, where you can open his or her information as a card and edit and add information as necessary.

Creating a Mailing List

You can use Mail to create a mailing list, which is an address entry consisting of more than one e-mail address in a single group. Usually you create a mailing list when you regularly send messages to a group of people.

Sharon frequently sends messages to each member of the maintenance department. She asks you to create a mailing list in her address book so she can type one nickname for the mailing list, instead of typing each address separately.

REFERENCE WINDOW   RW

Creating a Mailing List In Netscape Mail

- Click Tasks on the menu bar, and then click Address Book.
- In the Address Book window, click the New List button on the toolbar.
- In the Mailing List dialog box, type a name for the mailing list in the List Name text box. Type a nickname for the mailing list in the List Nickname text box, and then type an optional description for the mailing list in the Description text box.
- Click the Type names or drag addresses into the mailing list below box, and then type the first e-mail address to store in the mailing list. Continue adding names to the mailing list until you have added all mailing list members.
- Click the OK button, and then close the Address Book window.

To add a mailing list to the address book:

1. Click **Tasks** on the menu bar, and then click **Address Book**. The Address Book window opens. If necessary, maximize the Address Book window.

2. Click the **New List** button on the toolbar. The Mailing List dialog box opens.

3. Click in the List Name text box, type **Maintenance List**, and then press the **Tab** key to move the insertion point to the List Nickname text box.

4. Type **Maintenance** in the List Nickname text box. This nickname will represent the group.

5. Press the **Tab** key twice to move the insertion point to the Type names or drag addresses into the mailing list below box, and then type **C**. A menu of e-mail addresses in your address book and beginning with the letter "C" opens. You can click an address in the list or continue typing.

6. Click the entry for **Chris Breed**. Mail adds Chris's card to the mailing list and creates a new entry for the next name.

7. Press the **Tab** key to enter Chris's name, and then type **J**. Mail opens a list of addresses in the address book that begin with the letter "J."

8. Click the entry for **Jenny Mahala**, press the **Tab** key, and then add Richard Forrester's address to the mailing list. See Figure 3-34.

Figure 3-34 **CREATING A MAILING LIST**

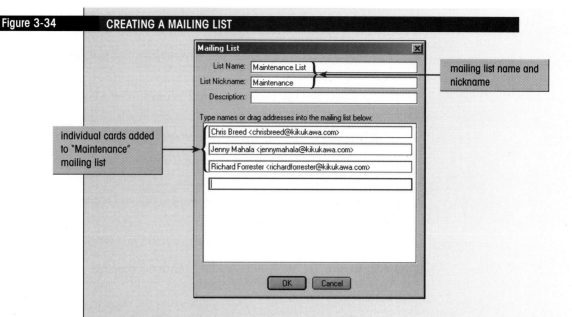

mailing list name and nickname

individual cards added to "Maintenance" mailing list

9. Click the **OK** button to close the Mailing List dialog box. The Maintenance List entry appears in the Address Book.

10. Click the **Close** button on the Address Book window title bar to close it.

Now, test the mailing list by creating a new message.

To address a message to a mailing list and close Mail:

1. Click the **New Msg** button on the toolbar. The Compose window opens. If necessary, maximize the Compose window.

2. Type **Maintenance** in the To field. As you type the first two or three letters, Mail's autocompletion feature might complete your entry for you by selecting the Maintenance mailing list.

3. Press the **Tab** key to enter the Maintenance list in the To field. Now when Sharon sends mail to the maintenance department members, she can type the group name "Maintenance" in any of the message's fields (To, Cc, or Bcc) instead of typing each address individually.

4. Click the **Close** button on the Compose window title bar to close the new message.

5. Click **File** on the menu bar, and then click **Exit**. Mail closes.

6. If necessary, log off your Internet connection.

When you need to modify a mailing list's members, you can delete one or more cards from the mailing list by opening the address book, double-clicking the mailing list entry, selecting the card to delete, and then clicking the Remove button. Similarly, you can add cards to the mailing list by entering new names in the Mailing List dialog box.

Session 3.3 QUICK CHECK

1. The folder that stores messages you have written but have not yet sent is the _____ folder.

2. True or False: You can use the Account Wizard to set Mail so it remembers your e-mail account password.

3. What happens when Mail queues a message?

4. When you receive a message with an attachment, what three options are available for the attached file?

5. When you delete a message from the Inbox, can you recover that message? Why or why not?

6. What information can you store about a person in a card?

If your instructor assigned Session 3.4, continue reading. Otherwise, complete the Review Assignments at the end of this tutorial.

SESSION 3.4

In this session, you will learn how to use Hotmail to send and receive e-mail. You will use Hotmail to print, file, save, delete, respond to, and forward e-mail messages. Finally, you will organize e-mail addresses in an address book.

Hotmail

Hotmail is a Web-based e-mail service powered by MSN.com that you use to send and receive e-mail. To use Hotmail, you must use a Web browser, such as Microsoft Internet Explorer or Netscape Navigator, to make a connection to the Internet. Then you navigate to the Hotmail home page, where your e-mail messages are stored.

Most people who use Hotmail and other Web-based e-mail services have Internet access from their employer, school, public library, or a friend. The Hotmail service is free, but you must have a way to access it using a Web browser and an existing Internet connection, which someone else might supply for you. Many public and school libraries provide free Internet access where you can access your Hotmail account. No matter where you are in the world, if you can connect to the Internet, you can access your Hotmail account. This portability makes Web-based e-mail a valuable resource for people who travel or who do not have their own computers.

You are eager to begin your evaluation of e-mail service for Sharon. To begin using Hotmail, you need to use your Web browser to connect to the Hotmail Web site. Then you will create a user account and send and receive messages.

Setting Up a Hotmail User Account

Cost is not a consideration because Hotmail is a free service. The steps in this session assume that you have a Web browser and can make an Internet connection. Before you can use Hotmail, you'll need to establish a user account. A user account establishes your name and Hotmail e-mail address so that you can use Hotmail to send and receive e-mail messages.

To begin setting up a Hotmail user account:

1. Start your Web browser and if necessary, log on to your Internet account.

TROUBLE? You must have an Internet connection to set up a Hotmail user account. If you cannot connect to the Internet, ask your instructor or technical support person for help.

2. Select any text in your browser's Address bar, type **www.msn.com**, press the **Enter** key, and then click the **Hotmail** link on the MSN.com home page. The home page for Hotmail opens in your browser. See Figure 3-35.

Figure 3-35	HOTMAIL SIGN-IN PAGE

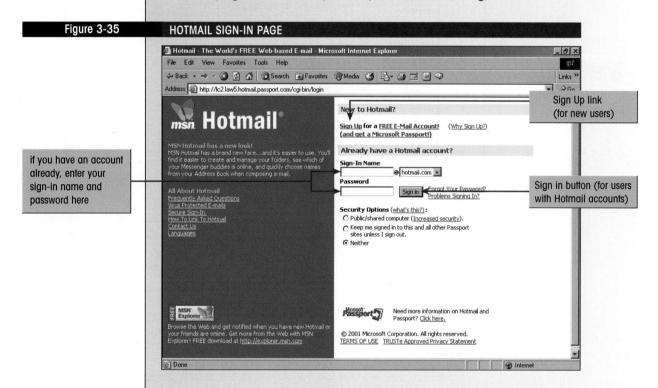

TROUBLE? If you already have a Hotmail account, log on to your account, and then skip to the next set of steps.

3. In the New to Hotmail? section, click the **Sign Up** link. The Hotmail Registration page shown in Figure 3-36 opens. This page changes occasionally, so your page might look different. However, you will need to supply the same information identified in the steps to create your Hotmail user account.

Figure 3-36	HOTMAIL REGISTRATION PAGE

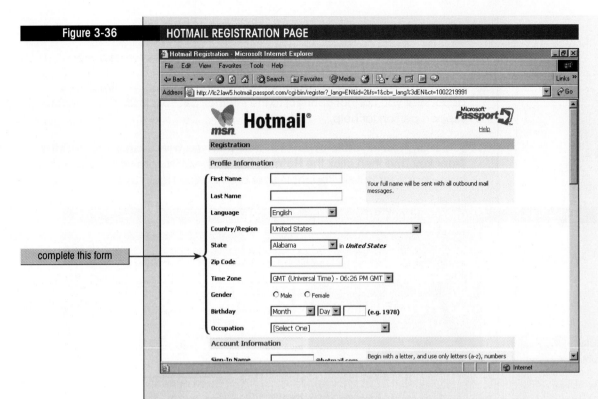

complete this form

4. With the insertion point in the First Name text box, type your first name, press the **Tab** key to move to the Last Name text box, and then type your last name. The note to the right of the First Name and Last Name text boxes indicates that your full name will appear in all Hotmail messages that you send.

5. If necessary, click the **Language** list arrow and select your preferred language setting. The default setting is English.

6. If necessary, click the **Country/Region** list arrow, and select the country in which you live. The default setting is United States.

   TROUBLE? If you live outside the United States, a new page might open in which you select an individual state, province, or other location in your country. Follow the on-screen instructions.

7. If you live in the United States, click the **State** list arrow, and then click the state in which you live. The default setting is Alabama because this state appears first in the alphabetical list of states.

8. Click in the **Zip Code** text box, and then type your zip code. Hotmail will use this information to provide you with additional services, such as local weather forecasts, that you might request in the future.

9. If necessary, click the **Time Zone** list arrow, and then click the time zone in which you live. Hotmail will use this setting to provide accurate date and time information in your e-mail messages.

10. Click the Male or Female option button in the Gender section.

11. Use the **Month** and **Day** list arrows in the Birthday section to indicate the month and date of your birth, click in the **text box** to the left of the Day list box, and then type the four-digit year of your birth.

12. Click the **Occupation** list arrow, and then click an appropriate choice in the list. If you are a student, click **Student**.

Now that you have provided some personal information to Hotmail, you need to create your user name, which Hotmail calls a sign-in name. Your sign-in name must begin with a letter. A sign-in name can contain letters, numbers, and underscore characters (_), but it cannot contain any spaces. After creating a sign-in name, you must create a password containing letters and/or numbers, but no spaces. You'll enter your password twice to ensure that you typed it correctly. Finally, to help you remember your password in the event that you forget it, you'll enter a secret question and its answer so the Hotmail server can verify your identity in the future as necessary.

To finish setting up a Hotmail user account:

1. Scroll down the Hotmail Registration Web page so the "Account Information" heading appears at the top of the browser window. See Figure 3-37.

Figure 3-37	SELECTING A SIGN-IN NAME

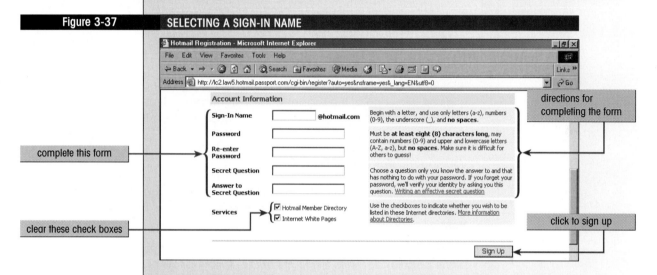

2. Click in the **Sign-In Name** text box, and then type a user name. You can use any sign-in name that you like, but it must be unique. You can try your first and last names, separated by an underscore character, followed optionally by your birth date or year of birth, such as sharon_kikukawa or sharon_kikukawa0922.

3. Press the **Tab** key, and then type a password. Make sure that your password contains at least eight characters. The most effective passwords are ones that aren't easily guessed and that contain letters and numbers. As you type your password, asterisks appear in the Password text box to protect your password from being seen by other users.

4. Press the **Tab** key, and then type your password again. Make sure to type letters in the same case; for example, media3456 and Media3456 are different passwords.

5. Press the **Tab** key, and then type a secret question. Try to ask a question to which only you know the answer, so another user couldn't easily answer your question.

6. Press the **Tab** key, and then type the answer to your secret question. Your answer must contain at least five characters.

7. In the Services section, click the **Hotmail Member Directory** and **Internet White Pages** check boxes to clear them.

8. Click the **Sign Up** button. If you selected a unique sign-in name, the Hotmail Sign Up Successful! page shown in Figure 3-38 opens.

Figure 3-38	HOTMAIL SIGN UP SUCCESSFUL! PAGE

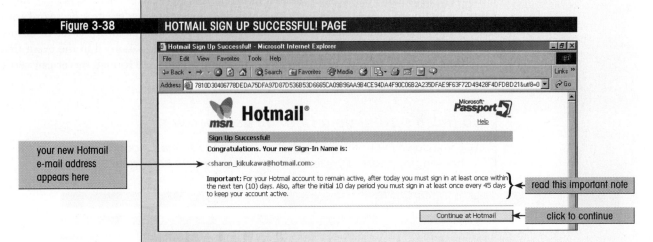

TROUBLE? If a page opens and tells you that the sign-in name that you selected is in use, click one of the suggested sign-in names or type another one in the text box, and then click the Submit New Sign-In Name button.

TROUBLE? If a Confirm dialog box opens and asks if you want to remember your logon, click the No button.

9. Read the information in the page before continuing, and then click the **Continue at Hotmail** button. A page opens describing the terms of use for a Hotmail account.

10. Read the Terms of Use page, and then click the **I Accept** button at the bottom of the page to agree to the terms of use. A Hotmail WebCourier Free Subscriptions page opens.

11. Without making any selections, scroll to the bottom of the page, and then click the **Continue** button. A Hotmail Special Offer Newsletters page opens.

12. Without making any selections, scroll to the bottom of the page, and then click the **Continue to E-mail** button. The Hotmail Home page opens. See Figure 3-39.

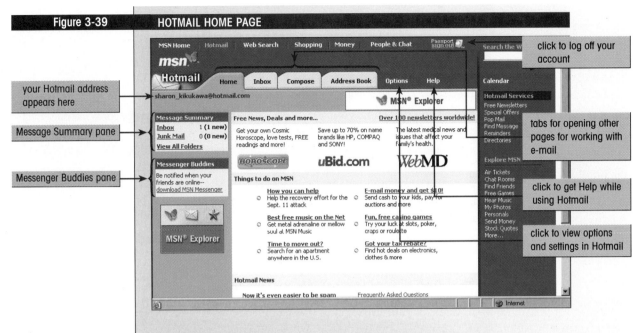

Figure 3-39 HOTMAIL HOME PAGE

TROUBLE? Your Hotmail Home page might look different from the one shown in Figure 3-39. This difference causes no problems.

The Hotmail Home page shown in Figure 3-39 displays the Home, Inbox, Compose, and Address Book tabs. The **Home tab** shows a page with links to news, shopping opportunities, and general links to other MSN sites. In addition, the Home tab displays a **Message Summary pane**, which shows you how many messages are stored in the specified folders. Clicking a folder name or the View All Folders link opens that folder and displays its contents. The **Messenger Buddies pane** contains a link to download MSN Messenger, a service that alerts you when a specific Internet user name has logged on, so you can send an instant message to that user. When you download and use this service, you can send a message to a friend when he logs on to the Internet, and the message appears on his screen in a special window. This service lets you "chat" in real time, with the help of e-mail.

The **Inbox tab** displays a list of messages that you have received. "Hotmail Staff" will send a message to you with the subject "Welcome New Hotmail User!" or a similarly worded subject when you first access your Hotmail account. The **Compose tab** contains options for creating a new message by displaying the message header options (To, Cc, Bcc, and Subject). The **Address Book tab** contains options for managing your address book of contacts. You can click the Options and Help links to open pages containing program options and help for Hotmail users, respectively.

Now that you have created a Hotmail user account, you are ready to send a message to Sharon. *Note:* In this tutorial, you will send messages to a real mailbox with the address sharonkikukawa@yahoo.com. Follow the instructions carefully and use the correct address. Messages sent to this mailbox are deleted without being opened or read.

Sending a Message Using Hotmail

You are ready to use Hotmail to send a message with an attached file to Sharon. You will send a carbon copy of the message to your own e-mail address to make sure that the message and attached file are sent correctly.

REFERENCE WINDOW   RW

Sending a Message Using Hotmail

- Open the Hotmail Home page, log on to your account, and then click the Compose tab.
- In the To text box, type the recipient's e-mail address. To send the message to more than one recipient, separate additional e-mail addresses with commas.
- Type the e-mail address of any Cc of Bcc recipients in the appropriate text boxes. Separate multiple recipients' e-mail addresses with commas.
- If necessary, click the Add/Edit Attachments button, click the Browse button to locate the file to attach, click the Attach button, and then click the OK button.
- In the message body, type your message.
- Check your message for spelling and grammatical errors.
- Click the Send button.

To send a message with an attachment:

1. Click the **Compose** tab. A blank message opens. See Figure 3-40.

Figure 3-40   **HOTMAIL COMPOSE PAGE**

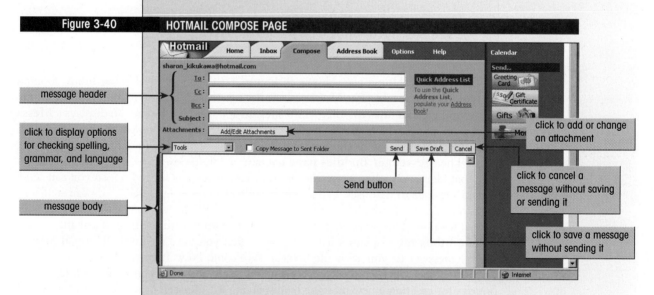

TROUBLE? Depending on the speed on your Internet connection, it might take a few seconds to open new pages. Check your browser's status bar to make sure that pages have fully loaded before using them.

2. In the To text box, type **sharonkikukawa@yahoo.com**, and then press the **Tab** key to move to the Cc text box.

TROUBLE? Make sure that you use the address sharonkikukawa@yahoo.com, instead of sharonkikukawa@kikukawa.com. If you type Sharon's e-mail address incorrectly, your message will be returned as undeliverable.

3. Type your full e-mail address in the Cc text box. When you send this message, you and Sharon will both receive copies.

TROUBLE? If you make a typing mistake on a previous line, use the arrow keys or click the insertion point to return to a previous line so you can correct your mistake. If the arrow keys do not move the insertion point backward or forward in the message header, press Shift + Tab or the Tab key to move backward or forward, respectively.

4. Press the **Tab** key twice to move the insertion point to the Subject text box, and then type **Test**.

5. Click the **Add/Edit Attachments** button. The Hotmail Attachments page opens. You can use Hotmail to send file attachments, but you are limited to a maximum file size of 1024 KB per message.

6. Make sure your Data Disk is in the appropriate drive, click the **Browse** button, and then use the **Look in** list arrow in the Choose file dialog box and select the drive that contains your Data Disk.

7. Double-click the **Tutorial.03** folder, double-click **Physicals**, click the **Attach** button and wait for the Physicals.wri file to appear in the Attachments box, and then click the **OK** button. The Hotmail Compose page now shows the attached file's name in the Attachments section.

8. Click the insertion point in the message display area, and then type **Please let me know when you receive this message and if you are able to view the attached file. I'm testing Hotmail and want to make sure that it is working properly.**

9. Press the **Enter** key twice, and then type your first and last names to sign your message. See Figure 3-41.

Figure 3-41	COMPLETED TEST MESSAGE

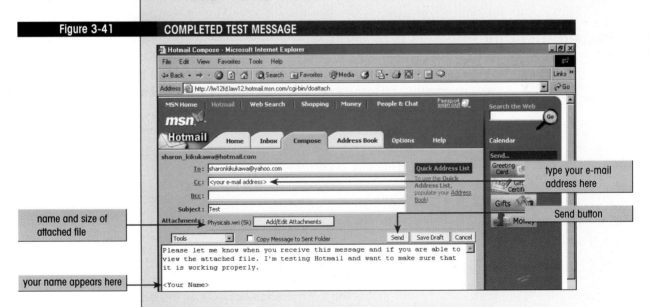

name and size of attached file

your name appears here

type your e-mail address here

Send button

10. Click the **Tools** list arrow, and then click **Spell Check**. If necessary, correct any errors. If your message is free of spelling errors, no dialog box or other indicator will appear.

11. Click the **Send** button to mail the message. The Hotmail Sent Message Confirmation page opens and shows that your message has been sent. See Figure 3-42. Note that the delivery of the message that you sent to yourself might also appear on this screen, depending on how fast the delivery of your Hotmail is.

Figure 3-42	HOTMAIL SENT MESSAGE CONFIRMATION PAGE

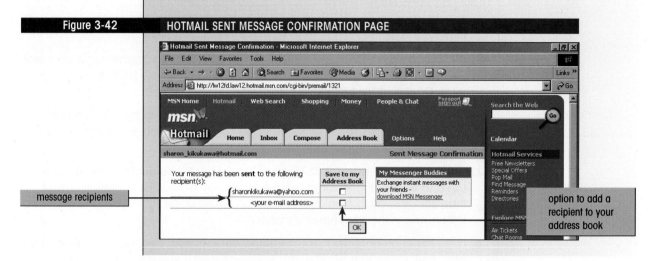

Because the e-mail addresses that you used in your Test message do not appear in your Hotmail address book, Hotmail provides an option for you to add these addresses by selecting the check box(es) in the Save to my Address Book column. You will add addresses to the address book later, so no action is necessary now.

Receiving and Reading a Message

When you receive new mail, messages that you have not opened have closed envelope icons, and messages that you have opened have open envelope icons. You will check for new mail next.

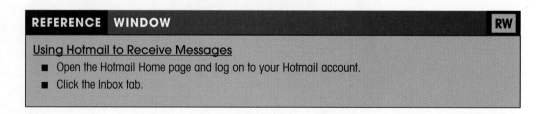

REFERENCE WINDOW   **RW**

Using Hotmail to Receive Messages
■ Open the Hotmail Home page and log on to your Hotmail account.
■ Click the Inbox tab.

To check for incoming mail:

1. Click the **Inbox** tab. The Test message appears on the Inbox tab. The sender's name is formatted as a hyperlink. To read the message, you click the hyperlink.

2. Click the sender's name for the **Test** message. The Hotmail Folder: Inbox page opens and displays the Test message. See Figure 3-43.

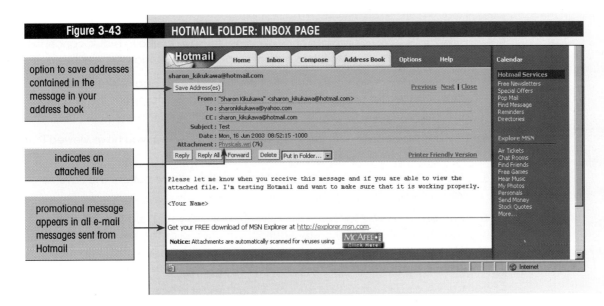

Figure 3-43   HOTMAIL FOLDER: INBOX PAGE

option to save addresses contained in the message in your address book

indicates an attached file

promotional message appears in all e-mail messages sent from Hotmail

You received your copy of the test message that you sent to Sharon. The filename in the Attachment section indicates that you received an attached file with the message. When you receive a message with one or more attachments, you can open the attachment or save it.

Viewing and Saving an Attached File

You want to make sure that your attached file was sent properly, so you decide to open it. Then you will save the file on your Data Disk.

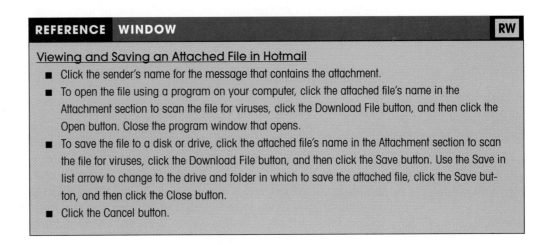

REFERENCE WINDOW   **RW**

<u>Viewing and Saving an Attached File in Hotmail</u>
- Click the sender's name for the message that contains the attachment.
- To open the file using a program on your computer, click the attached file's name in the Attachment section to scan the file for viruses, click the Download File button, and then click the Open button. Close the program window that opens.
- To save the file to a disk or drive, click the attached file's name in the Attachment section to scan the file for viruses, click the Download File button, and then click the Save button. Use the Save in list arrow to change to the drive and folder in which to save the attached file, click the Save button, and then click the Close button.
- Click the Cancel button.

To view and save the attached file:

1. Click the **Physicals.wri** link in the Attachment section. Hotmail automatically scans the file for viruses to protect your computer. A message appears indicating that no virus was found in the file.

TROUBLE? If Hotmail finds a virus in the file, follow the instructions on the screen to continue.

2. Click the **Download File** button. The File Download dialog box opens. You can open the file using a program on your computer, save the file to a disk, cancel the download, or click the More Info button to open a Help window for your browser.

3. Click the **Open** button, and then click the **Open** button again. WordPad or another text editor program on your computer starts and opens the attached file. If necessary, maximize the program window that opens.

4. Click the **Close** button on the program window. Now that you have viewed the attachment, you can save it on your Data Disk.

5. Click the **Download File** button, and then click the **Save** button. The Save As dialog box opens.

6. If necessary, browse to locate the drive containing your Data Disk, open the **Tutorial.03** folder, click the **Save** button, and then click the **Yes** button to overwrite the existing file with the same name on your Data Disk. The Download complete dialog box opens when the file has been transferred.

7. Click the **Close** button, and then click the **Cancel** button.

When you receive a message with an attached file, you can view and save the attachment for as long as you store the message. When you delete the message, you will delete the file attached to the message. However, because you saved the attachment on your Data Disk, the file exists there for as long as you need it.

Replying to and Forwarding Messages

You can forward any message you receive to one or more e-mail addresses. Similarly, you can respond to the sender of a message quickly and efficiently by replying to a message. Replying to and forwarding messages are common tasks for e-mail users.

Replying to an E-Mail Message

To reply to a message, click the Reply button to reply only to the sender, or click the Reply All button to reply to the sender and other people who received the original message (those e-mail addresses listed in the To and Cc text boxes). Hotmail will open the Hotmail Reply page and place the original sender's address in the To text box; other e-mail addresses that received the original message will appear in the To and Cc text boxes as appropriate. You can leave the Subject text box as is or modify it. Most programs, including Hotmail, will copy the original message and place it in the response window. A > (greater than) symbol appears to the left of the response to indicate the text of the original message. Figure 3-44 shows a reply to the Test message.

Figure 3-44 REPLYING TO A MESSAGE

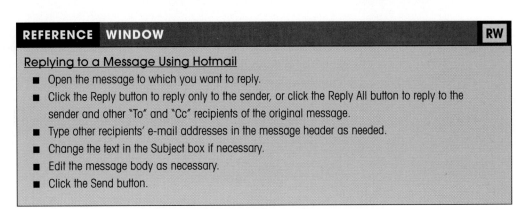

recipient's reply

sender's original
message

message automatically
addressed to sender

REFERENCE **WINDOW** **RW**

Replying to a Message Using Hotmail

- Open the message to which you want to reply.
- Click the Reply button to reply only to the sender, or click the Reply All button to reply to the sender and other "To" and "Cc" recipients of the original message.
- Type other recipients' e-mail addresses in the message header as needed.
- Change the text in the Subject box if necessary.
- Edit the message body as necessary.
- Click the Send button.

Forwarding an E-Mail Message

When you forward a message, you are sending a copy of your message to one or more recipients who were not included in the original message. To forward an existing mail message to another user, open the message you want to forward, and then click the Forward button. The Hotmail Forward page opens, where you can type the address of the recipient in the To text box. If you want to forward the message to several people, type their addresses, separated by commas, in the To text box (or Cc or Bcc text boxes). Hotmail inserts a copy of the original message in the message display area (as it does when you reply to a message) with a > mark to its left. Figure 3-45 shows a forwarded copy of the Test message.

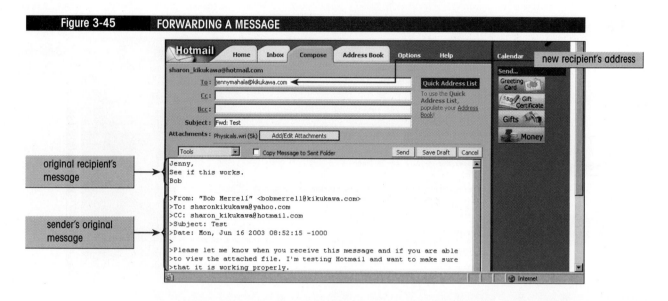

Figure 3-45   FORWARDING A MESSAGE

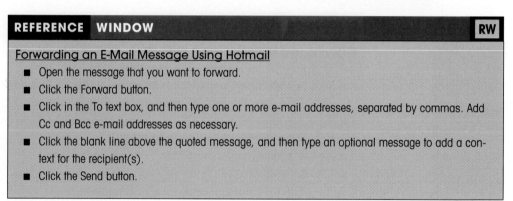

Forwarding an E-Mail Message Using Hotmail

- Open the message that you want to forward.
- Click the Forward button.
- Click in the To text box, and then type one or more e-mail addresses, separated by commas. Add Cc and Bcc e-mail addresses as necessary.
- Click the blank line above the quoted message, and then type an optional message to add a context for the recipient(s).
- Click the Send button.

Occasionally, you will receive important messages, so you want to make sure that you can print and file them as needed.

Filing and Printing an E-Mail Message

You can use the Hotmail folders to file your e-mail messages by category. When you file a message, you move it to another folder. You will file Sharon's message in a new folder named "FAA" for safekeeping. Later, you can create other folders to suit your style and working situation.

To create the new folder:

1. Click the **Home** tab, and then click the **View All Folders** link in the Message Summary pane. The Hotmail Folders page opens. See Figure 3-46.

Figure 3-46 HOTMAIL FOLDERS PAGE

options for renaming, deleting, and creating a folder

default Hotmail folders

information about the messages in each folder

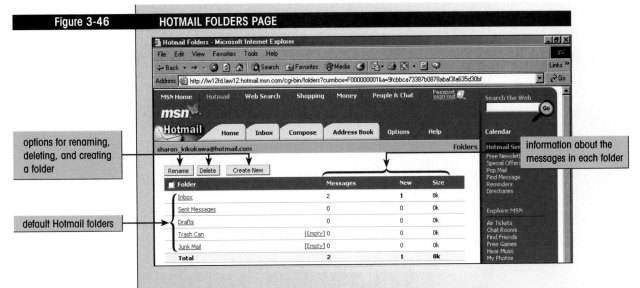

By default, Hotmail includes five folders: Inbox stores your new messages, Sent Messages stores messages that you have sent when you set it to do so, Drafts stores messages that you have written and saved but have not yet sent, Trash Can stores messages that you have deleted, and Junk Mail stores e-mail messages from senders that you specify as bulk mailers, advertisers, or any site from which you don't want to receive mail.

2. Click the **Create New** button. The Hotmail Create New Folder page opens.

3. With the insertion point in the New Folder Name text box, type **FAA**, and then click the **OK** button. The FAA folder appears in the list of folders.

4. Click the **Inbox** tab.

After you create the FAA folder, you can transfer messages to it. Besides transferring mail from the Inbox folder, you can select messages in any other folder and then transfer them to another folder.

To file the Test message:

1. Click the sender's name for the **Test** message to open it.

2. Click the **Put in Folder** list arrow, and then click **FAA**. After a moment, the message is transferred to the FAA folder.

3. Click the **Inbox** tab, and then click the **FAA** folder in the list of folders. The Test message is transferred to the FAA folder.

You will print the message before deleting it.

To print the e-mail message:

1. Click the **Inbox** tab, click the **FAA** folder in the list of folders, and then click the sender's name for the **Test** message to open it.

2. Click the **Printer Friendly Version** link. A new page opens, displaying only the message.

3. Click the **Print** button on the browser's toolbar. The message is printed.

TROUBLE? Depending on how your printer is set up, a Print dialog box might open. If so, click the OK or Print button to print the message.

4. Click the **Inbox** link to return to the Inbox tab.

You can print a message at any time—when you receive it, before you send it, or after you file it.

Deleting **an E-Mail Message and Folder**

When you don't need a message any longer, you can delete it by opening the message and clicking the Delete button. You can delete a folder by selecting it on the Hotmail Folders page and then clicking the Delete button. When you delete a message, you are simply moving it to the Trash Can folder; when you delete a folder you send the folder and its contents to the Trash Can folder. To remove items permanently, you must also delete them from the Trash Can folder.

REFERENCE WINDOW

Deleting an E-Mail Message Using Hotmail

- Open the folder that contains the message you want to delete, click the check box to the left of the message to select it, and then click the Delete button.
- To delete items permanently, open the Trash Can folder, click the Empty Folder button, and then click the OK button.

To delete the message:

1. Click the **FAA** folder in the list of folders.

2. Click the **check box** to the left of the Test message. This action selects the message.

3. Click the **Delete** button. The message is deleted from the FAA folder and is moved to the Trash Can folder.

4. Click the **Trash Can** folder in the list of folders. The Test message appears in the folder.

5. Click the **Empty Folder** button, and then click the **OK** button. All messages are deleted from the Trash Can folder.

To delete the FAA folder, you must open the Hotmail Folders page.

REFERENCE WINDOW   RW

Deleting a Hotmail Folder
- Click the Manage Folders button on the Inbox tab.
- Click the check box to the left of the folder that you want to delete.
- Click the Delete button twice.

To delete the FAA folder:

1. Click the **Manage Folders** button to open the Hotmail Folders page. The values of zero in the Messages, New, and Size columns all indicate that this folder is empty.

2. Click the **check box** to the left of the FAA folder to select it, click the **Delete** button, and then click the **Delete** button again. The FAA folder is permanently deleted from Hotmail.

Maintaining an Address Book

As you use e-mail to communicate with business associates and friends, you will want to save their addresses in an address book to make it easier to address your messages.

Adding a Contact to the Address Book

You can open the Hotmail address book by clicking the Address Book tab. To create a new address, you open the address book, click the Create New button, and then use the text boxes to enter a person's information. Each individual address must have a quickname (nickname), a first and last name, and an e-mail address; the rest of the information is optional.

REFERENCE WINDOW   RW

Adding a Contact to the Hotmail Address Book
- Click the Address Book tab.
- Click the Create New button.
- Enter the person's quickname, first name, last name, and e-mail address in the appropriate text boxes. Use the other text boxes as necessary to enter other information about the person.
- Click the OK button at the bottom of the page.

You are eager to add information to your address book. You'll begin by adding Sharon Kikukawa's contact information to your address book.

To add a contact to your address book:

1. Click the **Address Book** tab. The Hotmail Address Book page opens.

2. Click the **Create New** button. The Hotmail Create New Individual page opens. At a minimum, you need to enter a quickname for the person, as well as the person's first and last names and e-mail address. Other information on this page is optional.

3. With the insertion point in the Quickname text box, type **Sharon**.

4. Press the **Tab** key to move the insertion point to the First text box, type **Sharon**, press the **Tab** key to move the insertion point to the Last text box, and then type **Kikukawa**.

5. Click the **Business** option button in the E-mail Address section, press the **Tab** key, and then type **sharonkikukawa@yahoo.com**. Sharon's contact is complete. See Figure 3-47.

Figure 3-47   **HOTMAIL CREATE NEW INDIVIDUAL PAGE**

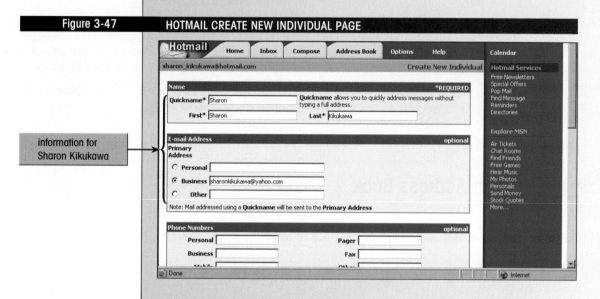

information for
Sharon Kikukawa

---

6. Scroll to the bottom of the page, noticing the optional information that you can store about an individual, and then click the **OK** button. Sharon's contact now appears in the address book.

7. Repeat Steps 2 through 6 to create new contacts for the following Kikukawa Air employees:

Quickname	First	Last	Business e-mail address
Chris	**Chris**	**Breed**	**chrisbreed@kikukawa.com**
Jen	**Jenny**	**Mahala**	**jennymahala@kikukawa.com**
Rich	**Richard**	**Forrester**	**richardforrester@kikukawa.com**

8. When you are finished entering the contacts, click the **Compose** tab. The quicknames for contacts stored in the address book appear in the Quick Address List.

Now that these e-mail addresses are stored in the address book, you can click a quickname in the Quick Address List to enter it into a text box in the message header.

When you send mail to someone who is not in your address book, the Hotmail Sent Message Confirmation page will include a Save to my Address Book check box for that address. Clicking the check box for a new contact and then clicking the OK button opens the Hotmail Save Address page, where you can add the person's quickname and first and last names to the address book.

Adding a Group to the Address Book

You can use Hotmail to create a **group**, or a mailing list, which is an address book entry consisting of more than one e-mail address. Usually you create a group when you regularly send messages to a group of people.

Sharon frequently sends messages to each member of the maintenance department. She asks you to create a group of contacts in her address book so she can type one quickname for the group of e-mail addresses, instead of having to type each address separately.

REFERENCE WINDOW　　　　　　　　　　　　　　　　　　　　　　　**RW**

Adding a Group to the Hotmail Address Book
- Click the Address Book tab.
- Click the Groups tab, and then click the Create New button.
- Type a group name for the group in the Group Name text box.
- Click in the Group Members list box, type the e-mail address for the first group member, type a comma, and continue adding names to the group until you have entered the e-mail addresses for all group members.
- Click the OK button.

To add a group to your address book:

1. Click the **Address Book** tab, and then click the **Groups** tab.

2. Click the **Create New** button. The Hotmail Create New Group page opens. On this page, you enter the group name and enter the individual e-mail addresses for members of the group. To separate individual e-mail addresses, press the spacebar or type a comma.

3. Click in the **Group Name** text box, and then type **Maintenance**. This quickname will represent the individual e-mail addresses of members of the maintenance department.

4. Press the **Tab** key to move the insertion point to the Group Members list box, and then type **chrisbreed@kikukawa.com**. Chris is the first member of the group.

5. Type a **comma**, press the **spacebar**, and then type **jennymahala@kikukawa.com**.

6. Type a **comma**, press the **spacebar**, and then type **richardforrester@kikukawa.com**. The group now contains three e-mail addresses.

7. Click the **OK** button. The Hotmail Address Book page now shows the quickname for the group and the e-mail addresses of its group members. See Figure 3-48.

| Figure 3-48 | HOTMAIL ADDRESS BOOK PAGE |

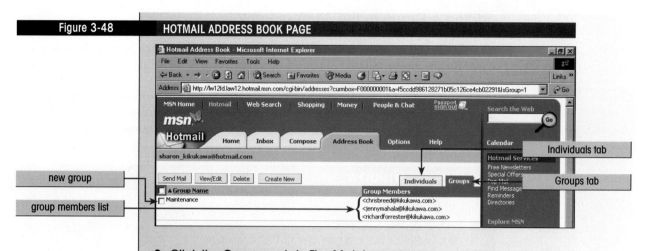

8. Click the **Compose** tab. The Maintenance group appears in the Quick Address List.

Now, test the new group by creating a new message.

To address a message to a group:

1. Click in the **To** text box to select it, and then click the **Maintenance** entry in the Quick Address List. Hotmail adds the individual e-mail addresses from the Maintenance group to the To text box.

When your Quick Address List contains many names, you'll need to use the Show All button to view the entire list.

2. Click the **Show All** button below the Quick Address List. The Insert Addresses window opens.

3. Click the **Cc** check box for Sharon, and then click the **OK** button. Hotmail closes the Insert Addresses window and adds Sharon's e-mail address to the Cc text box. See Figure 3-49.

| Figure 3-49 | USING THE QUICK ADDRESS LIST |

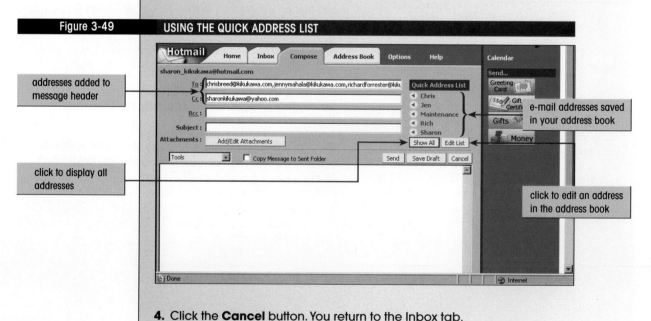

4. Click the **Cancel** button. You return to the Inbox tab.

When you need to modify a group's members, you can delete one or more members from the group by opening the address book, clicking the check box to the left of the group name, and then clicking the View/Edit button, which opens the Hotmail View/Edit Group page, where you can make changes to the group.

You are finished evaluating Hotmail, so you need to log off your Hotmail account and close your browser. It is important that you log off before closing the browser to ensure the security of your e-mail and to prevent unauthorized access.

To log off Hotmail and close your browser:

1. Click the **Passport sign out** link at the top of the page. A Hotmail page opens while your account is logged off, and then the MSN.com home page opens. To log back onto your Hotmail account, click the Hotmail link on the MSN.com home page, type your hotmail sign-in name in the Sign-In Name text box, type your password in the Password text box, and then click the Sign in button.

2. Click the **Close** button on your browser's title bar to close the browser.

3. If necessary, log off your Internet connection.

Session 3.4 QUICK CHECK

1. To set up a Hotmail account, what information must you provide to MSN.com?

2. True or False: If you are using a computer in a public library to access your Hotmail, you should log off your account when you are finished viewing your messages to protect your privacy.

3. Does Hotmail queue a message or send it right away?

4. When you receive a message with an attachment, what two options are available for the attached file?

5. When you delete a message from the Inbox, can you recover that message? Why or why not?

6. What information can you store about a person using the Hotmail address book?

Now you are ready to complete the Review Assignments using the e-mail program of your choice.

REVIEW ASSIGNMENT

Now that you have learned about different types of e-mail programs, Sharon asks you to submit a recommendation about which program to use for Kikukawa Air. Sharon also wants to see how graphics are sent over the Internet, so she asks you to send her the Kikukawa Air logo to simulate how it will appear when sent by Kikukawa employees. To evaluate e-mail alternatives for Sharon, complete the following steps.

1. Start your e-mail program or log on to your Hotmail account.

2. Add your instructor's full name and e-mail address to the address book. Create an appropriate nickname that will be easy for you to remember.

3. Add a mailing list to the address book using the full names and e-mail addresses of three of your classmates. Create appropriate nicknames for each person.

4. Create a new message. Use nicknames to send the message to Sharon and to your instructor. Send a carbon copy of the message to yourself, and use the mailing list address you created to send a blind carbon copy of the message to your classmates. Use the subject "E-mail Recommendation" for the message.

Explore 5. In the message body, type three or more sentences describing your overall impressions about the different e-mail alternatives you have explored. Recommend the program that Kikukawa Air should use based on the program's features, ease of use, and other important considerations that you determine.

6. In the message body, press the Enter key twice, and then type your full name and e-mail address on separate lines.

7. Attach the file named **KAir.gif** from the Tutorial.03 folder on your Data Disk to the message.

8. Check your spelling before you send the message and correct any mistakes. Proofread your message and verify that you have created it correctly, and then send the message.

9. Wait about 30 seconds, check for new mail (and enter your password, if necessary), and then open the message you sent to Sharon and your instructor. Print the message.

Explore 10. In a new message addressed only to your instructor, describe the appearance of the file you attached to the message. Use the subject "Attached Graphics File" and in the message body, explain your findings in terms of attaching a graphic to an e-mail message. Send the message.

Explore 11. Permanently delete the messages you received and *sent* from your e-mail program. (*Hint:* Delete messages from the folder where you receive messages and also from the folder that stores a copy of all sent messages. Make sure to delete messages from the folder that stores your deleted messages, as well.)

12. Exit your e-mail program. If necessary, log off your Internet connection.

CASE PROBLEMS

Case 1. Grand American Appraisal Company You are the office manager for Grand American Appraisal Company, which is a national real-estate appraisal company with its corporate headquarters in Los Angeles. Grand American handles real-estate appraisal requests from all over the United States and maintains a large list of approved real-estate appraisers located throughout the country. When an appraisal request is phoned into any regional office, an office staff member phones or faxes the national office to start the appraisal process. The appraisal order desk in Los Angeles receives the request and is responsible for locating a real-estate appraiser in the community in which the property to be appraised is located. After the Los Angeles office identifies and contacts an appraiser by phone, the appraiser has two days to perform the appraisal and either phone or fax the regional office with a preliminary estimate of value for the property. The entire process of phoning the regional office and then phoning or faxing the national office is both cumbersome and expensive.

Your supervisor asks you to use your e-mail program to set up an account for yourself so you can use e-mail for the appraisal requests instead of the current fax system. You will create a signature file to attach to your messages to identify your name, city, e-mail address, and appraiser license number by completing the following steps.

1. Start your e-mail program or log on to your Hotmail account.

2. Obtain the e-mail address of a classmate, who will assume the role of the Los Angeles order desk. Add your classmate's full name, nickname, and e-mail address to the address book.

3. If necessary, add your instructor's full name, nickname, and e-mail address to the address book.

4. Use your classmate's nickname to address a new message to him or her. Type your e-mail address and your instructor's nickname on the Cc line, and then type "Request for appraisal" on the Subject line.

5. Type a short message that requests the assignment of an appraiser. Include your street address and the request date in the message.

Explore   6. Use the Help system to learn how to create a signature file with your first and last names on the first line, your city and state on the second line, your e-mail address on the third line, and "License number" plus any six-digit number on the fourth line. (*Hint:* If you are using Outlook Express, search Help using the Index tab for "signatures, personal" and then follow the directions. Do not select the option to attach your signature to all outgoing messages. If you are using Mail, use WordPad or another text editor to create a signature file, and then save the file as **signature.txt** (make sure that you save it as a text file) in the Tutorial.03 folder on your Data Disk. Use the Account Settings dialog box to attach your signature file to outgoing messages. If you are using Hotmail, click the Options link to learn how to create a signature file.)

Explore   7. Include your signature file in the new message. (*Hint:* In Outlook Express, click Insert on the menu bar, and then click Signature. Mail and Hotmail will attach your signature file automatically.)

8. Send the message, wait a few seconds, and then retrieve your messages from the server. Print the message you sent to your classmate.

Explore   9. Permanently delete the message you received and *sent* from your e-mail program. (*Hint:* Delete the message from the folder where you receive messages and also from the folder that stores a copy of all sent messages. Make sure to delete messages from the folder that stores your deleted messages, as well.)

Explore   10. If you are using Outlook Express or Mail, delete your signature file. (*Hint:* In Outlook Express, select your signature on the Signatures tab in the Options dialog box, and then click the Remove button. In Mail, use the Account Settings dialog box to remove the path to your signature file.)

11. Exit your e-mail program. If necessary, log off your Internet connection.

Case 2. Bridgefield Engineering Company Bridgefield Engineering Company (BECO) is a small engineering firm in Somerville, New Jersey, that manufactures and distributes heavy industrial machinery for factories worldwide. Because BECO has difficulties reaching its customers around the world in different time zones, the company has installed an e-mail system to facilitate contact between BECO employees and their customers. As the president's assistant, your first task is to send a test message to several managers to ensure that the new system is working correctly. You will create and send the message by completing the following steps.

1. Start your e-mail program or log on to your Hotmail account.

2. Add to your address book the full name, nickname, and e-mail address of your instructor and two classmates.

3. Create a mailing list for the two classmates you added to the address book in Step 2 using the nickname "managers."

4. Create a new message addressed to your instructor. On the Cc line, enter the mailing list nickname you added to the address book in Step 3. On the Bcc line, enter your e-mail address. Use the subject "Testing new BECO e-mail system."

5. In the message display area, type a short note telling the recipients that you are conducting a test of the new e-mail system and asking them to respond to you when they receive your message. Sign your message with your first and last names.

6. Send the message, wait a few seconds, and then retrieve your messages from the server. Print the message you sent to your instructor.

Explore   7. If you are using Outlook Express or Mail, save the message in the Tutorial.03 folder on your Data Disk, using the message's subject as the filename. Choose the option to save the file in HTML format.

8. Create a mail folder or mailbox named BECO, and then file the message you received in the BECO folder.

Explore   9. Permanently delete the message you received and *sent* from your e-mail program and the BECO folder. (*Hint:* Delete the folder and message, delete the message you sent from the folder that stores sent messages, and then empty the folder that stores deleted items.)

10. Exit your e-mail program. If necessary, log off your Internet connection.

Case 3. Recycling Awareness Campaign You are an assistant in the Mayor's office in Cleveland, Ohio. The mayor has asked you to help with the recycling awareness campaign. Your job is to use e-mail to increase awareness of the recycling centers throughout the city and to encourage Cleveland's citizens and businesses to participate in the program. You will send an e-mail message to members of the city's chamber of commerce with an invitation to help increase awareness of the program by forwarding your message and its attached file to their employees and colleagues by completing the following steps.

1. Start your e-mail program or log on to your Hotmail account.

2. Add the full names, e-mail addresses, and nicknames of five classmates to your address book to act as chamber of commerce members. After creating individual entries in the address book for your classmates, add them to a mailing list named "Chamber" in your address book. Then add the full name, e-mail address, and nickname of your instructor to your address book.

3. Create a new message and address it to the Chamber mailing list. Add your instructor's nickname to the Cc line and your e-mail address to the Bcc line. Use the subject "Recycling campaign for businesses—please get the word out!"

Explore   4. Write a two- or three-line message urging the chamber members to promote the city's new business recycling campaign by forwarding your message and the attached file to local businesses. Make sure to thank them for their efforts on behalf of the Mayor's office.

5. Attach the file named **Recycle.wri** located in the Tutorial.03 folder on your Data Disk to the message.

Explore   6. Use the Help system in your e-mail program to learn how to create and use a signature file. Your signature should include your full name on the first line, the title "Assistant to the Mayor" on the second line, and your e-mail address on the third line. (*Hint:* If you are using Outlook Express, search Help using the Index tab for "signatures, personal" and then follow the directions. Do not select the option to attach your signature to all outgoing messages. If you are using Mail, use WordPad or another text editor to create a signature file, and then save the file as **signature.txt** (make sure that you save it as a text file) in the Tutorial.03 folder on your Data Disk. Use the Account Settings dialog box to attach your signature file to outgoing messages. If you are using Hotmail, click the Options link to learn how to create a signature file.)

Explore   7. Include your signature file in the new message. (*Hint:* In Outlook Express, click Insert on the menu bar, and then click Signature. Mail and Hotmail will attach your signature file automatically.)

8. Proofread and spell check your message, and then send your message. After a few moments, retrieve your e-mail message from the server and print it.

9. Forward the message to one of the classmates in your address book. Add a short message to the forwarded message that asks the recipient to forward the message to appropriate business leaders per your program objectives.

Explore   10. Save a *copy* of your message in a new subfolder of the Inbox named Recycling, and then delete the message from the Inbox.

Explore   11. Permanently delete the message you received and *sent* from your e-mail program and the Recycling folder. (*Hint:* Delete the folder and message, delete the message you sent from the folder that stores sent messages, and then empty the folder that stores deleted items.)

Explore   12. If you are using Outlook Express or Mail, delete your signature file. (*Hint:* In Outlook Express, select your signature on the Signatures tab in the Options dialog box, and then click the Remove button. In Mail, use the Account Settings dialog box to remove the path to your signature file.)

13. Exit your e-mail program. If necessary, log off your Internet connection.

Case 4. Student Study Group In two weeks, you have a final exam, and you want to organize a study group with your classmates. Everyone in your class has an e-mail account on the university's computer. You want to contact some classmates to find out when they might be available to get together in the next week to study for the exam. To create a study group, you'll complete the following steps.

1. Start your e-mail program or log on to your Hotmail account.

2. Obtain the e-mail addresses of at least four classmates, and then enter them on the To line of a new message. On the Cc line, enter your e-mail address, and then on the Bcc line, enter your instructor's e-mail address. Do *not* add these names to your address book.

3. Use the subject "Study Group" for the message. In the message body, tell your classmates about the study group by providing possible meeting times and locations. Ask recipients to respond to you through e-mail by a specified date if they are interested. Sign the message with your full name and e-mail address.

4. Proofread and spell check your message, and then send your message. After a few moments, retrieve your e-mail message from the server and open it.

Explore   5. Add each address on the To and Bcc lines to your address book.

Explore   6. Create a new "study group" mailing list using the addresses you added to your address book in Step 5. Then forward a copy of your message to the study group mailing list.

7. Send your message. After a few moments, retrieve your e-mail message from the server and print it.

Explore

8. Permanently delete the messages you received and *sent* from your e-mail program. (*Hint:* Delete the messages from the Inbox, delete the message you sent from the folder that stores sent messages, and then empty the folder that stores deleted items.)

9. Exit your e-mail program. If necessary, log off your Internet connection.

Case 5. Murphy's Market Research Services You work part-time for Murphy's Market Research Services, a company that surveys students about various topics of interest to college students. A local music store, CD Rocks, wants you to send a short survey via e-mail to students at your university to learn more about student-buying habits for music CDs. You need to find out the names of three of their favorite music CDs, where they prefer to shop for music CDs, and how much time they spend each day listening to music. You will create the survey using any word-processing program, such as Microsoft Word, WordPad, or WordPerfect, and then you'll attach the survey to your e-mail message. You need to receive the survey results within three weeks, so you'll ask the respondents to return the survey via e-mail within that time period. You will create and send the survey by completing the following steps.

1. Using any word-processing program, create a new document named **Survey** with the program's default filename extension in the Tutorial.03 folder on your Data Disk.

2. Create the survey by typing the following questions (separate each question with two blank lines) in the new document:
   a. What are the titles of your three favorite music CDs?
   b. Where is the best place (online or bricks-and-mortar) to shop for music CDs?
   c. Approximately how much time per day do you spend listening to music?

3. At the bottom of the document, type a sentence that thanks respondents for their time, and then on a new line, type your first and last names. Save the document, and then close your word-processing program.

4. Start your e-mail program or log on to your Hotmail account.

5. Obtain the e-mail addresses of three classmates, and then enter them on the To line of a new message. On the Cc line, enter your e-mail address, and then on the Bcc line, enter your instructor's e-mail address. Do *not* add these names to your address book.

6. Use the subject "Music Survey" for the message. In the message body, ask recipients to open the attached file and to complete the survey by typing their responses into the document. Make sure that recipients understand that you need them to return the survey within three weeks. As an incentive for completing the survey, ask recipients to return the survey via e-mail but to print their completed survey and bring it to their local CD Rocks outlet for a $2 discount on any purchase. Sign the message with your full name, the company name (Murphy's Market Research Services), and your e-mail address.

7. Attach the survey to your e-mail message, and then send the message. After a few moments, retrieve your e-mail message from the server.

Explore

8. Open the attached file, and then complete the survey. Before saving the file, use your word-processing program's Print command to print the document.

Explore

9. In your word-processing program, click File on the menu bar, and then click Save As. Navigate to the Tutorial.03 folder on your Data Disk, and then save the file as **Completed Survey**, using the program's default filename extension. Close your word-processing program.

10. Forward the message to your instructor, attach the **Completed Survey** file to the message, make sure that the original message text appears in the message body, type a short introduction (such as "Here is my completed survey."), sign your message with your full name and e-mail address, and then send the message.

Explore ▷ 11. Permanently delete the messages you received and *sent* from your e-mail program. (*Hint:* Delete the messages from the Inbox, delete the message you sent from the folder that stores sent messages, and then empty the folder that stores deleted items.)

12. Exit your e-mail program. If necessary, log off your Internet connection.

LAB ASSIGNMENTS

E-Mail E-mail that originates on a local area network with a mail gateway can travel all over the world. That's why it is so important to learn how to use it. In this Lab, you will use an e-mail simulator, so even if your school's computers don't provide you with e-mail service, you will learn the basics of reading, sending, and replying to electronic mail. See the Read This Before You Begin page for information on installing and starting this Lab.

1. Click the Steps button to learn how to work with e-mail. As you proceed through the Steps, answer all of the Quick Check questions that appear. After you complete the Steps, you will see a Quick Check summary report. Follow the instructions on the screen to print this report.

2. Click the Explore button. Write a message to re@films.org. The subject of the message is "Picks and Pans." In the body of your message, describe a movie you have recently seen. Include the name of the movie, briefly summarize the plot, and give it a thumbs up or a thumbs down. Print the message before you send it.

3. Look in your In Basket for a message from jb@music.org. Read the message, then compose a reply indicating that you will attend. Carbon copy mciccone@music.org. Print your reply, including the text of JB's original message before you send it.

4. Look in your In Basket for a message from leo@sports.org. Reply to the message by adding your rating to the text of the original message as follows:

Equipment:	Your rating:
Rollerblades	2
Skis	3
Bicycle	1
Scuba gear	4
Snowmobile	5

Print your reply before you send it.

5. Go into the lab with a partner. You should each log on to the E-mail Lab on different computers. Look at the Addresses list to find the user ID for your partner. You should each send a short e-mail message to your partner. Then, you should check your mail message from your partner. Read the message and compose a reply. Print your reply before you send it. *Note:* Unlike a full-featured mail system, the e-mail simulator does not save mail in mailboxes after you log off.

QUICK | CHECK ANSWERS

Session 3.1

1. True
2. protocols
3. header, body
4. Type a comma or semicolon between e-mail addresses.
5. False
6. Yes; you can attach the Word document file to an e-mail message.
7. The account name (or user name) identifies a specific individual and a computer name (or host name) identifies the computer on which that individual's account is stored.
8. By deleting unnecessary messages, you clear space on the drive or server on which your e-mail messages are stored.
9. A group, or mailing list group is a single nickname that represents two or more individual e-mail addresses.

Session 3.2

1. Drafts
2. True
3. Outlook Express holds messages that are queued until you connect to your ISP and click the Send/Recv button on the toolbar.
4. You can view the attached file if your computer has a program that can open it, or you can save the attached file on your computer.
5. Yes, you can recover the message because it is stored in the Deleted Items folder.
6. name, e-mail address, nickname, address, business information, personal information, and so on.

Session 3.3

1. Drafts
2. False
3. Mail holds messages that are queued until you connect to your ISP and click the Send button on the toolbar.
4. You can view the attached file if your computer has a program that can open it, you can save the attached file on your computer, and you can save all attached files on your computer at once.
5. Yes, you can recover the message because it is stored in the Trash folder.
6. name, e-mail address, nickname, address, phone numbers, notes, and so on

Session 3.4

1. Your name, preferred language, country, state, zip code, time zone, gender, birth-day, and occupation; you must also submit a unique sign-in name, a password, and a secret question and answer.

2. True

3. Hotmail sends messages right away because all work is completed with a live Internet connection.

4. You can view the attached file if your computer has a program that can open it, or you can save the attached file on your computer.

5. Yes, you can recover the message because it is stored in the Trash Can folder.

6. name, e-mail address, quickname, address, business information, personal information, and so on.

New Perspectives on

THE
INTERNET

3rd Edition

Read This Before You Begin

To the Student

Data Disks

To complete the Level II tutorials, Review Assignments, and Case Problems in this book, you need one Data Disk. Your instructor will either provide you with a Data Disk or ask you to make your own. You will also need to create a Tutorial.06 folder on your computer's hard drive or a personal network drive. In Tutorial 6, you will download several files and programs to your folder. Because the size of these files exceeds the amount of space on a floppy disk, you must download the files to another drive.

If you are making your own Data Disk, you will need **one** blank, formatted, high-density disk. You will need to copy a set of files and/or folders from a file server, a standalone computer, or the Web onto your disk. Your instructor will tell you which computer, drive letter, and folders contain the files you need. You could also download the files by going to **www.course.com** and following the instructions on the screen.

The information below shows you which folders go on your disks, so that you will have enough disk space to complete all the tutorials, Review Assignments, and Case Problems:

Data Disk 3

Write this on the disk label:
Data Disk 3: Tutorial 6

Put this folder on the disk:
Tutorial.06

Refer to the "File Finder" chart at the back of this text for more detailed information on which files are used in the tutorials. See the inside front or inside back cover of this book for more information on Data Disk files, or ask your instructor or technical support person for assistance.

Using Your Own Computer

If you are going to work through this book using your own computer, you need:

■ **Computer System** Netscape Navigator 4.0 or higher or Microsoft Internet Explorer 4.0 or higher and Windows 95 or higher must be installed on your computer. This book assumes a complete installation of the Web browser software and its components, and that you have an existing e-mail account and an Internet connection. Because your Web browser may be different from the ones used in the figures or the book, your screens may differ slightly at times.

■ **Data Disks** You will not be able to complete the tutorials or exercises in this book using your own computer until you have a Data Disk.

Visit Our World Wide Web Site

Additional materials designed especially for you are available on the World Wide Web.
Go to www.course.com/NewPerspectives.

To the Instructor

The Data Disk files are available on the Instructor's Resource Kit for this title. Follow the instructions in the Help file on the CD-ROM to install the programs to your network or standalone computer. For information on creating Data Disks, see the "To the Student" section above. To complete the tutorials in this book, students must have a Web browser, an e-mail account, and an Internet connection.

You are granted a license to copy the Data files to any computer or computer network used by students who have purchased this book.

In this tutorial you will:

- Determine whether a research question is specific or exploratory
- Learn how to formulate an effective Web search strategy to answer research questions
- Learn about Web search tools and how they work
- Create various kinds of search expressions
- Find information using search engines, directories, and other Web research tools

SEARCHING THE WEB

Using Search Engines and Directories Effectively

Midland News Business Section

The *Midland News* is a top-rated daily newspaper that serves the Midland metropolitan area. The *News* is especially proud of its business section, which has won a number of awards for business reporting and analysis over the years. Anne Hill is the business editor at the *News* and has recruited an excellent staff of editors, reporters, and columnists, who each specialize in different areas of business. Anne has hired you to fill an intern position as her staff assistant. The writers in the business section offices use computers to write and edit the newspaper. Recently, each writer gained access to the Internet on his or her computer. Anne would like you to work with Dave Burton, who is the paper's international news reporter, and Ranjit Singh, who writes a syndicated column on current economic trends. Dave and Ranjit are busy and do not have time to learn how to use the Internet for the quick, reliable research that they need to create and support their writing.

Anne expects you to begin by doing most of the Web searching for Ranjit and Dave yourself; eventually, she wants you to train them to use the Web. You tell Anne that you are just learning to use the Web yourself, but she explains that this will be your full-time job during your internship and she is counting on you to become skilled in Web searching. Anne also reassures you by telling you that she has been working with the Web quite a bit herself and would be happy to help you with questions you might have as you find your way around the Web.

SESSION 4.1

In this session, you will learn about two types of search questions, how to create search expressions, and how to use Web search engines and directories. Also, you will use other Web resources to find answers to your questions or information related to topics in which you are interested.

Types of Search Questions

Anne is present at your first meeting with Dave and Ranjit. Dave asks about what kinds of Web information can help him do his job better. You reply that Dave's Internet connection provides him with information about every country in the world and on most major businesses and industries. No matter what type of story he is writing, you probably can find relevant facts that he can use. Dave mentions that his stories always can use more facts. Anne agrees and says that one of the most frequent editor comments on reporters' stories is to "get the facts."

Ranjit says that his columns do not rely as much on current events and facts—they are longer, more thought-provoking pieces about broad economic and business issues. Quick access to facts is not nearly as important to him as it is to a business news reporter like Dave. Ranjit hopes that the Web can provide him with new ideas that he could explore in his columns. So, instead of fast answers to specific questions, Ranjit explains that he wants to use the Web as a resource for interesting concepts and ideas. He knows that the Web is a good way to find unusual and interesting views on the economy and general business practices. Ranjit is always looking for new angles on old ideas, so he is optimistic that you can find many useful Web resources for him.

Both writers were happy to have an eager assistant "working the Web" for them. Anne explained to you that the writers will need different kinds of help because of their different writing goals. Dave will need quick answers to specific questions. For example, he might need to know the population of Bolivia or the languages spoken in Thailand. Ranjit will need to find Web sites that contain, for example, collected research papers that discuss the causes of the Great Depression.

You can use the Web to obtain answers to both of these question types—specific and exploratory—but each question type requires a different search strategy. A **specific question** is a question that you can phrase easily and one for which you will recognize the answer when you find it. In other words, you will know when to end your search. The search process for a specific question is one of narrowing the field down to the answer you seek. An **exploratory question** is an open-ended question that can be harder to phrase; it also is difficult to determine when you find a good answer. The search process for an exploratory question requires you to fan out in a number of directions to find relevant information. You can use the Web to find answers to both kinds of questions, but each requires a different search strategy.

Specific questions require you to start with broad categories of information and gradually narrow the search until you find the answer to your question. Figure 4-1 shows this process of sequential, increasingly focused questions.

Figure 4-1	SPECIFIC RESEARCH QUESTION SEARCH PROCESS

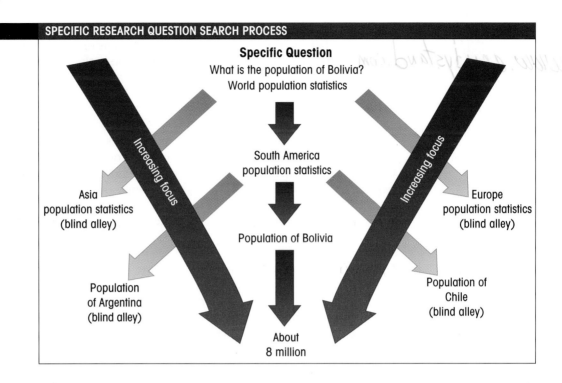

As you narrow your search, you might find that you are heading in the wrong direction, or down a blind alley. In that case, you need to move back up the funnel shown in Figure 4-1 and try another path.

Exploratory questions start with general questions that lead to other, less-general questions. The answers to the questions at each level should lead you to more information about the topic in which you are interested. This information then leads you to more questions. Figure 4-2 shows how this questioning process leads to a broadening scope as you gather information pertinent to the exploratory question.

Figure 4-2	EXPLORATORY RESEARCH QUESTION SEARCH PROCESS

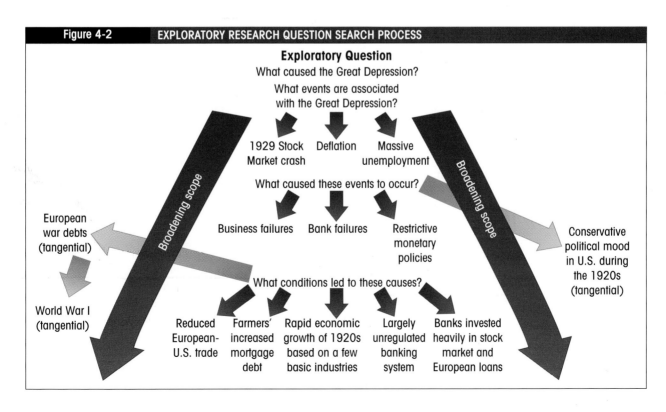

As your search expands, you might find yourself collecting tangential information that is somewhat related to your topic but does not help answer your exploratory question. The boundary between useful and tangential information is often difficult to identify precisely.

Web Search Strategy

Now that you understand the different types of questions that Ranjit and Dave will ask as you begin to work for them, Anne suggests that you learn something about searching the Web. You tell her that you know the Web is a collection of interconnected HTML documents and that you know how to use Web browser software to navigate the hyperlinks that connect these documents. Anne explains that the search tools available on the Web are an integral part of these linked HTML documents, or Web pages.

To search the Web effectively, you should first decide whether your question is specific or exploratory. The steps are the same for each type of question, but the determination of when your search process is completed is different for the two types of questions.

The Web search process includes four steps. First, you should carefully formulate and state your question. The second step is to select the appropriate tool or tools to use in your search. After obtaining your results from a Web search tool, you need to evaluate these results to determine if they answer your question. To continue the search, you can refine or redefine your question and then select a different search tool to see if you get a different result. Figure 4-3 shows the search process.

Figure 4-3	WEB SEARCH PROCESS

1. Formulate and state the question.
2. Select the appropriate Web search tool. *Google*
3. Evaluate the search results.
4. Repeat the previous steps until you find the answer (for a specific question) or until you have gathered enough information about the topic (for an exploratory question).

You can repeat this process as many times as necessary until you obtain the specific answer or the range of information regarding your exploratory topic that you find satisfactory. Sometimes, you might find that the nature of your original question is different than you had originally thought. You also might find that you need to reformulate, or more clearly state, your question. As you restate your question, you should try to think of synonyms for each word. Unfortunately, many words in the English language have multiple meanings. If you use a word in your search that is common and has many meanings, you can be buried in irrelevant information or be led down many blind alleys. Identifying unique phrases that relate to your topic or question is a helpful way to avoid some of these problems. *search other search engines*

Web Search Tools

To implement any Web search strategy, you will use one or more Web search tools. The four broad categories of Web search tools include search engines, directories, meta-search engines, and other Web resources. The Additional Information section of the Student Online Companion page for Tutorial 4 includes hyperlinks to many of these Web search tools. In this section, you will learn the basics of using each type of search tool. Remember that searching the Web is a challenging task for any of these tools. No one knows exactly how many pages exist on the Web, but the number is now in the billions. Each of these pages might have thousands of words, images, or links to downloadable files. Thus, the content of the Web is far greater than any library. Unlike the content of a library, however, the content of the Web is not indexed in any standardized way. Fortunately, the tools you have to search the Web are powerful.

Using Search Engines

A Web **search engine** is a special kind of Web site that finds other Web pages that match a word or phrase you enter. The word or phrase you enter, called a **search expression** or a **query**, might include instructions that tell the search engine how to search. A search engine does not search the Web to find a match; it only searches its *own* database of information about Web pages that it has collected, indexed, and stored. This information includes the URL of the Web page (recall from Tutorial 2 that a Web page's URL, or uniform resource locator, is its address). If you enter the same search expression into different search engines, you will get different results because each search engine has collected a different set of information in its database and each search engine uses different procedures to search its database. Most search engines report the number of hits they find. A **hit** is a Web page that is indexed in the search engine's database and contains text that matches your search expression. All search engines provide a series of **results pages**, which are Web pages that contain hyperlinks to the Web pages that contain text that matches your search expression.

Each search engine uses a Web robot to build its database. A **Web robot**, also called a **bot** or a **spider**, is a program that automatically searches the Web to find new Web sites and update information about old Web sites that already are in the database. One of a Web robot's more important tasks is to delete information in the database when a Web site no longer exists. The main advantage of using an automated searching tool is that it can examine far more Web sites than an army of people ever could. However, the Web changes every day, and even the best search engine sites cannot keep their databases completely updated. When you click hyperlinks on a search engine results page, you will find that some of the Web pages no longer exist.

Most search engines allow Web page creators to submit the URLs of their pages to search engine databases. This gives search engine sites another way to add Web pages to their databases. Most search engine operators screen such Web page submissions to prevent a Web page creator from submitting a large number of duplicate or similar Web pages. When the search engine receives a submission, it sends its Web robot out to visit the submitted URL and the robot performs its usual data gathering tasks.

The business firms and other organizations that operate search engines often sell advertising space on the search engine Web page and on the results pages to sponsors. An increasing number of search engine operators also sell paid placement rights on results pages. For example, Toyota may want to purchase rights to the search term "car." When you enter a search expression that includes the word "car," the search engine creates a results page that will have a link to Toyota's Web site at or near the top of the results page. Most, but not all, search engines label these paid placement links as "sponsored."

Search engine sites use the advertising revenue to generate profit after covering the costs of maintaining the computer hardware and software required to search the Web and to create and search the database. The only price you pay for access to these excellent tools is that you will see advertising banners on many of the pages, and you might have to scroll through some sponsored links at the top of results pages; otherwise, your usage is free.

You just received an e-mail message from Dave with your first research assignment. He wants to mention the amount of average rainfall in Belize to make a point in a story that he is writing. This search question is a specific question, not an exploratory question, because you are looking for a fact and you will know when you have found that fact. You can use the four steps from Figure 4-3 as follows:

1. Formulate and state the question. You have identified key search terms in the question that you can use in your search expression: *Belize*, *rainfall*, and *annual*. You will use these terms because they should each appear on any Web page that

www.CANdystand.com

includes the answer to Dave's question. None of these terms are articles, prepositions, or other common words. None of the words have multiple meanings. The term *Belize* should be especially useful in narrowing the search to relevant Web pages.

2. Because the question is very specific but could require a search of many categories in a directory, you decide that a search engine might return the answer more efficiently than a search of directories.

3. When you obtain the results, you will review and evaluate them and then decide whether they provide an acceptable answer to your question.

4. If the results do not answer the question to your satisfaction, you will redefine or reformulate the question so it is more specific or exploratory and then conduct a second search using a different tool, question, or search expression.

www.altavista.com/

To find the average annual rainfall in Belize:

1. Start your Web browser, open the Student Online Companion page at **www.course.com/newperspectives/internet3**, click the hyperlink for your book, click the **Tutorial 4** link, and then click the **Session 4.1** link. Click the **AltaVista** link and wait while the browser opens the AltaVista Web page.

2. Type **Belize annual rainfall** in the Search for text box, as shown in Figure 4-4.

| Figure 4-4 | TYPING THE SEARCH EXPRESSION INTO THE ALTAVISTA SEARCH ENGINE |

click here to begin search

search expression

3. Click the **Search** button to start the search. The search results appear on a new page—the page that appears in your browser should state that there are millions of Web pages that might contain the answer to your question.

4. Scroll down the results page and examine your search results. Click some of the links until you find a page or several pages that provide annual rainfall information for Belize. If you do not find any useful links on the first page of search results, click the numbers at the bottom of the page identified as links to more **Result Pages**. Click the **Back** button on your Web browser to return to the results page after going to each hyperlink. You should find that Belize has several climate zones and that the annual rainfall ranges from 50 to 170 inches, or 130 to 430 centimeters.

Dave had expected that you would find one rainfall amount that would be representative for the entire country, which is not the case. Web searches often disclose information that helps you adjust the assumptions you made when you formulated the original research question. Remember that the Web changes constantly and information is updated continuously, so you might find somewhat different information than the results shown here. Dave wants you to check another source to confirm your results, so you decide to search for the same information in HotBot, which is another search engine.

To conduct the same search using the HotBot search engine:

1. Return to the Student Online Companion page for Session 4.1, and then click the **HotBot** link to open the HotBot search engine page.

2. Type **Belize annual rainfall** in the Search Smarter text box, as shown in Figure 4-5.

| Figure 4-5 | TYPING THE SEARCH EXPRESSION INTO THE HOTBOT SEARCH ENGINE |

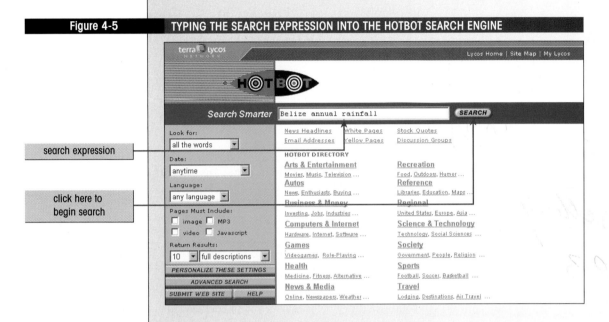

3. Click the **SEARCH** button to start the search. The search results appear on a new page, and this time, your search returns a few thousand hits. The HotBot results page may not show this number on the first results page, but the total number of hits at the top of the second and subsequent results pages.

4. Scroll down the results page and examine your search results, and then click some of the links until you find a page that provides the average annual rainfall for Belize. Return to the results page after going to each hyperlink. Once again, you should find that Belize has several climate zones and that the annual rainfall ranges from 50 to 170 inches, or 130 to 430 centimeters.

HotBot returned substantially fewer Web pages than the AltaVista search engine for two reasons: First, each search engine includes different Web pages in its database; second, the HotBot search engine, by default, only returns hits for pages that include *all* of the words you enter in a search expression. The AltaVista search engine's default is to return hits for pages that include *any* of the words. You found the same information after running both searches, so you can give Dave an answer with the second confirmation he requested.

You may have noticed that many of the links on the results pages led to Web sites that had no information about Belize rainfall at all. That is why most researchers routinely use several search engines. Answers that are difficult to find using one search engine are often easy to find with another.

Search engines databases store different collections of information about the pages that exist on the Web at any given time. Many search engine robots do not search all of the Web pages at a particular site. Further, each search engine database indexes the information it has collected from the Web differently. Some search engine robots only collect information from a Web page's title, description, keywords, or HTML tags; others only read a certain amount of the HTML code in each Web page. Figure 4-6 shows the HTML code from a Web page that contains information about electronic commerce.

Figure 4-6	META TAGS FOR A WEB PAGE

```
<HEAD>

<TITLE>
Current Developments in Electronic Commerce
</TITLE>

<META NAME ="description" CONTENT="Current
news and reports about electronic commerce
developments.">

<META NAME ="keywords" CONTENT ="electronic
commerce, electronic data interchange,
value added reseller, EDI, VAR, secure
socket layer, business on the internet">

</HEAD>
```

The description and keywords tags are examples of HTML META tags. A **META tag** is HTML code that a Web page creator places in the page header for the specific purpose of informing Web robots about the content of the page. META tags do not cause any text to appear on the page when a Web browser loads it; rather, they exist solely for the use of search engine robots.

The information contained in META tags can become an important part of a search engine's database. For example, the keywords META tag shown in Figure 4-6 includes the phrase "electronic data interchange." These keywords could be a very important phrase in a search engine's database because the three individual words *electronic*, *data*, and *interchange*, are common terms that often are used in search expressions that have nothing to do with electronic commerce. The word *data* is so common that many search engines might be programmed to ignore it. A search engine that includes the full phrase "electronic data interchange" in its database will greatly increase the chances that a user interested in that topic will find this particular page.

If the terms you use in your search expression are not in the part of the Web page that a search engine stores in its database, the search engine will not return a hit for that page. Some search engines store the entire content of every Web page they place in their databases. This practice is called **full text indexing**. Many search engines, even those that claim to be full text indexed search engines, omit common words such as *and*, *the*, *it*, and *by* from their databases. These are called **stop words**. You can find out if a particular search engine omits stop words by examining the Help pages provided by the search engine Web site. Many search engine sites include information about their search engines, robots, and databases on their Help or About pages. You will learn more about several of the major search engines in Session 4.2.

One recent advance in search engine technology is page ranking. **Page ranking** is a way of grading Web pages by the number of other Web pages that link to them. A page that has more Web pages linking into it is given a higher ranking than a page that has fewer pages linking into it. In complex page ranking schemes, the value of each link varies with the linking page's rank.

For example, a Web page with many inbound links might have a lower ranking than another Web page that has fewer inbound links if the second page's inbound links are from Web pages that, in turn, each have a large number of inbound links themselves. As you can imagine, calculating page ranks can be very complex! The URLs of Web pages with high rankings are presented first on the search results page. One search engine that has been a leader in the use of page ranking is Google. You decide to see how page ranking might affect your search results and run your query about Belize rainfall on the Google search engine.

To examine page ranking effects at Google:

1. Return to the Student Online Companion page for Session 4.1, and then click the **Google** link and wait while your browser opens the Google search engine page.

2. Type **Belize annual rainfall** in the search text box, as shown in Figure 4-7.

Figure 4-7	TYPING THE SEARCH EXPRESSION INTO THE GOOGLE SEARCH ENGINE

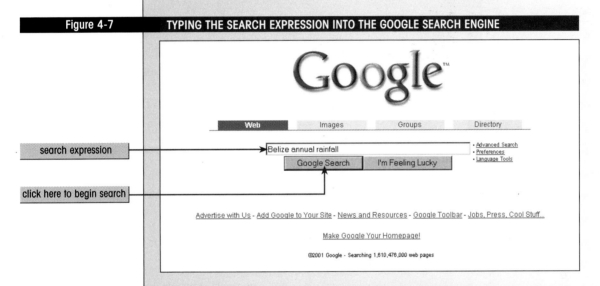

3. Click the **Google Search** button to start the search. The search results appear on a new page and should include a few thousand hits.

4. Scroll down the results page to examine your search results, and then click some of the links to determine whether Google's page ranking approach has provided a better set of search results. Return to the results page after going to each hyperlink.

Another feature that search engine sites are including in their pages is natural language querying. A **natural language query interface** allows users to enter a question exactly as they would ask a person that question. The search engine then analyzes the question using knowledge it has been given about the grammatical structure of questions and uses that knowledge to convert the natural language question into a search query. This procedure of converting a natural language question into a search expression is sometimes called **parsing**. One of the first search engines to offer a natural language query interface was Ask Jeeves. You decide to see how Ask Jeeves handles the Belize rainfall question.

To examine the natural language query interface at Ask Jeeves:

1. Return to the Student Online Companion page for Session 4.1, and then click the **Ask Jeeves** link to open the Ask Jeeves search engine page.

2. Type **What is the annual rainfall in Belize?** in the Ask text box, as shown in Figure 4-8.

Figure 4-8	TYPING THE NATURAL LANGUAGE QUESTION INTO THE ASK JEEVES SEARCH ENGINE

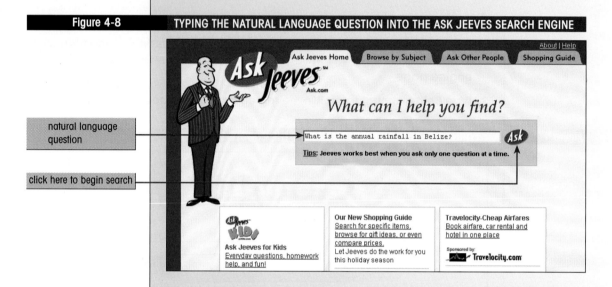

natural language question

click here to begin search

3. Click the **Ask** button to run the search. The search results appear on a new page, and should include a few hundred hits.

4. Scroll down the results page and examine your search results, and then click some of the links to determine whether Ask Jeeves' natural language query interface has provided a good list of search results. Note that the first page contains several alternative reformulations of your natural language query. You can click these to see if any of these reformulated search queries offers better results than your original question. Return to the results page after going to each hyperlink.

Using Directories and Hybrid Search Engine Directories

Search engines provide a powerful tool for executing keyword searches of the Web. However, because most search engine URL databases are built by computers running programs that perform the search automatically, they can miss important classification details that you would notice instantly. For example, if a search engine's robot found a Web page with the title "Test Data: Do Not Use," it would probably include content from the page in the search engine database. If you were to read such a warning in a Web page title, *you* would know not to include the page's contents. However, keep in mind that with billions of Web pages on the Web, the volume of data that a search engine robot obtains as it travels the Web makes it impossible to have people screen every Web page.

Web directories use a completely different approach from search engines to build useful indexes of information on the Web. A **Web directory** is a listing of hyperlinks to Web pages that is organized into hierarchical categories. The difference between a search engine and a Web directory is that *people* select the Web pages to include in a Web directory. These people, who are knowledgeable experts in one or more subject areas and skilled in various classification techniques, review candidate Web pages for inclusion in the directory. When the experts decide that a Web page is worth listing in the directory, they determine the appropriate category in which to store the hyperlink to that page. Many directories allow a Web page to be indexed in several different categories. The main weakness of a directory is that you must know which category is likely to yield the information you desire. If you begin searching in the wrong category, you might follow many hyperlinks before you realize that the information you seek is not in that category. Some directories overcome this limitation by including hyperlinks in category levels that link to lower levels in other categories.

One of the oldest and most respected directories on the Web is **Yahoo!** (see Figure 4-9). Two Stanford doctoral students, David Filo and Jerry Yang, who wanted a way to keep track of interesting sites they found on the Internet, started Yahoo! in 1994. Since 1994, Yahoo! has grown to become one of the most widely used resources on the Web. Yahoo! currently lists hundreds of thousands of Web pages in its categories—a sizable collection, but only a small portion of the billions of pages on the Web. Although Yahoo! does use some automated programs for checking and classifying its entries, it relies on human experts to do most of the selection and classification work.

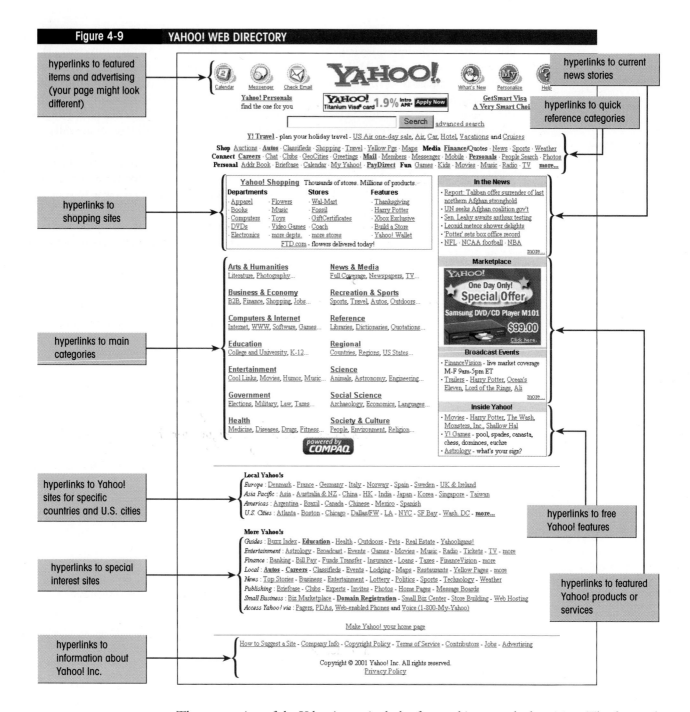

Figure 4-9   YAHOO! WEB DIRECTORY

The top section of the Yahoo! page includes featured items and advertising. The featured items change regularly and usually highlight timely topics that the Yahoo! editors believe will interest many of the site's visitors.

The search tool that appears below the advertising banner is a search engine within the Yahoo! directory. You can enter search terms into this tool, and Yahoo! will search its listings to find a match. This combination of search engine and directory is sometimes called a **hybrid search engine directory**; however, most directories today include a search engine function, so many people just call these sites directories. No matter what it is called, the combination of search engine and directory provides a powerful and effective tool for searching the Web. Using a hybrid search engine directory can help you identify which category in the directory is likely to contain the information you need. After you enter a category, the search

www. DOGPILE. COM .

engine is useful for narrowing a search even further; you can enter a search expression and limit the search to that category.

The next section of the Yahoo! page includes quick reference categories, which are commonly used categories that might otherwise be hard to find because they would be buried several layers under a main category heading. Also, users might find it difficult to guess which main categories might include these items. For example, "weather" might be classified under the main category headings "News & Media" or "Science." The quick reference section makes often-sought information categories easier to find.

The Yahoo! Shopping section includes hyperlinks to sites that offer goods and services for sale on the Web. Some of these sites are operated by Yahoo!, which rents the space to businesses. Others are independent sites operated by major companies that have paid Yahoo! for this hyperlink space on the Yahoo! page.

The main categories section of the Yahoo! page is the primary tool for searching the directory's listings. Under each of the 14 main categories, Yahoo! lists several subcategories. These are not the only subcategories; they are just a sample of those that are the largest or most used. You can click a main category hyperlink to see all of the subcategories under that category.

The right side of the page includes four sections. The first includes hyperlinks to current news stories. The second includes hyperlinks to featured Yahoo! products or services. The third includes hyperlinks to radio, television, and other multimedia features. The fourth includes links to free Yahoo! features designed to encourage you to return to the site frequently.

The lower section of the Yahoo! main page includes hyperlinks to Yahoo! directories for other countries and large U.S. cities. The lower section also has a collection of hyperlinks to other parts of the directory that contain Yahoo! specialized categories of hyperlinks, such as the Yahooligans! site, which is a version of Yahoo! designed for children. The very bottom of the page includes links to Yahoo! Inc., the company that operates the site.

Just as you are becoming familiar with the layout of the Yahoo! directory, Dave calls you. He is up against a deadline and needs some background information on an organization that does research on business issues named The Conference Board. You tell Dave that you will call him back as quickly as possible. Following your guidelines for searching on the Web, you decide that Dave's question is about a specific fact and:

1. Identify key search terms—Conference Board, business, and organization— that you will use in your search.

2. Use a Web directory to find the answer, so you can search in the business directory instead of searching the entire Web.

3. Examine the results and decide whether a second search using a different category or search terms is necessary.

4. Plan to repeat the first three steps until you determine whether The Conference Board provides any information about itself on the Web.

To find The Conference Board on the Web:

1. Return to the Student Online Companion page for Session 4.1, and then click the **Yahoo!** link and wait while your browser opens the Yahoo! home page.

   You consider the main categories on the Yahoo! page and determine that you could probably find your information in the Business & Economy category.

2. Click the **Business & Economy** category hyperlink, and wait while your browser opens the Yahoo! Business and Economy page shown in Figure 4-10. This page includes hyperlinks to lower levels in the hierarchy and to other points in the

hierarchies of other categories. The hyperlinks to lower-levels in this hierarchy include numbers in parentheses that indicate the number of Web pages included in each lower-level category. The hyperlinks that include the "@" symbol are links to other points in the hierarchies of other categories. New categories and categories that include new Web pages are indicated by a "NEW!" icon.

| Figure 4-10 | YAHOO! BUSINESS AND ECONOMY CATEGORIES PAGE |

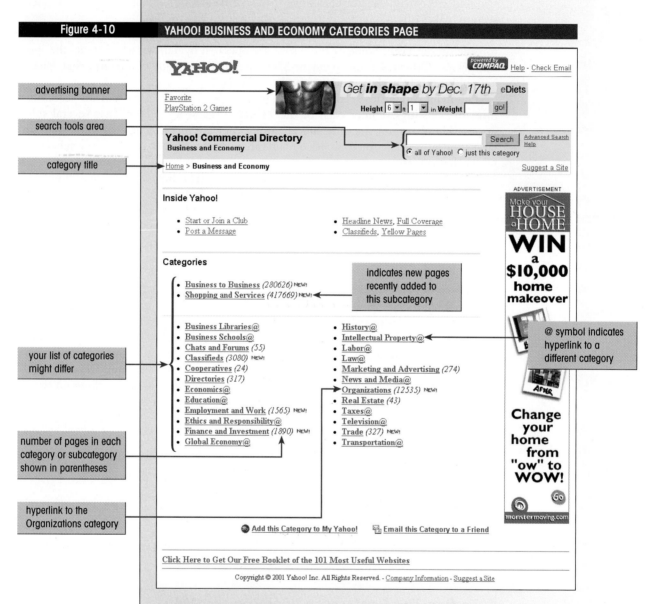

3. Click the **Organizations** category link, and wait while your browser opens the Organizations page.

4. Type **Conference Board** in the search text box, click the **just this category** option button, and then click the **Search** button.

5. The results page opens and lists the hits. See Figure 4-11. The results include a small number of category and Web page hits. Using the search tools within the directory lets you complete your search faster and more efficiently.

Figure 4-11	SEARCH RESULTS PAGE

search restriction reminder

links to categories

links to Web pages of paying advertisers

links to Web pages

Yahoo! search results page showing:

Search Results — Your search: **conference board**

This search was restricted to **Organizations**. For more matches, try searching all of Yahoo!.

Category Matches   1 - 2 of 2
- Business Organizations > The Conference Board
- Conference Board of Canada @

Sponsor Matches   (What are Sponsor Matches?)
- SupplyWorks - Manufacturing eProcurement - SupplyWorks is the only vendor focused on ... www.supplyworks.com
- Business-Supply: Next Day at No Charge - All your office essentials. Free shipping, most ... www.business-supply.com
- Chart of the Day - Conference Board - Does a drop in consumer expectations bode well for ... www.chartoftheday.com

Web Site Matches   1 - 6 of 6

1. **Conference Board**, The - non-profit business membership and research organization for senior executives internationally; produces the Consumer Confidence Index, and Leading Economic Indicators. http://www.conference-board.org/ More sites about: Business Organizations > The **Conference Board**

2. **Conference Board** of Canada - not-for-profit and independent applied research organization. Seeks to help members, from business, government, and public-sector organizations, to anticipate and respond to the changing global economy. http://www.conferenceboard.ca More sites about: **Conference Board** of Canada@

3. Ron Brown Award for Corporate Leadership - presented annually by the President of the United States to honor companies for corporate citizenship. http://www.ron-brown-award.org/ More sites about: Business Organizations > The **Conference Board**

4. Canadian Tourism Research Institute - provides interpretation and timely communication of travel research information. http://www2.conferenceboard.ca/ctri/wr_default.htm More sites about: **Conference Board** of Canada@

5. Association for Information and Image Management International - AIIM provides services to the document management community including trade shows/**conference**s, standards activities, publications, and a bulletin **board** service. http://www.aiim.org/ More sites about: Business and Economy Organizations > Trade Associations

6. National Human Resources Association - offers programs and services including news, **conference**s, career resources, message **board**s and more. http://www.humanresources.org More sites about: Human Resources Organizations > Professional@

1-6 of 6

5. Click one or more of the links leading to sites sponsored by The Conference Board to determine if any of them provide background information on the organization.

You should find information about The Conference Board at one or more of the sites listed, so you can call Dave back with the information and help him beat his deadline. Now that you have seen how to use a search engine and a hybrid search engine directory, you are ready to use an even more powerful combination of Web research tools: the meta-search engine.

Using Meta-Search Engines

A **meta-search engine** is a tool that combines the power of multiple search engines. Some meta-search tools also include directories. The idea behind meta-search tools is simple. Each search engine on the Web has different strengths and weaknesses because each search engine

- Uses a different Web robot to gather information about Web pages,
- Stores a different amount of Web page text in its database,
- Selects different Web pages to index,
- Has different storage resources,
- Interprets search expressions somewhat differently.

You saw how these differences cause different search engines to return vastly different results for the same search expression. To perform a complete search for a particular question, you might need to use several individual search engines. Using a meta-search engine lets you search several engines at the same time, so you need not conduct the same search many times. A meta-search engine accepts your search expression and transmits it to several search engines, such as the AltaVista and HotBot search tools you used earlier in this session. These search engines run the search expression against their databases of Web page information and return results to the meta-search engine. The meta-search engine reports consolidated results from all of the search engines it queried. Meta-search engines use the same kinds of programs to run their queries, but they do not have their own databases of Web information.

You want to learn how to use meta-search engines so you can access information faster. You decide to test a meta-search engine using Dave's Belize rainfall question. **Dogpile** is one of the more comprehensive meta-search engines available; it forwards your queries to more than a dozen major search engines and directories, including About.com, AltaVista, FindWhat, LookSmart, Open Directory, Overture, Yahoo!, and several others. The list of search engines and directories might be different when you use this tool because newer and better search tools become available and old favorites disappear over time. MetaCrawler reports results from each search engine or directory separately and does not eliminate duplicate hits. The list of hyperlinks returned by each search engine remains in the order that the search engine reports them to Dogpile. Like most regular search engines, Dogpile now includes a directory feature.

REFERENCE WINDOW   **RW**

Using the Dogpile Meta-search Engine

- Formulate your search question.
- Open the Dogpile home page in your Web browser.
- Enter the search expression into the Dogpile search text box.
- Evaluate the results, and decide whether to revise the question or your choice of search tools.

To use the Dogpile meta-search engine:

1. Return to the Student Online Companion page for Session 4.1, and then click the **Dogpile** link and wait while your browser opens the Dogpile Web engine page.

2. Type **Belize annual rainfall** in the Dogpile search text box, as shown in Figure 4-12.

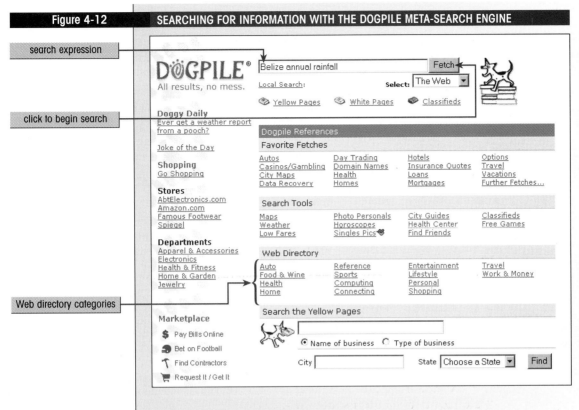

| Figure 4-12 | SEARCHING FOR INFORMATION WITH THE DOGPILE META-SEARCH ENGINE |

3. Click the **Fetch** button to run the search. After the search is complete, a Metasearch Results page opens and shows the hits for each search engine.

4. Examine and evaluate your search results.

As you scroll through the search results pages, you can see that there is a wide variation in the number and quality of the results provided by each search engine and directory. You might see many hits but no hyperlinks. You also might notice a number of duplicate hits; however, most of the Web pages returned by one search tool are not returned by any other. You can click the **Next** button that appears at the bottom of the results page to see the hits returned by other search engines.

Using Other Web Resources

A variety of other resources are available for searching the Web that do not fit exactly into the three preceding categories. These search resources are similar to bibliographies, but instead of listing books or journal articles, they contain lists of hyperlinks to Web pages. Just as some bibliographies are annotated, many of these resources include summaries or reviews of Web pages.

These other resources can be very useful when you want to obtain a broad overview or a basic understanding of a complex subject area. A search for such resources that uses a search engine or directory is likely to turn up a narrow list of references that are too detailed and that assume a great deal of prior knowledge. For example, using a search engine or directory to find information about quantum physics will probably give you many references to technical papers and Web pages devoted to current research issues in quantum physics. However, your search probably will yield very few Web pages that provide an introduction to the topic. A Web bibliography page can offer hyperlinks to information regarding a particular subject that is presented at various levels. Many of these resources include annotations and reviews of the sites they list. This information can help you identify Web pages that fit your level of interest.

Some of the names used to identify these Web bibliographies include **resource lists**, **guides**, **clearinghouses**, and **virtual libraries**. Many of these bibliographies are general references, such as the Librarian's Index to the Internet, Information Please, the Scout Report Signpost, and the Argus Clearinghouse. Others are more focused, such as Martindale's The Reference Desk, which emphasizes science-related links. You can visit any of these Web sites by clicking their links on the Tutorial 4 page of the Student Online Companion. The hyperlinks for these resources appear in the Additional Information section of the page under the Other Search Tools and Resources heading.

Ranjit stops by your office and asks for your help. He is planning to write a series of columns on the business and economic effects of current trends in biotechnology. The potential effects of genetic engineering research particularly intrigue him, but he admits that he does not know much about any of these topics. Ranjit wants you to find some Web sites that he could explore to learn more about biotechnology trends in general and genetic engineering research in particular. He mentions that it would be nice, but not essential, to find some recent news summaries about biotechnology and business. You decide to use the Argus Clearinghouse site as a resource to work on the exploratory question that Ranjit has given you. The **Argus Clearinghouse** reviews and provides hyperlinks to subject guides. You determine that Ranjit's request is an exploratory search. You know that biotechnology is a branch of the biological sciences, so you identify three category terms: *biotechnology*, *genetic engineering*, and *biology* to use as your search categories.

REFERENCE WINDOW   **RW**

Using the Argus Clearinghouse Web Site
- Identify categories and search terms that might lead you to the desired information resources.
- Open the Argus home page in your Web browser.
- Explore the Argus categories that are related to the categories and search terms you identified.
- Follow the category hyperlinks to subcategories and Web pages.
- Evaluate the results and decide whether to revise your categories or choice of Web resources.

To use Argus to conduct an exploratory search:

1. Return to the Student Online Companion page for Session 4.1, and then click the **Argus Clearinghouse** link and wait while the browser opens The Argus Clearinghouse home page.

As you scan the main categories on the Argus Clearinghouse home page, you do not see any of your search categories listed; however, you know that biology is a science.

2. Click the **Science & Mathematics** link.

3. Click the **biology** link that appears on the Science & Mathematics subcategory page. You see two of your search terms in the keywords list on the biology page and decide to follow both of them.

4. Click the **biotechnology** keyword hyperlink to open the Web page shown in Figure 4-13. The National Biotechnology Information Facility hyperlink is the most highly rated site, as indicated by its five dark check marks, so you decide to open the page.

Figure 4-13   BIOTECHNOLOGY SUBCATEGORY IN ARGUS CLEARINGHOUSE

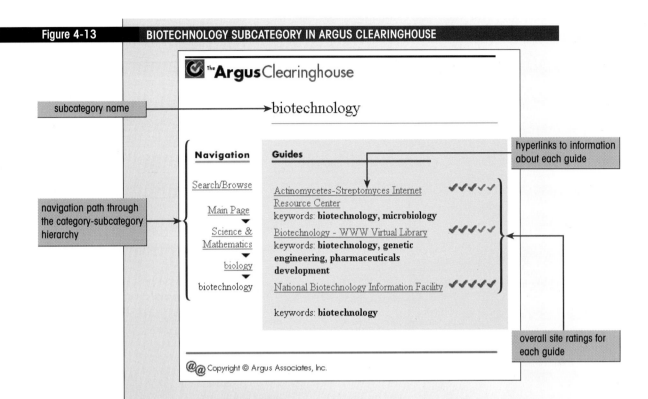

5. Click the **National Biotechnology Information Facility** link to open the Guide Information page for the site shown in Figure 4-14. The Guide Information page includes a hyperlink to the Web site, indexing keywords, information about the author of the site, and detailed ratings on several dimensions. You can follow this site to gather specific information for Ranjit or give him the site's URL and let him explore the site. You might want to gather the URLs of this and other sites that you find and send them all to Ranjit in one e-mail message. You have explored the biotechnology subcategory; next, you will explore the genetic engineering subcategory.

Figure 4-14   INFORMATION ABOUT THE BIOTECH GUIDE WEB SITE

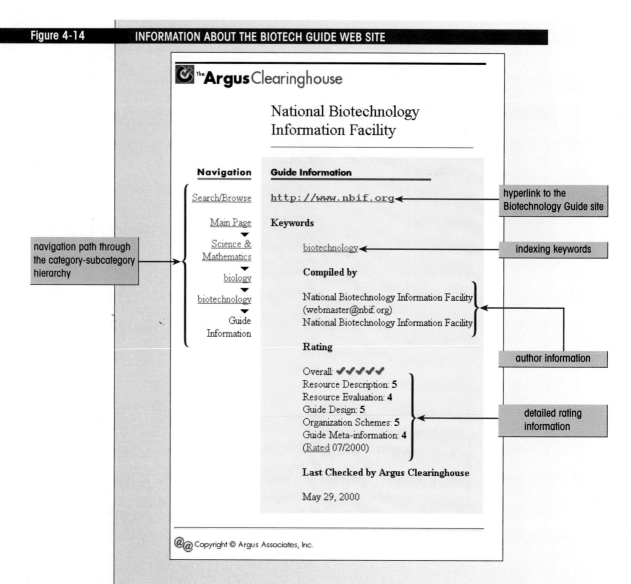

6. Click the **biology** hyperlink that appears in the Navigation path on the left side of the Web page to return to the list of biology keywords.

7. Click the **genetic engineering** hyperlink in the Keywords list to open the genetic engineering page. There are three entries provided in the Guides list. One of these entries is the Biotechnology - WWW Virtual Library page, which also appeared on the biotechnology Guides page shown in Figure 4-13.

8. Click the **Biotechnology - WWW Virtual Library** hyperlink to explore the resources at that site. Remember that Ranjit does not expect you to understand the contents of the Web pages you find; he just wants you to identify resources to help him learn more about trends in this area of scientific research.

9. Examine your search results and determine whether you have gathered sufficient useful information to respond to Ranjit's request.

10. Close your browser, and if necessary, log off your Internet connection.

You have completed your search for Web sites that might help Ranjit. Many of these sites contain hyperlinks to other useful sites that Ranjit might want to explore. You can deliver information from these pages to Ranjit by printing copies of the Web pages, sending the URLs by e-mail, or saving the Web pages and attaching them to an e-mail message. Because your answer to Ranjit's question involves so many pages at different sites, your best approach would be to send an e-mail message with a list of relevant URLs.

Session 4.1 QUICK CHECK

1. What are the key characteristics of an exploratory search question?

2. True or False: Web search engine operators use advertising revenue to cover their expenses and to earn a profit.

3. The part of a search engine site that searches the Web to collect information for the search engine's database is called a(n) _robot, bot spider_

4. A search engine that uses page ranking will list a Web page nearer the top of search results pages if that page has many _inbound link_

5. True or False: Most search engines index all Web page words in their databases.

6. List one advantage and one disadvantage of using a Web directory instead of a Web search engine to locate information.

7. How does a hybrid search engine-directory overcome the disadvantages of using either a search engine or a directory alone?

8. How does a meta-search engine process the search expression you enter into it?

9. What are the key features offered by Web bibliographies?

SESSION 4.2

Although you can find the answers to many research questions on the Web with a simple search using one of the tools described in Session 4.1, some questions are more complex. In this session, you will learn how to use the advanced features of Web search engines, directories, and other Web resources to answer complex questions. Many of these Web search tools use Boolean logic and other filtering mechanisms to select and sort search results; however, many of these search tools implement these mechanisms differently. After learning the basics of Boolean logic and filtering techniques, you will use those techniques in a variety of Web search tools.

Boolean **Logic and Filtering Techniques**

The most important factor in getting good results from a search engine, a meta-search engine, or a search tool within a hybrid search engine-directory is to select carefully the search terms you use. When the object of your search is straightforward, you can choose one or two words that will work well. More complex search questions require more complex queries, which you can use along with Boolean logic, search expression operators, or filtering techniques, to broaden or narrow your search expression. In the next three sections, you will learn how to use each of these techniques.

Boolean Operators

When you enter a single word into a Web search tool, it searches for matches to that word. When you enter a search expression into a Web search tool that includes more than one word, the search tool makes assumptions about the words that you enter. You learned in Session 4.1 that the AltaVista search engine assumes that you want to match any of the keywords in your search expression, whereas HotBot assumes that you want to match all of the keywords. These different assumptions can make dramatic differences in the number and quality of hits returned. Many search engine operators, realizing that users might want to match all of the keywords on one search and any of the keywords on a different search, have designed their search engines to offer these options. The most common way of implementing these options is to offer Boolean operators as part of their search engines.

George Boole was a nineteenth century British mathematician who developed a branch of mathematics and logic that bears his name, **Boolean algebra**. In Boole's algebra, all values are reduced to one of two values. In most practical applications of Boole's work, these two values are *true* and *false*. Although Boole did his work many years before practical electrically powered computers became commonplace, his algebra was useful to computer engineers and programmers. At the very lowest level of analysis, all computing is a manipulation of a single computer circuit's on and off states. Unlike the algebra you might have learned in your math classes, Boolean algebra does not use numbers or mathematical operators. Instead, Boolean algebra uses words and logical relationships.

Some parts of Boolean algebra are also useful in search expressions. **Boolean operators**, also called **logical operators**, are a key part of Boolean algebra. Boolean operators specify the logical relationship between the elements they join, just as the plus sign arithmetic operator specifies the mathematical relationship between the two elements it joins. Three basic Boolean operators—AND, OR, and NOT—are recognized by most search engines. You can use these operators in many search engines by simply including them with search terms. For example, the search expression "exports AND France" returns hits for pages that contain both words, the expression "exports OR France" returns hits for pages that contain either word, and "exports NOT France" returns hits for pages that contain the word *export* but not the word *France*. Some search engines use "AND NOT" to indicate the Boolean NOT operator.

Figure 4-15 shows several ways to use Boolean operators in more complex search expressions that contain the words *exports*, *France*, and *Japan*. The figure shows the matches that a search engine will return if it interprets the Boolean operators correctly. Figure 4-15 also describes information-gathering tasks in which you might use these expressions.

Figure 4-15	USING BOOLEAN OPERATORS IN SEARCH EXPRESSIONS	
SEARCH EXPRESSION	**SEARCH RETURNS PAGES THAT INCLUDE**	**USE TO FIND INFORMATION ABOUT**
exports AND France AND Japan	All of the three search terms.	Exports from France to Japan or from Japan to France
exports OR France OR Japan	Any of the three search terms.	Exports from anywhere, including France and Japan, and all kinds of information about France and Japan
exports NOT France NOT Japan	Exports, but not if the page also includes the terms *France* or *Japan*.	Exports to and from any countries other than France or Japan
exports AND France NOT Japan	Exports and France, but not Japan.	Exports to and from France to anywhere else, except exports shipped to Japan

Other Search Expression Operators

When you join three or more search terms with Boolean operators, it is easy to become confused by the expression's complexity. To reduce the confusion, you can use precedence operators, a tool you probably learned in basic algebra, along with the Boolean operators.

A **precedence operator**, also called an **inclusion operator** or a **grouping operator**, clarifies the grouping within a complex expression and is usually indicated by the parentheses symbols. Some search engines use double quotation marks to indicate precedence grouping; however, other search engines use double quotation marks to indicate search terms that must be matched exactly as they appear (that is, search for the exact search phrase) within the double quotation marks. Figure 4-16 shows several ways to use precedence operators with Boolean operators in search expressions.

Figure 4-16	USING BOOLEAN AND PRECEDENCE OPERATORS IN SEARCH EXPRESSIONS	
SEARCH EXPRESSION	**SEARCH RETURNS PAGES THAT INCLUDE**	**USE TO FIND INFORMATION ABOUT**
exports AND (France OR Japan)	Exports and either France or Japan.	Exports from or to either France or Japan.
exports OR (France AND Japan)	Exports or both France and Japan.	Exports from anywhere, including France and Japan, and all kinds of other information about France and Japan.
exports AND (France NOT Japan)	Exports and France, but not if the page also includes Japan.	Exports to and from France, except those going to or from Japan.

Some search engines recognize variants of the Boolean operators, such as "must include" and "must exclude" operators. For example, a search engine that uses the plus sign to indicate "must include" and the minus sign to indicate "must exclude" would respond to the expression "exports + France - Japan" with hits that included anything about exports and France, but only if those pages did not include anything about Japan.

Another useful search expression tool is the location operator. A **location operator**, or **proximity operator**, lets you search for terms that appear close to each other in the text of a Web page. The most common location operator offered in Web search engines is the NEAR operator. If you are interested in French exports, you might want to find only Web pages in which the terms *exports* and *France* are close to each other. Unfortunately, each search engine that implements this operator uses its own definition of how close "NEAR" is. One search engine might define NEAR to mean "within 10 words," whereas another search engine might define NEAR to mean "within 20 words." To use the NEAR operator effectively, you must read the search engine's help file carefully.

Wildcard Characters and Search Filters

Most search engines support some use of a wildcard character in their search expressions. A **wildcard character** allows you to omit part of the search term or terms. Many search engines recognize the asterisk (*) as the wildcard character. For example, the search expression "export*" would return pages containing the terms *exports*, *exporter*, *exporters*, and *exporting* in many search engines. Some search engines let you use a wildcard character in the middle of a search term. For example, the expression "wom*n" would return pages containing both *woman* and *women*.

Many search engines allow you to restrict your search by using search filters. A **search filter** eliminates Web pages from a search. The filter criteria can include such Web page attributes as language, date, domain, host, or page component (URL, hyperlink, image tag, or title tag). For example, many search engines provide a way to search for the term *exports* in Web page titles and ignore pages in which the term appears in other parts of the page.

Advanced Searches

Most search engines implement many of the operators and techniques you have learned about, but search engine syntax varies. Some search engines provide separate advanced search pages for these techniques; others allow you to use advanced techniques such as Boolean operators on their simple search pages. Next, you will learn how to conduct complex searches using the advanced search features of several different search engines.

Advanced Search in AltaVista

Ranjit is working on a series of columns about the role that trade agreements play in limiting the flow of agricultural commodities between countries. This week's column concerns the German economy. He wants you to find some Web page references for him that might provide useful background information for his column. Ranjit is especially interested in learning more about the German perspective on trade issues, but he cannot read German.

You recognize this as an exploratory question and decide to use the advanced query capabilities of the AltaVista search engine to conduct a complex search for Web pages that Ranjit might use for his research. You want to provide Ranjit with a reasonable number of hyperlinks to Web pages, but you do not want to inundate him with thousands of URLs, so you decide to use Boolean and precedence operators to create a search expression that will focus on useful sites. To create a useful search expression, you must identify search terms that might lead you to appropriate Web pages. Some terms you might use are *Germany*, *trade*, *treaty*, and *agriculture*. You decide to use Boolean and precedence operators to combine your search terms. You also decide to use the wildcard character to allow the search to find plural and extended forms of the terms *treaty* (such as *treaties*) and *agriculture* (such as *agricultures*, *agricultural*, and *agriculturally*). Ranjit's primary interest is in trade issues, so you decide to rank the hits returned by *trade*.

REFERENCE WINDOW

Conducting a Complex Search Using AltaVista
- Open the AltaVista search engine in your Web browser.
- Select the Advanced Search option.
- Choose a language filter.
- Formulate and enter a suitable search expression.
- Click the Search button.
- Evaluate the results, and if necessary, revise your search expression.

To perform an advanced search using AltaVista:

1. Start your Web browser, open the Student Online Companion page at **www.course.com/newperspectives/internet3**, click the hyperlink for your book, click the **Tutorial 4** link, click the **Session 4.2** link, and then click the **AltaVista** link and wait while the browser opens the AltaVista home page.

2. Click the **Advanced Search** hyperlink on the AltaVista page. Ranjit only reads English, so you need to filter the language.

3. Click the **list arrow** to the right of the box that displays the text "any language," and then click **English**.

4. Click in the **Boolean query** text box, and then type **Germany AND (trade OR treat*) AND agricult***.

5. If necessary, scroll down the page, and then click the **Search** button to start the search. The search settings and results appear in Figure 4-17. The search returns more than 100,000 hits, so you need to refine your search expression. You examine some of the descriptions provided for the first search results listed and find that many of them include information about fertilizer treatments. You decide that narrowing the search to exclude those sites would make the search results more useful to Ranjit.

Figure 4-17	COMPLEX SEARCH USING ALTAVISTA

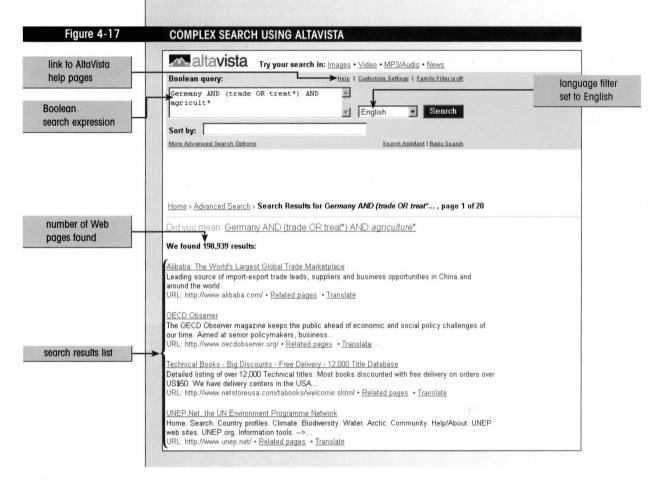

Getting Help and Refining an Advanced Search in AltaVista

Each search engine follows different rules and offers different features. To obtain help for a particular search engine, examine its home page and look for a hyperlink to help pages for that search engine. The AltaVista Advanced Search page includes a hyperlink titled "Help." You decide to exclude the word *treatment* from your Boolean search expression and, to obtain a narrower search that focuses better on the German viewpoint, you decide to restrict the domain to German Web sites.

To obtain help and refine an advanced search in AltaVista:

1. Scroll down the results page, and then click the **Help** hyperlink and wait while the browser opens the AltaVista Advanced Search page.

2. Click the **Advanced Cheat Sheet** link.

3. Scroll down the Web page and look for **domain:***domainname* in the Advanced Search Cheat Sheet table. In AltaVista, the domain filter is "domain:" followed by the name of the domain to which you want to limit your search. Ranjit tells you that the domain name for Germany is "de."

4. Click your browser's **Back** button twice to return to the AltaVista - Advanced Search page.

5. Change your Boolean search expression (at the top of the page) to **Germany AND (trade OR treat*) AND agricult* AND NOT treatment AND domain:de**, and then click the **Search** button. AltaVista returns a much smaller number of hits this time.

6. Examine your search results and determine whether you have gathered sufficient useful information to respond to Ranjit's request. There are many sites to explore. You could give Ranjit this list or define the search expression further to reduce the number of hits.

Advanced Search in HotBot

Dave stops by your office to tell you he is working on a story for tomorrow's edition about the effect of unusual weather patterns and recent rainstorms on Southeast Asian rice crops during the past six months. You decide to use the HotBot search engine to run a complex query for Dave. Although HotBot offers a SuperSearch page with a wide array of search options (to use SuperSearch, click the More Search Options button on the HotBot main page), you can perform Boolean and filtered searches from HotBot's main search page.

REFERENCE WINDOW	RW

Conducting a Complex Search Using HotBot
- Open the HotBot search engine page in your Web browser.
- Open the HotBot Advanced Search page.
- Set the Look For field to allow Boolean operators.
- Select a date and geographic region filters.
- Formulate and enter a suitable search expression.
- Click the SEARCH button.
- Evaluate the results, and if necessary, revise your search expression.

To perform a complex search using HotBot:

1. Return to the Student Online Companion page for Session 4.2, and then click the **HotBot** link and wait while the browser opens the HotBot home page.

2. Click the **ADVANCED SEARCH** button to open the HotBot SuperSearch page that appears in Figure 4-18.

Figure 4-18   ADVANCED SEARCH FEATURES OF THE HOTBOT MAIN SEARCH ENGINE PAGE

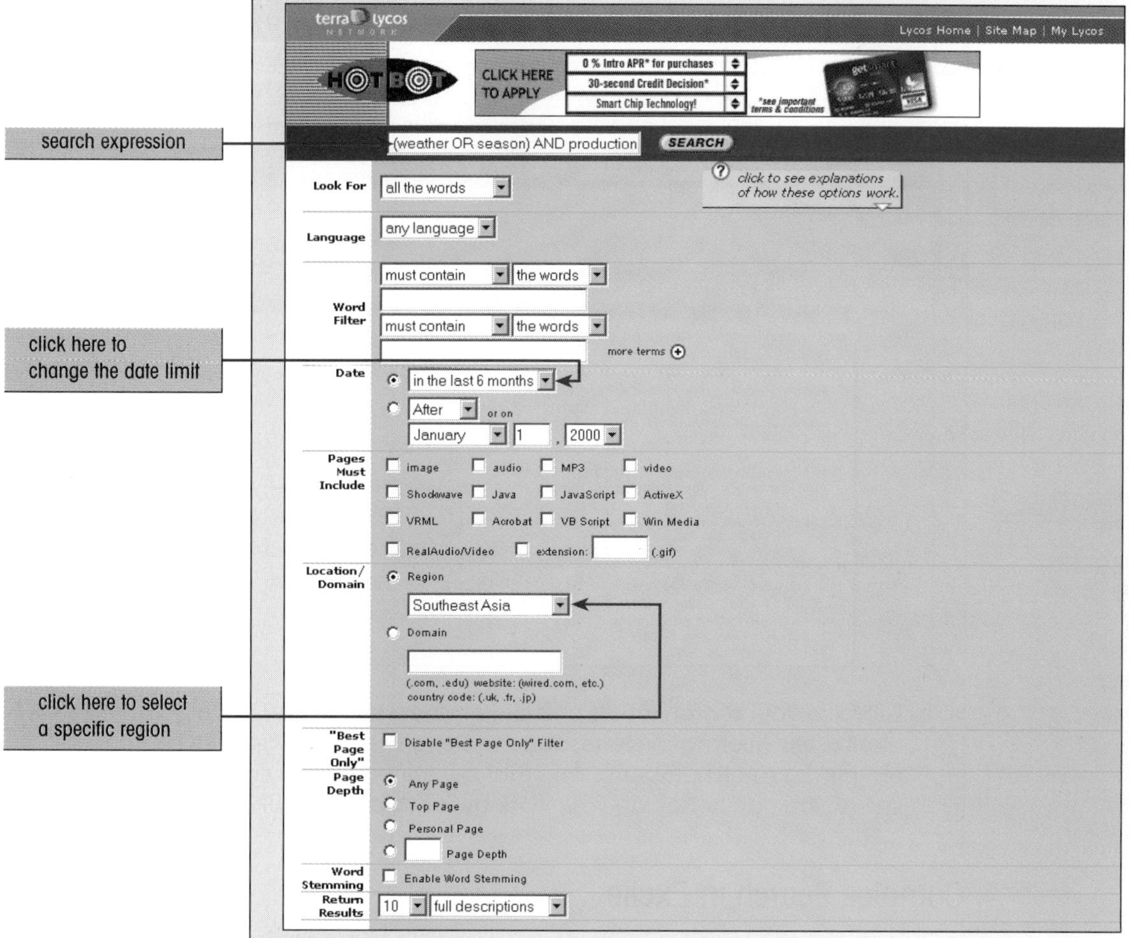

search expression

click here to change the date limit

click here to select a specific region

3. Click the **Look For** list arrow, and then click **boolean phrase** in the list.

4. Click the **Date** list arrow, and then click **in the last 6 months** to change the Date limit from *anytime*.

5. Click the **Location/Domain** list arrow, and click **Southeast Asia** to specify the Region option

To create a useful search expression, you must identify search terms that might lead you to appropriate Web pages. Some terms you might use are *rice*, *weather*, and *production*. Dave told you that Southeast Asia has a rainy season, so the term *season* might appear instead of *weather* on Web pages that contain information that Dave could use. You decide to use Boolean and precedence operators to combine your search terms. HotBot does not recognize wildcard characters, but it does allow you to set precedence operators.

6. Click in the search text box, and then type **rice AND (weather OR season) AND production**.

7. Click the **SEARCH** button to start the search. Figure 4-19 shows the search results page, where you can see part of the search expression, the filter settings, information about the search, and a partial list of hyperlinks to related Web pages. The description also includes the date each page was last updated.

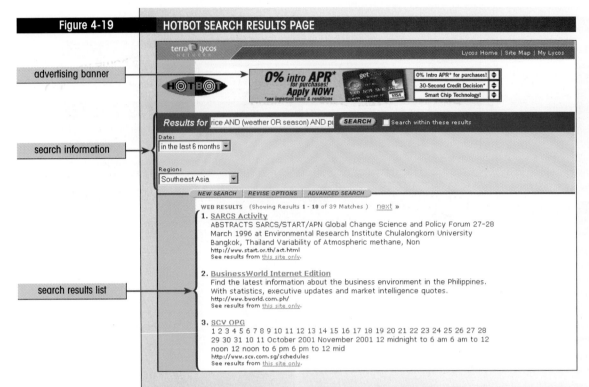

Figure 4-19   HOTBOT SEARCH RESULTS PAGE

advertising banner

search information

search results list

8. Examine your search results and determine whether you have gathered sufficient useful information to respond to Dave's request. Since the search
returned a small number of links that contained information relevant to Dave's
query, you can conclude your work by forwarding the URLs to Dave.

Complex Search in Excite

Dave calls and has a quick request for your research help. He is working on a story about
Finland and remembers that he met a professor who taught graduate business students there.
He does not remember the professor's name or the name of the university at which the professor teaches. Dave is confident that he would recognize the university's name if he saw it
again. He would like to interview the professor for his story. Dave asks if you can find some
Finnish university names on the Web. After evaluating Dave's request, you decide to use the
Excite search engine for this task. To create a useful search expression, you must identify
search terms that might lead you to appropriate Web pages. Some terms you might use
include *Finland*, *university*, and *business*. You consider that a university with a graduate business
program might have an academic unit, "school," so you add that to your search expression as an
alternative to "university." Hopeful that someone might have placed a list of universities on the
Web, you decide to include *list* as a search term, too. The Excite search engine permits Boolean
operators in its main page, so you decide to use that page for your query.

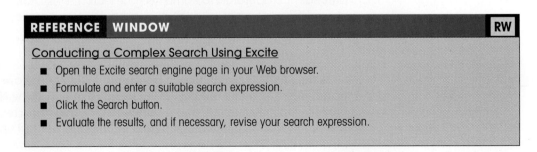

REFERENCE WINDOW   RW

Conducting a Complex Search Using Excite
■ Open the Excite search engine page in your Web browser.
■ Formulate and enter a suitable search expression.
■ Click the Search button.
■ Evaluate the results, and if necessary, revise your search expression.

To perform an advanced search using Excite:

1. Return to the Student Online Companion page for Session 4.2, and then click the **Excite** link and wait while the browser opens the Excite home page.

2. Click in the **Search for** text box at the top of the page, and then type **finland AND list AND (university OR school) AND business**.

3. Click the **Search** button to start the search. Figure 4-20 shows the results page.

Figure 4-20	EXCITE SEARCH RESULTS PAGE

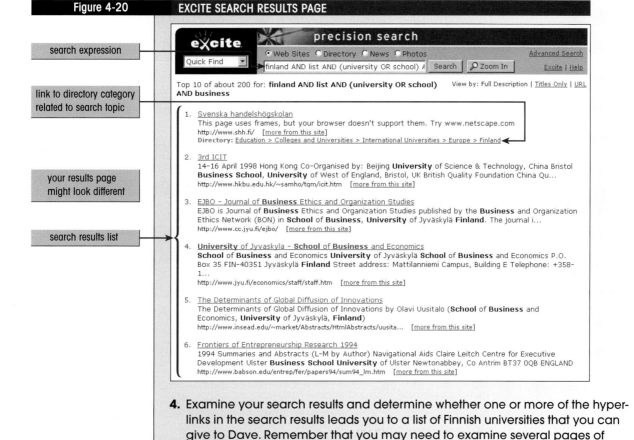

4. Examine your search results and determine whether one or more of the hyperlinks in the search results leads you to a list of Finnish universities that you can give to Dave. Remember that you may need to examine several pages of search results to find exactly what you need.

Complex Search in Northern Light

Ranjit is working on a series about fast-food franchises in various developing countries around the world. He would like to feature this industry's experience in Indonesia in his next column and asks you for help. He mentions that he would like to use industry publications in addition to Web sites for his research on this column. You know that the Northern Light search engine indexes not only the Web, but also a collection of periodicals. Therefore, you decide to run this search for Ranjit on the Northern Light search engine. To create a useful search expression, you must identify search terms that might lead you to appropriate Web pages. Some terms you might use include *fast*, *food*, *franchise*, and *Indonesia*. You are not interested in Web pages that have the individual terms *fast* and *food* as much as you are interested in Web pages that contain the phrase "fast food." The Northern Light search engine does not support full Boolean logic, so you will enter a simple expression and use Northern Light's folders feature to filter your results.

REFERENCE WINDOW   RW

Conducting a Complex Search Using Northern Light

- Open the Northern Light search engine page in your browser.
- Formulate and enter a suitable search expression.
- Click the Search button.
- Evaluate the results, and if necessary, revise your search expression.

To perform a complex search using Northern Light:

1. Return to the Student Online Companion page for Session 4.2, and then click the **Northern Light** link and wait while your browser opens the Northern Light Search page.

2. Click in the search text box, and then type **"fast food" franchise Indonesia**. Make sure that you type the quotation marks, so you find the phrase "fast food," instead of the individual terms.

3. Click the **Search** button to start the search. Figure 4-21 shows the search results page; these hyperlinks look promising.

Figure 4-21	NORTHERN LIGHT SEARCH RESULTS PAGE

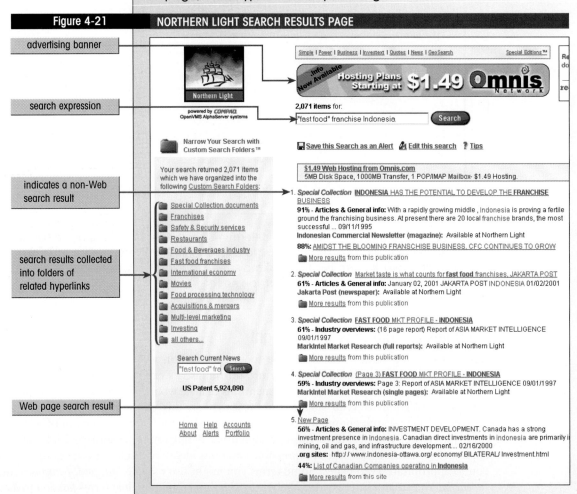

advertising banner

search expression

indicates a non-Web search result

search results collected into folders of related hyperlinks

Web page search result

4. In the list of Custom Search Folders links at the left side of the page, click the folders that look promising. Examine your search results from each folder and

> determine whether you have gathered enough information about the fast-food industry in Indonesia for Dave.
>
> **5.** Close your Web browser, and if necessary, log off your Internet connection.

Northern Light provides hyperlinks to Web pages and to its own collection of several thousand journals, books, and other print resources. It provides a hyperlink to Web pages it finds and provides a summary of the print resources in its collection. For a fee, you can purchase the right to download and print an item from its collection. However, you can often find the original source in your school or company library if you do not want to purchase the item from Northern Light. Downloading the item would be a nice convenience if you used this search engine frequently.

The first four hyperlinks that appear in the results shown in Figure 4-21 begin with the words "Special Collection" to indicate that they are from Northern Light's own collection. The other hyperlinks are to Web pages.

Another unique feature of Northern Light is that it collects search results into folders, as shown in Figure 4-21. These folders are organized collections of related hyperlinks found in the search. Clicking one of these folders—for example "Food processing technology"—will narrow your results page to include only those hits that fit that category. Your search provides Dave with the information he needs and he congratulates you on a job well done.

Future of Web Search Tools

A number of different companies and organizations are working on ways to make searching the Web easier for the increasing number of people who use the Web. Work on natural language interfaces continues as search engine sites strive to make the job of searching even easier for users. An increasing number of search engines offer natural language querying as an option for entering search expressions. Although it is unlikely that these interfaces will provide the same power as Boolean searches anytime soon, they are much easier for infrequent Internet searchers to use.

One company, **About.com**, hires people with expertise in specific subject areas to create and manage their Web directory entries in those areas. Although Yahoo! uses subject matter experts this way, About.com takes the idea one step further and identifies their experts. Each of the About.com experts, called Guides, hosts a page with hyperlinks to related Web pages, moderates discussion areas, and provides an online newsletter. This creates a community of interested persons from around the world that can participate in maintaining the Web directory. The **Open Directory Project** uses the services of volunteer editors (more than 40,000 of them) who maintain listings in their individual areas of interest.

Dave and Ranjit are pleased with the information that you collected for them. They are anxious to start using search engines, directories, meta-search engines, and other Web resources to help them write their stories. Anne is so impressed with your work that she wants you to conduct some short classes to demonstrate the use of Web search tools to all staff members.

Session 4.2 QUICK CHECK

1. The three basic Boolean operators are _____, _____, and _____.

2. Write a search expression using Boolean and precedence operators that returns Web pages that contain information about wild mustang horses in Wyoming but not information about the Ford Mustang automobile.

3. True or False: The NEAR location operator always returns phrases that contain all keywords within 10 words of each other in a search expression.

4. True or False: In most search engines, the wildcard character is a * symbol.

5. Name three kinds of filters you can include in a HotBot search run from its main search page.

6. In an advanced or Boolean search expression, parentheses are an example of a(n) _____ operator.

7. Name one distinguishing feature of the Northern Light search engine.

REVIEW ASSIGNMENTS

Dave and Ranjit are keeping you busy at the Midland News. Your internship will be over soon, so you would like to leave Anne and the News with hyperlinks to some resources that the international business news section might want to use after you leave. To create those hyperlinks, complete the following steps:

1. Start your Web browser, open to the Student Online Companion page at www.course.comnewperspectives/internet3, click the hyperlink for your book, click the Tutorial 4 link, and then click the Review Assignments link and wait while the browser loads the page. The Review Assignments page contains links to search engines, directories, and meta-search engines.

2. Choose at least one search tool from each category and conduct a search using the search expression "international" and "business."

3. Extend or narrow your search using each tool until you find 10 Web sites that you believe are comprehensive guides or directories that Anne, Dave, and Ranjit should include in their bookmark or favorites lists to help them get information about international business stories.

4. For each Web site, record the URL and write a paragraph that explains why you believe the site would be useful to an international business news writer. Identify each site as a guide, directory, or other resource.

5. When you are finished, close your Web browser, and if necessary, log off your Internet connection

CASE PROBLEMS

Case 1. Key Consulting Group You are a manager at Key Consulting Group, a firm of geological and engineering consultants who specialize in earthquake-damage assessment. When an earthquake strikes, Key Consulting Group sends a team of geologists and structural engineers to the quake's site to examine the damage in buildings and determine what kinds of reconstruction will be needed. In some cases, the buildings must be demolished. An earthquake can occur without warning in many parts of the world, so Key Consulting Group needs quick access to information about local conditions in various parts of the world, including the temperature, rainfall, money exchange rates, demographics, and local customs. It is early July when you receive a call that an earthquake has just occurred in Northern Chile. To obtain information about local mid-winter conditions there so Key Consulting Group can prepare its team, complete the following steps.

1. Start your Web browser, open the Student Online Companion page at www.course.com/newperspectives/internet3, click the hyperlink for your book, click the Tutorial 4 link, and then click the Case Problems link and wait while your browser opens the page. The Case Problems section contains links to search engines, directories, and meta-search engines.

2. Use one of the search tools to conduct searches for information on local conditions in Northern Chile in July.

3. Prepare a short report that includes the daily temperature range, average rainfall, the current exchange rate for U.S. dollars to Chilean pesos, and any information you can obtain about the characteristics of the local population.

4. When you are finished, close your Web browser, and if necessary, log off your Internet connection.

Case 2. Lightning Electrical Generators, Inc. You work as a marketing manager for Lightning Electrical Generators, Inc., a firm that has built generators for over 50 years. The generator business is not as profitable as it once was, and John Delaney, the firm's president, has asked you to investigate new markets for the company. One market that John would like to consider is the uninterruptible power supply (UPS) business. A UPS supplies continuing power to a single computer or to an entire computer system if the regular source of power to the computer fails. Most UPSs provide power only long enough to allow an orderly shutdown of the computer. John wants you to study the market for UPSs in the United States. He also wants to know which firms currently make and sell these products. Finally, he would like some idea of what the power ratings and prices are of individual units. To provide John the information he needs, complete the following steps.

1. Start your Web browser, open the Student Online Companion page at www.course.com/newperspectives/internet3, click the hyperlink for your book, click the Tutorial 4 link, and then click the Case Problems link and wait while your browser opens the page. The Case Problems section contains links to search engines, directories, and meta-search engines.

2. Use one of the search tools to conduct searches for information about UPSs for John. You should design your searches to find the manufacturers' names and information about the products that they offer.

3. Prepare a short report that includes the information you have gathered, including the manufacturer's name, model number, product features, and suggested price for at least five UPSs.

4. When you are finished, close your Web browser, and if necessary, log off your Internet connection.

Case 3. Dunwoody Cams, Inc. Gunther Dunwoody is the founder of Dunwoody Cams, Inc., a manufacturer of automobile parts. Buyers for the major auto companies frequently visit Dunwoody's factory Web page to obtain quotes on parts. Gunther would like you to find Web pages that contain information about the history of the automobile so he can place hyperlinks to those pages on the Dunwoody Web page, so the site is more interesting to use. He is especially interested in having links to Web sites that have photographs of old autos. To gather the automobile-related information that Gunther wants, complete the following steps.

1. Start your Web browser, open the Student Online Companion page at www.course.com/newperspectives/internet3, click the hyperlink for your book, click the Tutorial 4 link, and then click the Case Problems link and wait while your browser opens the page. The Case Problems section contains links to search engines, directories, and meta-search engines.

2. Use one of the search tools to find Web sites that contain historical information about automobiles and automobile manufacturing.

3. Prepare a list of at least five URLs that Gunther might want to include on the Dunwoody Web page. Be sure that at least one of the URLs is for a Web site that includes photographs of old automobiles.

4. When you are finished, close your Web browser, and if necessary, log off your Internet connection.

Case 4. Glenwood Employment Agency You work as a staff assistant at the Glenwood Employment Agency. Eric Steinberg, the agency's owner, wants you to find Web resources for finding open positions in your geographic area. Eric would like this information to gauge whether his own efforts are keeping pace with the competition. He wants to monitor a few good pages but does not want to conduct exhaustive searches of the Web every week. To help Eric find current employment information, complete the following steps.

1. Start your Web browser, open the Student Online Companion page at www.course.com/newperspectives/internet3, click the hyperlink for your book, click the Tutorial 4 link, and then click the Case Problems link and wait while your browser opens the page. The Case Problems section contains links to search engines, directories, and meta-search engines.

2. Use one of the search tools to find Web sites that contain information about job openings in your geographic area. You can use search expressions that include Boolean and precedence operators to limit your searches.

3. Prepare a list of at least five URLs of pages that you believe would be good candidates for Eric's monitoring program.

4. For each URL that you find, write a paragraph that explains why you selected it and then identify any particular strengths or weaknesses of the Web site based on Eric's intended use.

5. When you are finished, close your Web browser, and if necessary, log off your Internet connection.

Case 5. Lynda's Fine Foods For many years, Lynda Reuss has operated a small store that sells specialty foods, such as pickles and mustard, and related gift items. Lynda is thinking about selling her products on the Web because they are small, relatively expensive, and easy to ship. She believes that people who buy her products might appreciate the convenience of ordering via the Web. Lynda would like to find some specialty food store sites on the Web so she can determine what the competition might be and to obtain some ideas that she might use when she creates her own Web site. To research selling specialty food items on the Web, complete the following steps.

1. Start your Web browser, open the Student Online Companion page at www.course.com/newperspectives/internet3, click the hyperlink for your book, click the Tutorial 4 link, and then click the Case Problems link and wait while your browser opens the page. The Case Problems section contains links to search engines, directories, and meta-search engines.

2. Use one of the search engine tools to find Web sites that offer gift items such as pickles or mustard. You can use search expressions that include Boolean and precedence operators to limit your searches.

3. Repeat your search using one of the Web directory tools.

4. Compare the results you obtained using a search engine and using a Web directory. Explain in a memorandum of about 100 words which search tool was more effective for this type of search.

5. When you are finished, close your Web browser, and if necessary, log off your Internet connection.

QUICK | CHECK ANSWERS

Session 4.1

1. open-ended, hard to phrase, difficult to determine when you have found a good answer
2. True
3. Web robot, bot, or spider.
4. many inbound links from other Web pages.
5. False. Most search engines exclude stop words such as *and* or *the*.
6. Advantage: Experts have selected, examined, and classified the entries in a Web directory. Disadvantage: You must know which category to search to find information.
7. The power of the search engine operates on the expert-selected and classified entries in the directory.
8. It forwards the expression a number of other search engines, and then presents and organizes the search results it receives from them.
9. They offer lists of hyperlinks to other Web pages, frequently including summaries or reviews of the Web sites, organized by subject.

Session 4.2

1. AND, OR, NOT
2. One possibility is: (mustang OR horse) AND Wyoming NOT (Ford OR automobile OR auto OR car)
3. False
4. True
5. time period, language, pages that include a specific type of media
6. inclusion, grouping
7. It includes non-Web search results from its special collection and organizes search results into folders of related hyperlinks.

INFORMATION RESOURCES ON THE WEB

Finding, Evaluating, and Using Web Information Resources

Cosby Promotions

You just started a new position as the executive assistant to the president of Cosby Promotions, Marti Cosby. Cosby Promotions is a growing booking agency that handles promotion and concert contract negotiations for musicians and bands. Cosby Promotions works with a wide variety of music acts. Their current clients include bands that play pop, Latin, heavy metal, techno, industrial, and urban. The agency does not currently handle many country music acts, but Marti wants to expand their country music business over the next few years. Marti explains that the music business is fast moving—the popularity of musical artists often changes rapidly. The promotion and booking strategies that will work best for a particular client one month might not work well the next month. Promotional tie-ins and sponsorships are also important revenue sources for music acts and the needs of specific sponsors change with shifts in the preferences of their customers.

Your main job is to help Cosby Promotions' staff members stay current on news items and trends that might affect their clients. Marti expects you to use your basic understanding of Web searching techniques to help the firm identify and track important information about the agency's clients and potential sponsors. Your other duties will include updating agency executives and clients about local conditions at travel destinations and working with the firm's Web site design team to develop an effective Web presence for the firm.

In addition to working with Marti and the executive team, you will work closely with Susan Zhu, the firm's research director. Susan has worked at Cosby Promotions for six years in a variety of research jobs. The research department undertakes background investigations related to issues that arise in the firm's dealings with its clients. For example, whenever Marti starts working on a booking for a concert hall or other venue that is new for the firm, she asks Susan to provide background on the venue. Susan is looking forward to having you work with her as part of the Cosby Promotions research team.

SESSION 5.1

In this session, you will search for current news, weather, and travel information. You will find individual and business listings in directories. Finally, you will find multimedia resources and learn about some common Web multimedia formats.

Current Information

In earlier tutorials, you learned how to use search engines, directories, and other resources to find information on the Web. As you begin your new job, Marti explains that many of your assignments will be to find recent news and information about clients, potential sponsors, performance venues, and changes in the music industry.

To help you find current news and information, many search engines and directories include a hyperlink to a "What's new" page. The Yahoo! directory, for example, includes hyperlinks titled "News," "Sports," and "Weather" at the top of its home page. The Excite directory's main page includes a collection of hyperlinks to current events as shown in Figure 5-1.

Figure 5-1	EXCITE'S MAIN SEARCH PAGE

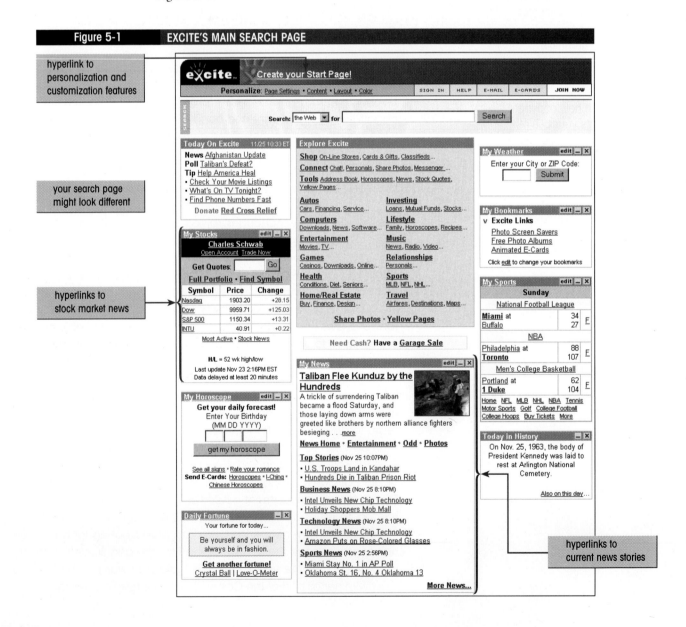

You can see Excite's stock market and current news hyperlinks in Figure 5-1. The page also includes hyperlinks for sports news, weather, and even horoscopes. If you are willing to register with Excite, you can follow the Create your Start Page or Join Now hyperlink (near the top of the Web page) to personalize the page. This personalization feature lets you specify the kind of information that appears on this page when you log on.

Search engines can be useful tools for finding current news stories, too. Many search engines, including HotBot and AltaVista, allow you to choose a date range when you enter a search expression. HotBot provides two ways to do this. On its main page, you can specify one of a range of time options, such as "in the last week" or "in the last 3 months," to limit your search to sites that were last modified within your selected time period. HotBot's Advanced Search page includes the same range of time options as the main page, but it also lets users limit searches to dates before or after a specific date. To open the HotBot Advanced Search page shown in Figure 5-2, click the ADVANCED SEARCH button that appears on the HotBot search engine's main page.

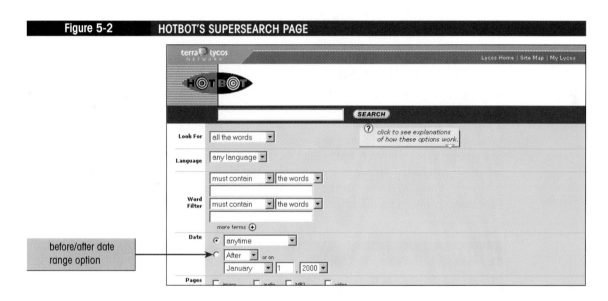

Figure 5-2   HOTBOT'S SUPERSEARCH PAGE

before/after date range option

In the section of the HotBot Advanced Search page that is visible in Figure 5-2, you can see the before/after date range option. HotBot, even on its SuperSearch page, does not provide a way to search for sites *within* a specific date range. For example, you could not limit a HotBot search to sites modified between April 24, 2000, and November 11, 2000. As you learned in Tutorial 4, a good Internet researcher will always know how to use more than one search engine. The AltaVista search engine does not have the pre-set range of time options that HotBot offers, but it does allow you to set an exact "between" date range on its advanced search page. Figure 5-3 shows the AltaVista advanced search page with an exact date range set.

Figure 5-3   **DATE RANGE SETTINGS IN AN ALTA VISTA ADVANCED SEARCH**

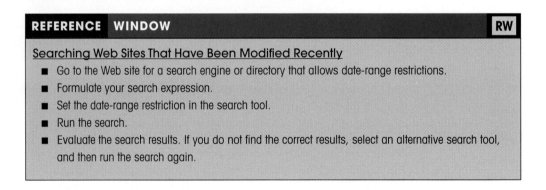

exact "between" date range settings

Marti calls to tell you that she has been negotiating with Honda on behalf of one of Cosby Promotions' heavy metal bands. Honda wants to increase its appeal to younger drivers and is looking to sponsor a band that will appeal to that market. Marti knows that other agencies will be pitching bands to Honda for this sponsorship, so she wants as much background information on Honda as possible before she meets with them next week. She would like you to search the Web and collect the URLs of any sites that mention Honda and she is especially interested in learning more about the kinds of promotional activities that Honda is already doing. Marti needs the most recent information available, so you will search for sites that have been modified within the last three months.

REFERENCE WINDOW   **RW**

Searching Web Sites That Have Been Modified Recently
- Go to the Web site for a search engine or directory that allows date-range restrictions.
- Formulate your search expression.
- Set the date-range restriction in the search tool.
- Run the search.
- Evaluate the search results. If you do not find the correct results, select an alternative search tool, and then run the search again.

Consider the search tools available. Your search term—Honda—is a brand name, so it is likely that directory builders will collect many useful sites that include that term in their databases. Yahoo! is a directory that includes a date-range restriction option, so you decide to use it for your first search. Remember, if you do not find what you are looking for with one search tool, you can try your search again using different tools until you are satisfied with your results.

To find specific Web pages based on last modified dates:

1. Start your Web browser, and then go to the Student Online Companion page at **http://www.course.com/newperspectives/internet3**, click the hyperlink for your book, click the **Tutorial 5** link, and then click the **Session 5.1** link. Click the **Yahoo!** hyperlink and wait while the browser loads the Yahoo! home page.

2. Click the **advanced search** hyperlink to the right of the Search button to open the Yahoo! Search Options page.

3. Type **Honda** in the search text box.

4. Click the **Find only new listings added during the past** list arrow to open the list of choices (see Figure 5-4), click **3 months**, and then click the **Search** button to start the search.

Figure 5-4	SEARCHING THE YAHOO! DIRECTORY USING DATE CRITERIA

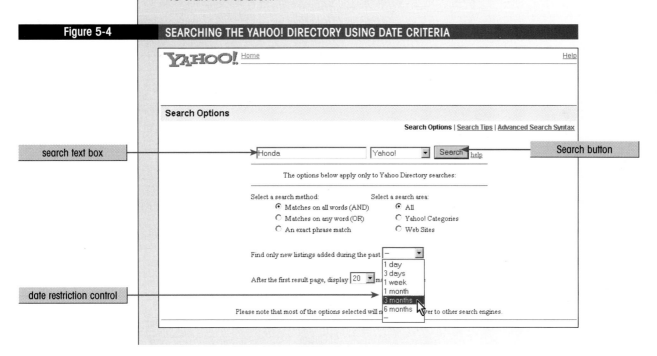

Your search should return fewer than 100 hits and will include the Web pages of Honda motorcycle and automobile dealers. After examining the results, you decide that you did not find what Marti needs. Susan suggests that you try your search again using HotBot because HotBot is a search engine and might return more hits than a directory such as Yahoo!.

To search for last modified dates using HotBot:

1. Use your browser's **Back** button or the history list to return to the Student Online Companion page for Session 5.1, and then click the **HotBot** hyperlink and wait for the HotBot home page to load in your Web browser.

2. Type **Honda AND promotion** in the Search Smarter text box to search for URLs of Web pages that relate to Honda's auto manufacturing operations.

3. Click the **Look for** list arrow, and then click **boolean phrase**.

4. Click the **Date** list arrow, and then click **in the last 3 months** to search for URLs that have been modified in the last three months. The search parameters you have specified appear in the portion of the HotBot search page shown in Figure 5-5.

| Figure 5-5 | SETTING SEARCH CRITERIA IN HOTBOT |

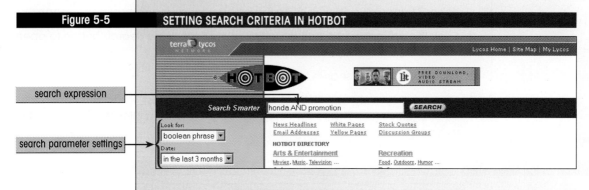

5. Click the **SEARCH** button to start the search. Your search should return many more pages than Yahoo! based on the specified criteria. You are certain that Marti can find the information she is looking for from your list of URLs.

You can send the URLs to Marti in an e-mail message, or you can tell her how to obtain the same search results. For now, you decide to cut and paste the URLs that look promising and then send them to her in an e-mail message.

Getting the News

Marti stops by to see you the day after you send her the URLs she requested. She is pleased with many of the recently modified Web pages you found. Now, she asks you to find any recent news stories about Honda that might not appear as part of a recently modified Web page.

Finding current news stories on the Web is an easy task. Almost every search engine and Web directory includes a list of current news hyperlinks to broadcast networks, wire services, and newspapers. A **wire service** (also called press agency or a news service) is an organization that gathers and distributes news to newspapers, magazines, broadcasters, and other organizations that pay a fee to the wire service. Although there are hundreds of wire services in the world, most news comes from the four largest wire services: United Press International (UPI) and the Associated Press (AP) in the United States, Reuters in Great Britain, and Agence France-Presse in France.

All of the major U.S. broadcasters, including ABC, CBS, CNN, Fox, MSNBC (the Microsoft-NBC joint venture), and National Public Radio (NPR) have Web sites that carry news features. Broadcasters in other countries, such as the BBC, also provide news reports on their Web pages. The Reuters Web page includes current news stories in addition to the news services that it sells. Major newspapers, such as *The New York Times*, *The Washington Post*, and the *London Times*, have Web sites that include current news and many other features from their print editions. Many of these broadcast news, wire service, and newspaper Web sites include search features that allow you to search the site for specific news stories. However, not many search tools are available on the Web to search multiple news sources at the same time. You begin to think about the time it will take to do a comprehensive search of just the major news sites for Marti and you begin to worry.

Susan tells you that the **Internet Public Library – Online Newspapers** site includes hyperlinks to hundreds of international and domestic newspapers. Figure 5-6 shows a portion of the Internet Public Library Web site.

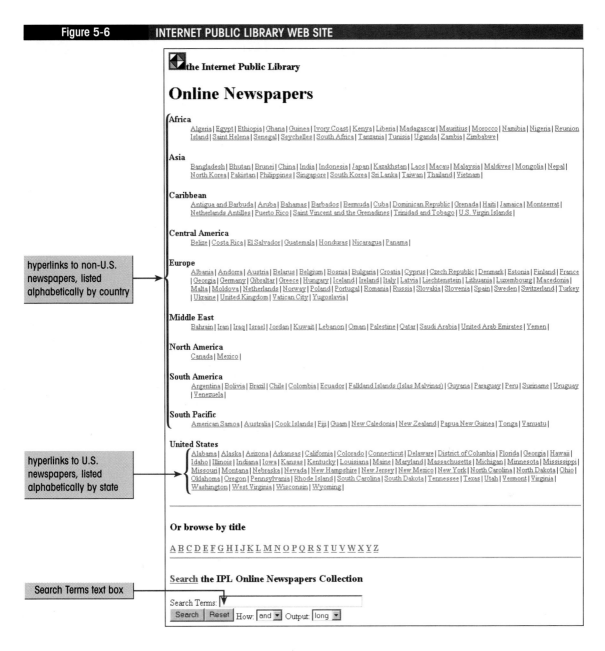

| Figure 5-6 | INTERNET PUBLIC LIBRARY WEB SITE |

As you can see in Figure 5-6, this site has a search field, but it searches only the title and the main entry for each newspaper and does not search the newspaper sites' contents. Therefore, you could use it to identify all of the newspapers in New Jersey or all of the newspapers that had the word *Tribune* in their titles, but you could not use it to find news stories that include the word *Honda*.

Fortunately, several Web sites let you search the content of current news stories in multiple publications and wire services.

Yahoo! News includes the AP and Reuters wire services along with news it purchases from other leading newspapers and magazines. The Northern Light Current News site includes the AP and UPI wire services in its offerings. VPOP Technologies' NewsHub site updates its news database with information from a number of wire services every 15 minutes. To obtain both breadth and currency of coverage, you might want to run the same query using more than one of these search tools.

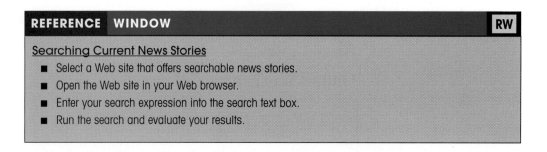

REFERENCE WINDOW RW

Searching Current News Stories
- Select a Web site that offers searchable news stories.
- Open the Web site in your Web browser.
- Enter your search expression into the search text box.
- Run the search and evaluate your results.

You would like search coverage that is both current and broad, so you decide to use the NewsHub, Yahoo!, and Northern Light news search tools.

To find recent news stories on the Web that mention Honda:

1. Return to the Student Online Companion Web page for Session 5.1, and then click the **NewsHub** hyperlink and wait while your Web browser loads the NewsHub page that appears in Figure 5-7.

Figure 5-7 NEWSHUB HOME PAGE

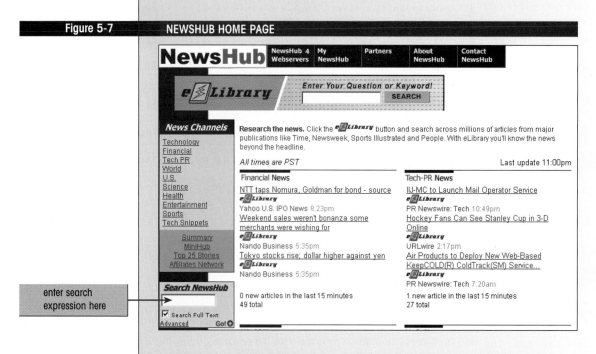

enter search expression here

TROUBLE? If a Privacy dialog box opens about a privacy icon appearing on your taskbar, click OK.

2. Type **Honda** in the **Search NewsHub** text box (do not use the eLibrary search tool at the top of the page), and then click the **Go!** button. Examine the Web pages that NewsHub found, and note the URLs of any pages that might interest Marti. You want to make sure you find enough relevant hits, so you decide to try the other news search tools.

TROUBLE? If your search does not yield many useful results, try using different combinations of words in the search expression. For example, you might find that entering "Honda sponsor" or "Honda promotion" works better than the word "Honda" alone.

3. Return to the Student Online Companion Web page for Session 5.1, and then click the **Yahoo! News** hyperlink to load that page in your Web browser.

4. Type **Honda** in the search text box (you might need to scroll down the page to see the search text box), and then click the **Search** button to start your search. As in Step 2, you can try other words if your search does not yield useful results.

5. Return to the Student Online Companion Web page for Session 5.1, and then click the **Northern Light Current News Search** hyperlink to load the page shown in Figure 5-8.

Figure 5-8	NORTHERN LIGHT CURRENT NEWS SEARCH PAGE

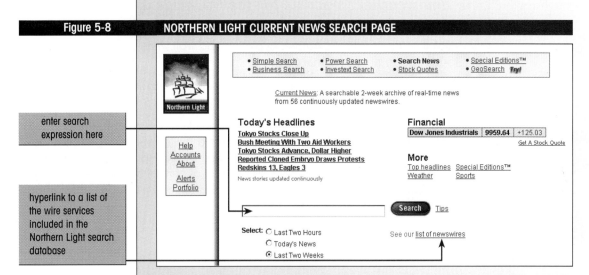

6. Type **Honda** in the search text box, and then click the **Search** button to start your search. The Northern Light results page might include links to its Special Collection pages in addition to Web page results. Also, the search results will be collected in Northern Light's customized folders. Recall that you learned about these two features of the Northern Light search engine in Tutorial 4.

Now you have accumulated a respectable list of URLs about Honda's current promotional and sponsorship activities for Marti. You have gained experience in searching for current topics by examining Web pages that have been modified recently and by using three tools that search the Web specifically for news reports.

Weather Reports

Marti will travel to Nashville later in the week to meet with some new country music artists that she hopes to sign as clients for the agency. Marti already has made her travel plans, and she is interested in the weather forecast for the area. You decide to check two sources for the information because you know that meteorology is not an exact science—forecasts from different sources can differ.

Finding a Weather Forecast

■ Open the weather information Web site you would like to use in a Web browser.

■ Locate the weather report for the city or area in which you are interested.

■ Repeat the steps to find other weather information in different Web sites.

To find weather forecasts for the Nashville area:

1. Return to the Student Online Companion Web page for Session 5.1, and then click the **The Weather Channel** hyperlink and wait while your Web browser loads the Weather Channel page.

2. Type **Nashville** in the Enter city or US zip code text box, and then click the **GO** button.

3. A page appears showing a number of hyperlinks to U.S. cities named "Nashville." You are interested in weather in Nashville, Tennessee, so click that hyperlink to open a page similar to the one shown in Figure 5-9. The Weather Channel page for Nashville includes a report of current conditions and a ten-day forecast for the Nashville area. The page includes a Doppler radar image and links to many more radar and satellite images.

| Figure 5-9 | WEATHER CHANNEL NASHVILLE LOCAL FORECAST PAGE |

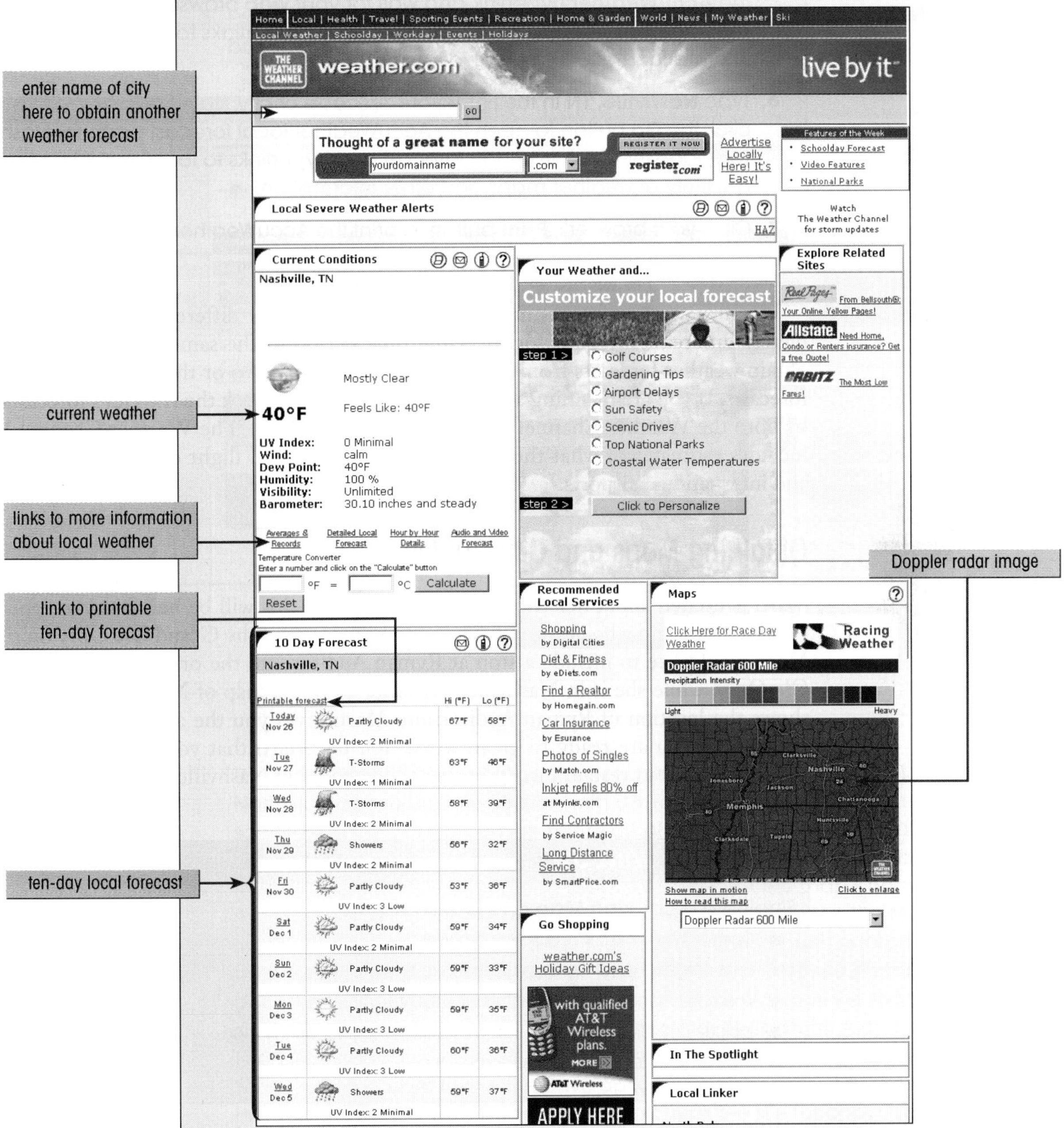

enter name of city here to obtain another weather forecast

current weather

links to more information about local weather

link to printable ten-day forecast

ten-day local forecast

Doppler radar image

TROUBLE? If a small Web page in the form of a dialog box opens, click that page's Close button to dismiss it. The site may also open small Web pages that contain ads. You can click the Close button on those pages also.

TROUBLE? If the Local Weather page for Nashville opens in another window, close the one you used to click the Nashville, Tennessee link.

4. Scroll the page, if necessary, and then click the **Printable forecast** hyperlink to open a page that only shows the ten-day forecast. Later, you can click your browser's **Print** button to print the forecast for Marti. Now, use a different weather source to search for weather conditions in Nashville.

REFERENCE   WINDOW   **RW**

Obtaining Travel Destination Information
- Go to a city guide Web site in your Web browser.
- Search the site for your destination city, region, or country.
- Explore the hyperlinks provided by the site for your destination.

To obtain information about Nashville and the Ryman Auditorium:

1. Return to the Student Online Companion Web page for Session 5.1, and then click the **CitySearch** hyperlink and wait while your Web browser loads the Web page.

2. Click the **Nashville** hyperlink in the list of City Guides.

3. Type **Ryman Auditorium** in the Search for ANYTHING text box, and then click the **GO!** Button (the GO! button is to the right of the ANYWHERE search box.)

4. Click the **Ryman Auditorium** hyperlink that appears on the search results page to open the Web page shown in Figure 5-11.

Figure 5-11 CITYSEARCH WEB PAGE

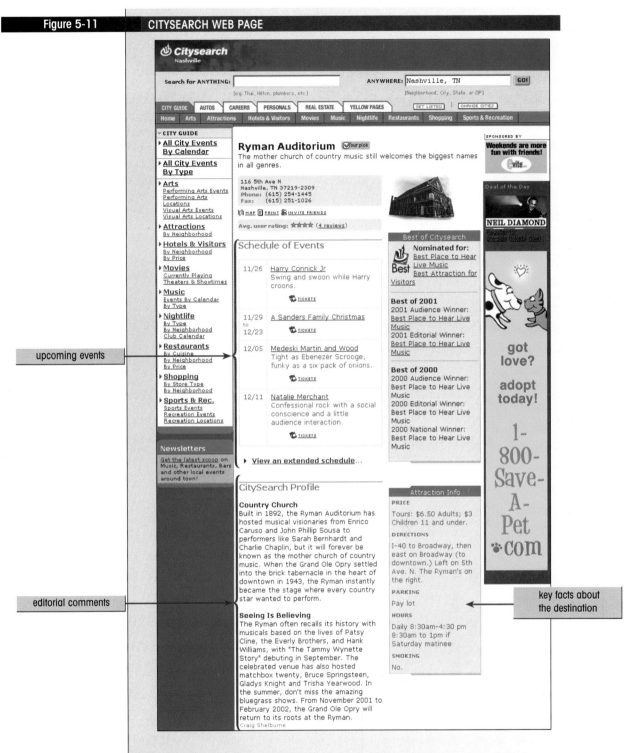

Figure 5-11 shows hyperlinks and other useful information that Marti can use for her trip. The key facts presented include the auditorium's telephone number, hours of operation, and tour prices. The page includes hyperlinks to a map of the local area—provided by MapQuest—and a seating diagram for the venue. The editorial comments provide a short history of the building and its role in the development of country music. The page also includes information about upcoming events scheduled at the auditorium. The hyperlinks at the top of the page link to information about restaurants, nightclubs, bars, theaters, and movies in the area.

You are satisfied that you have found more than enough information to make Marti's Nashville trip memorable and successful.

Finding Businesses

Over the next few years, Marti is interested in developing reciprocal relationships with local booking agencies in Nashville. She would like to make some initial contacts during this trip and asks you to search the Web to find a list of booking agencies in Nashville.

Many search engines on the Web specialize in finding people and businesses. The sites that store only information about businesses are often called **yellow pages** sites. One of these search engines is the **SuperPages.com** site operated by Verizon. You decide to use SuperPages.com to create the booking agency list for Marti.

REFERENCE WINDOW   RW

Finding Business Listings on the Web
- Navigate to a page that provides business listings or a business listing search engine in your Web browser.
- Enter information about the nature and geographic location of the business that you want to find.
- Run the search.
- Examine and evaluate the results to determine whether you should revise your search or try another search engine.

To find Nashville booking agencies on the Web:

1. Return to the Student Online Companion Web page for Session 5.1, and then click the **SuperPages.com** hyperlink and wait while your Web browser loads the Web page.

2. Because you are not sure how booking agents will be listed in the SuperPage.com database, you decide to use a general term to begin your search. Type **Agents** in the Category text box.

3. Press the **Tab** key twice, and then type **Nashville** in the City text box.

4. Click the **State** list arrow, and then click **TN**.

5. Click the **Find It** button to begin the search. The results page includes a list of links to a number of related categories.

6. Click the **Artists, Managers, & Agencies** category link to open a page similar to the one that appears in Figure 5-12.

Figure 5-12   **SUPERPAGES.COM SEARCH RESULTS PAGE**

list of booking
agencies in Nashville

Your search should find booking agencies included in the listings from this SuperPages.com category. The listings include the name, address, telephone number, and a hyperlink to a map for each firm. SuperPages.com also provides a hyperlink to listed firms' Web sites. Some or all of the booking agencies listed in the results pages might not have Web sites and, therefore, your results pages might not include any hyperlinks. Now, you are ready to prepare a report for Marti that contains the agencies' information so she can investigate potential relationships with those agencies.

Finding People and Related Privacy Concerns

Many Web sites let you search for individuals' names, addresses, and telephone numbers. These sites often are called **white pages** sites. One comprehensive site that includes search tools for finding information about businesses and individuals is **Switchboard**. Switchboard collects information from published telephone directories and other publicly available information and indexes it by last name.

Many people expressed concerns about privacy violations when this type of information became easily accessible on the Web. In some cases, Web sites made unpublished and unlisted telephone numbers available for public use. Some sites grouped individual listings by category, including categories such as religious or political affiliations. In response to these privacy concerns, most white pages sites offer people a way to remove their listings. For example, Switchboard will accept a list removal request sent via its Web page, e-mail, or a letter. You might want to determine whether white pages sites have a correct listing for you and whether you want your listing to appear in a white pages site.

REFERENCE WINDOW   **RW**

Searching for Your White Pages Listing

- Open a white pages Web site in your Web browser.
- Enter your name and part of your address.
- Run the search, and then examine the search results.
- Consider repeating the search with various combinations of partial address information or variants of the correct spelling of your name.

To search for your listing on the Switchboard white pages site:

1. Return to the Student Online Companion Web page for Session 5.1, and then click the **Switchboard** hyperlink and wait while your Web browser loads the Web page.

2. Click the **Find a Person** hyperlink to open the Find a Person Web page.

3. Click in the **Last Name** text box, and then type your last name.

4. Press the **Tab** key to move to the City text box, and then type the name of the city in which you live.

5. Press the **Tab** key to move to the State text box, and then type the two-letter U.S. Postal Service abbreviation for the state in which you live.

6. Click the **Search** button. Your name might appear in the first results page. If it does not appear, click the **Next Matches** hyperlink to go to the next page.

   TROUBLE? If your telephone number is listed in another person's name, use that person's name to find your listing.

   TROUBLE? If you do not find your listing, click the Modify Search hyperlink, add more information to the search text boxes, and then search again. If you still cannot find your listing, try searching for a friend's listing or your parents' listing.

7. Close your browser and, if necessary, log off your Internet connection.

You might need to run the search several times using different information to find your listing. If you do not want Switchboard to list your name and information, return to the Switchboard start page, click the My Personal Listing hyperlink near the bottom of the page, and then click the Remove your personal listing hyperlink. Follow the instructions on the page that appears to remove your listing from the Switchboard directory.

The Student Online Companion page for Tutorial 5 contains hyperlinks to other white pages Web sites. You can search those sites for your listing and follow similar steps to remove or change it, if you want.

You have accomplished many tasks and helped Marti quite a bit. You look forward to your meeting with Susan tomorrow morning to discuss the research department's guidelines for evaluating the validity and quality of the information that you obtain during your searches of the Web.

Session 5.1 QUICK CHECK

1. Reuters is an example of a _____ .

2. True or False: NewsHub updates its news stories twice each day.

3. Explain why you might want to consult two or three Web resources for weather information before leaving on an out-of-town trip.

4. List two advantages of using a Web map server instead of a paper map or atlas.

5. Describe three types of information that you might obtain from a city guide Web page.

6. True or False: City guide Web sites are usually created by an agency of the city government.

7. A Web site that helps people find businesses by name or category is often called a _____ .

8. A Web site that helps people find the telephone numbers or e-mail addresses of other individuals is often called a _____ .

Now that you know more about where to find information on the Web, you need to learn how to evaluate that information. In Session 5.2, you will learn how to assess the validity and quality of the information you find on the Web.

SESSION 5.2

In this session, you will learn how to evaluate the quality of Web research resources based on a site's author, content, and appearance. You will then learn how to use library research resources to find information about a specific topic. You will learn how to find multimedia resources on the Web and how copyright laws affect your ability to use those resources. You also will learn about the future of electronic publishing.

Evaluating the Validity and Quality of Web Research Resources

In your morning meeting with Susan, you reviewed some of the research department's standards and practices for information that the firm collects using the Internet. One of the most important issues in doing Web research is assessing the validity and quality of the information provided on the Internet. Because the Web has made publishing so easy and inexpensive, it allows virtually anyone to create a Web page on almost any subject. Research published in scientific or literary journals is subjected to peer review. Books and research monographs are often reviewed by peers or edited by experts in the appropriate subject area. Information on the Web is seldom subjected to this review and editing process that has become a standard practice in print publishing.

When searching the Web for entertainment, general information, news, or weather information, you are not likely to encounter a site that someone has intentionally created to misinform you. Further, the potential damage caused by a bad weather report or false news is not great. When you are searching the Web for an answer to a serious research question, however, the risks can be significant.

You can reduce your risks by carefully evaluating the quality of any Web resource on which you plan to rely for information related to an important judgment or decision. To develop an opinion about the quality of the resource, you can evaluate three major components of any Web page. These three components are the Web page's authorship, content, and appearance.

Author Identity and Objectivity

The first thing you should try to do when evaluating a Web research resource is to determine who authored the page. If you cannot easily find authorship information on a Web site, you should question the validity of the information included on that site. A Web site that does not identify its author has very little credibility as a research resource. Any Web page that presents empirical research results, logical arguments, theories, or other information that purports to be the result of a research process should identify the author *and* present the author's background information and credentials. The information on the site should be sufficient to establish the author's professional qualifications. You also should check secondary sources for corroborating information. For example, if the author of a Web page indicates that he or she is a member of a university faculty, you can find the university's Web site and see if the author is listed as a faculty member. The Web site should provide author contact information, such as a street, e-mail address, or telephone number, so you can contact the author or consult information directories to verify the addresses or telephone numbers.

In some cases, it can be difficult to determine who owns a specific Web server or provides the space for the Web page. You can make a rough assessment, however, by examining the domain identifier in the URL. If the site claims affiliation with an educational or research institution, the domain should be .edu for educational institution. A not-for-profit organization would most likely have the .org domain, and a government unit or agency would have the .gov domain. These are not hard and fast rules, however. For example, some perfectly legitimate not-for-profit organizations have URLs with a .com domain.

You also should consider whether the qualifications presented by the author pertain to the material that appears on the Web site. For example, the author of a Web site concerned with gene-splicing technology might list a Ph.D. degree as a credential. If the author's Ph.D. is in history or sociology, it would not support the credibility of the gene-splicing technology Web site. If you cannot determine the specific areas of the author's educational background, you can look for other examples of the author's work on the Web. By searching for the author's name and terms related to the subject area, you should be able to find other sites that include the author's work. The fact that a Web site author has written extensively on a subject can add some evidence—though not necessarily conclusive—that the author has expertise in the field.

In addition to identifying the author's identity and qualifications, the author information should include details about the author's affiliations—either as an employee, owner, or consultant—with organizations that might have an interest in the research results or other information included in the Web site. Information about the author's affiliations will help you determine the level of independence and objectivity that the author can bring to bear on the research questions or topics. For example, research results supporting the contention that cigarette smoke is not harmful that are presented in a site authored by a researcher with excellent scientific credentials might be less compelling if you learn that the researcher is the chief scientist at a major tobacco company. By reading the page content carefully, you might be able to identify any bias in the results that is not justified by the evidence presented.

Content

Content is a criterion that is much more difficult to judge than the author's identity and objectivity; after all, you were searching for Web sites so you could learn more about your search topic, which implies that you probably are not an expert in that content area. However, you can look for some things in the Web site's presentation to help determine the quality of information. If the Web page has a clearly stated publication date, you can determine the timeliness of the content. You can read the content critically and evaluate whether the included topics are relevant to the research question at hand. You might be able to determine whether important topics or considerations were omitted. You also might be able to assess the depth of treatment the author gives to the subject.

Form and Appearance

The Web does contain pages full of outright lies and misinformation that are nicely laid out, include tasteful graphics, and have grammatically correct and properly spelled text. However, many pages that contain low-quality or incorrect information are poorly designed and not well edited. For example, a Web page devoted to an analysis of Shakespeare's plays that contains spelling errors indicates a low-quality resource. Loud colors, graphics that serve no purpose, and flashing text are all Web page design elements that often suggest a low-quality resource.

Having explained how these principles of assessing Web page quality are applied to the research team's work at Cosby Promotions, Susan asks you to evaluate a Web page. One of the bands that the agency represents has received a request to perform at a fund-raising concert for an environmental protection group that is concerned about global warming. Susan has been gathering a list of URLs from which she plans to take information to include in a briefing report for the talent manager who will be deciding whether the band should perform at the fund-raising concert. Susan would like you to evaluate the quality of a URL titled "Environmental Health Update" that is on her list.

REFERENCE WINDOW   RW

Evaluating a Web Research Resource
- Open the Web page in your Web browser.
- Identify the author, if possible. If you can identify the author, evaluate his or her credentials and objectivity.
- Examine the content of the Web site.
- Evaluate the site's form and appearance.
- Draw a conclusion about the site's overall quality.

To evaluate the quality of the environmental health update Web page:

1. Start your Web browser, if necessary, and then go to the Student Online Companion page by entering the URL **http://www.course.com/newperspectives/internet3** in the appropriate location in your Web browser. Click the hyperlink for your book, click the **Tutorial 5** link, and then click the **Session 5.2** link. Click the **PSR Program Update** link and wait while the browser loads the Web page that appears in Figure 5-13. Examine the content of the Web page; read the text, examine the titles and headings, and consider the page's appearance.

Figure 5-13	PSR PROGRAM UPDATE WEB PAGE

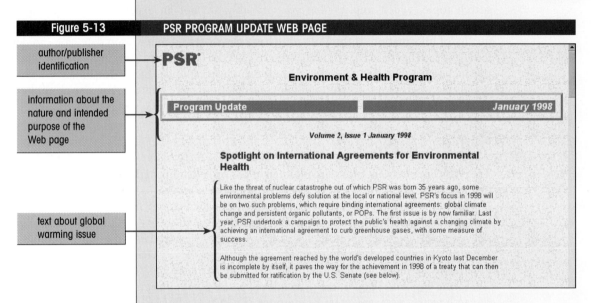

author/publisher identification

information about the nature and intended purpose of the Web page

text about global warming issue

You can see in Figure 5-13 that the author or publisher of the page is identified only as "PSR" and the page has a simple, clear design. The .org domain in the URL tells you that the publisher is a not-for-profit organization. You note that the grammar and spelling are correct, and that the content—although it clearly reflects a strong specific viewpoint on the issue—is not inflammatory or overly argumentative. As you read more of the page, you see that this style of layout and content is consistent in passages related to global warming and other issues discussed on the page. You note that the text cites such authorities as the U.S. National Oceanic and Atmospheric Administration and the *New England Journal of Medicine*. The reputable references and the consistent style of the page suggest that this might be a high-quality site. You also note that the date on the page has been published and kept on the Web for several years. Although this fact alone would not increase your assessment of the page's validity, taken with the other content on the page, it does add help corroborate the quality of the page.

2. Use your browser's scroll bar to scroll to the bottom of the page, which looks like Figure 5-14.

Figure 5-14	IDENTIFYING INFORMATION IN THE PSR PROGRAM UPDATE WEB PAGE

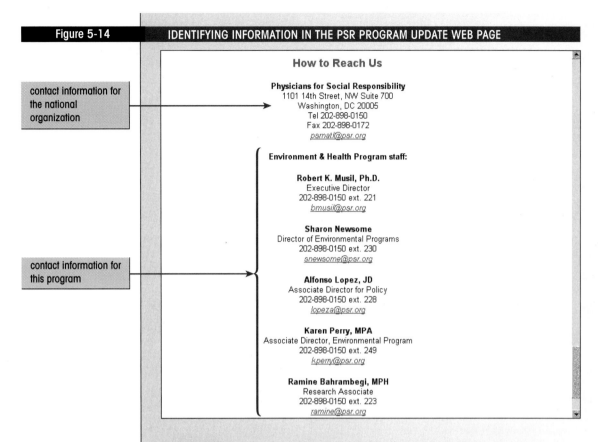

contact information for the national organization

contact information for this program

How to Reach Us

Physicians for Social Responsibility
1101 14th Street, NW Suite 700
Washington, DC 20005
Tel 202-898-0150
Fax 202-898-0172
psrnatl@psr.org

Environment & Health Program staff:

Robert K. Musil, Ph.D.
Executive Director
202-898-0150 ext. 221
bmusil@psr.org

Sharon Newsome
Director of Environmental Programs
202-898-0150 ext. 230
snewsome@psr.org

Alfonso Lopez, JD
Associate Director for Policy
202-898-0150 ext. 228
lopeza@psr.org

Karen Perry, MPA
Associate Director, Environmental Program
202-898-0150 ext. 249
kperry@psr.org

Ramine Bahrambegi, MPH
Research Associate
202-898-0150 ext. 223
ramine@psr.org

Now you can see that PSR is an acronym for the Physicians for Social Responsibility organization. Further, you can see that the organization's address, telephone number, and e-mail address are listed along with contact information for key individuals in the PSR's Environment and Health Program. To find more information about PSR, you might want to visit the organization's home page. The Web page shown in Figure 5-14 does not include a home page hyperlink, but you can guess that it might be the first part of the URL for this page.

3. Click in your browser's Location field or Address Bar, and then delete all of the text to the right of the .org/ domain name portion of the URL. Press the **Enter** key to load the Web page shown in Figure 5-15 with the shortened URL.

Figure 5-15   **PSR HOME PAGE**

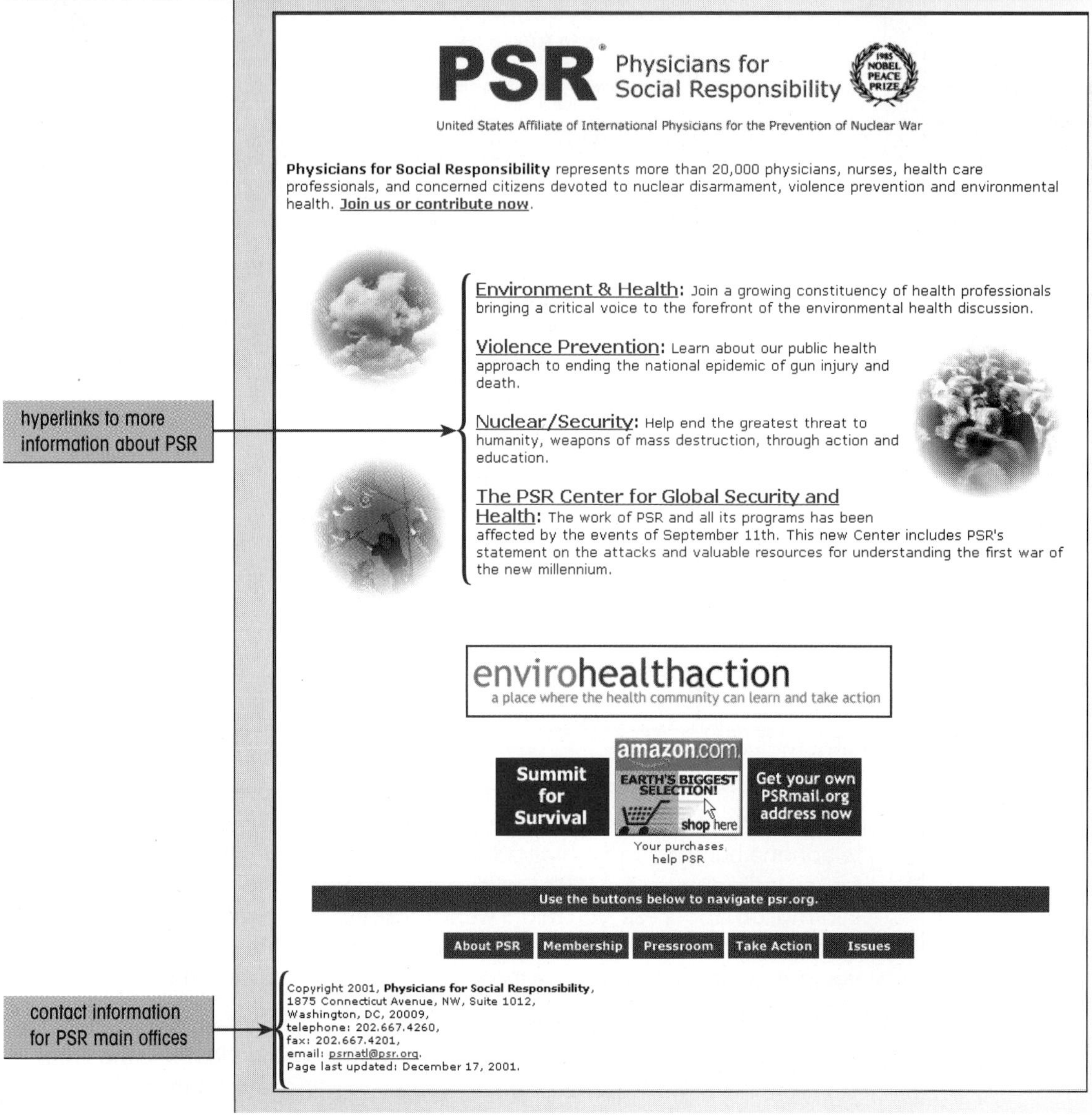

The Web page shown in Figure 5-15 is, in fact, the U.S. National PSR Office home page that includes hyperlinks to information about the organization, its goals, activities, directors, and membership. The page even indicates that the organization was awarded the Nobel Peace Prize in 1985. This information will allow you to make an accurate evaluation of the site and help Susan to determine how she can use its contents to prepare her report to the Cosby Promotions talent manager.

Library **Resources**

Susan is very happy with your evaluation of the environmental health update Web page and needs you to do more work for the research department. You ask Susan about the future of traditional libraries, given that so much information is available on the Web. She admits that she might be biased, having worked in a library for several years, but says that libraries will likely be around for a long time. In fact, the Web has made existing libraries more accessible to more people. As traditional libraries and online collections of works that have serious research value begin to recognize each other as complementary rather than as competing, library users should see many new and interesting research resources. One example of this is the **LibrarySpot** Web site, which is a collection of hyperlinks organized in the same general way that a physical library might arrange its collections.

To explore the LibrarySpot Web site:

1. Return to the Student Online Companion Web page for Session 5.2, and then click the **LibrarySpot** hyperlink and wait while your Web browser loads the Web page shown in Figure 5-16.

| Figure 5-16 | LIBRARYSPOT WEB SITE |

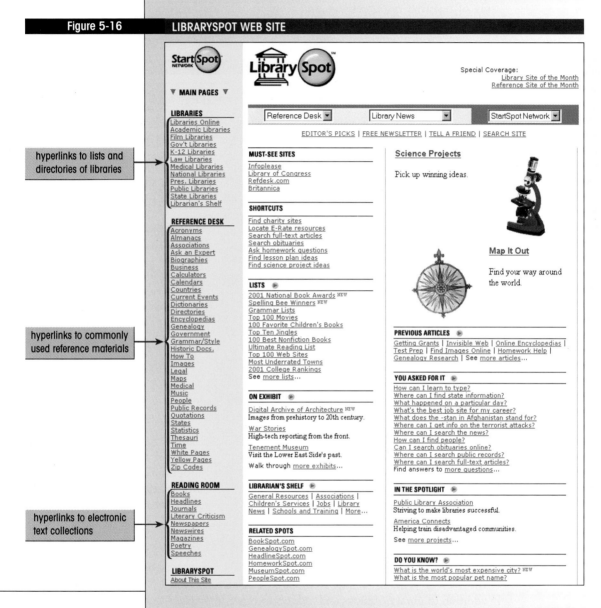

Figure 5-16 shows that the LibrarySpot includes many of the same things you would expect to find in a public or school library. This library is, however, open 24 hours a day and seven days a week. The LibrarySpot site lets you access reference materials, electronic texts, and other library Web sites from one central Web page.

2. Close your browser, and if necessary, log off your Internet connection.

The Student Online Companion page for Tutorial 5 contains many other hyperlinks to useful library and library-related Web sites in the Additional Information section under the "Library Information Sites" heading. Feel free to explore the libraries of the Web the next time you need to complete a research assignment for school or your job.

Figure 5-17 shows the U.S. Library of Congress Web site, which includes links to a huge array of research resources, ranging from the Thomas legislative information site to the Library of Congress archives.

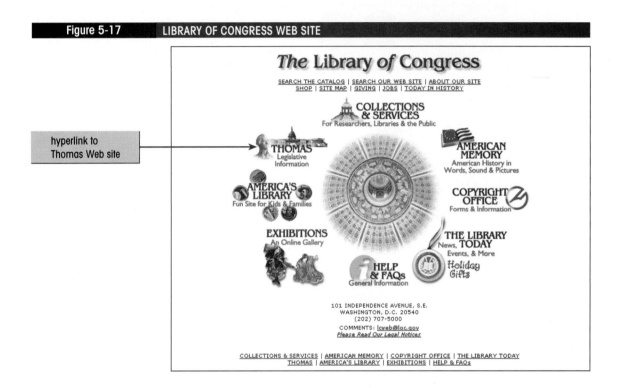

Figure 5-17   LIBRARY OF CONGRESS WEB SITE

The Thomas Web site provides you with search access to the full text of bills that are before Congress, the *Congressional Record*, and Congressional Committee Reports. The American Memory hyperlinks lead you to archived photographs, sound and video record-ings, maps, and collections of everything from seventeenth-century dance instruction man-uals to baseball cards. The Exhibitions hyperlink leads you to information about current and past displays sponsored by the Library of Congress.

Text and Other Archives on the Web

In addition to library catalogs and indexes to other information, the Web contains a number of text resources, including dictionaries, thesauri, encyclopedias, glossaries, and other refer-ence works. Many people find reference works easier to use when they have a computerized search interface. For example, when you open a dictionary to find the definition of a specific word, the structure of the bound book actually interferes with your ability to find the answer you seek. A computer interface allows you to enter a search term—in this case, the word to be defined—and saves you the trouble of scanning several pages of text to find the correct entry.

Of course, publishers sell dictionaries and encyclopedias on CDs, but the Web provides many alternatives. These alternatives range in quality from very low to very high. Many of the best resources offered on the Web require you to pay a subscription fee. The free refer-ence works on the Web are worth investigating, however; they are good enough to provide acceptable service for many users. In addition to dictionaries and encyclopedias, the Web includes grammar checkers, thesauri, rhyming dictionaries, and language-translation pages. The Student Online Companion page for Tutorial 5 includes a collection of hyperlinks to a number of these reference resources in the Additional Information section.

The Web also offers a number of full text copies of works that are no longer protected by copyright. Two of the most popular Web sites for full text storage are the **Project Gutenberg** and **Project Bartleby** Web sites. These volunteer efforts have collected the contributions of many people throughout the world who have spent enormous amounts of time entering or converting printed text into electronic form.

The Web itself has become the subject of archivists' attention. The **Internet Archive Wayback Machine** provides researchers a series of snapshots of Web pages as they were at various points in the history of the Web. The Student Online Companion page for Tutorial 5 includes hyperlinks to these and several other Web sites that offer electronic texts and archives in the Additional Information section.

Citing Web Research Resources

As you search the Web for research resources, you should collect information about the sites so you can include a proper reference to your sources in any research report you write based on your work. As you collect information, you should record the URL and name of any Web site that you use, either in a word-processor document, as a Navigator bookmark, or as an Internet Explorer favorite. Citation formats are very well-defined for print publications, but formats for electronic resources are still emerging. For academic research, the two most widely followed standards for print citations are those of the **American Psychological Association (APA)** and the **Modern Language Association (MLA)**. Various parties have proposed a number of additions to these two styles, but without reaching a consensus. The APA Style information page for Electronic References appears in Figure 5-18.

Figure 5-18	APA ELECTRONIC REFERENCES STYLE PAGE

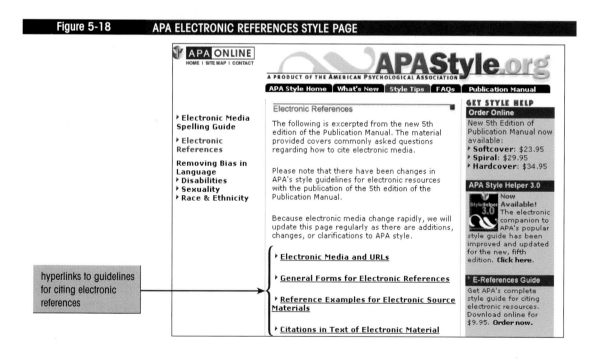

hyperlinks to guidelines for citing electronic references

One of the problems that both standards face is the difficulty of typesetting long URLs in print documents. No clear standards that specify where or how to break long URLs at the end of a print line have emerged. Another typesetting problem is how to distinguish between punctuation that is included in the URL and punctuation that is part of the sentence in which the URL appears. One solution used by some publishers is to enclose the URL with chevron symbols (< >); however, this solution is not generally accepted. The Additional Information section of the Student Online Companion page for Tutorial 5 includes hyperlinks to several citation style and formatting resources on the Web. You can check these Web pages periodically for updates to these changing standards. You also can request specific guidance from your instructor, if your research report is for a course requirement, or from the editor of the publication to which you plan to submit your work.

Any method of citing Web pages faces one serious, yet-unsolved problem—moving and disappearing URLs. The Web is a dynamic medium that changes constantly. The citation systems that academics and librarians use for published books and journals work well because the printed page has a physical existence. A Web page exists only in an HTML document on a Web server computer. If that file's name or location changes, or the Web server is disconnected from the Internet, the page is no longer accessible. Perhaps future innovations in Internet addressing technologies will solve this problem. You thank Susan for providing you with so much information about evaluating and citing Web information resources.

Multimedia **Resources**

Marti would like to create Web pages for each musical artist that the agency represents. Many of the bands have their own Web pages, but Marti would like to have a page for each band on the Cosby Promotions Web site with a standard set of information (that could include a link to the band's own Web page). She would like you to undertake a long-term assignment for her by paying close attention to the multimedia elements of the Web pages you view as you undertake searches for the agency's staff members. She asks you to note any particularly effective uses of Web page design elements and forward any relevant URLs to her. So that you will understand how these elements work and be better able to gather this information for him, Marti has asked Susan to give you a tour of multimedia elements in Web pages. The first issue Susan wants to discuss with you is how copyright law governs the use of these elements.

Copyright Violation and Plagiarism

Susan explains that when you use your Web browser to see a graphic image, listen to a sound, or view a video clip, your Web browser downloads the multimedia element from the Web server and stores it in a temporary file on your computer's hard drive. This process creates a new, intermediate level of ownership that did not exist before the emergence of the Web. For example, when you go to an art gallery and view a picture, you do not take possession of the picture in any way; in fact, if you went around touching all of the pictures in the gallery, a security guard would probably ask you to leave. When you visit an online art gallery, however, your Web browser takes temporary possession of a copy of the file containing the image. As you have learned in earlier tutorials, it is easy to make a permanent copy of Web page images—even though your copy might violate the image owner's rights.

Making a photocopy of a picture that appears in a book can be a copyright violation. Because computer files are even easier to copy than a picture in a book, the potential for Web copyright violations is much greater. Some Web site owners disclaim liability by storing only hyperlinks to other Web pages that contain copyright-violating multimedia elements; whether this is an effective shield against liability is not clear.

In most cases, scanning a copy of a popular cartoon from a newspaper or magazine and placing it on a Web page is a violation of the owner's copyright. Some cartoonists regularly search the Web, looking for unauthorized copies of their work. They threaten or take legal action when they find Web sites that appear to violate their copyrights.

Some uses of multimedia elements do not present a copyright violation. For example, some sites provide graphics files that are in the **public domain**, which means that you are free to copy the files without requesting permission from the source. Even though you can freely use public domain information, you should check the site carefully for requirements about if and how you acknowledge the source of the material when it is used. Acknowledging a source can be especially important when you use public domain material in papers, reports, or other school projects. Failure to cite the source of material that you use (even though it is in the public domain and not protected by copyright) is called **plagiarism** and can be a serious violation of your school's academic honesty policy.

Other sites offer some files free as samples and offer other files for sale. The free files often carry a restriction against selling or redistributing them, even though you may be able to use them without cost on your own personal Web page. You must carefully examine any site from which you download multimedia files to determine what usage limitations apply. If you cannot find a clear statement of copyright terms or a statement that the files are in the public domain, you should not use them on your Web page or anywhere else.

Images and Graphics

The Student Online Companion page for Session 5.1 contains several hyperlinks to Web pages that offer photographs and images. Some of these sites permit downloading of at least some of the files for personal or commercial use.

Most images on the Web are in one of two file formats, GIF and JPEG. **GIF**, an acronym for **Graphics Interchange Format**, is an older format that does a very good job of compressing small- or medium-sized files. Most GIF files you find on the Web have a .gif extension. This file format can store only up to 256 different colors. The GIF format is widely used on the Internet for images that have only a few distinct colors, such as line drawings, cartoons, simple icons, and screen objects. Some of the more interesting screen objects on the Web are animated GIF files. An **animated GIF file** combines several images into a single GIF file. When a Web browser that recognizes the animated GIF file type loads this type of file, it cycles through the images in the file and gives the appearance of cartoon-like animation. The size and color-depth limitations of the GIF file format prevent animated GIFs from delivering high-quality video, however. **JPEG**, an acronym for **Joint Photographic Experts Group**, is a newer file format that stores many more colors than the GIF format—over 16 million more, in fact—and more colors yields a higher-quality image. The JPEG format is particularly useful for photographs and continuous-tone art; that is, images that do not have sharp edges. Most JPEG files that you find on the Web usually have a .jpg file extension.

Both of these formats offer file compression, which is important on the Web. Uncompressed graphics files containing images of significant size or complexity are too large to transmit efficiently. JPEG file compression is "lossy." Any **lossy compression** procedure erases some elements of the graphic so that when it is displayed, it will not resemble the original image. The greater the level of compression, the more graphic detail is lost.

Graphic images on the Web also use many other file formats—including Windows bitmap file format (.bmp), Tagged Image File Format (or TIFF) format (.tif), PC Paintbrush format (.pcx), and the new Portable Network Graphics (or PNG) format (.png)—but most images you encounter will be in either the JPEG or GIF formats. The Windows bitmap, TIFF, and PC Paintbrush formats are all uncompressed graphics formats. Web page designers usually avoid these formats because a Web browser takes too long to download them. The PNG format is a new format that the World Wide Web Consortium has approved as a standard. Although its promoters hope that it will become the prevailing Web standard, it is not yet widely used.

One of the best Web resources for the fine arts is the **WebMuseum** site, which occasionally features special exhibitions. The WebMuseum's mainstay is its Famous Paintings collection, which includes images of artwork from around the world. Susan wants you to see the museum's portrait of Vincent van Gogh so you can gain experience using and searching for graphics files at a museum Web site.

REFERENCE   WINDOW

Viewing an Image in an Online Museum
- Open the online museum Web page in your Web browser.
- Follow the directory's hyperlinks or use the site's search engine to find the artist or work in which you are interested.
- Art works are often presented as small images called thumbnails that you can click to open a larger version of the image.

To view Vincent van Gogh's self-portraits at the WebMuseum site:

1. Return to the Student Online Companion Web page for Session 5.2, and then click the **WebMuseum** hyperlink and wait while your Web browser loads the Web page.

2. Scroll down the WebMuseum main page to the General Exhibitions section, and then click the **Famous Paintings** collections hyperlink.

3. Click the **Artist Index** hyperlink.

4. Scroll down the list of artists to find the **Gogh, Vincent van** hyperlink, and then click it.

5. Click the **Self-Portraits** hyperlink to open the page shown in Figure 5-19.

Figure 5-19	WEBMUSEUM WEB PAGE

narrative

click thumbnail image
to see a larger image

information about the
picture

This page, devoted to van Gogh's self-portraits, includes a narrative about
these works; the title, date created, file size, media, size of the original; and
information about the work's owner (if it is a public institution). You can click
any of the small (or thumbnail) images to view a larger version of the image.

6. Close your Web browser, and if necessary, log off your Internet connection.

Finding image files on the Web can be difficult because the robots that gather information for search engines do not read graphics files to identify their attributes. A search
engine, therefore, cannot find all images that contain a particular shade of green, for example. Search engines rely on HTML image tags that Web page builders include in their
HTML documents that contain terms that describe the image. One Web site that can help
you find clip-art images is the **Clip Art Searcher**, shown in Figure 5-20. The Student
Online Companion page for Tutorial 5 contains a link to the Clip Art Searcher Web site in
the Additional Information section under the heading "Photographs and Images."

Figure 5-20   SEARCHING FOR CLIP ART

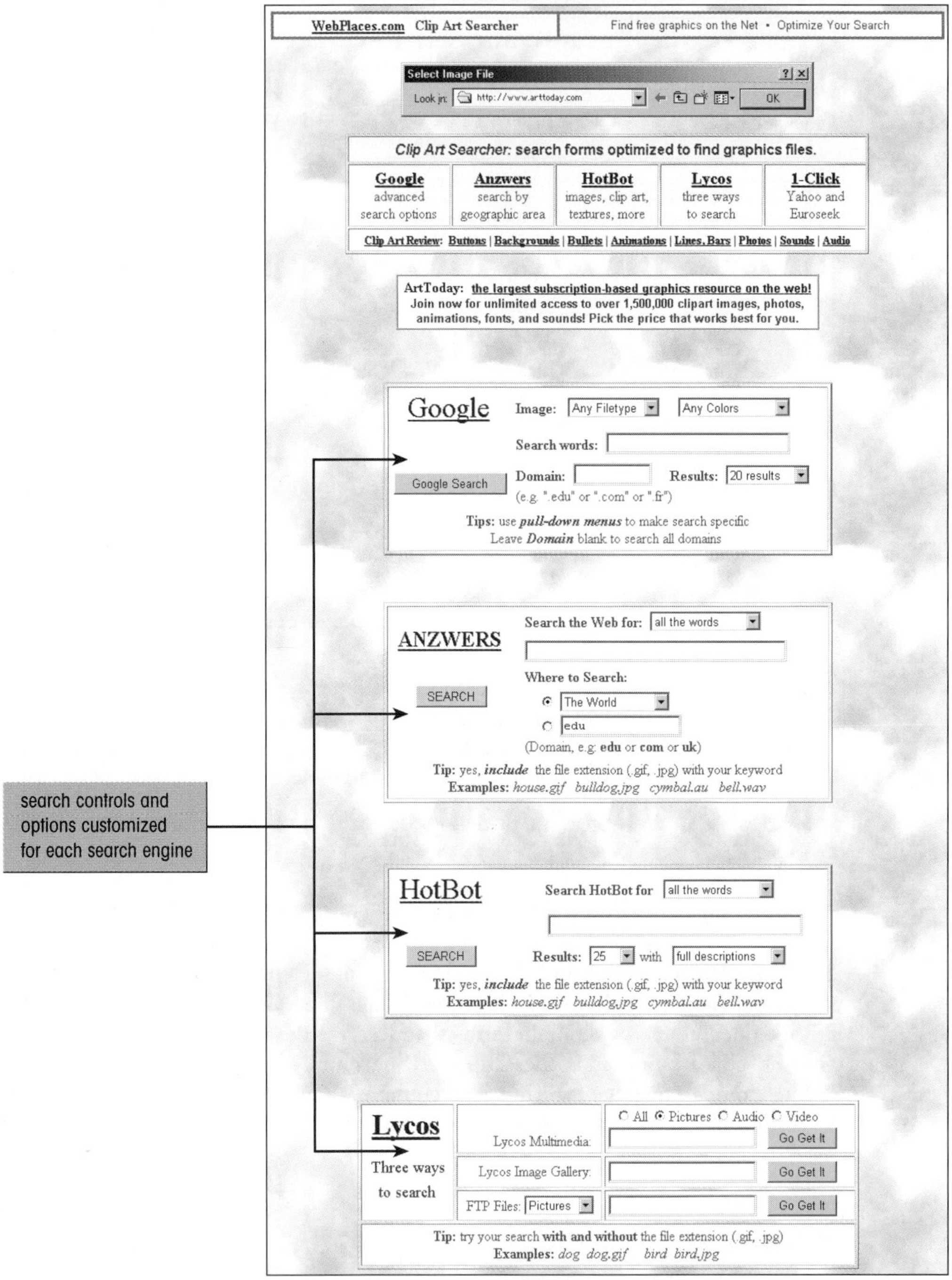

The Clip Art Searcher Web page is not a search engine, but it includes customized search controls for six search engines and directories. These search controls are optimized for each search engine or directory to help you locate the specific types of graphics files you want to find.

Sounds, Music, and Video Clips

The animated GIF format has only a limited ability to present moving graphics and cannot store audio information along with the video animation. Many Web site designers include sound or video clips to enhance the information on their pages. Unlike graphics files, sound and video files appear on the Web in many different formats and often require that you add software extensions to your Web browser. These software extensions, or **plug-ins**, are usually available as free downloads. The firms that offer media players as free downloads earn their profits by selling encoding software to developers who want to include audio and video files in that format on their Web sites. Each firm that creates a format has an incentive to promote its use, so no clear standards for using audio or video files on the Web have emerged. Another difficulty that you might encounter when playing audio files is that your computer must be equipped with a sound card and either a speaker or earphones. The computers in your school's lab or in your employer's offices might not have a sound card installed; if that's the case, you will not be able to listen to sounds.

One widely used audio file format is the **Wave** format, which was jointly developed by Microsoft and IBM. **Wave (WAV)** files digitize audio waveform information at a user-specified sampling rate and play on any Windows computer that supports sound. WAV files that are recorded at a high sampling rate (the higher the sampling rate, the higher the sound quality) can be very large. A WAV file that stores one minute of CD-quality sound can be over 1 megabyte in size. The size of WAV files limits their use on the Web to situations that require only short, lower-quality audio information. You can recognize a WAV file on the Web by its .wav file extension.

Another commonly used Web file format is the MIDI format. The **MIDI (Musical Instrument Digital Interface)** format is a standard adopted by the music industry for controlling devices that create and read musical information. The MIDI format does not digitize the sound waveform. Instead, it digitally records information about each element of the sound, including its pitch, length, and volume. Most keyboard synthesizers use MIDI so that music recorded on one synthesizer can be played on other synthesizers or on computers that have a MIDI interface. It is much easier to edit music recorded in the MIDI format than music recorded in the WAV format because you can manipulate the individual characteristics of the sound with precision. MIDI files are much smaller than WAV files and are, therefore, often used on the Web. Usually, MIDI files have either a .midi or .mid file extension.

Because the Web originated mostly on computers running the UNIX operating system, that system's audio file format still appears on the Web. Both Navigator and Internet Explorer can read this format, which is known as the AU format because its file extension is normally .au. These files are approximately the same size as WAV files that store the same information.

A very popular technique for transferring both sound and video files on the Web is called streaming transmission. In a **streaming transmission**, the Web server sends the first part of the file to the Web browser, which begins playing the file. While the browser is playing the file, the server is sending the next segment of the file. Streaming transmission allows you to access very large audio or video files in much less time than the download-then-play procedure requires because you start playing the file before you finish downloading. RealNetworks, Inc. has pioneered this technology and developed the RealAudio format for audio files and the RealVideo format for video files. To play these files, which you can recognize by their .ra or .ram file extensions, you must download and install one of the Real file players from the firm's Web site. The RealNetworks formats are compressed to increase further the efficiency with which they can be transferred over the Internet. For example, you can compress a 1-megabyte WAV file into a 30-kilobyte RealAudio file.

Video files are also available in older formats on the Web. Windows computers are able to play Microsoft's **AVI (Audio Video Interleaved)** format files and, with the proper software downloaded and installed, also can play Apple's **QuickTime** format files. One minute of video and sound recorded in either of these formats results in a file that is about 6 megabytes, which is a very large file to transmit over slower types of Internet connections. Because of the larger file sizes, development of better ways to transmit video files over the Internet continues. The International Standards Organization's **Moving Picture Experts Group (MPEG)** has created a series of standards for compressed file formats. As in JPEG graphic files, this compression technique deletes information from the file and can deteriorate quality.

The audio portion of the MPEG file format was responsible for one of the greatest revolutions in online music that has occurred in the history of the Web. The MPEG format's audio track, called **MPEG Audio Layer 3 (MP3)** became wildly popular just as disk storage on personal computers dropped in price and CD writers (also called CD burners) became affordable for home use. Files in the MP3 format are lower in quality than WAV format files, but they are 90 percent smaller. Thus, a CD that might hold 15 popular songs in high quality WAV format (about 40 megabytes per song) could hold 150 popular songs in MP3 format (about four megabytes per song).

Their smaller size made MP3 files easy to send from one person to another through the Internet. File sharing software, such as Napster, became very popular. Companies in the recording industry and the recording artists themselves were not very happy. People could now copy music from CDs that they had purchased and convert that music into MP3 files to exchange with others on the Internet. Recording companies and artists filed suits against Napster and other file-sharing sponsors for violating copyright laws and were generally successful in obtaining court orders or out-of-court settlements that are preventing further copyright violations in many cases. Many individuals, however, still violate the law and share MP3 files that contain copyrighted works.

Sites such as **MP3.com** do offer free downloads of music in MP3 format. The music that is available on such sites is recorded by new or relatively unknown bands (in most cases) and made available to promote the live tours or other recordings of those bands. Many of Cosby Promotions' client bands and musical artists have released MP3 recordings and make them available on their own Web sites and on sites such as MP3.com. The MP3.com Web site appears in Figure 5-21.

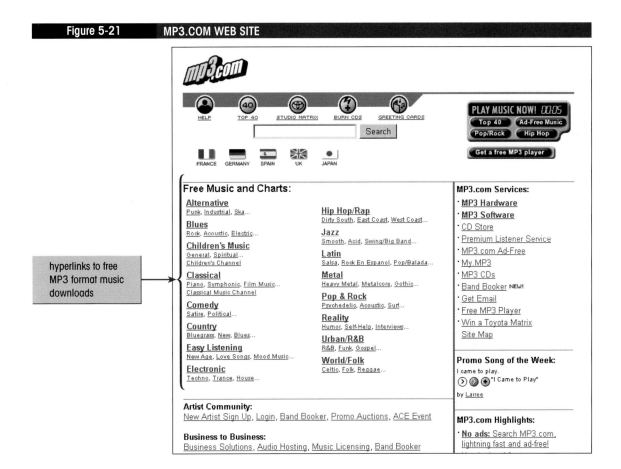

Figure 5-21   **MP3.COM WEB SITE**

hyperlinks to free MP3 format music downloads

Future of Electronic Publishing

One of the key changes that the Internet and the Web have brought to the world is that information can now be disseminated more rapidly than ever in large quantities with a low required investment. The impact of this change is that firms in the public relations business—firms that spend great amounts of time and money trying to present their clients through the major media in the best possible light—might be facing a significantly changed business environment. Many industry analysts believe that the ease of publishing electronically on the Web might help reduce the concentration of media control that has been developing over the past three decades as newspapers merged with each other and, along with radio and television stations, were purchased by large media companies.

To be successful in print media publishing—such as a monthly magazine—a publisher must have a large subscription market. The fixed costs of composing and creating the magazine are spread over enough units so that the publisher can earn a profit. The costs of publishing a Web page are very low compared to printing magazines or newspapers. Therefore, the subscription market required for a Web publication to be successful can be very small or even nonexistent. If a Web-based magazine, or an **e-zine**, can attract advertisers, it can be financially successful with no subscribers and a small number of readers. As a result, e-zines are appearing on the Web in increasing numbers. An e-zine does not require a large readership to be successful, so these electronic publications can focus on very specialized, narrow interests. E-zines have become popular places for publishing new fiction and poetry, for example. The Additional Information section of the Student Online Companion page for Tutorial 5 includes hyperlinks to several e-zine Web sites that you might want to explore.

Session 5.2 QUICK CHECK

1. Explain why it is important to determine a Web page author's identity and credentials when you plan to use the page's information as a research resource.

2. What information about Web page authors can help you assess their objectivity with respect to the contents of their Web pages?

3. True or False: Domain names in URLs can help you assess the quality of Web pages.

4. How can you assess the quality of a Web page that deals with a subject area in which you are not very knowledgeable?

5. Briefly describe two ways that libraries use the Web.

6. What are the advantages of using online reference works such as dictionaries or encyclopedias instead of print editions?

7. True or False: Music stored in a WAV file format would be of lower quality and would result in a smaller file than the same music stored in an MP3 formatted file.

When you need to use the Web to find information for your classes or your job, remember to return to the Additional Information section of the Student Online Companion page for Tutorial 5 for a comprehensive list of Web information resources.

REVIEW ASSIGNMENTS

Marti is preparing to visit a new techno band that she would like to sign in Chicago, Illinois. While in Chicago, she would like to visit a number of clubs that feature blues artists.

Do the following:

1. Start your Web browser, go to the Student Online Companion (http://www.course.com/newperspectives/internet3), click the link for your book, click the Tutorial 5 link, and then click the Review Assignments link.

2. Obtain weather forecasts for the Chicago area from the Weather Channel and CNN Weather. Print the forecasts from each site.

3. The band is renting practice space in a warehouse near the corner of West 35th Street and South Morgan Street on the South side of Chicago. Print two maps from the MapQuest site: one street-level map and one higher-level map that shows the surrounding area in Chicago.

4. Use the Trip.com site's Destination Guides to locate information about restaurants in the Chicago area. Prepare a report that lists three restaurants that would be good choices for Marti to entertain clients while in Chicago.

5. Use the Trip.com site's Destination Guides to locate at least two blues clubs that Marti can visit while she is in Chicago.

6. When you are finished, close your Web browser and if necessary, log off your Internet connection.

CASE PROBLEMS

Case 1. Portland Concrete Mixers, Inc. You are a sales representative for Portland Concrete Mixers, Inc., a company that makes replacement parts for concrete mixing equipment. This equipment is mounted on trucks that deliver ready-mixed concrete to buildings and other job sites. You have been transferred to the Seattle area and would like to plan your first sales trip there. Because you plan to drive to Seattle, you need information about the best route as well as a map of Seattle. You hope to generate some new customers on this trip and, therefore, need to identify sales-lead prospects in the Seattle area. Companies that manufacture concrete are good prospects for you.

Do the following:

1. Start your Web browser, go to the Student Online Companion (http://www.course.com/newperspectives/internet3), click the link for your book, click the Tutorial 5 link, and then click the Case Problems link.

2. Click the MapQuest hyperlink to open the MapQuest Web page.

3. Click the Driving Directions hyperlink to obtain driving directions. Your starting address is Portland, OR, and your destination address is Seattle, WA. Type these city and state names in the appropriate boxes.

4. Click the GET DIRECTIONS button. Print the new Web page that opens.

5. Click the first map on the Web page to zoom in and obtain a more detailed route from Portland to Seattle, and then print it.

6. To obtain a map of Seattle, click the Re-center option button below the map image, and then click Seattle on the map. You can click the plus and minus sign icons in the Map Level settings area to adjust the map to the level of detail you desire.

7. To identify sales leads in Seattle, return to the Student Online Companion and then click the YP.Net hyperlink. Type concrete in the Keywords box, and then click the SEARCH button. Click the View by Business Location button, and then click the link to Washington(WA). On the page that opens, click the link to SEATTLE-BELLE-VUE-EVERETT. On the page that opens, click the link to SEATTLE.

8. The results page contains contact information for a number of companies in the concrete business in Seattle. Copy the names and addresses of at least three sales prospects to a document that you will carry with you on your trip.

9. When you are finished, close your Web browser and, if necessary, log off your Internet connection.

Case 2. Ragtime Tonight You are the owner of a popular nightclub, Ragtime Tonight, near the convention center. Although you have a good local following with the nightclub's program of stand-up comedy and ragtime piano music, many of your patrons are visitors to the city who stay in hotels near the convention center. You realize that an increasing number of these travelers are making airline, hotel, and car-rental reservations using the Web, and you would like to create a Web site that could help you reach these customers. As you are designing the site, you decide that you would like to add some ragtime audio clips that play when the site is opened using a Web browser. You have heard that single musical instruments, particularly pianos, sound realistic when synthesized in the MIDI format and you would, therefore, like to find some ragtime pieces in that format. Of course, you are willing to locate the composer and performer of any MIDI file you use and obtain the necessary permissions before adding the sound clip to your Web page.

Do the following:

1. Start your Web browser, go to the Student Online Companion (http://www.course.com/newperspectives/internet3), click the link for your book, click the Tutorial 5 link, and then click the Case Problems link.

2. Click one or more of the MIDI music links provided for this Case Problem.

3. Evaluate the files offered on these Web pages or the pages to which they lead. Write a short report summarizing your experience. In your report, describe what copyright restrictions are described on the Web site that offers the file or files that you would like to use.

4. When you are finished, close your Web browser and, if necessary, log off your Internet connection.

Case 3. Toddle Inn owns and operates a chain of day-care centers in several Midwestern states from its headquarters in Minneapolis, Minnesota. The directors are interested in undertaking a national expansion program that will require outside financing and an effective public relations program that integrates with their strategic marketing plans. You are an intern in the office of Joan Caruso, a public relations consultant that does work for Toddle Inn. Joan has asked you to help her with some background research as she creates a proposal for the Toddle Inn board of directors next meeting that integrates a Web site into their public relations program.

Do the following:

1. Start your Web browser, go to the Student Online Companion (http://www.course.com/newperspectives/internet3), click the link for your book, click the Tutorial 5 link, and then click the Case Problems link.

2. Use the NewsHub and Northern Light news search engines to find at least three current (within the past three months) news reports about the child-care industry. Write a memo to Joan that summarizes the major issues identified in these reports.

3. Joan would like you to conduct an evaluation of the Child Care Parent/Provider Information Network Web site. Prepare an evaluation of that site that considers the author's or publisher's identity and objectivity, and the site's content, form, and appearance.

4. One of the things that any public relations campaign must consider is the impact of pending legislation. Joan asks you to see if there are any bills pending in the U.S. Congress that will affect the child-care industry. Use the link on the Student Online Companion to open the Thomas legislative information Web site, type "child care" (without quotation marks) in the By Word/Phrase text box and then click the Search button. Read one of the bills listed and prepare a one-paragraph summary for Joan of the bill's likely effects on the child-care industry.

5. When you are finished, close your Web browser and if necessary, log off your Internet connection.

Case 4. Arnaud for Senate Campaign You work for the campaign team of Lisa Arnaud, who is running for a seat in the state senate. One issue that promises to play a prominent role in the upcoming election campaign is her opponent's position on privatization of the state prison system. It is important for Lisa to establish a clear position on the issue early in the campaign, and she has asked you to prepare a briefing document for her to consider. Lisa tells you that she has no particular preference on the issue and that she wants you to obtain a balanced set of arguments for each side. Once the campaign takes a position, however, she will need to defend it. Therefore, Lisa wants to have an idea of the quality of the information you gather. You decide to do part of your research on the Web.

Do the following:

1. Start your Web browser, go to the Student Online Companion (http://www.course.com/newperspectives/internet3), click the link for your book, click the Tutorial 5 link, and then click the Case Problems link.

2. Click the AltaVista hyperlink to open that search engine.

3. Type the words "privatization prisons" (without the quotation marks) in the Search for text box, and then click the Search button.

4. Examine your list of search results for authoritative sites that include positions on the issue. You might need to follow a number of results page hyperlinks to find suitable Web pages. In general, you should avoid current news items that appear in the results list.

5. Find one Web page that states a clear position in favor of privatization and another that states a clear position against privatization. Print a copy of each.

6. For each page, prepare a three-paragraph report that evaluates the quality of the page on each of the three criteria: author identity and objectivity, content, and form and appearance.

7. When you are finished, close your Web browser and, if necessary, log off your Internet connection.

Case 5. Dalton Precision Castings You are the office manager for Dalton Precision Castings, a company that makes metal parts for packaging machinery and sells them throughout the world. Two of Dalton's major customers, one from Portugal and one from Italy, are arriving next week for a briefing on new technologies and products. Tom Dalton, the company's president, has asked you to help make these visitors feel welcome. He would like to have a local artist create replicas of the Portuguese and Italian flags as gifts for the visitors. He would like you to find images of the flags from which the artist can create the replicas. You decide to do your research on the Web.

Do the following:

1. Start your Web browser, go to the Student Online Companion (http://www.course.com/newperspectives/internet3), click the link for your book, click the Tutorial 5 link, and then click the Case Problems link.

2. Click the Clip Art Searcher hyperlink to open that Web site.

3. Type the word "flag" (without the quotation marks) in the search text box for the first search engine that appears on the Clip Art Searcher page.

4. Examine your list of search results for sites that might include images of the Portuguese or Italian flags. You might need to follow a number of results page hyperlinks to find suitable Web pages.

5. If you do not find any suitable pages, repeat your search using the search terms "flag Portugal" and "flag Italy" (again, type the terms without the quotation marks). You can also try your search in the Clip Art Searcher search controls for the other search engines on its Web page.

6. When you find a Web page or pages that offer suitable images, examine the Web site to determine what copyright or other restrictions exist regarding your use of the images.

7. Prepare a one-paragraph report for each flag that describes the source you plan to use. Include the URL of the site where you found the flag image and a summary of the restrictions on Dalton's use of that image. If the Web site does not include any description of restrictions, refer to the text and state your opinion regarding what restrictions might exist on Dalton's use of the image.

8. Close your Web browser and, if necessary, log off your Internet connection.

Quick | Check answers

Session 5.1

1. a major wire service (or press agency or news service) based in Great Britain
2. False. NewsHub updates its stories every 15 minutes.
3. Different meteorologists often predict different weather conditions for the same location; gathering several forecasts provides a range of likely weather conditions.
4. You can change the map's scale, and you can e-mail the map or save it to your PDA.
5. any three of: recommendations and reviews of restaurants, entertainment (or nightlife), sports, shopping, landmarks, and other visitor information
6. False
7. yellow pages site
8. white pages site

Session 5.2

1. Author identity and credentials help establish the credibility of Web page content.
2. their employment or other professional affiliations
3. True
4. timeliness, inclusion of relevant topics, depth of treatment
5. by adding online resources to their collections and by making their collections accessible to remote users and other libraries
6. available 24 hours a day, seven days a week; can be easier and faster to search
7. False

OBJECTIVES

In this tutorial you will:

- Learn what FTP is and how it works

- Learn how to compress and decompress files and to check them for viruses

- Navigate an FTP site using a Web browser

- Download an FTP client program using a Web browser

- Download programs using an FTP client program

- Trace the connection between your computer and a remote computer

- Explore file-based storage options on the Internet

- Use Yahoo! Briefcase to upload and download a file

- Examine the future of subscription software models

FTP
AND DOWNLOADING
AND STORING DATA

Using FTP and Other Services to Transfer and Store Data

CASE

Sound Effects, Inc.

One of the things that Milt Spangler enjoys most about being a musician is being able to manipulate music electronically to create customized sounds. After graduating from the University of Southern California with a degree in business administration, Milt started Sound Effects, Inc., a company that produces sounds and voiceovers for local advertising agencies and other businesses that use digitally produced and created sounds. Soon Milt's business sufficiently expanded so that he could rent a warehouse with a built-in sound studio. As part of the expansion, Milt hired professional actors to do voiceover work and other speaking roles, such as recording characters' voices in CD-ROM games and educational programs for children. Milt soon began receiving contracts from out-of-state businesses, educational software manufacturers, and advertising agencies as his work became nationally recognized. As a result of his success, he needed to expand his pool of actor talent beyond the Los Angeles area.

Sound Effects operates with only a few permanent employees in the Los Angeles area, but many of the actors who provide voiceover work live elsewhere in the United States and in all provinces of Canada. These actors record their material for Milt in studios near their homes. Because their work is produced digitally, Milt needs a way to transfer files from studios in the actors' hometowns to the Los Angeles office, where the files can be edited and finalized for clients. The large file sizes of digitally produced files and the high cost of sending files prohibit Milt from relying on e-mail attachments and overnight delivery services as options for transporting files. He asks you to help him find new ways to send large files using another method.

SESSION 6.1

In this session, you will learn how to use FTP to transmit files between your computer and a computer connected to the Internet. You will learn about the different types of FTP access and the different methods by which you can access an FTP site. You will use a Web browser to navigate an FTP site. Finally, you will learn about file transfer modes, file types and extensions, decompressing files, and checking files for viruses.

Using File Transfer Protocol

You already know that you can use e-mail attachments to send files over the Internet. E-mail is often a good way of transporting a file from one location to another, or even to yourself. For example, if you're in the university computer lab working on a report and forget to bring your disk, you can attach the report to an e-mail message to yourself; when you get home and download your e-mail messages the file arrives on your home computer. This method works for sending files to other people as well. However, many e-mail servers limit the size of files you attach to a single e-mail message. E-mail servers might also limit the types of files you can send. For example, some servers will not accept file attachments that can execute programs for fear that these types of attachments could damage the e-mail server.

To address storage issues and issues related to transmitting large files from one location to another, you can use FTP. **FTP**, or **File Transfer Protocol**, is one of several services built into and supported by the Internet suite of protocols. You can think of FTP as a means of accessing a hard drive to which you connect via the Internet. In some cases, you only can read (view) the files; in other cases you can read and write (edit) the files. FTP is the protocol that transfers files from one computer that is connected to the Internet to another computer that is connected to the Internet. The site to which you are sending files and from which you are receiving files is usually called an **FTP site** or a **remote computer**; when you use your computer to connect to an FTP site it is called the **local computer**. When a file is transferred over the Internet—whether you are viewing it with a Web browser or not—FTP is responsible for sending the file between computers. You can send any file type to an FTP site, including spreadsheet, picture, video, MP3, program, and text files.

When you send a file using FTP, you **upload** a file to send it from your computer to the FTP site. When you receive a file, you **download** the file from an FTP site and send it to your computer. Downloading is more common because people usually receive more files than they send. Whether files are uploaded or downloaded, FTP is the protocol that accomplishes the transfer. FTP can run from a Web browser, with an FTP client program, or through a command-line interface. A **command-line interface** is one in which you enter a command and press the Enter key; the receiving computer then acts on the command you sent. This process continues until you have typed enough single-line commands to complete a task. An **FTP client program** is a Windows program that resides on your PC and transfers files between your computer and an FTP site connected to the Internet. Like other Windows programs, most FTP client programs have menu bars and toolbars with buttons to help you execute commands. Figure 6-1 shows a popular FTP client program, WS_FTP LE, which is communicating with a remote computer.

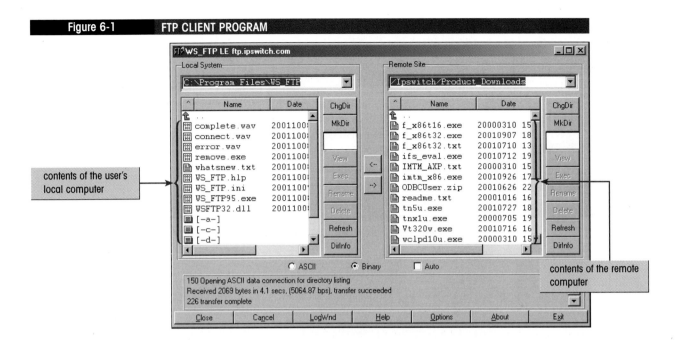

Figure 6-1   FTP CLIENT PROGRAM

FTP programs that you execute using a command-line interface are more difficult to use because you have to know the commands, such as *get*, *put*, *cd*, and others, to transfer files. The **Telnet Client** is a Windows program that uses the Telnet protocol and a command-line interface to access a remote computer. To start Telnet, click the Start button on the Windows taskbar, click Run, type Telnet in the Open text box of the Run dialog box, and then click the OK button. Then you can type the commands to request and transfer files between the local and remote computers.

Like other Internet protocols, FTP follows the standard client/server model. When you want to download or upload a file, you connect to a remote computer and request that the FTP site either receive files from your computer or transfer files from the remote computer to your computer. An **FTP server program** receives file transfer requests and then acts on those commands. The FTP server program manages the details of transferring files between your computer and the FTP site. FTP is operating system neutral. For example, your PC might use FTP and Windows XP to communicate with a large minicomputer running the FTP server on a UNIX operating system. It makes no difference that the operating systems are different on each computer; FTP seamlessly transfers files between the computers. Web browsers support FTP and provide a simple and familiar interface for you to locate and download files. In this tutorial, you will learn how to transfer files using an FTP client program and a Web browser.

Accessing an FTP Server

To transfer files between your PC and a remote computer, you must first connect to the remote computer. You can can connect to a remote computer by logging on to it using your Web browser or an FTP client program. Microsoft Internet Explorer and Netscape Navigator both recognize the FTP protocol. To use a remote computer, you must identify yourself, or **log on**, by supplying your user name and a password. Some computer systems provide public access to their computers, which means anyone can connect to the FTP site. When you connect to a public FTP site, your access is restricted to only those files and folders designated for access by public users. Other systems allow restricted access to their computers. To access these computers, you must have an account on the computer.

Anonymous FTP

Logging on to one of the many publicly accessible, remote computers connected to the Internet is known as an **anonymous login** because you type *anonymous* as your user name. You do not need a password to access a public computer. However, it is both customary and polite to enter your full e-mail address when you are prompted for your password. That way, the hosting organization can identify which groups are accessing the public areas of its computer. When you download or upload files using an anonymous login, you are participating in an **anonymous FTP session**. Figure 6-2 shows an example of an anonymous login using a command-line interface.

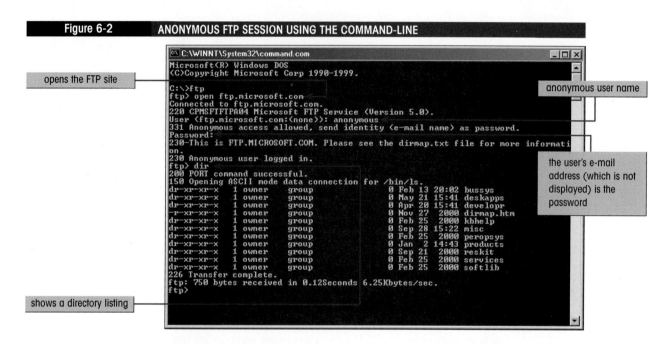

Figure 6-2   ANONYMOUS FTP SESSION USING THE COMMAND-LINE

You can use many of the anonymous FTP computers connected to the Internet to download files to your PC. In most cases, public FTP sites impose limits on uploading files or provide only one publicly accessible directory to which you can upload files. Public FTP sites also limit your access to selected directories and files on their systems. People using FTP sites with anonymous logins cannot open and view all the directories and files on the site. You can determine which directories you can access by experimenting. If you attempt to open directories or examine files that are not accessible to anonymous users, you will receive an error or warning message indicating that you do not have access to the requested file or directory. Experimenting with your access is allowable, but you should obey all rules and regulations regarding anonymous access. Remember that you are using another person's or organization's computer at no cost to download files for your use.

When you connect to a public FTP site using a Web browser, the browser automatically supplies the user name *anonymous* and an appropriate password to access the site and handles all FTP communications with the site. If the site requires you to enter a user name and password, the browser will prompt you for these items. Figure 6-3 shows a browser with a connection to the Netscape FTP site. Notice that the protocol in the site's URL is ftp:// instead of http:// and that the site's URL indicates an FTP site (ftp) instead of a Web site (www).

Figure 6-3	ANONYMOUS FTP SESSION USING A WEB BROWSER

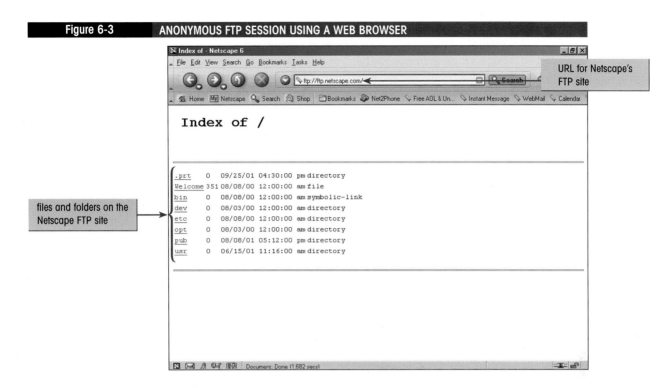

Students and other users frequently use FTP to upload group projects to university or other publicly accessible sites so each member of the group can access the project files. Most files must be placed in the public directory, and they often have a maximum life span of a few days or weeks. The site's manager determines how long files can remain in the public directory. Usually, the file-deletion schedule and other policy statements are stored in the readme.txt file in the public directory. If you find a file by that or a similar name, be sure to read it carefully.

Full-Privilege FTP

When you need to access an FTP site that is not public, such as one for your school or employer, you will use **full-privilege FTP**, or **named FTP**, where you have been given full access to its content with a user name and password. Even though you might have an account on a particular FTP site, your access might be limited to transferring files in a specific directory. When you log on to a computer with your user name and password, the system automatically directs you to a particular directory on that computer in which you have full read and write access rights. When you have an account on a computer that is connected to the Internet, you can usually store larger files for longer periods than you can on a public FTP site.

FTP **Programs**

The choice of FTP program depends on your situation. You can use a command-line FTP program, an FTP client program, or a Web browser to transfer files using FTP.

Command-Line FTP

If you have dial-up access to a computer running the UNIX operating system, then the only choice for transferring files is to use command-line FTP. You use command-line FTP by typing *ftp* at the command prompt and entering a series of one-word commands to establish your FTP session and transfer files. In order to use command-line FTP, you must either have a command-line FTP program installed on your PC (such as the Telnet Client) or access to a host computer that has a command-line FTP program. As you are working, it is important to remember that if you use FTP on a UNIX computer, all commands are case-sensitive; that is, *FTP* and *ftp* are different commands. Figure 6-4 shows some common FTP commands that FTP client programs and browsers issue automatically.

Figure 6-4	COMMON FTP COMMANDS	
COMMAND	**DESCRIPTION**	
binary	Sets the transfer mode to binary	
cd *directory*	Changes the remote directory to *directory*	
close	Disconnects from the current remote computer	
get *filename*	Downloads *filename* from the remote computer	
help	Displays Help on various FTP topics	
lcd *directory*	Changes the current local directory to *directory*	
ls or dir	Displays the current folder's filenames and directory names	
open *remote*	Connects to a remote FTP site on *remote*	
put *filename*	Uploads *filename* to a remote computer	
quit	Exits the FTP program and logs off the remote server	

REFERENCE WINDOW   RW

Downloading a File Using Command-Line FTP

- Start your FTP program and then type *open ftp address* where *ftp address* is the address of the remote FTP site.
- Log in using *anonymous* as the user name and your e-mail address as the password for public access or using your user name and password for full-privilege FTP.
- Navigate to the file you want to download. Type the *cd* and *dir* commands at the command prompt to change directories and list directory contents, respectively.
- Set the transfer mode to binary by typing the *binary* command at the command prompt, and then press the Enter key.
- Download the file by typing the *get* command and the filename you want to download at the command prompt, and then press the Enter key.
- When the download is complete, disconnect from the remote site by typing the *quit* command, and then press the Enter key.

FTP Client Programs and Web Browsers

Both FTP client programs and Web browsers issue FTP commands automatically so you do not need to learn how to issue commands manually as you would when using command-line FTP. You can use either an FTP client program or a Web browser to download files from an FTP site. FTP client programs usually transfer files faster than Web browsers. When you use a Web browser to transfer a file, the browser automatically determines the file's format and transfers the file in that mode. If the browser determines the file's type incorrectly, the file may become corrupted during the transfer, rendering the file unusable. FTP client programs do not make file type determinations, so *you* must determine a file's type and set its transfer properly.

Web browsers and FTP client programs both allow you to download files from FTP sites, but you can't use a Web browser to upload files to an FTP site. If you need to upload files, you'll need to use an FTP client program.

A Web browser lets you open files by clicking or double-clicking folders and files to open them. The browser handles most simple FTP commands easily, but if you use FTP frequently, you might need the power and additional commands found in an FTP client program. Many FTP client programs are either free or inexpensive. FTP client programs allow you to log on anonymously or with a user name and password. FTP client programs provide many features that vary from one program to another. An FTP client program provides the following desirable features, although some FTP client programs support only a few of these features:

- Provides a multipane display so you can see both the local and remote computer directories simultaneously.
- Allows you to transfer many files in one FTP session.
- Permits drag and drop file transfers so you can use the mouse to drag and drop files between the local and remote computers.
- Simplifies the process of deleting directories and files on local and remote computers.
- Displays an interface similar to that found in Windows Explorer for both the local and remote computers.
- Allows you to set up scheduled file transfers at a future date and time so selected files can be transmitted automatically.
- Recovers interrupted file transfers by continuing the transfer process from the point where it was interrupted.
- Reconnects automatically to sites that disconnect your transfer when your connection exceeds the maximum allotted time.

Now that you have reviewed some basic facts about FTP, Milt asks you to show him how to use a Web browser to navigate an FTP site. Because Microsoft frequently stores program updates on its public FTP site, you will show him this site first.

Using a Web Browser to Navigate an FTP Site

Because most Internet users are adept at using a Web browser and know how hyperlinks work, they will have no difficulty navigating an FTP site in search of files. Using FTP is especially easy when you use a Web browser to log on to a public FTP site because the browser automatically supplies the anonymous login. If you need to upload files to a site requiring full-privilege FTP access rights, then you will need to use an FTP client program.

When you visit an FTP site, your first goal should be to become familiar with its organization. FTP sites are organized hierarchically, much like the folders and files on a computer's hard drive. When you access an FTP site, you usually enter at the site's **root directory**, also called the **home directory** or **top-level directory**. The root directory contains other directories that contain files and other directories, as shown in Figure 6-5. Most sites prevent users with anonymous logins from accessing some files and directories in the root directory. When you enter a root directory for the first time, a message might appear indicating which file contains important information about navigating the site.

Figure 6-5 FTP SITE'S HIERARCHICAL STRUCTURE

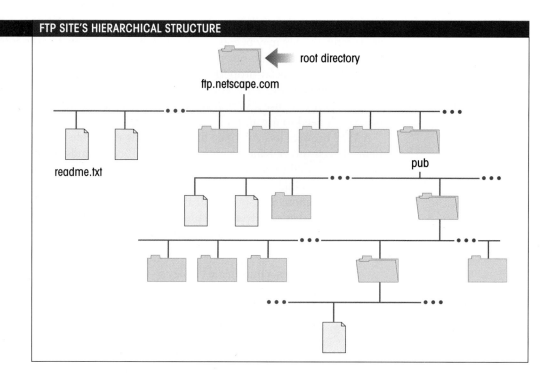

An FTP site usually stores two items—directories (folders) and files—that you either single- or double-click to open. If you use Internet Explorer to access the site, you double-click a directory or file to open it. If you are using Navigator, you will click a link to open a directory or file. Double-clicking a file or clicking a hyperlink to a file either opens the file in a new browser window or a program window so you can view the file or begins downloading it to your computer. Most FTP client programs display directory and file links with different icons or notations so you can distinguish directories from files.

Depending on what software you are using to access an FTP site, you might use a different method for moving up one level in the hierarchy. In Internet Explorer, you click the Up button on the toolbar; in Navigator, you click the set of dots at the top of the page. In both cases, the browser moves up one level and displays that folder's contents. Some FTP client programs display a toolbar button that you can click to move up one level.

Milt asks you to show him how a Web browser opens an FTP site. You'll demonstrate how easy it is to access and navigate an FTP site next.

To open an FTP site using a Web browser:

1. Start your Web browser, open the Student Online Companion page at **www.course.com/newperspectives/internet3**, click the hyperlink for your book, click the **Tutorial 6** link, and then click the **Session 6.1** link. Click the **Microsoft FTP** link and wait while the browser loads the page. Figure 6-6 shows the directories and files in the root directory of Microsoft's FTP site when accessed using Internet Explorer. A yellow folder icon identifies directories; files are identified with a file icon that indicates the file's type. Because the contents of this site change regularly, your screen might look different.

| Figure 6-6 | MICROSOFT'S FTP SITE ROOT DIRECTORY IN INTERNET EXPLORER |

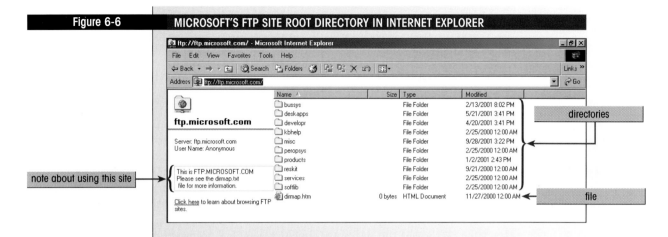

| Figure 6-7 | MICROSOFT'S FTP SITE ROOT DIRECTORY IN NAVIGATOR |

If you are using Navigator, directories and files both appear as hyperlinks. Each hyperlink is identified using the word "directory" or "file," as shown in Figure 6-7, to indicate its contents.

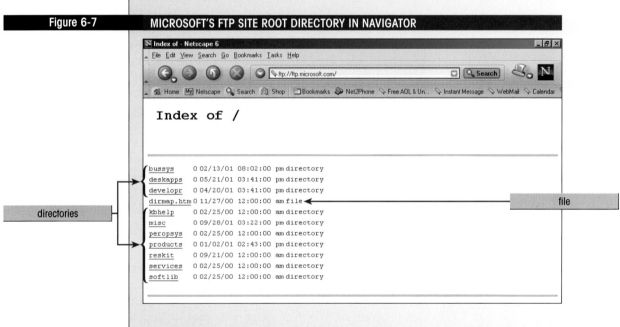

2. Locate the **deskapps** directory. If you are using Internet Explorer, double-click **deskapps** to open it; if you are using Navigator, click **deskapps** to open it. The deskapps directory opens and displays several directories and a file. The new page displays directories with familiar names, such as access, excel, and word.

3. Double-click or click the **readme.txt** file and then read the file that opens and describes the files and directories available in the deskapps directory. Sometimes you might find site information in the readme.txt or about.txt file. You might encounter other names, but they all serve the same function—that is, to provide an overview of the site's structure and file locations.

4. If you are using Internet Explorer, click the **Close** button on the title bar to close the readme.txt file; if you are using Navigator, click the **Back** button on the toolbar. You return to the deskapps directory listing.

5. If you are using Internet Explorer, click the **Up** button to move up one level; if you are using Navigator, click the set of dots (**. .**) at the top of the page. You return to the root directory.

6. Close your browser, and if necessary, log off your Internet connection.

If you get lost in an FTP directory structure, there is a simple way to determine your location and get back to the root directory. The URL in your browser's address field lists all the directories that lead to your current location. As you move deeper down the directory hierarchy, a forward slash (/) separates the individual directory names. To move back toward the root directory, click at the end of the URL, press the Backspace key to delete the right-most (or current) directory name, and then press the Enter key to move up to the previous directory. Figure 6-8 shows a URL indicating that the user is viewing the ie directory, which is a subdirectory of the deskapps directory, which is a directory in the root directory at ftp.microsoft.com. To return to the deskapps directory, you can delete the /ie directory from the URL and then press the Enter key. Using the URL to move up one level is the same as clicking a button or link to move up one level.

Figure 6-8	USING THE URL TO MOVE TO THE ROOT DIRECTORY

Milt now sees that a Web browser easily handles downloading files from an FTP site to a local computer. However, he and his staff frequently will need to upload *and* download files, so he asks you to identify some issues related to using an FTP client program for transferring files.

Downloading **Files Using an FTP Client Program**

You can use FTP to download programs, data files, and software patches (programs that correct known problems in a particular application) from many different sites. Using either an FTP client program or a Web browser is an easy way to locate and download files. With an FTP client program or a Web browser, you click or double-click items to open and download them.

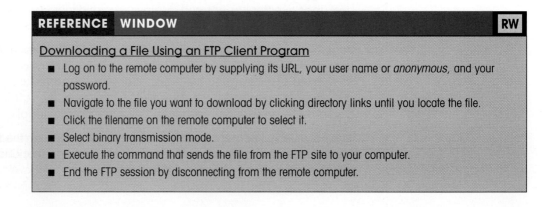

REFERENCE WINDOW   **RW**

Downloading a File Using an FTP Client Program
- Log on to the remote computer by supplying its URL, your user name or *anonymous,* and your password.
- Navigate to the file you want to download by clicking directory links until you locate the file.
- Click the filename on the remote computer to select it.
- Select binary transmission mode.
- Execute the command that sends the file from the FTP site to your computer.
- End the FTP session by disconnecting from the remote computer.

Milt is curious about the transmission modes available for transferring files.

File Transfer Modes

Many files, including Web pages and e-mail messages, consist of ASCII (plain) text. **ASCII text** contains symbols typed from the keyboard but does not include any nonprintable, binary codes. Besides ASCII, many files, such as pictures, movies, sound files, and graphics, are **binary**. Any file created by a word-processing program or a file containing character formatting, such as bold or italics, is binary. FTP can transfer both ASCII and binary files. You select which of the two **file transfer modes**—ASCII or binary—that you want to use before transferring the file. Choose **ASCII mode** to transfer plain-text files; choose **binary mode** for transferring everything else. People usually read plain-text files, whereas computer programs, such as Word or Excel, read binary files. It is important to distinguish between the two types of files, but they are also related. ASCII characters or codes are actually a subset of the larger binary code set. That is, all ASCII characters are also binary characters. The opposite is not true; not all binary representations or codes are ASCII characters. People cannot read many binary codes—only programs can make sense of them. If you download and open a file and it contains a bunch of codes, then you have chosen the wrong transfer mode. Simply execute the FTP operation again using the correct transfer mode.

File Types and Extensions

The decision to transfer a file using binary or ASCII mode is largely determined by noting a file's type, much like Windows programs do. Programs such as Excel, Word, or Internet Explorer determine a file's type by the file extension. A **file extension** is the last three characters following the period in the filename. You can download files with a file extension of .txt in ASCII mode. You should download files with other file extensions in binary mode. It is helpful to understand the relationship between a file's extension and programs that manipulate that file type so you can determine a file's general use and assess your ability to read the file before you download it.

File extensions are added automatically by the program that created them based on a widely agreed-upon convention for associating files with programs. Filenames without periods (called "dots") do not have file extensions. Your PC operating system (Windows, for example) keeps track of most file extension associations and maintains a list of file extensions and programs that can open files with those extensions. Each computer that you use maintains different information about the file types stored on that computer. You can use Windows Explorer to learn about the file associations for your computer.

To view Windows file extension associations:

1. Click the **Start** button on the Windows taskbar, point to **Programs**, point to **Accessories**, and then click **Windows Explorer** to start the program.

2. Click **Tools** on the menu bar, and then click **Folder Options**. The Folder Options dialog box opens.

3. Click the **File Types** tab to see your computer's registered file types and the programs it uses to open those files. Figure 6-9 shows the registered file types for one user's computer; your list will probably differ. The file types are registered each time you install a new software program, so your list of registered file types depends on what programs are installed on your computer. Clicking a registered file type in the list displays more information about that file extension, such as the program that opens the file and a description of the file's purpose.

| Figure 6-9 | VIEWING REGISTERED FILE TYPES |

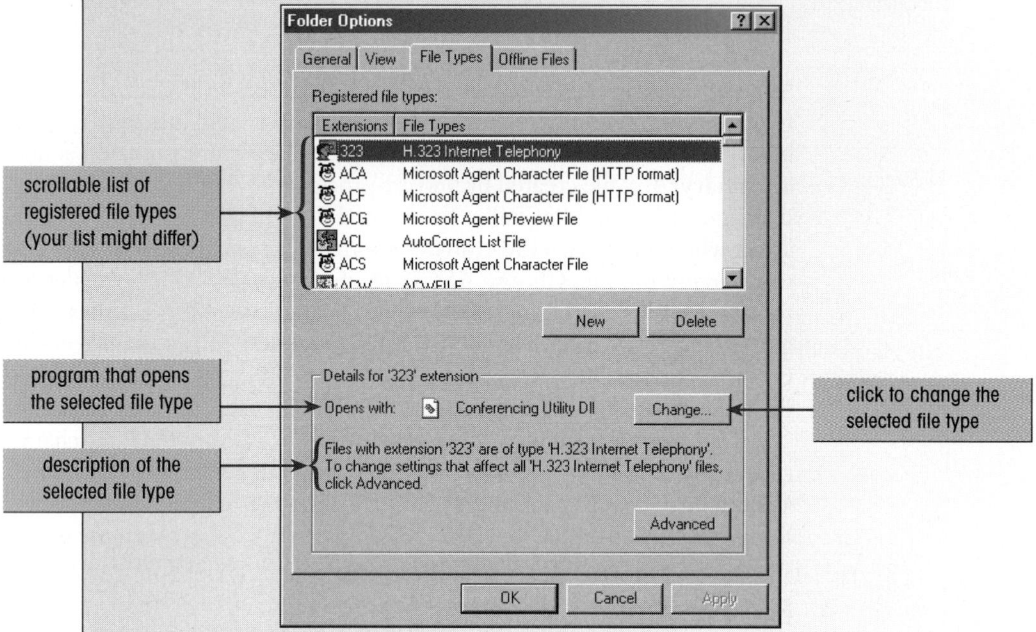

scrollable list of registered file types (your list might differ)

program that opens the selected file type

description of the selected file type

click to change the selected file type

4. Scroll down the list to view all of the registered file types, and then click the **Cancel** button to close the dialog box without making any changes.

5. Close Windows Explorer by clicking its **Close** button.

Figure 6-10 shows several filenames with common file extensions, transfer modes, and programs that open them. Don't worry about remembering all of the different file extensions. In practice, you might encounter only a few of the listed extensions. Most often, you will see files on the Internet with extensions of .doc, .exe, .html, .txt, or .zip.

| Figure 6-10 | COMMON INTERNET FILE EXTENSIONS, TRANSFER MODES, AND ASSOCIATED PROGRAMS |

FILENAME AND EXTENSION	EXTENSION	TRANSFER MODE	TYPE OF FILE
Picture.bmp	.bmp	Binary	Microsoft Paint picture
Readme.doc	.doc	Binary	Word document
Spinner.exe	.exe	Binary	Program
Starship.gif	.gif	Binary	Picture
Index.html or Index.htm	.html or .htm	ASCII	Web page
Employee.mdb	.mdb	Binary	Access database
Help.pdf	.pdf	Binary	Acrobat Portable Document Format
Marketing.ppt	.ppt	Binary	PowerPoint presentation
Readme.txt	.txt	ASCII	Text file
Profit.xls	.xls	Binary	Excel worksheet
File.zip	.zip	Binary	Compressed file

Sometimes you will need to translate the file format of downloaded files into another form before you can read and use them. To translate files, you use a **file utility program**, which is a program that transforms the downloaded file into another format. The most common file type that you find on the Internet is a compressed file. There are many file utility programs that you can use to read compressed files.

Decompressing **Downloaded Files**

Internet files of all types are frequently stored in compressed form. **Compressed files** use less space when stored, and they take less time to be transferred from one computer to another. For example, you might be able to compress a 1,200 KB file to 400 KB and thereby decrease its download time by over 50%. Compression will be especially important to Milt, because many of his contractors connect to the Internet using dial-up connections with slow upload and download times.

You can use a **file compression program** to decrease the original size of nearly any file. Some widely used file compression programs are WinZip and PKZIP. After you download a compressed file, you must use a program to restore the file to its original state before you can open or execute it. The process of restoring a compressed file to its original state is called **file decompression**, or **file expansion**. FTP recognizes most compressed files by their extensions. The most common extension is .zip, which is why some people refer to compressed files as **zip files** or **zipped files**. The Additional Information section of the Student Online Companion for this tutorial contains links to file compression programs.

Before you install any file or program that you downloaded from another computer, you must first check it for viruses. Milt will want to ensure the health of the computers at Sound Effects, so he wants you to help him locate several options for checking its computers.

Checking **Downloaded Files for Viruses**

For anyone using the Internet, computer viruses pose a real and potentially costly threat. Computer viruses made their debut shortly after 1985 and have evolved from a nuisance to a hazard for your computer. Computer **viruses** are programs that "infect" your computer and cause harm to your disk or programs. People create viruses by coding programs that invisibly attach themselves to other programs on a computer. Some viruses simply display an annoying or silly message on your screen and then go away, whereas others can cause real harm by reformatting a hard drive or changing all of its file extensions. You have to know how to detect and eradicate viruses if you plan to download anything—including data, programs, or e-mail attachments from either reputable or questionable sources—from the Internet.

Virus detection software, also called **antivirus software**, regularly scans the files on your computer and looks for any infected files by comparing your files to a signature that known viruses carry. A **virus signature** is a sequence (string) of characters that is always present in a particular virus program. A virus detection program can scan a single file or folder or your entire computer to search for infected files. When the virus detection software spots a virus signature, the program warns you. You can either delete the file containing the virus or ask the virus detection program to remove the virus. Most virus detection programs can clean infected files, which removes the virus from the files and renders them "healthy" again. The Additional Information section of the Student Online Companion for this tutorial lists resources for obtaining and using a virus detection program.

Uploading Files

Milt and his associates will need to upload files to remote computers as a means of transporting the files from one location to another. The process of uploading a file is the reverse of downloading one. First, you should check the file for viruses. If your file is large, or if you want to combine several files into one file, then you should compress the files before uploading them to reduce the transfer time and space on the remote computer. With full-privilege access to another computer, you can send the file to a particular folder. Without full-privilege access, you are restricted to uploading a file to the public directory. In any case, you must use an FTP client or command-line program to upload files.

REFERENCE WINDOW   **RW**

Uploading a File Using FTP

- Log on to the remote computer by entering its URL, your user name or *anonymous,* and your password.
- Navigate to the directory on the remote computer to which you want to upload the file.
- Click the filename of the file to upload from the local computer.
- Select the appropriate transmission mode.
- Click the button or execute the command that sends the file from your PC to the remote computer.
- End the FTP session by logging off and disconnecting from the remote computer.

Using a Public Directory

Milt won't require the use of a public directory because all of the files transmitted to and from Sound Effects will be proprietary in nature. However, some public FTP sites allow users with anonymous FTP access to view only one directory and any files or other directories it contains. That directory is traditionally named *pub* (for public). Besides permitting download access by anonymous users, the site's manager, also referred to as the **webmaster**, might allow users to upload files, making them available to anyone who can connect to the site. Frequently, public directories provide a temporary location for users to upload and share data or programs that they think others might find useful. One problem with sites permitting users with upload privileges is that the webmaster must monitor the files uploaded to a public directory on a regular basis. In addition to worrying about viruses that might be hidden in uploaded files, the webmaster must find and delete any copyrighted files that were illegally uploaded to the site for public use. For example, uploading a program such as Microsoft Word to a public directory is a clear copyright violation because Microsoft's license agreement prohibits you from sharing the program with other users. Many FTP sites have specific policies that force you to acknowledge, before uploading any files, that you are the owner of the material or that its transfer to the FTP site will not violate any copyright or intellectual property restrictions. There are many legitimate uses for public directories, such as sharing data or research with other users. However, it is your responsibility to ensure that someone else does not hold the copyright to the data or research you are sharing.

Most sites have clearly stated rules and policies about the acceptable use of FTP. Be sure to read the site's readme files to learn any rules about acceptable use when you enter an FTP site.

In Session 6.2, you will use the Internet to download an FTP client program that Milt can use to transfer files between his Los Angeles studio and contractors in different areas of the United States and Canada. You will also download a file compression program and a program for reading files saved in the PDF format, investigate the use of a virus detection program, and visit Web sites that provide reviews and information about current releases of different categories of software.

Session 6.1 QUICK CHECK

1. True or False: Only an FTP client program is capable of downloading files from the Internet.

2. When a user logs on to a publicly accessible computer connected to the Internet, what is the customary password that the user should supply?

3. True or False: An FTP client program automatically determines the transfer mode for files that you download.

4. What two types of items might you find in the root directory of an FTP site?

5. What would you type in your browser's address field to open the FTP site at zdnet.com?

6. What type of file uses the .ppt file extension?

7. Programs that reduce a file's size and subsequently its transmission time are known as _____ programs.

SESSION 6.2

In this session, you will visit several Web sites and search for and download software from them. You will use a browser to download and install an FTP client program, and then you will use the FTP client program to download Adobe Acrobat Reader and WinZip. Finally, you will learn how to determine the virtual distance between computers connected to the Internet.

Locating Software Download Sites

Now that Milt understands how FTP works, he is eager to begin using it to transfer files between his Los Angeles studio and its contractors. The computers in the Los Angeles office use Windows 2000 Professional. Because Milt will need to upload and download files, he is most interested in obtaining an FTP client program that can handle both transactions. To help Milt make his decision about an FTP client program, your first goal is to make sure that the software you will download and install is reliable. Cost is not a high-priority issue for Milt at this time, although it is always nice to save money when you can. Perhaps equally important is how various software tools stack up against each other, so you need to find some sort of ratings system that will guide you in making good decisions about which of several software product alternatives to choose.

A good way of locating software on the Internet is to use one or more Internet search engines. If you are searching for FTP client programs, you can look for reviews or comparisons of the software by users or vendors. For example, several popular PC magazines feature articles comparing Internet utility programs and designating one or more programs in a class as the "best of the class" or a "best buy." The criteria these sites use to judge which program is best might be different from your criteria. However, it never hurts to review the ratings when you can. You decide to use a search engine to find information about FTP client programs, so Milt can make an informed choice when selecting an FTP client program.

To use a search engine to find information about FTP client programs:

1. Start your Web browser, open the Student Online Companion page at **www.course.com/newperspectives/internet3**, click the hyperlink for your book, click the **Tutorial 6** link, and then click the **Session 6.2** link. Click the **HotBot** link and wait while the browser opens the HotBot home page.

2. Type **FTP client** in the Search Smarter text box, and then click the **SEARCH** button to start the search. Figure 6-11 shows the first page of search results.

| Figure 6-11 | FTP CLIENT PROGRAMS RETURNED BY HOTBOT |

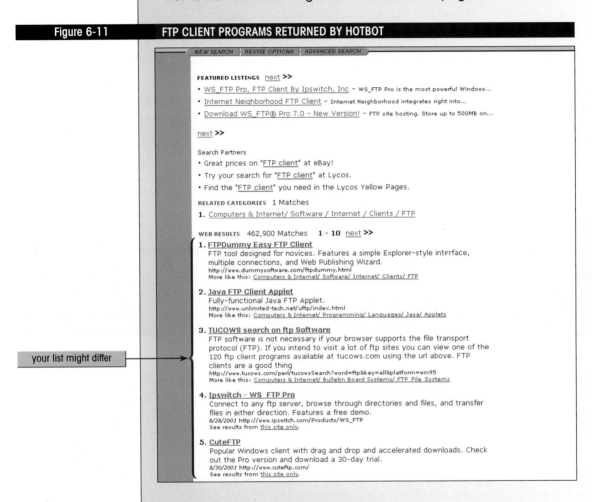

your list might differ

3. Click the first few links on the results page to learn more about FTP client programs.

As you explore some of the links returned by HotBot, you will find that some are relevant and others are not. PC magazines frequently review software using their specially designed software testing laboratories, conduct product comparisons, and report the results. They should not have a vested interest in the outcome, but always view the results with a critical eye to identify any biases. The Additional Information section of the Student Online Companion for this tutorial contains links to publishers of software and hardware product reviews.

You can also try searching for software download sites using the search phrase "software download." The search engine will return a list of sites that contain links to software that you can download from the Internet.

Visiting and Using Popular Download Sites

Several Web sites provide links to freeware and shareware programs; some of these same sites also allow you to download programs directly. To find a list of FTP client programs and reviews about their usage, you decide to visit DOWNLOAD.COM, which contains many freeware and shareware programs organized in different categories.

To browse the DOWNLOAD.COM Web site:

1. Return to the Student Online Companion Web page for Session 6.2, and then click the **DOWNLOAD.COM** hyperlink and wait while your Web browser loads the Web page.

2. Type **FTP client** in the Search text box, as shown in Figure 6-12. Alternatively, you could select a category in which to search, such as Games or Web Authoring. Each category contains subcategories so you can narrow your search.

Figure 6-12	SEARCHING FOR FTP CLIENT PROGRAMS USING DOWNLOAD.COM

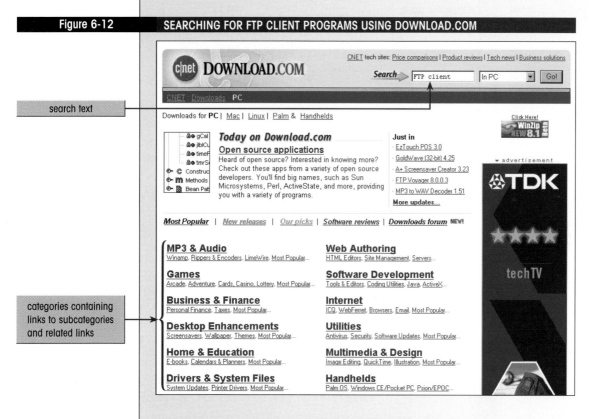

search text

categories containing links to subcategories and related links

3. Click the **Go!** button to search for FTP client programs. Figure 6-13 shows the search results and the different FTP client programs that are available for download from DOWNLOAD.COM. (Your list might differ.) The search returns the date when the files were uploaded to the site and the current number of times each file has been downloaded. Sometimes the download count is a good resource for discovering popular and useful programs because popular programs usually have larger download counts.

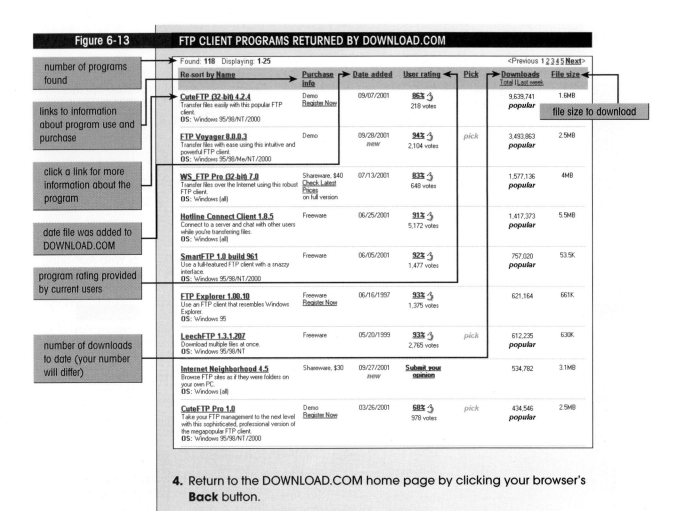

Figure 6-13 · FTP CLIENT PROGRAMS RETURNED BY DOWNLOAD.COM

4. Return to the DOWNLOAD.COM home page by clicking your browser's **Back** button.

Another CNET site, Shareware.com, also provides search capabilities for freeware, shareware, and limited edition software. The two sites complement each other, but DOWNLOAD.COM provides more information about downloadable software and advanced search techniques, so that site might provide the best value.

As part of your initial investigation using DOWNLOAD.COM, you find several good FTP client programs for Milt. Before leaving the site, you will explore the category listings to see if they might provide another easy way of searching for downloads.

To browse for Internet software on DOWNLOAD.COM:

1. Click the **Internet** link in the categories list on the DOWNLOAD.COM home page. The Internet category page shown in Figure 6-14 opens and displays a list of Internet software by subcategory. Clicking any of the subcategory links opens a new page that lists related software.

Figure 6-14   DOWNLOAD.COM SUBCATEGORIES

links to subcategories

2. Click the **Tools & Utilities** link in the subcategories list to open a page of Internet software tools and utility programs. (You may need to scroll down to find this link.) See if you can find any programs that Milt can use, and then explore the links to those sites, but do not download any programs yet.

3. Click your browser's **Back** button as necessary to return to the DOWNLOAD.COM home page.

Tucows (which stands for "The Ultimate Collection Of Winsock Software" and is pronounced "two cows") is another popular site that provides quick access to free, inexpensive, and licensed software. Tucows lists its software products by type. You decide to search the Tucows site to see if you can find software that would help Milt.

To browse the Tucows Web site:

1. Return to the Student Online Companion Web page for Session 6.2, and then click the **Tucows** link and wait while your Web browser loads the Web page.

   You can search for software for different operating systems; you will search for Windows 2000 software because that is what Milt and his staff use.

2. Click the **Windows** link. The Choose a Region page opens. Tucows is a busy site with worldwide servers, so you need to click the link for the server closest to you.

3. Click the list arrow for your country, and then select the state, country, or province in which you live. The Choose a Mirror page opens, in which you select the city closest to where you live. You might see only one mirror listed, depending on the location of the country, state, or province in which you live.

4. Click the link of the mirror name in a location close to you. The Welcome to Tucows page shown in Figure 6-15 opens. Because you already selected Windows software, this page lists products for Windows.

Figure 6-15	WELCOME TO TUCOWS PAGE

Internet tab

TROUBLE? You might see more than one link for your location. You can click any entry to open the Welcome to Tucows page. If you cannot open a link, try another state or region until you succeed.

5. Click the **Internet** tab at the top of the page to open a page listing categories of Internet programs, similar to what you viewed using DOWNLOAD.COM.

6. Scroll down the page to examine its contents. Each category contains links that open pages containing more links to detailed information about the individual software programs you can download.

When Milt needs to download files, he might use his browser instead of an FTP client program. You'll need to make sure that he has the most current browser available to ensure the best quality and security available. You'll visit Microsoft's Download Center to investigate new browser programs and updates.

To locate Microsoft Internet Explorer files on Microsoft's Web site:

1. Return to the Student Online Companion Web page for Session 6.2, and then click the **Microsoft Download Center** link and wait while your Web browser loads the Web page shown in Figure 6-16.

Figure 6-16   **MICROSOFT DOWNLOAD CENTER PAGE**

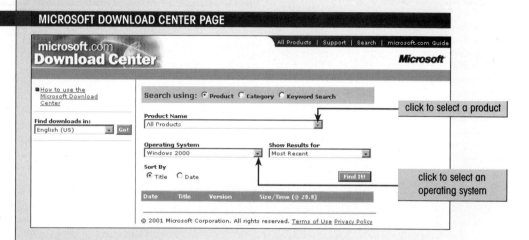

2. Click the **Product Name** list arrow, and then scroll down the list and click **Internet Explorer 6** (or a higher version number if one is available).

3. Click the **Operating System** list arrow, scroll down the list as necessary and click **Windows 2000**, and then click the **Find It!** button. The page that opens lists the files you can download for Internet Explorer version 6 and Windows 2000. Review the links, but do not download any files.

Milt just asked you about another software download site that is maintained by ZDNet. ZDNet tests and reviews information technology products and reports its findings on its Web site. ZDNet issues ratings based on tests and evaluations of users who send their impressions of the software via e-mail to the publisher. Because ZDNet is well regarded for its thorough reviews, you decide to search for antivirus software and use the ratings to identify programs that will provide security for Milt's file transfers.

To search the ZDNet Software Library Web site for antivirus software:

1. Return to the Student Online Companion Web page for Session 6.2, and then click the **ZDNet Downloads** link and wait while your Web browser loads the Web page.

2. Locate the Search For text box near the top of the page, type **antivirus** in the text box, and then click the **GO** button. A search results page opens and returns a list of links to antivirus software programs, as shown in Figure 6-17. Your results might be different from those shown in Figure 6-17, but you should find many antivirus programs in the list.

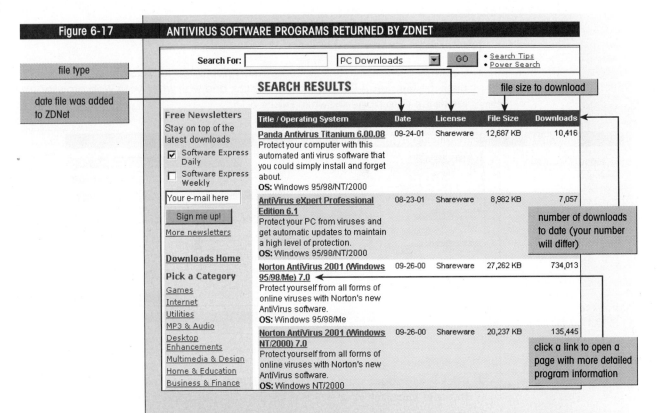

Figure 6-17   ANTIVIRUS SOFTWARE PROGRAMS RETURNED BY ZDNET

TROUBLE? If the search results page does not list any files, type "virus" or "antivirus" (without the quotation marks) in the Search For text box, and then click the GO button again. You might need to search several times using different search expressions to find antivirus software.

3. Click the hyperlink for the program named **Norton AntiVirus 2001 (Windows NT/2000) 7.0** to open the page shown in Figure 6-18, which supplies more information about the program, including a detailed description and its compressed file size. You can use this page to download the program by clicking the Download Now link. You can also click the Add to Basket link to place the program in your virtual shopping cart so you can continue selecting programs and download all of them at once.

TROUBLE? If you cannot find the Norton AntiVirus 2001 (Windows NT/2000) 7.0 link, scroll to the bottom of the page, and then click the Hits 27-52 button to view the next group of links.

| Figure 6-18 | NORTON ANTIVIRUS 2001 PRODUCT PAGE |

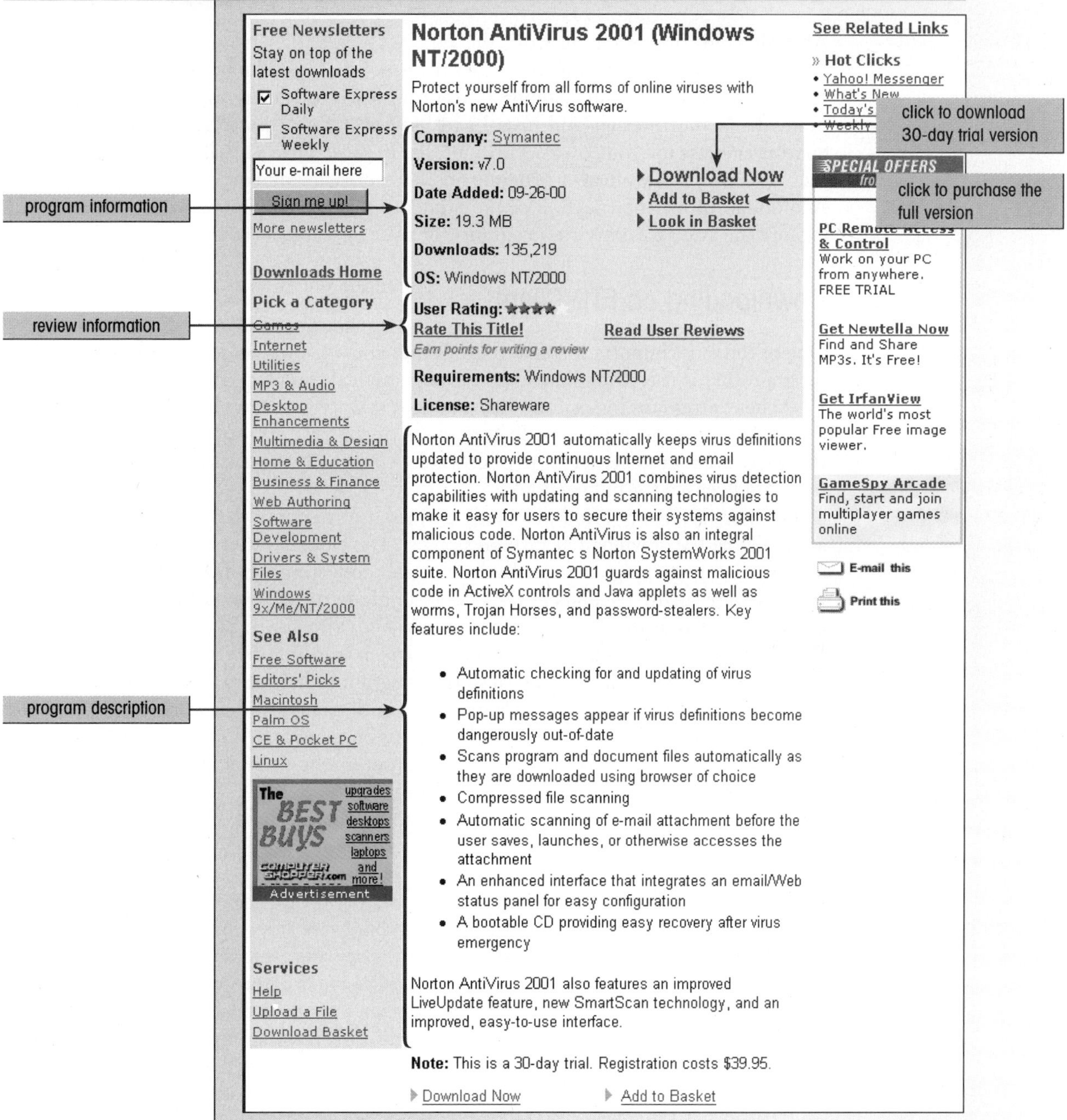

Free Newsletters
Stay on top of the latest downloads
☑ Software Express Daily
☐ Software Express Weekly

[Your e-mail here]
[Sign me up!]
More newsletters

Downloads Home

Pick a Category
Games
Internet
Utilities
MP3 & Audio
Desktop Enhancements
Multimedia & Design
Home & Education
Business & Finance
Web Authoring
Software Development
Drivers & System Files
Windows 9x/Me/NT/2000

See Also
Free Software
Editors' Picks
Macintosh
Palm OS
CE & Pocket PC
Linux

The BEST BUYS
upgrades
software
desktops
scanners
laptops
and more!
COMPUTERSHOPPER.com
Advertisement

Services
Help
Upload a File
Download Basket

program information →
review information →
program description →

Norton AntiVirus 2001 (Windows NT/2000)
Protect yourself from all forms of online viruses with Norton's new AntiVirus software.

Company: Symantec
Version: v7.0
Date Added: 09-26-00
Size: 19.3 MB
Downloads: 135,219
OS: Windows NT/2000

▸ **Download Now**
▸ **Add to Basket**
▸ **Look in Basket**

click to download 30-day trial version

click to purchase the full version

User Rating: ★★★★
Rate This Title!   **Read User Reviews**
Earn points for writing a review

Requirements: Windows NT/2000
License: Shareware

Norton AntiVirus 2001 automatically keeps virus definitions updated to provide continuous Internet and email protection. Norton AntiVirus 2001 combines virus detection capabilities with updating and scanning technologies to make it easy for users to secure their systems against malicious code. Norton AntiVirus is also an integral component of Symantec s Norton SystemWorks 2001 suite. Norton AntiVirus 2001 guards against malicious code in ActiveX controls and Java applets as well as worms, Trojan Horses, and password-stealers. Key features include:

- Automatic checking for and updating of virus definitions
- Pop-up messages appear if virus definitions become dangerously out-of-date
- Scans program and document files automatically as they are downloaded using browser of choice
- Compressed file scanning
- Automatic scanning of e-mail attachment before the user saves, launches, or otherwise accesses the attachment
- An enhanced interface that integrates an email/Web status panel for easy configuration
- A bootable CD providing easy recovery after virus emergency

Norton AntiVirus 2001 also features an improved LiveUpdate feature, new SmartScan technology, and an improved, easy-to-use interface.

Note: This is a 30-day trial. Registration costs $39.95.

▸ Download Now   ▸ Add to Basket

See Related Links
» **Hot Clicks**
- Yahoo! Messenger
- What's New
- Today's
- Weekly

SPECIAL OFFERS
from

PC Remote Access & Control
Work on your PC from anywhere. FREE TRIAL

Get Newtella Now
Find and Share MP3s. It's Free!

Get IrfanView
The world's most popular Free image viewer.

GameSpy Arcade
Find, start and join multiplayer games online

✉ **E-mail this**
🖨 **Print this**

Now that you have identified several evaluation versions of an FTP client program, browser updates, and an antivirus program, you are ready to locate and download them for Milt so he can begin using them. You begin by using a Web browser to download an FTP client program.

Downloading Programs

After downloading anything from the Internet—even files from reputable sources—your first priority is to scan the file for viruses to ensure that installing or opening the program or file will not damage your computer. You can download many high quality antivirus programs from the Internet and install and use them for a limited time to determine their appropriateness for your own security needs. Because most antivirus programs are large in size, you won't download a program in this tutorial, but you can click the links in the Additional Information section of the Student Online Companion page for this tutorial to explore the available antivirus programs for your operating system.

Downloading an FTP Client

One of the most important software tools that you want to locate for Milt is an FTP client program that is user-friendly and contains many features. You conducted your research on FTP client programs by visiting sites that review software searching and read articles about different FTP client programs. In the course of conducting your research, you have found that there are four general classes of downloaded software: freeware, shareware, limited edition, and licensed (or full version).

Internet surfers are often pleasantly surprised to discover that many Internet programs are available for download at little or no cost. Developers often make their software available for free in exchange for user feedback. After collecting user feedback and improving the free software, many developers provide an upgrade of the free version for a nominal fee. Software that is available to users at no cost and with no restrictions is called **freeware**. Freeware users must accept the implicit or explicit warning that the software might contain errors, called **bugs**, which could cause the program to halt or malfunction or even damage the user's computer. The main risk associated with using freeware is that its limited testing often results in a program that contains a lot of bugs, and the software's developer is rarely liable for any damage that the freeware program might cause. On the other hand, a lot of good-quality commercial software started as freeware. Before you use freeware, you should use a Web search engine to locate reviews before you download, install, virus check, and use any freeware program to see what kinds of successes and problems its users have reported.

Shareware is similar to freeware, but it is not entirely free and usually is available only for a short evaluation period. After that evaluation period expires—usually either a specified number of days or a specific number of uses—shareware stops functioning. Shareware users are expected to stop using the shareware after the specified initial trial period and uninstall it from their computers. Otherwise, anyone who likes the program and wants to continue using it can purchase a license. There are three popular ways to turn shareware users into paying customers. The first way is to build a counter into the program that keeps track of the number of times they have used a program. After users have reached a usage limit, the software is disabled. The second way is by inserting an internal date checker as a time-expiration technique that causes the shareware to stop working after a specific time period from the installation date has elapsed, such as 30 days. Third, many shareware developers use a "nag" screen that appears each time you start the program to encourage users who do not purchase a license to stop using the shareware, although the program may continue to work. The screen usually displays a message with the developer's name and Web address and asks you to abide by the licensing agreement and to submit payment for the shareware version of the product.

Shareware is usually slightly more reliable than freeware because the shareware developer is sometimes willing to accept responsibility for the program's operation. Usually, shareware developers have an established way for users to report any bugs and receive free or low-cost software upgrades and bug fixes.

Some developers distribute restricted versions of their software for free to let people use it without risk. A restricted version of a shareware program is called a **limited edition** (or **LE**), and it provides most of the functionality of the full version that is for sale. However, LE software omits one or more useful features of the full version. You can sometimes download an LE version and use it for free. If you really like the LE, then you can purchase the full version. The FTP client program WS_FTP LE is one example of a free limited edition of the full WS_FTP program. The limited edition performs all the standard FTP tasks but omits some of the advanced features that make the full product especially attractive. Because the complete versions of limited edition software are inexpensive, most users of the limited edition will purchase the upgraded, comprehensive version so they can use its additional capabilities.

Regardless of which type of software you use to evaluate a product, most developers provide you with a means of contacting them to purchase a license to use the full version of the evaluation copy. Purchasing a license usually involves paying a fee to get a code to unlock the software and render it fully functional.

From your studies, you conclude that the WS_FTP LE FTP client program is the best choice for Milt, so you will download it next.

To download the WS_FTP LE program:

1. Return to the Student Online Companion Web page for Session 6.2, and then click the **Ipswitch** link and wait while your Web browser loads the Ipswitch home page shown in Figure 6-19.

Figure 6-19   IPSWITCH HOME PAGE

Download Evaluations link

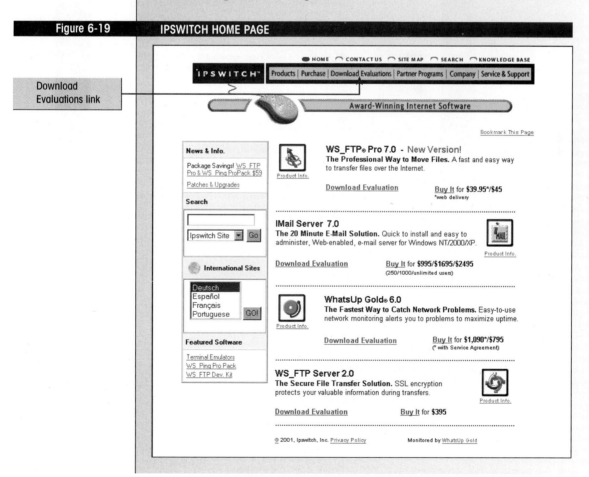

2. Locate and click the **Download Evaluations** link on the link bar that appears at the top of the page. The Download Evaluations page opens.

3. Scroll down the page and locate the WS_FTP LE 5.08 link in the Other Products section.

   TROUBLE? If you see a higher version of the WS_FTP LE program, use that version instead of the one included in Steps 3 and 4.

4. Click the **WS_FTP LE 5.08** link. Your browser opens the page at FTPplanet.com as shown in Figure 6-20. You'll download the WS_FTP LE program from this site.

| Figure 6-20 | FTPPLANET.COM HOME PAGE |

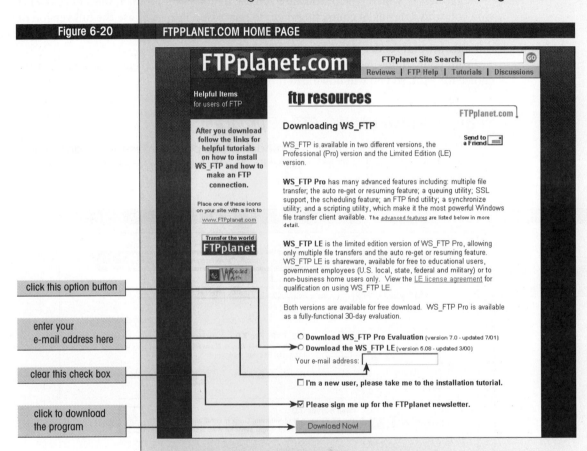

5. Read the page that opens, click the **Download the WS_FTP LE** option button to select it, type your e-mail address in the Your e-mail address text box, clear the check box for signing up to receive the FTPplanet newsletter, and then click the **Download Now!** button.

   TROUBLE? If a dialog box opens and asks if you would like to open or save the file, click the Save button.

6. Make sure your Data Disk is in the appropriate drive, click the **Save in** list arrow and select the appropriate drive, and then double-click the **Tutorial.06** folder to open it. You will accept the default filename of ws_ftple.exe.

> **7.** Click the **Save** button to begin downloading the file to your Data Disk. After a few moments, the compressed file that contains the FTP client program is stored on your Data Disk.
>
> TROUBLE? If a dialog box opens to indicate that the download is complete, click the Close button.

After you download the program's executable file, you should check it for viruses, and then you must install the program on your computer to use it. You can use Windows Explorer to check the Tutorial.06 folder on your Data Disk to make sure that it contains the ws_ftple.exe file.

Note: If your instructor or technical support person permits you to install and use the program, complete the next set of steps to install the software. If your lab policy prohibits you from installing the program, read the following steps so you know how to install the software, but do *not* complete the steps at the computer.

To install WS_FTP LE on your computer:

1. Make sure that your Data Disk is in the appropriate drive, click the **Start** button on the Windows taskbar, click **Run**, and then type **A:\Tutorial.06\ws_ftple.exe** in the Open list box.

TROUBLE? If your Data Disk is not in drive A, substitute your drive letter in the Open list box.

2. Click the **OK** or **Open** button (as instructed) to start the installation process. An installation screen appears.

TROUBLE? If the on-screen instructions for WS_FTP LE differ from those shown in the steps, follow the on-screen instructions.

3. Click the **Continue** button. A second dialog box opens asking you to identify your status.

4. Click the option button to indicate that you are a student, and then click the **Next** button. A dialog box opens and asks how you plan to use the program.

5. Click the **At school** check box to select it, click the **For academic work** check box to select it, and then click the **Next** button. A dialog box opens, displaying the license agreement for using WS_FTP LE. (As a business owner, Milt would choose the appropriate option and follow the license agreement to use the software.)

6. Read the license agreement, and then click the **Accept** button to indicate that you accept the terms of the agreement. (If you do not accept the terms of the license agreement, then the installation process stops.) A WS_FTP LE Installation dialog box opens with a default destination folder for installing the program.

7. Click the **OK** button to accept the default folder in which the program files will be stored, and then click the **OK** button again to accept the default folder for file transfers. (The default directory is C:\Program Files\WS_FTP.) The Program Manager Group dialog box opens.

8. Click the **OK** button to accept the suggested name, WS_FTP LE, for the Program Manager group. (WS_FTP is the name of the Program Manager group folder that will appear on the Programs menu.)

9. Click the **OK** button to complete the installation process. A window opens with the shortcuts for using the WS_FTP LE program.

10. Close the WS_FTP LE window by clicking its **Close** button.

After you are finished installing the program, you may want to read the WS_FTP LE Release Notes file to learn how to use the program, or you can use the program's Help files for program instructions. After installing the product, Milt can use it to send files via FTP to other computers.

Downloading Adobe Acrobat Reader

Sound Effects, Inc. is planning to change the format in which its scripts and other written documents are prepared. **Portable Document Format (PDF)**, developed by Adobe Corporation, provides a convenient, self-contained package for delivering and displaying documents containing text, graphics, charts, and other objects. PDF files and compressed files are both special formats for storing files, but they are not related. PDF files simply provide a universal and convenient way to represent documents, whereas compressed files condense files so they occupy much less space. Compressed files cannot be viewed until you decompress them.

When you download a PDF file, you do not need to use the same program as the file's creator to display, browse, and print the document; you use the **Adobe Acrobat Reader** program to view the document. For example, if you download a PDF file that was created in Microsoft Word, you can use Acrobat Reader to access the document, even if you don't have Word installed on your computer. Most Web browsers can start the Acrobat Reader program so you can use your Web browser to view PDF documents without downloading them first, or you can download the Acrobat Reader program separately to read files that you have already downloaded.

Acrobat Reader is a free, simple to install program. You will use DOWNLOAD.COM's site to search for and download Acrobat Reader so Milt will have it on his computer for testing purposes when he begins using PDF files to prepare scripts and other communications.

Note: You cannot download the Acrobat Reader program to a floppy disk because the program's size (approximately eight megabytes) exceeds the disk's storage capacity. Your instructor might ask you to download the program to your hard drive or to simply read the following steps without actually downloading the file.

To download the Acrobat Reader from DOWNLOAD.COM:

1. Return to the Student Online Companion Web page for Session 6.2, and then click the **DOWNLOAD.COM** link and wait while your Web browser loads the Web page.

2. Type **Acrobat Reader** in the Search text box, and then click the **Go!** button. Your search results page should look similar to Figure 6-21.

Figure 6-21	ADOBE ACROBAT READER LINKS RETURNED BY DOWNLOAD.COM

Found: **7** Displaying: **1-7**

Re-sort by Name	Purchase info	Date added	User rating	Pick	Downloads Total I Last week	File size
Adobe Acrobat Reader (32-bit) 5.0 Read Adobe PDF files from the Web. **OS**: Windows (all)	Freeware Check Latest Prices on full version	04/19/2001	92% 5,596 votes	*pick*	6,096,749 *popular*	8.6MB
Adobe Acrobat 4.05 Update 2 Update your version of Acrobat 4.05. **OS**: Windows 95/98/NT	Freeware	07/26/2000	97% 1,708 votes		544,551 *popular*	2.8MB
Adobe Acrobat Reader (16-bit) 3.01 Browse Adobe PDF files for the Web. **OS**: Windows 3.x	Freeware	08/28/1997	87% 491 votes		376,516 *popular*	3.7MB
Adobe Acrobat Reader OCX Update 1.0 Fix Adobe Acrobat to work properly with Internet Explorer 4.0. **OS**: Windows 3.x	Freeware	11/18/1997	91% 36 votes		62,708 *popular*	1.2MB
Adobe Acrobat Distiller Update 3.02 Fix bugs with a tool included in Adobe Acrobat. **OS**: Windows 95/98/NT/2000	Freeware	10/05/2000	75% 36 votes		30,902 *popular*	1MB
Adobe Acrobat Forms Plug-in 3.5 View and print forms created with the Author plug-in. **OS**: Windows 3.x	Freeware	01/29/1998	76% 13 votes		23,576 *popular*	2.3MB
Make Accessible Plug-In 5.0 Create tagged PDF files easily with this Acrobat plug-in. **OS**: Windows 95/98/NT/2000	Freeware	04/19/2001	84% 25 votes		11,647	1.9MB
Re-sort by Name	Purchase info	Date added	User rating	Pick	Downloads Total I Last week	File size

Found: **7** Displaying: **1-7**

Filter list by [All OSs ▼] [All categories ▼] [All licenses ▼] [Update]

links to Adobe Acrobat Reader programs (your list might differ)

The Downloads column displays the number of downloads that have occurred to date—a larger number generally indicates that the software is popular and reliable, whereas a smaller number indicates that the software could be relatively new.

TROUBLE? Software vendors update and improve their programs regularly, so your Acrobat Reader program version number might be different. If you see a higher version number than the ones shown in Figure 6-21, download that program in Step 3, which is a more current version.

3. Click the **Adobe Acrobat Reader (32-bit) 5.0** link (or the link for the latest version of Windows) to open the page shown in Figure 6-22. This page provides details about the program and a link to download it.

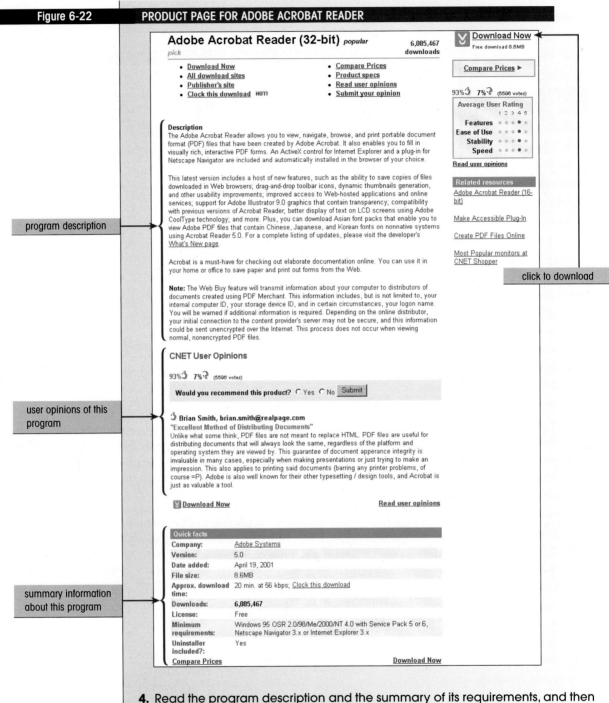

Figure 6-22 | **PRODUCT PAGE FOR ADOBE ACROBAT READER**

4. Read the program description and the summary of its requirements, and then click the **Download Now** link. DOWNLOAD.COM will select a download site for you automatically.

5. If a dialog box opens and asks if you want to open or save the file, click the **Save** button. If this dialog box does not open, then your browser will automatically choose to save the file to disk.

TROUBLE? Ask your instructor or technical support person if you can download the file to your hard drive. If you cannot download the file, or if you are unsure about downloading the file, then click the Cancel button now and read the rest of the steps without completing them at the computer.

6. In the Save As dialog box, click the **Save in** list arrow, click the drive and folder in which to save the file, and then click the **Save** button. Figure 6-23 shows the dialog box that Internet Explorer displays while it downloads the file. (Navigator displays a different dialog box.)

| Figure 6-23 | FILE DOWNLOAD DIALOG BOX IN INTERNET EXPLORER |

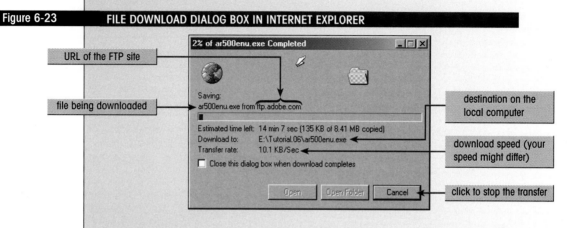

URL of the FTP site

file being downloaded

destination on the local computer

download speed (your speed might differ)

click to stop the transfer

7. After the download is complete, click the **Close** button (if necessary) to close the dialog box that opens.

8. Close your browser, but do not disconnect from your Internet connection.

The time it takes to transfer the program file varies based on the speed of your Internet connection. If you are on a local area network (LAN) with a T1 Internet connection, then the transfer time is a few seconds. If you are using a modem and a dial-up connection, then the transfer time could take several minutes. Another factor in the download time is the amount of traffic at the FTP site. Many simultaneous users (more than 4,000 for example) can directly affect the download process. If you encounter problems while downloading a file, stop the process by clicking the Cancel button and try again later.

Now the downloaded Acrobat Reader file is saved on your hard drive. You can install the program by double-clicking its filename in Windows Explorer and then following the on-screen steps. After installing the Acrobat Reader program, you can delete the downloaded executable file from the drive and folder to which you downloaded it, or you can keep it in case you need to reinstall the program.

Downloading WinZip

Milt is very interested in compressing files to decrease the amount of space they require on an FTP site and also to decrease the time it takes to upload and download files. Many file compression programs available on the Internet are reliable and easy to use. One popular program is WinZip, which is available for free during your evaluation. WinZip has been downloaded millions of times and has received many awards from computing magazines and other sources.

To test the FTP client program that you downloaded earlier, you will use it to connect to the WinZip FTP site so you can download an evaluation copy of the program. When you establish a connection to an FTP site, you can save the site's host address and your user name and password so you can easily return to the site later. When you use an FTP client program to save this information, you are creating an **FTP session profile**.

Note: In the following steps, you will use the WS_FTP LE program to download the WinZip program. If you do not have an FTP client or cannot install one on your school's computer, then read the steps without completing them at the computer.

To establish and save an FTP session profile:

1. Click the **Start** button on the Windows taskbar, point to **Programs**, point to **WS_FTP**, and then click **WS_FTP95 LE** to start the WS_FTP LE program. The Session Properties dialog box opens.

   TROUBLE? If you do not see WS_FTP on the Programs menu, make sure that you downloaded and installed the WS_FTP LE program earlier in this session.

2. Click the **New** button in the Session Properties dialog box to create a new FTP session profile.

3. In the Profile Name text box, type **WinZip** to name the new FTP session profile so you can easily recognize it later.

4. Press the **Tab** key to move to the Host Name/Address text box, and then type **ftp.winzip.com**. This address is the URL to the FTP site for WinZip. You can usually find the FTP address for an FTP site by replacing the "www" in a site's Web address with "ftp". Some companies list their FTP site addresses on their Internet Web pages, as well.

5. Click the **Anonymous** check box to select it. WS_FTP LE automatically adds the anonymous logon to the User ID text box and a default password to the Password text box. You'll change the default password to your e-mail address as is customary on the Internet to identify your use of the site.

6. Select the default password in the Password text box, and then type your full e-mail address. Figure 6-24 shows the Session Properties dialog box settings to establish an anonymous login to the WinZip FTP site.

Figure 6-24	SESSION PROPERTIES DIALOG BOX FOR WINZIP

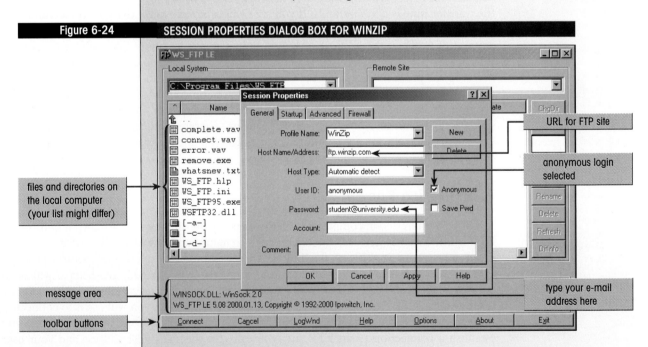

files and directories on the local computer (your list might differ)

message area

toolbar buttons

URL for FTP site

anonymous login selected

type your e-mail address here

7. Click the **Apply** button to save the WinZip session profile without connecting to the WinZip FTP site.

Now you can easily visit the WinZip FTP site the next time by clicking the Profile Name list arrow in the Session Properties dialog box and then clicking WinZip. With the URL and user information entered, you are ready to log on to the FTP site anonymously and download the WinZip program.

Note: You cannot download the WinZip 8.0 program to a floppy disk because the program's file size (approximately two megabytes) exceeds the disk's storage capacity. Your instructor might ask you to download the program to your hard drive or to simply read the following steps without actually downloading the file.

To log on anonymously and download the file:

1. Click the **OK** button to log on to the WinZip FTP site. Several messages scroll in the message area at the bottom of the WS_FTP LE window. You can use the scroll arrows to view the messages passed between your client and the FTP server.

2. If necessary, click the **Maximize** button to maximize the program window. The Local System pane displays the drives and folders on your computer (the local computer) and the Remote Site pane displays the contents of the WinZip FTP site (the remote computer). You use the buttons to the right of each directory listing to change, make, view, rename, delete, and refresh the directories and files.

3. Click the **ChgDir** button in the Local System pane. The Input dialog box opens and requests the local folder name that you would like to display. See Figure 6-25.

| Figure 6-25 | CHANGING THE LOCAL DIRECTORY |

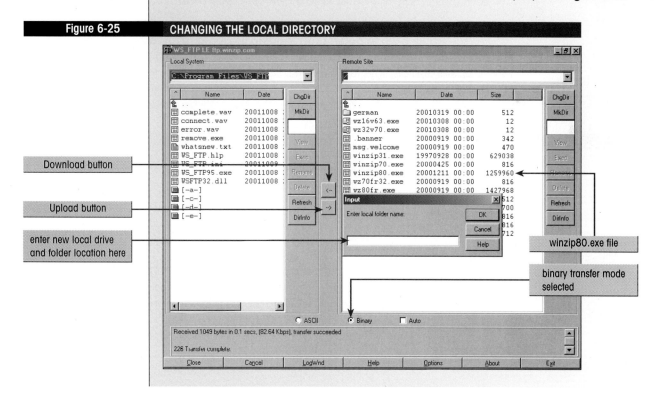

4. Type the drive letter and folder for the location to which you will download the file in the text box (see Figure 6-25), and then click the **OK** button. The Local System pane changes and displays the files and folders on the drive you selected. By changing the drive and folder on the local computer, files you download will be stored in that location.

TROUBLE? If you cannot establish a connection with the WinZip FTP server, then click the Close button at the bottom of the window, click the Connect button to open the Session Properties dialog box, click the Profile Name list arrow, and then click WinZip. Make sure you entered ftp.winzip.com in the Host Name/Address text box. Click the OK button to connect, and then follow the steps.

TROUBLE? If you tried more than once to connect to the WinZip site without success, the site might be busy. When the number of anonymous logins exceeds a large number, the WinZip site rejects all subsequent anonymous FTP sessions. Try again later, or just read the steps so you understand how to use an FTP client to download files.

The file you want to download, winzip80.exe, appears in the Remote Site pane.

5. If necessary, click the **Binary** option button to ensure that the program file is transferred correctly.

6. In the Remote Site pane, locate and then click **winzip80.exe** to select it.

7. Click the **Download** button between the Local System and Remote Site panes (see Figure 6-25) to begin downloading the file from the WinZip FTP site to the location you specified. As shown in Figure 6-26, a Transfer Status dialog box opens and displays information about the status of the download. When the Transfer Status dialog box closes, the message window will display the message "Transfer complete," and the winzip80.exe file will be saved on your computer.

Figure 6-26	TRANSFER STATUS DIALOG BOX

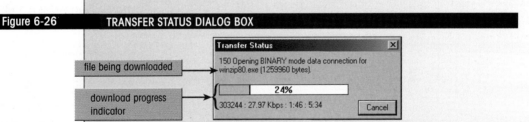

file being downloaded

download progress indicator

TROUBLE? WS_FTP LE might save a log file named WS_FTP.LOG on the drive and folder where you saved the winzip80.exe file. A log file indicates the status of the download operation; you can delete this file after the download is complete.

8. Click the **Exit** button at the bottom of the window to log off the WinZip FTP site and to close the WS_FTP LE program.

If you are allowed to install the WinZip program, open Windows Explorer, change to the drive and folder to which you downloaded the winzip80.exe file, double-click winzip80.exe, and then follow the on-screen instructions. (Ask your instructor or technical support person first before installing the program.) The WinZip file that you downloaded is an **evaluation version**, which means that you can use it to evaluate the software at no charge. Each time you start the program, it will remind you about your use of an evaluation copy that has not yet been registered. If you continue using the software, you can click a button in the reminder screen to purchase a license to use the full version.

Tracing **an Internet Route**

In this session, you have encountered Web sites that have asked you to select a download location, also known as a mirror site, from which to download a file. A **mirror site** is a replica of an existing server that provides an alternate location for downloading files. When you select a mirror site, you will usually begin by selecting a site close to you; for example, if you live in Tallahassee, Florida, you might choose a mirror site in Atlanta, Georgia rather than a site in Seattle, Washington. Because the Internet makes it feel as though you are accessing sites from very long distances in just a few seconds, you might think that the physical difference between you and another Internet site is unimportant, but it is. The Internet is a complex network of interconnected computers. Just as the distance between your PC and a remote computer might be measured in miles, the distance between your PC and a remote computer on the Internet is measured in hops. A **hop** is a connection between two computers. If a file travels through 15 computers before arriving at your PC, then the file has made 14 hops (the number of computers in the path minus one). Minimizing the number of hops between a remote computer and your PC reduces the total download time to transfer files between computers.

You can count the hops and identify the computers between your PC and a remote computer using the Windows **tracert** (for *trace route*) program. You can use the tracert program to make an informed choice between alternative download sites. Tracert will show you up to 30 hops and indicate the response time, the site name, and the IP address of each hop along the route. (If you do not have tracert installed on your computer, use a Web search engine to search for **ping**, or **Packet Internet Groper**, which is a program that tests a computer to determine if it is connected to the Internet. You can find several freeware and shareware ping programs that accomplish the same thing as tracert. In addition, the Additional Information section of the Student Online Companion for this tutorial includes links to other programs that trace routes.)

As Milt reviews additional software programs he might be given a list of mirror sites from which to download files; he can use tracert to determine if one mirror site might provide a more direct connection over others. Because many of the actors who provide voiceovers live in New York City, Milt asks you to use tracert to view the hops between your PC and the FTP site at New York University.

To view the hops between your PC and a remote computer:

1. Click the **Start** button on the Windows taskbar, click **Run**, type **command** in the Open list box, and then click the **OK** button. A DOS program window opens. If necessary, click the **Maximize** button on the program window's title bar to maximize it.

2. Type **tracert ftp.nyu.edu** at the command prompt, and then press the **Enter** key to list the hops between your PC and the server at the New York University in New York. Tracert produces a list of each computer's IP address on the path between your PC and the specified URL. When the trace is complete, the "Trace complete" message appears at the bottom of the site trace list. Figure 6-27 shows the hops from a user located in Texas; your trace will be different.

| Figure 6-27 | TRACERT COMMAND |

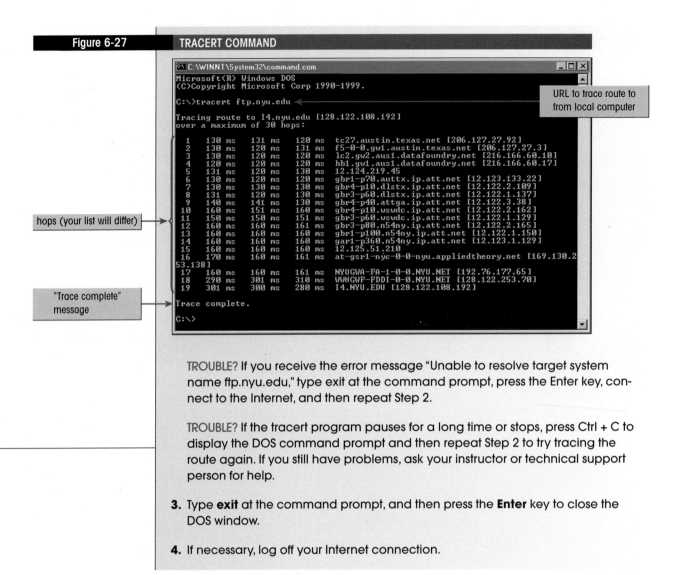

TROUBLE? If you receive the error message "Unable to resolve target system name ftp.nyu.edu," type exit at the command prompt, press the Enter key, connect to the Internet, and then repeat Step 2.

TROUBLE? If the tracert program pauses for a long time or stops, press Ctrl + C to display the DOS command prompt and then repeat Step 2 to try tracing the route again. If you still have problems, ask your instructor or technical support person for help.

3. Type **exit** at the command prompt, and then press the **Enter** key to close the DOS window.

4. If necessary, log off your Internet connection.

When you are downloading very large program files, you can use the tracert program any time—even while your browser is running—to find the path with the fewest hops, because that path might reduce your download time significantly. To trace a route while your browser is running, write down or copy the URL to the target site, click the Start button on the Windows taskbar, click Run, and then type *tracert* followed by the URL of the target site. Click the OK button to trace the route. Once the trace is complete, the tracert window closes immediately, so look quickly!

Milt is pleased with the programs that you have found. After testing the programs to make sure that they will satisfy the requirements at Sound Effects, Inc., Milt will fulfill any licensing agreements so he can install the full versions of the programs you downloaded on the office computers.

You successfully downloaded many programs from the Internet. In addition to its utility in transferring files between computers, FTP is an excellent way to share files with other users and to temporarily and permanently store files. In Session 6.3, you'll learn about online storage providers of these services.

Session 6.2 Quick Check

1. What is freeware, shareware, and limited edition software?

2. After downloading a program from the Internet, what should you do prior to installing it?

3. What is the file format that is used for storing documents on the Internet so users can print them without accessing the program used to create the documents?

4. What is the general name for a program that reduces the size of one or more files and that saves multiple files using a single filename?

5. What is a hop?

6. What Windows program determines the distance between computers connected to the Internet?

SESSION 6.3

In this session, you will visit the Web sites of some online storage providers and learn more about the services they provide. You will use Yahoo! Briefcase to upload and download a file and to send a link to a file in an e-mail message. Finally, you will examine the future of subscription models for delivering software products to end users.

Using Online Storage Services

Now that you've provided Milt with the tools he needs to transfer files on the Internet, where is he going to send those files? He can't upload his proprietary data and other sensitive information to a public directory on a publicly accessible FTP site, nor can he ask his contractors to do the same. Milt needs access to an FTP site that is both secure and password protected, with enough storage space so that files can remain on the site for as long as necessary. He also needs to provide access to this site to his contractors so they can upload and download files.

When you use an ISP for your Internet connection and e-mail services, you might also receive some free space to use to store a Web site or files. This space is useful to you, but your user name and password control access to the site. You probably won't want to share this space with other users, because by doing so you will need to give those other users full access to your account, including your e-mail messages. You would have no way of controlling access to the site or securing important data from other users.

Because FTP is easy to use and an efficient way of transferring files across the Internet, many services have evolved to meet the increased need for ways to store and share files. FTP sites are one way of sharing and storing files, but not everyone has full-privilege access to an FTP site. From this need, the creation of a new business model formed, where ISPs and other entities started providing 10 to 50 megabytes of storage space on their servers, either for free or for a fee. This space is secured with an account name and password and permits the sharing of files by many users. As the space sizes increased, so did the possibilities. Many businesses rely on these online storage services to send and receive large files while employees are traveling or as a normal course of business. In addition, the proliferation of large data files moving across the Internet has the potential to overload many networks and e-mail servers when these files are attached to e-mail messages, so these online storage providers provide an alternate to consuming a company's network resources.

At first, many of these services provided up to 50 megabytes of free storage space to registered users. As more registered users started accessing the sites, and as those users started storing large files and increasing the number of daily transfers, many sites experienced conflicts with users competing for the company's resources, so that the free model was in direct conflict with the paid model. As a result of bandwidth problems, many online storage providers changed their policies to limit the number of transfers and amount of space, charge a small monthly fee for the use of the space, or a combination of both. Most services provide additional space and transfers for an additional fee.

Using an online storage provider might be a good opportunity for Milt. As he reviews his requirements, he decides that he needs at least 50 to 100 megabytes of space and the capability to allow restricted and full access, depending on the user. Because the cost of maintaining his own FTP server would be an impediment to his overall operating budget, Milt is willing to pay a monthly fee for use of whichever provider matches his needs best. In addition, because Milt works with only a few contractors at a time, his space will not have a high number of transfers each day. Because Milt will require upload and download transfers, he will need to use an FTP client program or an easy-to-use Web page interface to execute the transfers. Being able to use any FTP client program or a Web browser to log on to the site—and not requiring any proprietary software from the online storage provider—will make it easier for Milt and his contractors to access and use the site. Finally, Milt wants to make sure that the provider will ensure the security of his data from unauthorized use.

You'll use the Internet to conduct your research to help Milt identify some potential providers for his online data storage needs. In the following sections, you will learn about some companies that provide online storage services.

Xdrive

Xdrive Technologies produces several versions of its online storage space for users in many categories, from large corporations to individuals. Many individuals use Xdrive Plus to store and share large files, such as MP3 files, that would otherwise be difficult to transfer across the Internet. Corporations use Xdrive to reduce the amount of traffic generated by large e-mail attachments on their network servers. Xdrive is also a simple way for people employed in satellite and home offices to transfer files to people working in corporate offices. Windows XP, which was released in late 2001, offers an integrated interface with Xdrive, making it very easy to transfer files to Xdrive and share them with other users. The optional Xdrive service, which costs less than $5 a month for most users, is available via the Windows XP Publishing Wizard for those users who purchase it.

Because Xdrive has been a popular service, you decide to investigate its Web site to determine if it might be a candidate for Milt.

To visit the Xdrive Web site:

1. Start your Web browser, open the Student Online Companion page at **www.course.com/newperspectives/internet3**, click the hyperlink for your book, click the **Tutorial 6** link, and then click the **Session 6.3** link. Click the **Xdrive** link and wait while the browser opens the Xdrive Technologies home page.

2. Point to **Products** in the link bar on the left, and then click **Products** in the menu that opens. The Products & Services page shown in Figure 6-28 opens.

Figure 6-28   **PRODUCTS & SERVICES PAGE**

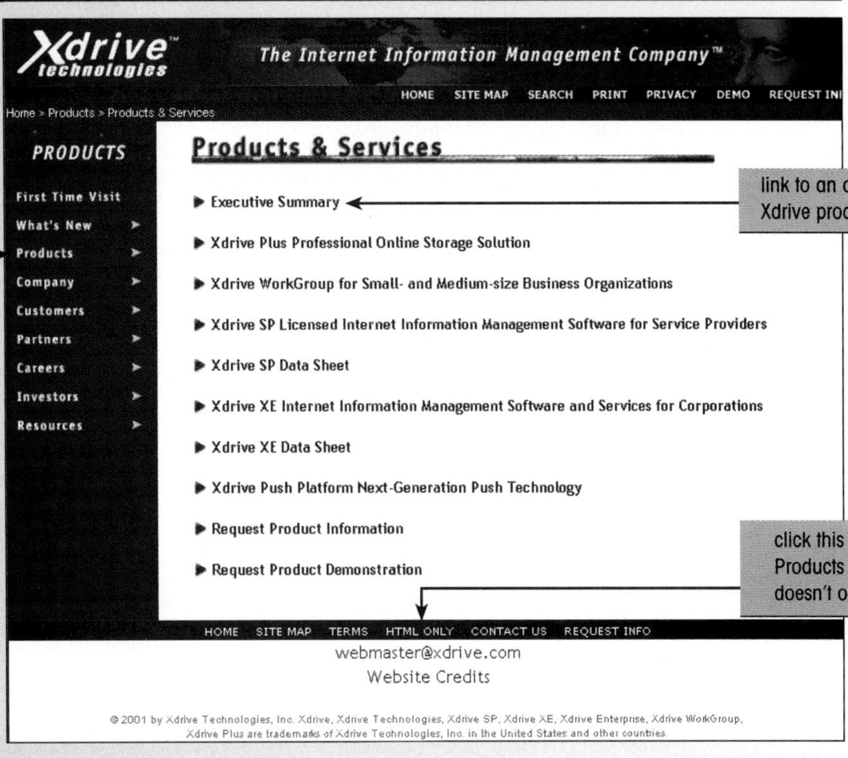

Products link

Xdrive technologies   *The Internet Information Management Company*™

HOME   SITE MAP   SEARCH   PRINT   PRIVACY   DEMO   REQUEST IN

Home > Products > Products & Services

PRODUCTS

First Time Visit
What's New
Products
Company
Customers
Partners
Careers
Investors
Resources

Products & Services

► Executive Summary   ←   *link to an overview of Xdrive products*

► Xdrive Plus Professional Online Storage Solution

► Xdrive WorkGroup for Small- and Medium-size Business Organizations

► Xdrive SP Licensed Internet Information Management Software for Service Providers

► Xdrive SP Data Sheet

► Xdrive XE Internet Information Management Software and Services for Corporations

► Xdrive XE Data Sheet

► Xdrive Push Platform Next-Generation Push Technology

► Request Product Information

click this link if the Products menu doesn't open

► Request Product Demonstration

HOME   SITE MAP   TERMS   HTML ONLY   CONTACT US   REQUEST INFO

webmaster@xdrive.com
Website Credits

© 2001 by Xdrive Technologies, Inc. Xdrive, Xdrive Technologies, Xdrive SP, Xdrive XE, Xdrive Enterprise, Xdrive WorkGroup,
Xdrive Plus are trademarks of Xdrive Technologies, Inc. in the United States and other countries.

TROUBLE? If a menu doesn't open, your browser might not support Java applet code. Scroll to the bottom of the page, and then click the HTML Only link to disable the Java applets so you can display and click links as you would in other Web pages.

Xdrive offers online storage in a variety of formats to address the needs of corporations, service providers, small- and medium-sized businesses, and individuals. You'll examine the Xdrive WorkGroup option, which is geared toward small- and medium-sized businesses, first.

3. Click the **Xdrive WorkGroup for Small- and Medium-size Business Organizations** link. A page opens and offers options for logging into Xdrive WorkGroup and for obtaining information about Xdrive WorkGroup.

4. Click the **Learn about Xdrive WorkGroup** link. Read the page that opens and describes this option. So far, this option might work well for Milt. It includes security features, individualized accounts, and file storage capabilities.

5. At the bottom of the page, click the **Benefits to Employees and Partners** link. Read the page that opens and describes how Xdrive WorkGroup might be used in a business.

Xdrive WorkGroup is a very powerful product and probably would deliver more features than Milt will ever need. You decide to investigate the option for individuals, Xdrive Plus.

To learn more about Xdrive Plus:

1. Click your browser's **Back** button as necessary to return to the Products & Services page, and then click the **Xdrive Plus Professional Online Storage Solution** link. The Xdrive Plus Online File Storage and Collaboration Solution for Individuals page opens.

2. Click the **Learn about Xdrive Plus** link. Read the page that opens and describes the features available in Xdrive Plus. This option would work well for Milt because it provides online storage, group access, and security features with a variety of storage limits at reasonable monthly rates.

Xdrive Plus appears to be a strong candidate for Milt's storage needs. He asks you to continue your search for an online storage provider so you can report back to him about other available options.

Driveway

Driveway Corporation is another provider of solutions for storing and transferring data across the Internet. Similar to Xdrive, Driveway offers several options based on the amount of data and type of storage required by its users.

To examine Driveway's file management options:

1. Return to the Student Online Companion Web page for Session 6.3, and then click the **Driveway** link and wait while your Web browser loads the Driveway Corporation home page shown in Figure 6-29.

| Figure 6-29 | DRIVEWAY CORPORATION HOME PAGE |

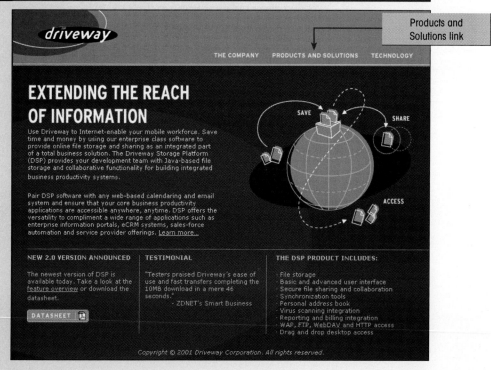

2. Click the **Products and Solutions** link at the top of the page. Read the page that opens and describes the Driveway storage platform service.

3. On the left side of the page, click the **Pricing and Services** link to open the Pricing and Services page. Read the page that opens. Because this service has a minimum fee requirement, it is probably not the best option for Milt.

4. Click the **Product Features** link on the left side of the page and read the page that opens and describes the file management features for Driveway. Notice that Driveway also requires users to download a program to access it.

Driveway is a powerful product, but it is probably too expensive for Milt to use. You'll look at another online storage provider, FreeDrive, next.

FreeDrive

FreeDrive was one of the first Web sites to offer free storage space to registered users. FreeDrive offers different levels of service, based on your usage and storage requirements. Membership is free and you must use a Web browser to transfer files. Although Milt's preference is to use an FTP client program or Web browser to transfer files, he wants you to find out more information about FreeDrive, especially because its basic membership and service are free.

To explore options at FreeDrive:

1. Return to the Student Online Companion Web page for Session 6.3, and then click the **FreeDrive** link and wait while your Web browser loads the FreeDrive home page.

2. On the left side of the page, click the **why sign up?** link and read the page that opens and describes how to use FreeDrive. See Figure 6-30.

Figure 6-30	FREEDRIVE INFORMATION PAGE

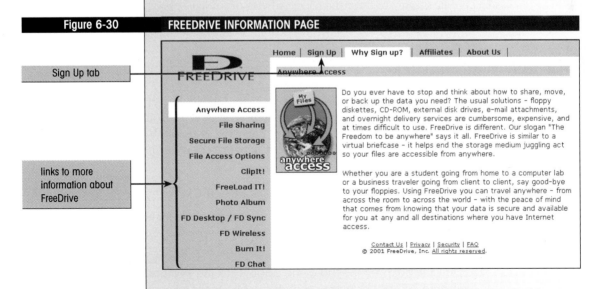

Sign Up tab

links to more information about FreeDrive

3. On the left side of the page, click the **Secure File Storage** link and read the page that opens. This service provides security features.

4. At the top of the page, click the **Sign Up** tab. The page shown in Figure 6-31 opens, describing the different membership plans for FreeDrive users. Scroll down the page to examine the membership plans for FreeDrive users.

Figure 6-31	FREEDRIVE MEMBERSHIP PLAN INFORMATION

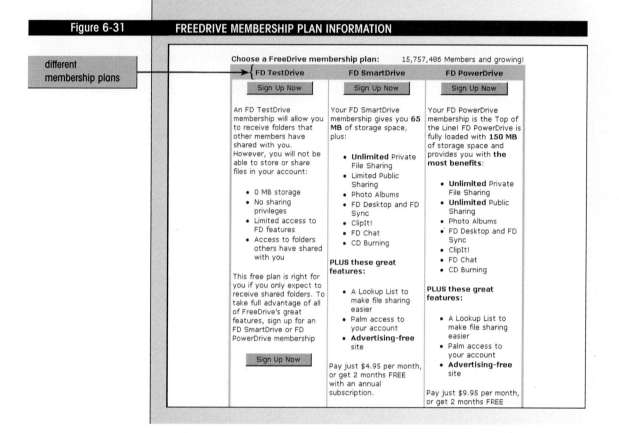

different membership plans

Choose a FreeDrive membership plan: 15,757,486 Members and growing!

FD TestDrive

Sign Up Now

An FD TestDrive membership will allow you to receive folders that other members have shared with you. However, you will not be able to store or share files in your account:

- 0 MB storage
- No sharing privileges
- Limited access to FD features
- Access to folders others have shared with you

This free plan is right for you if you only expect to receive shared folders. To take full advantage of all of FreeDrive's great features, sign up for an FD SmartDrive or FD PowerDrive membership

Sign Up Now

FD SmartDrive

Sign Up Now

Your FD SmartDrive membership gives you **65 MB** of storage space, plus:

- **Unlimited** Private File Sharing
- Limited Public Sharing
- Photo Albums
- FD Desktop and FD Sync
- ClipIt!
- FD Chat
- CD Burning

PLUS these great features:

- A Lookup List to make file sharing easier
- Palm access to your account
- **Advertising-free site**

Pay just $4.95 per month, or get 2 months FREE with an annual subscription.

FD PowerDrive

Sign Up Now

Your FD PowerDrive membership is the Top of the Line! FD PowerDrive is fully loaded with **150 MB** of storage space and provides you with **the most benefits**:

- **Unlimited** Private File Sharing
- **Unlimited** Public Sharing
- Photo Albums
- FD Desktop and FD Sync
- ClipIt!
- FD Chat
- CD Burning

PLUS these great features:

- A Lookup List to make file sharing easier
- Palm access to your account
- **Advertising-free site**

Pay just $9.95 per month, or get 2 months FREE

The SmartDrive option is a good candidate for Milt. It provides unlimited transfers, some public sharing of files, and 65 megabytes of storage space at a low monthly fee. You'll present this option to Milt for his storage needs and continue your research.

My Docs Online

My Docs Online is another service that provides individual accounts for transferring files. This service also permits access to your online storage drive from any computer connected to the Internet and also to wireless devices, such as a pager or Palm Pilot. For an additional charge, you can send, print, or fax your documents from your online drive.

To examine the My Docs Online services:

1. Return to the Student Online Companion Web page for Session 6.3, and then click the **My Docs Online** link and wait while your Web browser loads the My Docs Online home page.

2. In the link bar near the top of the page, click the **Features** link. The page shown in Figure 6-32 opens and describes the My Docs Online services. Scroll down the page to view the options.

Figure 6-32   **MY DOCS ONLINE SERVICES INFORMATION**

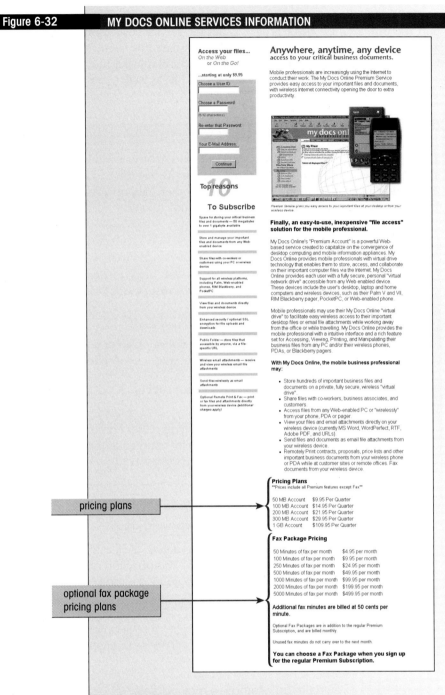

3. In the link bar near the top of the page, click the **FAQ** link. Click the hyperlinks to view some answers to frequently asked questions about the services. Make sure to view answers to questions that Milt may ask, such as "Why is using My Docs Online better than using e-mail attachments?", "How do I login to my account?", "How do I give files to others?", and "Can I give files to people who may not be My Docs Online users?"

My Docs Online provides many of the features that Milt has requested. It does not support use with an FTP client program, but the service is accessible from any Web browser and from most wireless devices. The option to share documents with users who are not My Online Docs users is attractive because he could still transfer files to people who do not have accounts. This service seems to be very affordable, as well.

Yahoo! Briefcase

Yahoo! Briefcase is the final online storage service that you will investigate for Milt. To use Yahoo! services, you must have a Yahoo! account. By creating an account at Yahoo!, you will set up an e-mail address and gain access to other Yahoo! services. To learn more about Yahoo! Briefcase, you will need to create a Yahoo! account.

To create a Yahoo! account:

1. Return to the Student Online Companion Web page for Session 6.3, and then click the **Yahoo!** link and wait while your Web browser loads the Yahoo! home page.

2. Click the **Briefcase** link. The Yahoo! Briefcase page opens.

   TROUBLE? If you already have a Yahoo! account, enter your Yahoo! ID and password on the Yahoo! Briefcase page, and then skip to the next set of steps.

3. Click the **Sign me up!** link in the New User section. A page opens and requests some basic information.

4. Click in the **Yahoo! ID** text box, and then type a user name, such as milt_spangler. If you have a common name, you might try using your name plus some digits (such as your year of birth), such as milt_spangler1980.

5. Press the **Tab** key, and then type a password. Yahoo! passwords are case-sensitive, so be sure and type letters using the correct case.

6. Press the **Tab** key, and then type your password again.

7. Click the **Security Question** list arrow, and then click a question in the list. If you forget your password, Yahoo! will ask you this question and if you respond correctly, Yahoo! will send your password to you via e-mail.

8. Type the answer to your secret question in the Answer text box.

9. Enter your birthday in the text boxes, and then type an alternate e-mail address in the Alternate Email text box (if you don't have an alternate e-mail address, skip this text box).

   TROUBLE? If you enter an alternate e-mail address, Yahoo! will send a confirmation message to that account.

10. Scroll down the page as necessary to the Customizing Yahoo! section, and then select your language, enter your zip or postal code, select your gender, select **college/graduate student** as your occupation, and select **education, research** as your industry.

11. Deselect the **Contact me occasionally** check box so you will not receive special offers from Yahoo!.

12. Scroll down the page to the Word Verification section, and then follow the instructions to enter the word you see in the box.

13. Click the **Submit This Form** button at the bottom of the page. If your Yahoo! ID is not in use, the page shown in Figure 6-33 opens and indicates that your registration is complete. Make sure to write down your Yahoo! ID so you won't forget it.

Figure 6-33	YAHOO! BRIEFCASE REGISTRATION COMPLETE PAGE

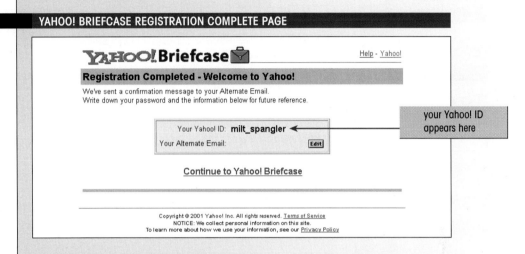

TROUBLE? If your Yahoo! ID is being used, follow the instructions on the screen to create a new ID, and keep resubmitting your application until you receive your Yahoo! ID.

Now that you have a Yahoo! ID, you can use it to send and receive e-mail messages; your e-mail address is your Yahoo! ID followed by @yahoo.com. You'll continue to the Briefcase next.

To set up your Yahoo! Briefcase:

1. Click the **Continue to Yahoo! Briefcase** link. The Yahoo! Briefcase – Account Setup page opens. You use this page to create your Briefcase and to indicate your preferences and the folders you would like it to contain.

2. In the Create Folders section, make sure that the **My Documents** check box is selected, that the other check boxes are not selected, and that the **Yahoo! Specials** check box is deselected. You will accept the default settings in the second section (Select View Preferences).

3. In the Enter Confirmation Code section, follow the instructions to enter your code, and then click the **Submit** button at the bottom of the page. The Yahoo! Briefcase home page shown in Figure 6-34 opens.

Figure 6-34	YAHOO! BRIEFCASE HOME PAGE

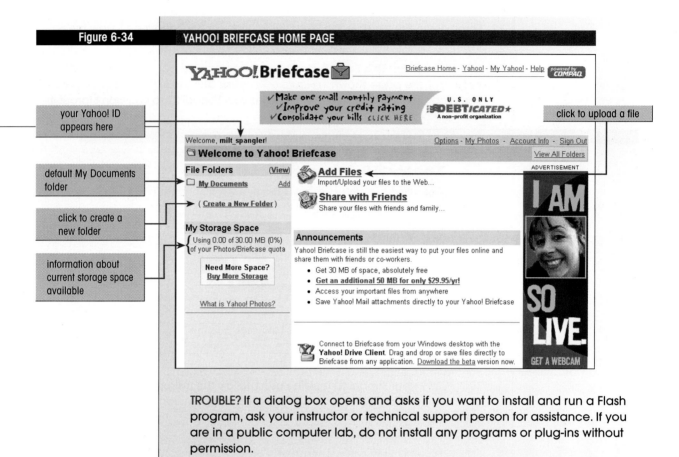

TROUBLE? If a dialog box opens and asks if you want to install and run a Flash program, ask your instructor or technical support person for assistance. If you are in a public computer lab, do not install any programs or plug-ins without permission.

Now that you've set up your account and Briefcase, you can upload a file.

Uploading a File to Yahoo! Briefcase

You can upload one file or multiple files to the default folders in your Briefcase, or you can use Briefcase to create new folders. After creating a new folder, you can change the folder's properties to public (so that all users can access it), private (so no other users can access it), or friends (so that only those users you specify can access it). Setting a folder's properties lets you control access to your Briefcase for other users.

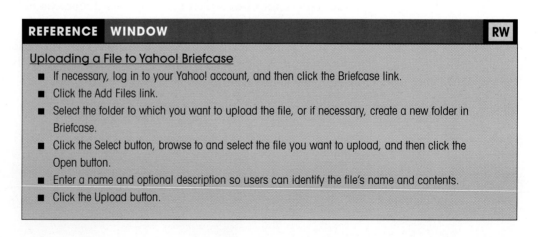

REFERENCE	WINDOW	RW

Uploading a File to Yahoo! Briefcase
- If necessary, log in to your Yahoo! account, and then click the Briefcase link.
- Click the Add Files link.
- Select the folder to which you want to upload the file, or if necessary, create a new folder in Briefcase.
- Click the Select button, browse to and select the file you want to upload, and then click the Open button.
- Enter a name and optional description so users can identify the file's name and contents.
- Click the Upload button.

You'll upload a file from your Data Disk to test the interface and its ease of use.

To upload a file to Yahoo! Briefcase:

1. Click the **Add Files** link. The Select Folder page opens, where you select the Briefcase destination for your files. You can also create a new folder using this page. See Figure 6-35.

Figure 6-35   SELECT FOLDER PAGE

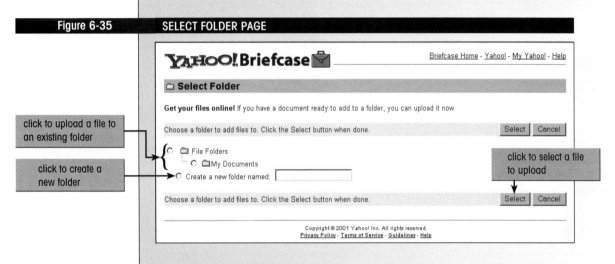

click to upload a file to an existing folder

click to create a new folder

click to select a file to upload

2. Click the **My Documents** option button to select this folder, and then click the **Select** button below the option button. The Add a File page opens. You'll upload a file from your Data Disk to the My Documents folder. You upload files one at a time or as a group; notice that the maximum file size for any single file is five megabytes.

3. Click the **Browse** button in the first section on the page. The Choose file dialog box opens.

4. Use the Look in list arrow to open to the **Tutorial.06** folder on your Data Disk, click the **Memorandum** file to select it, and then click the **Open** button. The path to the Memorandum.doc file on your Data Disk appears in the On your computer text box, as shown in Figure 6-36. (Your path might be different.)

Figure 6-36	ADD A FILE PAGE

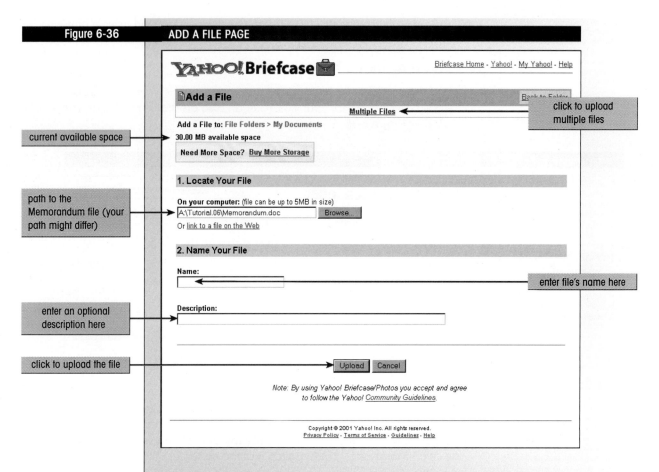

YAHOO! Briefcase

Briefcase Home - Yahoo! - My Yahoo! - Help

Add a File   Back to Folder

Multiple Files ←   click to upload multiple files

Add a File to: **File Folders > My Documents**

current available space →   **30.00 MB available space**

Need More Space? Buy More Storage

1. Locate Your File

path to the Memorandum file (your path might differ) →   **On your computer:** (file can be up to 5MB in size)

`A:\Tutorial.06\Memorandum.doc`   Browse...

Or link to a file on the Web

2. Name Your File

Name:

[   ] ←   enter file's name here

enter an optional description here →   **Description:**

[   ]

click to upload the file →   Upload   Cancel

Note: By using Yahoo! Briefcase/Photos you accept and agree to follow the Yahoo! Community Guidelines.

Copyright © 2001 Yahoo! Inc. All rights reserved.
Privacy Policy - Terms of Service - Guidelines - Help

After selecting the file to upload, you need to give it a name and an optional description. By doing so you make it easier for you and other users to identify the file and its contents.

5. Click in the **Name** text box, type **Memorandum**, press the **Tab** key, and then type **Memo to contractors about online storage.**

6. Click the **Upload** button at the bottom of the page. Depending on the speed of your Internet connection, it could take several moments to upload the file. After the file has been uploaded, the confirmation page shown in Figure 6-37 opens and tells you that the transfer is complete.

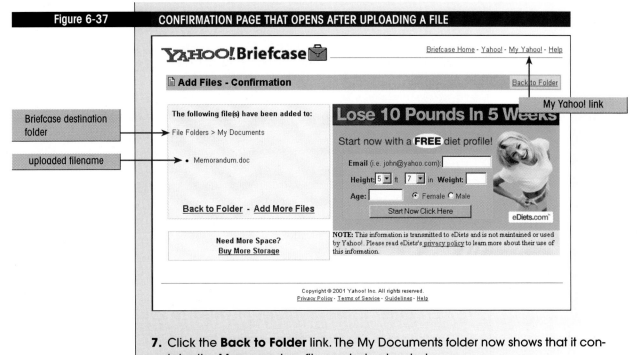

Figure 6-37   CONFIRMATION PAGE THAT OPENS AFTER UPLOADING A FILE

7. Click the **Back to Folder** link. The My Documents folder now shows that it contains the Memorandum file you just uploaded.

Now that you've uploaded the file, you need to learn how to make other users aware of it and how to access it.

Sending an E-Mail Message to a File in the Briefcase

When you upload a file to the Briefcase, you make other users aware of the file by selecting it and then sending an e-mail message from Briefcase to the users' e-mail addresses. You can select more than one file per message and up to 10 e-mail addresses at a time to which to send the message. You can also include a personal note in the message; Yahoo! adds the name and description of the file in the message, along with the URL to download it.

Before you can send a message to your Yahoo! e-mail address, you'll need to activate it.

To activate your Yahoo! mailbox:

1. Click the **My Yahoo!** link in the upper-right corner of the page. Your My Yahoo! page opens. Notice that your Yahoo! ID appears on the page, indicating that your account is active.

2. Find the Message Center pane on the My Yahoo! page, and then click the **Check Email** link.

3. Type your first and last names in the appropriate text boxes, and then click the **Set me up** button. A page opens and welcomes you to Yahoo! Mail.

4. Click the **Continue to Yahoo! Mail** button (if there are two buttons on the page, click either one). Your Yahoo! mailbox opens.

Now you can return to Briefcase and send an e-mail message.

REFERENCE WINDOW   **RW**

<u>Sending an E-Mail Message Linked to a File in Briefcase</u>
- Click the check box for the files that you want to include in the e-mail message.
- Click the Email button.
- Type your return e-mail address in the From text box.
- Type the e-mail address of the recipient in the To text box. If you are sending the message to multiple recipients, separate their addresses with commas or spaces.
- Type an optional message in the Message text box to identify the purpose of the message for the recipients.
- If necessary, click an option button in the Expiration Date section to set an expiration date for downloading the files.
- Click the Send Email button.

You will send the message to yourself to simulate how it will work for another user.

To alert other users of a file uploaded to your Briefcase:

1. Click the check box for the **Memorandum** file to select it. When your Briefcase contains more than one file, you can select multiple files by clicking their check boxes.

2. Click the **Email** button. The Email File Links page opens. You use this page to specify the address to use in the From text box, up to 10 e-mail addresses for the recipients, and an optional message. You can also set an expiration date for the users to have access to the file.

3. If necessary, type your Yahoo! e-mail address in the From text box.

4. Press the **Tab** key, and then type your Yahoo! e-mail address in the To text box. When you send the message to more than one recipient, separate the addresses with commas or spaces.

5. Press the **Tab** key twice, and then type **I am sending a link to a memo that I uploaded to Briefcase.** The completed page is shown in Figure 6-38.

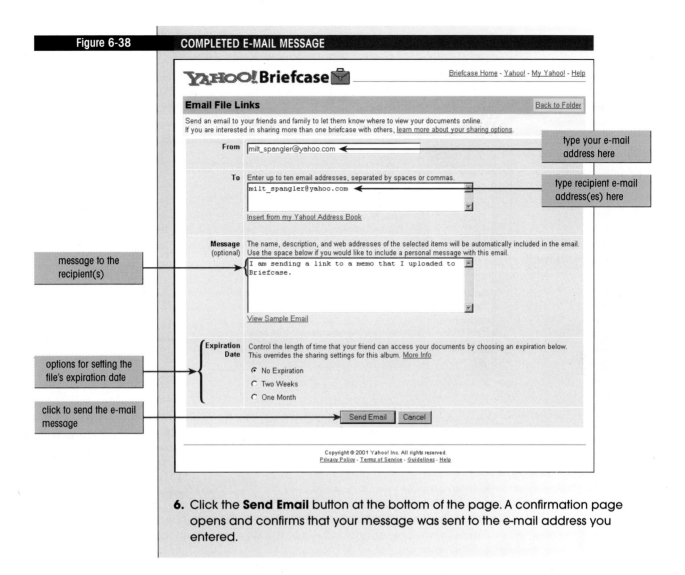

Figure 6-38 COMPLETED E-MAIL MESSAGE

6. Click the **Send Email** button at the bottom of the page. A confirmation page opens and confirms that your message was sent to the e-mail address you entered.

You'll retrieve your e-mail from Yahoo! to see the message another user would receive.

To view the e-mail message you sent:

1. Click the **My Yahoo!** link in the upper-right corner of the confirmation page. Your personalized Yahoo! page opens.

2. Scroll down the page so you can see the Message Center pane, which usually appears on the left side of the page. A new mail icon appears to indicate that you have new mail.

3. Click the **Check Email** link. Your Inbox opens and displays the message you received. Because you just signed up for Yahoo! Mail, you will also have a welcome message from Yahoo! in your mailbox.

4. Click the **Check Mail** link on the left side of the page to open your Inbox. Your message appears in the list.

5. Click the **Yahoo! Briefcase: <your name>'s file(s)** link to open your message, and then scroll down the page so you can see the text of the message. See Figure 6-39.

Figure 6-39	E-MAIL MESSAGE SENT FROM BRIEFCASE

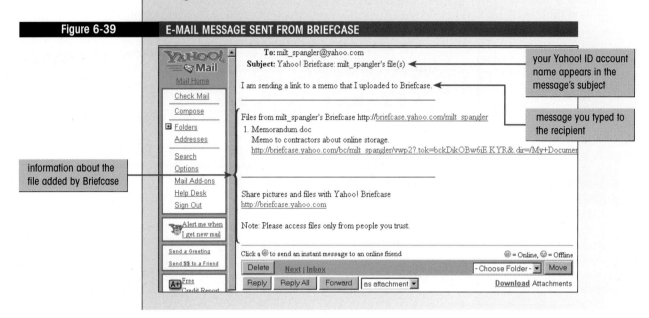

When you send a message from Briefcase, the message contains your message (if you added one), along with a link to the file you uploaded. You'll download the file next to see how it works.

To download the file from Briefcase and open it:

1. Click the link to the **Memorandum.doc** file in the e-mail message. A new browser window opens and shows the file in your Briefcase. See Figure 6-40.

Figure 6-40	LINK TO UPLOADED MESSAGE

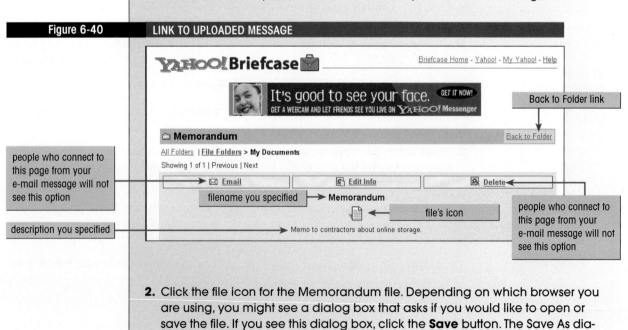

2. Click the file icon for the Memorandum file. Depending on which browser you are using, you might see a dialog box that asks if you would like to open or save the file. If you see this dialog box, click the **Save** button. The Save As dialog box opens.

3. If necessary, use the Save in list arrow to open the **Tutorial.06** folder on your Data Disk, change the filename to **Memorandum1**, and then click the **Save** button. A dialog box opens while the file is being downloaded. If necessary, close this dialog box when the "download complete" message appears.

4. Start Windows Explorer, open the **Tutorial.06** folder on your Data Disk, and then double-click the **Memorandum1** file to start Word or another program and view the file. The file opens.

5. After reading the memo, close Word.

After all users have downloaded the file or when you no longer require its storage in your Briefcase, you can delete the file.

Deleting a File from Briefcase

You downloaded and viewed the file. Now you can delete it.

REFERENCE WINDOW   **RW**

Deleting a File from Briefcase
- Open the Briefcase folder containing the file you want to delete.
- Click the check box for the file you want to delete.
- Click the Delete button.
- Click the Confirm Delete button.

Because you logged on to your Yahoo! account, you'll be able to delete the file from the screen that you are currently viewing. Other users will not have this option unless you specifically give them permission to change the files in your folder.

To delete the file from your Briefcase and log off:

1. Click the **Back to Folder** link. The contents of the My Documents folder appear.

2. Click the check box for the **Memorandum** file to select it.

3. Click the **Delete** button. A page opens and asks you to confirm the file's deletion.

4. Click the **Confirm Delete** button. The file is deleted and the My Documents folder no longer contains any files.

5. Click the **Sign Off** link near the top of the page. A page opens indicating that you have signed out of your Yahoo! account.

6. Close your browser, and if necessary, log off your Internet connection.

When you need to log back on to your Yahoo! account, return to the Yahoo! Web site at www.yahoo.com, click the link for the page or service that you want to open (Briefcase or Check Email), and then enter your Yahoo! ID and password. Always be sure to log off your account when you are finished using it, especially if you are using a public computer.

The last thing that you'll investigate for Milt is obtaining software updates online.

Subscription **Services**

For many years, computer manufacturers such as IBM, Hewlett-Packard, and Compaq have offered leases and other incentives to corporations in an effort to make replacing outdated hardware products with newer models more affordable. Recently this idea was carried forward to software programs, as well. When Microsoft announced the release of its Office XP product, its business and marketing plans included a new method of selling the software. A **subscription model**, also called a **subscription service**, is a method of selling software over the Internet in lieu of the traditional boxed product with CD-ROMs that you might purchase in a retail outlet. The software publisher has the advantage of controlling the number of unlicensed copies of the software—for example, when you borrow a friend's CD-ROM disc to install a program—and has a guaranteed source of revenue when new software versions are released. Regardless of the impact of the new software version—major or minor—the publisher is guaranteed that users will use it, because the decision to purchase and install the new software has already been made by way of the subscription. To the end user, a software subscription ensures an up-to-date product because product updates, enhancements, and patches are installed automatically over the Internet.

After careful analysis of the delivery system, Microsoft ultimately decided to offer its new subscription service to a few select locations in the world (mostly in Australia) in order to perfect its delivery system of products over the Internet. However, other software producers are following suit in an effort to offer the same subscription models to their customers. Some industry analysts estimate that by the year 2006, all Microsoft products will be delivered via the Internet. For now, however, you can still purchase your favorite product in a box at the local computer store.

Milt is pleased with the information that you have provided. His goal of finding the perfect online storage provider will be much easier now that he has your research in hand. He is confident that he will be able to find a suitable provider for him and his contractors.

Session 6.3 QUICK | CHECK

1. How might an online storage provider help a company to reduce its network activity and increase its productivity?

2. True or False: Some online storage providers offer free online storage for registered users.

3. True or False: Some online storage providers offer the ability to share files between registered and unregistered users.

4. Before using Yahoo! Briefcase, what must the Briefcase owner do?

5. Which folder is created by default in Yahoo! Briefcase?

6. True or False: You can use Yahoo! Briefcase to upload only one file at a time.

7. True or False: Microsoft offers a subscription license for Office XP products sold in the United States.

REVIEW ASSIGNMENTS

Milt has asked you to investigate the use of a new e-mail program, Eudora Pro, which is produced by Qualcomm. Your research reveals that you can download an evaluation copy of Eudora to evaluate the program. If Milt likes this program, he can inquire about purchasing licenses to the more powerful, commercial version of Eudora Pro for his staff. Before downloading the evaluation copy, you would like to read the user's manual to learn more about the program. Fortunately, you can download the user's manual in PDF. You will complete the following steps to download the user's manual.

1. Place your Data Disk in the appropriate drive.

2. Start the WS_FTP LE FTP client program on your computer. (*Note:* The Review Assignments are written for the WS_FTP LE FTP client program you downloaded in this tutorial. However, you can use any FTP client program or a browser to complete these steps by executing the equivalent steps in that program.)

3. Use the Profile Name list arrow to select the Eudora FTP session, or create a new session profile named Eudora. The host name or address is ftp.qualcomm.com. You will log on using an anonymous login and your full e-mail address as the password.

4. Connect and log on to the Qualcomm FTP server. (*Hint:* If necessary, make a dial-up connection before connecting to the Qualcomm server.)

5. If necessary, change the directory on the remote site to /eudora/eudoralight/windows/english.

6. Select the file named eul3manl.pdf on the remote site, and then download that file to your computer. This file contains the user's manual in PDF format.

7. After the download is complete, disconnect from the remote site, close your FTP client program, and then log off your Internet connection if necessary.

Explore   8. If you have an antivirus program installed on your computer, use it to scan the files you downloaded in this tutorial for viruses.

9. If necessary, install the Adobe Acrobat Reader program you downloaded in Session 6.2. (*Note:* Check with your instructor or technical support person before installing any program on your computer's hard drive.)

10. Open Windows Explorer, and then locate and double-click the eul3manl.pdf file that you just downloaded. Acrobat Reader will start and open the file.

Explore   11. Locate the pages that describe "Using a Signature" found somewhere in the first 30 pages. (*Hint:* In Acrobat Reader, use the Find command on the Edit menu to search for the three-word term. You'll find an entry in the Contents first, so you'll need to use Find again to locate the heading for this section.) The description of signature files may span more than one page. Print up to two pages describing signature files. (*Hint:* Use the Acrobat Reader's Help system to learn more about using the program to read Eudora's program documentation.)

12. Close Acrobat Reader.

CASE PROBLEMS

Case 1. County Assessor's Office Herb Merrell is the County Assessor for Lancaster County in eastern Nebraska. The county assessor's property office has a large database of information stored on an FTP site that the public can access for a small fee. Realtors and real-estate appraisers are the primary users of this information. However, many other businesses are taking advantage of this online access to Lancaster County property records. Herb has received complaints from customers in the southern part of the county about long delays in accessing the system. You are Herb's chief architect of the information system that supports the entire county assessor's online database. Herb wants you to investigate the system's processing delays. You realize that because the Lancaster system is stored on a network server, some delays are caused by general Internet traffic and, therefore, are unresolvable. Herb wants you to see if the problem is with one of the computer systems that is connected to the main computer that stores the county assessor's files.

You decide to begin your research by installing an Internet ping program to test the Internet connections for delays. You will complete the following steps to research and find programs that can identify processing problems, and then you will download the program.

1. Start your Web browser, open the Student Online Companion page at www.course.com/newperspectives/internet3, click the hyperlink for your book, click the Tutorial 6 link, and then click the Case Problems link. Click the Excite link for Case Problem 1 and wait while the browser loads the page.

Explore ▷ 2. Search for information about ping programs using the search phrase "Packet Internet Groper." Follow some of the hits, and then use your browser's Print button to print at least one page of a definition that you think is correct.

3. Return to the Student Online Companion page, and then click the Tucows link for Case Problem 1 to open that page. Use the links to connect to a server for your operating system and in a region or state that is the closest to your location.

4. Click the Internet tab to display a page of Internet categories, and then click the Finger and Ping link in the Network Protocols section.

Explore ▷ 5. Explore the links to programs in the Finger and Ping category to learn more about the programs you can download. Use the links in the Additional Information section of the Student Online Companion for Tutorial 6 to see if you can find a review of any of the programs. If you find a review, use your browser's Print button to print one or two pages.

6. Based on your research, locate a program on the Tucows Web site that will help Herb with his problem as described in the case problem description. Use your browser's Print button to print the page that describes the program you are recommending.

7. If you have permission to do so, download to the Tutorial.06 folder on your Data Disk or a hard drive the ping program you are recommending. (*Note:* Check with your instructor before downloading any files from the Internet. Before downloading the file, make sure that you have enough disk space to save it in the location you specify.)

Explore ▷ 8. If you are able to do so, scan the file you downloaded for viruses.

9. Close your browser, and if necessary, log off your Internet connection.

Explore ▷ 10. On a separate piece of paper, write a short memo to Herb that explains why you have chosen this program and list some advantages it has over other shareware programs available on the Tucows Web site.

Case 2. Internet Adventures Internet Adventures is a consulting company providing a variety of services to small- and medium-sized companies. Roxanna Kubovich, owner of Internet Adventures, charges an hourly rate to research and download information on the Internet. Roxanna is currently working with a large CPA firm that wants her to create bookmarks to Web sites that are of interest to tax preparers so the accountants can give them to their clients on disk. Because the firm's clients use Internet Explorer and Navigator to browse the Web, she needs to find a way to convert an existing set of Internet Explorer favorites to Navigator bookmarks. Roxanna remembers reading a review about several shareware products that might be able to maintain a library of common bookmarks that Internet Explorer and Navigator can share. To help Roxanna with her research, you'll complete the following steps.

1. Start your Web browser, open the Student Online Companion page at www.course.com/newperspectives/internet3, click the hyperlink for your book, click the Tutorial 6 link, and then click the Case Problems link. Click the Tucows link for Case Problem 2 and wait while the browser loads the page.

2. Click the link for your operating system, click the Internet tab, scroll down to the Web Browsers & Tools category, and then click the Bookmark Utilities link.

3. Use the links on the page that opens to find three programs that convert Internet Explorer favorites to Navigator bookmarks and vice versa. Review and print the documentation information for each program. Use the links in the Additional Information section of the Student Online Companion for Tutorial 6 to see if you can find a review of any of the programs. If you find a review, use your browser's Print button to print one or two pages.

4. If you have permission to do so, download to the Tutorial.06 folder on your Data Disk or a hard drive the converter program you are recommending for Roxanna. (*Note:* Check with your instructor before downloading any files from the Internet. Before downloading the file, make sure that you have enough disk space to save it in the location you specify.)

Explore   5. If you are able to do so, scan the file you downloaded for viruses.

6. Close your browser, and if necessary, log off your Internet connection.

Explore   7. On a separate piece of paper, write a short memo to Roxanna that explains why you have chosen this program and list some advantages it has over other shareware programs available on the Tucows Web site.

Case 3. Midwestern University Marco Lozario is director of computing at Midwestern University. He and his staff of three people ensure that the school's computer lab of 45 Windows-based computers function properly. Last week, a virus infected every computer in the lab, and Marco had to close the lab to prevent the virus from spreading to students' disks and to other computers. Some of the lab computers have McAfee Virus Scan software installed and others have Norton Antivirus, but the installed versions of both programs do not recognize and cannot eradicate the new virus pattern. Complete the following steps to locate the latest virus data files from McAfee and Symantec (the company that produces Norton Antivirus) so Marco can clean the infected computers.

1. Start your Web browser, open the Student Online Companion page at www.course.com/newperspectives/internet3, click the hyperlink for your book, click the Tutorial 6 link, and then click the Case Problems link. Click the McAfee link for Case Problem 3 and wait while the browser loads the page.

2. Use your browser to navigate to the readme.txt file at ftp.mcafee.com/pub/antivirus/datfiles/4.x.

3. Open the readme.txt file in this folder and review its contents. Use your browser or the program that opens to print the first page of this document, and then close the browser window or program that opened the file.

Explore   4. Use your browser's address field to return to the root directory, and then open the licensed folder. What happens?

5. Return to the Student Online Companion page, and then click the Symantec link and wait while your browser loads the page.

6. Use your browser to navigate to the update.txt file at ftp.symantec.com/public/english_us_canada/antivirus_definitions/norton_antivirus.

7. Open the update.txt file in this folder and review its contents. Use your browser or the program that opens to print the first page of this document, and then close the browser window or program that opened the file.

Explore   8. Marco needs some information about the Live Update product from Symantec so he can look into installing it on the lab's computers. He asks if you can find a text file that describes the Live Update setup. Browse the FTP site at ftp.symantec.com to find this file, and then save the file in the Tutorial.06 folder on your Data Disk. (*Hint:* Use the Save As command on your browser's File menu to save the file.)

9. Close your browser, and if necessary, log off your Internet connection.

Case 4. Englewood Health Club John Rowe owns the Englewood Health Club in Englewood, Colorado. His business transmits all of its employer data on tape to the Internal Revenue Service (IRS) and uses a wire transfer to deposit its employees' federal tax payments into the correct accounts. John just received a letter from the IRS indicating that the tape with his company's federal unemployment data for the third quarter of the year 2000 was lost or damaged in transmit, and that he needs to file submit this form again manually. Because this error was due to an IRS error, neither John nor the club will incur any penalty. John needs to download the correct form to use from the IRS FTP site. He asks you to help him find it and the instructions for its completion. To help John, you'll complete the following steps.

1. Start your Web browser, open the Student Online Companion page at www.course.com/newperspectives/internet3, click the hyperlink for your book, click the Tutorial 6 link, and then click the Case Problems link. Click the Internal Revenue Service link for Case Problem 4 and wait while the browser loads the page.

Explore   2. The IRS indicates on the site that the file 00-index.txt lists the descriptions of all files in each directory. Open this file in the pub directory and review its contents to learn the location of the directory that contains tax forms in PDF format for the year 2000.

Explore   3. Open the directory that you found in Step 2, and then open the file 00-index.txt in that directory to learn about the files it contains. Scan through the file to locate and write down the filenames for three files: Form 940 (Employer's Annual Federal Unemployment (FUTA) Tax Return), Form 940EZ (Employer's Annual Federal Unemployment (FUTA) Tax Return), and Form 941 (Employers Quarterly Federal Tax Return). (*Hint:* Use the Find command on the Edit menu or the Find in This Page command on the Search menu in the browser to find your search text in this file.)

Explore   4. Close the text file, and then locate the three PDF files that you noted in Step 3. Save these three files in the Tutorial.06 folder on your Data Disk. (*Hint:* In Internet Explorer, press and hold the Ctrl key, click each file, release the Ctrl key, click File on the menu bar, and then click Save As to save the files. In Navigator, right-click a file and click Save As on the shortcut menu to save each file individually.)

5. Open the PDF file for Form 941 in the browser. (*Note:* You must have Adobe Acrobat Reader to view this file. If your browser cannot open the file, try double-clicking the file you saved in the Tutorial.06 folder on your Data Disk to open it.) Use your browser's Print dialog box to print page 1 of the PDF file.

6. Close your browser, and if necessary, log off your Internet connection.

Case 5. Seaworthy Engineering Seaworthy Engineering is an engineering consulting group based in San Antonio, Texas. Judy Seaworthy, the company's chief technical officer, oversees the consultants' computer needs. Among her many duties, she is responsible for supplying each consultant with a notebook computer. Because the consultants spend up to 75% of their time in the field with engineering clients, the consultants must carry their computers with them to make appointments for service calls, produce reports to send to the main office, schedule travel between client locations, and access e-mail and Web sites. Most computers have Netscape Navigator 4.76 installed on them. Judy is considering upgrading to a newer version of Netscape. However, before she upgrades the computers, Judy asks you to learn more about a new browser, Opera, which is highly regarded by many of its users. She wants you to find some information about Opera and print a few pages of product information and ratings, if available, so she can investigate it further. To help Judy evaluate Opera, you'll complete the following steps.

1. Start your Web browser, open the Student Online Companion page at www.course.com/newperspectives/internet3, click the hyperlink for your book, click the Tutorial 6 link, and then click the Case Problems link. Click the ZDNet link for Case Problem 5 and wait while the browser loads the page.

2. Use the search text box on the ZDNet home page using the term "Opera." Click the link to Reviews, and then click the link to Opera. Print the page that opens (the Opera product review).

3. Return to the Student Online Companion page for Tutorial 6, and then click the PC World link and wait while the browser opens the page.

4. Use the search text box to search using the term "Opera," and then sort the results page with the most recent matches listed first. Locate and click a link that provides a product review of Opera, and then print the page that opens.

5. Return to the Student Online Companion page for Tutorial 6, and then click the DOWNLOAD.COM link and wait while the browser loads the page.

6. Search for an Opera product page, and then open and print it.

7. On the page that opens, locate and then click the link to the company's Web site (Opera Software). When the Opera Software home page opens, click the Buy Opera link and then print the page that describes the pricing options for Opera.

8. Click the Windows link at the top of the page, click the Features link to open a page listing the Opera browser's features, and then print this page.

9. Close your browser, and if necessary, log off your Internet connection.

Explore   10. In a memo addressed to Judy, make a recommendation about Opera. In your memo, be sure to include data from the research you conducted on the Web sites you visited. Make your recommendation based on a comparison of the features in your current Web browser and those you learned about using the Opera Software Web site. Make sure that you support your recommendation with facts, and consider ease of use, file sizes, download times, and cost.

QUICK CHECK ANSWERS

Session 6.1

1. False
2. their e-mail addresses
3. False
4. directories (folders) and files
5. ftp://ftp.zdnet.com
6. PowerPoint
7. file compression

Session 6.2

1. Freeware is free software that has no restrictions on its use or guarantees for its performance; shareware is free or for-fee software that usually is operable for a limited time period; limited edition software is a limited version of a complete program that either functions for a limited time or includes only core features.
2. scan it for viruses
3. Portable Document Format (PDF)
4. file compression program
5. A hop is a connection between two computers.
6. tracert

Session 6.3

1. A company can reduce its network activity by encouraging its employees to use an online storage provider instead of e-mail attachments to transport large files. A company can increase its productivity by offering online storage for traveling employees or those employees in satellite offices.
2. True
3. True
4. The user must register with Yahoo! and obtain a Yahoo! ID.
5. My Documents
6. False
7. False

managing, WEB 2.48
saving to disk, WEB 2.38
saving to folder, WEB 2.46–2.47
using, WEB 2.13, WEB 2.14
A feature of Navigator that allows you to save the URL of a specific page so you can return to it.

Bookmarks button, WEB 2.44

Bookmarks window, examining bookmark hierarchy in, WEB 2.45

Boole, George, WEB 4.24

Boolean algebra, WEB 4.24
A branch of mathematics and logic in which all values are reduced to one of two values—in most practical applications of Boolean algebra, these two values are true and false.

Boolean operators, WEB 4.23–4.25, WEB 4.26, WEB 4.30
In Boolean algebra, operators that specify the logical relationship between the elements they join. Also known as logical operators.

bots, WEB 4.07. *See also* **robots**

bugs, WEB 6.24
Errors found in software that can cause a program to halt, misbehave, or damage the user's computer.

Bush, Vannevar, WEB 1.15

businesses
.com domain identifier, 2.07, WEB 5.20
finding on the Web, WEB 5.16–5.17

byte, WEB 2.06

C

cable modems
connecting to Internet with, WEB 1.23
defined, WEB 1.23
Converts a computer's digital signals into analog signals that are similar to television transmission signals. The converted signals travel to and from the user's cable company, which maintains a connection to the Internet.

cable television, connecting to the Internet with, WEB 1.20, WEB 1.23

cables, connecting computers to Internet with, WEB 1.06–1.07

cache folder, WEB 2.13

Calliau, Robert, WEB 1.15, WEB 1.16

carbon copies (Cc)
e-mail responses and, WEB 3.13
in Hotmail, WEB 3.58
in Netscape Mail, WEB 3.39
in Outlook Express, WEB 3.18–3.20
A copy of an e-mail message sent to other people in addition to the primary recipient.

carbon copy (Cc) line, WEB 3.03, WEB 3.05, WEB 3.43

cards, adding to Address Book, in Netscape Mail, WEB 3.48–3.50

case-sensitivity, of URLs, WEB 2.08

Category 1 cable, WEB 1.06
A type of twisted-pair cable that telephone companies have used for years to carry voice signals. Category 1 cable is inexpensive and easy to install but transmits information much more slowly than other types of cable.

Category 5 (Cat-5) cable, WEB 1.06
A type of twisted-pair cable developed specifically for carrying data signals rather than voice signals. Category 5 cable is easy to install and carries signals between 10 and 100 times faster than coaxial cable.

CBS, WEB 5.06

cd *directory* **command, WEB 6.06**

CD writers (CD burners), WEB 5.34

Cerf, Vincent, WEB 1.09

CERN, WEB 1.15

chat, in Hotmail, WEB 3.57

chevron symbols ( ), WEB 5.28

circuit switching, WEB 1.08
A centrally controlled, single-connection method for sending information over a network.

circuits, WEB 1.08

citations, for Web resources, WEB 5.27–5.28

cities
finding information on, WEB 5.12, WEB 5.13–5.15
finding maps of, WEB 5.12–5.14

finding weather forecasts for, WEB 5.09–5.12

CitySearch, WEB 5.14–5.15

Clark, James, WEB 1.16

clearinghouses, WEB 4.20
A Web site that contains a list of hyperlinks to other Web pages that contain information about a particular topic or group of topics and often includes summaries or reviews of the Web pages listed. Also known as a guide, resource list, virtual library, or Web bibliography.

clients, WEB 1.05
Web, WEB 2.02
A computer that is connected to another, usually more powerful, computer called a server. The client computer can use the server computer's resources, such as printers, files, or programs. This way of connecting computers is called a client/server network.

client/server local area networks, WEB 1.05–1.06
A way of connecting multiple computers, called client computers, to a main computer, called a server computer in a limited geographical location, such as a single building. This connection method allows the client computers to share the server computer's resources, such as printers, files, and programs.

client/server structure, WEB 2.02

Clip Art Searcher, WEB 5.31–5.32

Close button, in Web browsers, WEB 2.10

close command, WEB 6.06

CNET, WEB 6.18

CNN, WEB 5.06

coaxial cable, WEB 1.06, WEB 1.07
An insulated copper wire that is encased in a metal shield and then enclosed in plastic insulation. The signal-carrying wire is completely shielded so it resists electrical interference much better than twisted-pair cable does. Coaxial cable also carries signals about 20 times faster than twisted-pair cable, but it is considerably more expensive.

.com domain identifier, 2.07, WEB 5.20

full-privilege FTP, WEB 6.05

The act of logging on to a computer on which you have an account (with a user name and password) and transferring files. Also known as named FTP.

Full Screen, Internet Explorer, WEB 2.18–2.19

full text indexing, WEB 4.10

A method that some search engines use for creating their databases in which the entire content of included Web pages is included in the database's index.

 G

Get Msg button, Netscape Mail, WEB 3.40

GIF files

animated, WEB 5.29, WEB 5.33

.gif extension, WEB 6.12

uses of, WEB 5.29

gigabits per second (Gbps), WEB 1.19

A measure of bandwidth; 1,073,741,824 bits per second (bps).

glossaries, WEB 5.26

Go menu, Netscape Navigator, WEB 2.50

Google

page ranking effects, WEB 4.11

A Web search engine.

government agencies, WEB 5.20

.gov domain identifier, WEB 2.07, WEB 5.20

graphical transfer process indicator, WEB 2.17

Element of the Internet Explorer status bar that indicates how much of a Web page has loaded from the Web server.

graphical user interface (GUI), WEB 1.16, WEB 2.09

A way of presenting program output to users that uses pictures, icons, and other graphical elements instead of just displaying text.

graphic images. *See* **images**

copyright violations, WEB 5.28

formats, WEB 5.29, WEB 5.33

on museum Web sites, WEB 5.30–5.31

searching for, WEB 5.31–5.32

Web site evaluation and, WEB 5.21

Graphics Interchange Format (GIF), WEB 5.29

A file format for graphics images that is widely used on the Internet for storing images that have only a few distinct colors, such as line drawings, cartoons, and simple icons.

group address entries. *See also* **mailing lists**

in Hotmail, WEB 3.69–3.70

in Outlook Express, WEB 3.32–3.33

grouping operators, WEB 4.25. *See also* **precedence operators**

group mailing lists, WEB 3.13. *See also* **mailing lists**

GUI. *See* **graphical user interface (GUI)**

guides, WEB 4.20. *See also* **clearinghouses**

Guides (About.com), WEB 4.33

 H

Help

in Internet Explorer, WEB 2.32–2.33

in Netscape Navigator, WEB 2.57–2.58

help command, WEB 6.06

hexidecimal numbering system, WEB 2.06

hierarchical structures

Bookmarks window, WEB 2.45

of FTP sites, WEB 6.08

The organized, inverted tree containing folders and files on a computer.

History button, Internet Explorer, WEB 2.27

history list, WEB 2.13

in Internet Explorer, WEB 2.27–2.28

in Netscape Navigator, WEB 2.50–2.51

A file in which the Web browser stores the location of each page you visit as you navigate hyperlinks from one Web page to another.

hits, WEB 4.07, WEB 4.19

A Web page that is indexed in a search engine's database and contains text that matches the search expression entered into the search engine. Search engines provide hyperlinks to hits on results pages.

Home button

in Internet Explorer, WEB 2.28

in Netscape Navigator, WEB 2.50–2.51

in Web browsers, WEB 2.11

home directory, of FTP sites, WEB 6.07

home pages. *See also* **start pages**

default

in Internet Explorer, WEB 2.28–2.29

in Netscape Navigator, WEB 2.51–2.53

defined, WEB 2.05

Hotmail, WEB 3.57

use of term, WEB 2.05

The main page that all of the pages on a particular Web site are organized around and to which they link; or the first page that opens when a particular Web browser program is started; or the page that a particular Web browser program loads the first time it is run. Home pages under the second and third definitions also are called start pages.

Home tab, Hotmail, WEB 3.57

hops, WEB 6.35

A connection between two computers on the Internet that measures the number of intermediate computers in the path. If a file travels through 15 computers on its way to your PC, then it has gone through 14 hops.

host names, WEB 3.07

A user-friendly name that uniquely identifies a computer connected to the Internet. You can use it in place of an IP address.

HotBot, WEB 4.24

advanced searches, WEB 4.28–4.30, WEB 5.04

conducting searches on, WEB 4.08–4.09

date range restrictions, WEB 5.03, WEB 5.05–5.06

TASK	PAGE #	RECOMMENDED METHOD	WHERE USED
HOTMAIL TASKS			
Address book, save to	WEB 3.67	See Reference Window: Adding a Contact to the Hotmail Address Book	Hotmail
Attached file, save	WEB 3.61	See Reference Window: Viewing and Saving an Attached File in Hotmail	Hotmail
Attached file, view	WEB 3.61	See Reference Window: Viewing and Saving an Attached File in Hotmail	Hotmail
Contact, add to address book	WEB 3.67	See Reference Window: Adding a Contact to the Hotmail Address Book	Hotmail
File, attach	WEB 3.59	Click the Add/Edit Attachments button, locate the file, click Attach	Hotmail
Group of contacts, add to address book	WEB 3.69	See Reference Window: Adding a Group to the Hotmail Address Book	Hotmail
Hotmail, start	WEB 3.53	Go to the MSN.com home page, click the Hotmail link, log into your account	
Hotmail account, set up	WEB 3.52	Start your browser, connect to the Internet, go to MSN.com home page, click the Hotmail link, click the Sign Up link	Hotmail
Mail, compose	WEB 3.58	Open the Hotmail Home page, log into your account, click the Compose tab	Hotmail
Mail, delete	WEB 3.66	See Reference Window: Deleting an E-Mail Message Using Hotmail	Hotmail
Mail, delete permanently	WEB 3.66	Open the Trash Can folder, click the Empty Folder button, click OK	Hotmail
Mail, forward	WEB 3.64	See Reference Window: Forwarding an E-Mail Message Using Hotmail	Hotmail
Mail, print	WEB 3.65	Select the message, click the Printer Friendly Version link, click the Print button	Hotmail
Mail, read	WEB 3.60	Log into your Hotmail account, click the Inbox tab	Hotmail
Mail, receive	WEB 3.60	See Reference Window: Using Hotmail to Receive Messages	Hotmail
Mail, reply to all recipients	WEB 3.63	See Reference Window: Replying to a Message Using Hotmail	Hotmail
Mail, reply to sender	WEB 3.63	See Reference Window: Replying to a Message Using Hotmail	Hotmail
Mail, send	WEB 3.58	See Reference Window: Sending a Message Using Hotmail	Hotmail

TASK	PAGE #	RECOMMENDED METHOD	WHERE USED
Mail, spell check	WEB 3.59	Click the Tools list arrow, click Spell Check	Hotmail
Mail folder, create	WEB 3.64	Click the Home tab, click the View All Folders link in the Message Summary pane, click the Create New button, type the name of the folder, click OK	Hotmail
Mail folder, delete	WEB 3.67	See Reference Window: Deleting a Hotmail Folder	Hotmail

MICROSOFT INTERNET EXPLORER TASKS

TASK	PAGE #	RECOMMENDED METHOD	WHERE USED
Address book, open	WEB 3.30	Click the Address button	Outlook Express
Attached file, save	WEB 3.22	See Reference Window: Viewing and Saving an Attached File in Outlook Express	Outlook Express
Attached file, view	WEB 3.22	See Reference Window: Viewing and Saving an Attached File in Outlook Express	Outlook Express
Contact, add to address book	WEB 3.30	See Reference Window: Adding a Contact to the Outlook Express Address Book	Outlook Express
Group of contacts, add to address book	WEB 3.32	See Reference Window: Adding a Group of Contacts to the Address Book	Outlook Express
Favorite, move to a new folder	WEB 2.24	See Reference Window: Moving an Existing Favorite into a New Folder	Internet Explorer
Favorites bar, open	WEB 2.21	Click the Favorites button	Internet Explorer
Favorites folder, create	WEB 2.22	See Reference Window: Creating a New Favorites Folder	Internet Explorer
File, attach in New Message window	WEB 3.18	Click the Attach button, locate the file, click Attach	Outlook Express
Full Screen, change to	WEB 2.19	Click View, click Full Screen	Internet Explorer
Help, get	WEB 2.32	See Reference Window: Opening Internet Explorer Help	Internet Explorer
History list, open	WEB 2.28	Click the History button	Internet Explorer
Home page, change default	WEB 2.28	See Reference Window: Changing the Default Home Page in Internet Explorer	Internet Explorer
Home page, return to	WEB 2.11	Click the Home button	Internet Explorer
Internet Explorer, close	WEB 2.10	Click the Close button	Internet Explorer, Outlook Express
Internet Explorer, start	WEB 2.16	Click the Start button, point to Programs, point to Internet Explorer, click Internet Explorer	
Internet Explorer window, maximize	WEB 2.10	Click the Maximize button	Internet Explorer, Outlook Express

TASK	PAGE #	RECOMMENDED METHOD	WHERE USED
Internet Explorer window, minimize	WEB 2.06	Click the Minimize button	Internet Explorer, Outlook Express
Internet Explorer window, restore maximized	WEB 2.10	Click the Restore button	Internet Explorer, Outlook Express
Mail, compose	WEB 3.18	Click the Create Mail button	Outlook Express
Mail, delete	WEB 3.29	See Reference Window: Deleting an E-Mail Message or a Folder in Outlook Express	Outlook Express
Mail, delete permanently	WEB 3.29	Open Deleted Items folder, click the message summary of the message to delete, click the Delete button, click the Yes button	Outlook Express
Mail, forward	WEB 3.26	See Reference Window: Forwarding an E-Mail Message Using Outlook Express	Outlook Express
Mail, move to another folder	WEB 3.27	Drag the message from the message list to a folder in the Folders pane	Outlook Express
Mail, print	WEB 3.28	Click the message summary, click the Print button, click OK	Outlook Express
Mail, read	WEB 3.21	Click the message summary	Outlook Express
Mail, receive	WEB 3.21	Click the Send/Recv button	Outlook Express
Mail, reply to	WEB 3.25	See Reference Window: Replying to a Message Using Outlook Express	Outlook Express
Mail, send	WEB 3.18	See Reference Window: Sending a Message Using Outlook Express	Outlook Express
Mail, send and receive	WEB 3.20	Click the Send/Recv button	Outlook Express
Mail, spell check in New Message window	WEB 3.20	Click the Spelling button	Outlook Express
Mail account, set up	WEB 3.16	Click Tools, click Accounts, click the Mail tab, click the Add button, click Mail, follow steps in the Internet Connection Wizard	Outlook Express
Mail folder, create	WEB 3.27	Right-click the Inbox folder, click New Folder, type the name of the folder, click OK	Outlook Express
Mail folder, delete	WEB 3.29	See Reference Window: Deleting an E-Mail Message or a Folder in Outlook Express	Outlook Express
Outlook Express, start	WEB 3.16	Click the Start button, point to Programs, click Outlook Express	
Start page, return to	WEB 2.28	Click the Home button	Internet Explorer
Toolbar, hide or show	WEB 2.19	See Reference Window: Hiding and Restoring the Toolbars in Internet Explorer	Internet Explorer

TASK	PAGE #	RECOMMENDED METHOD	WHERE USED
URL, enter and go to	WEB 2.20	See Reference Window: Entering a URL in the Address Bar	Internet Explorer
Web page, change print settings	WEB 2.30	Click File, click Page Setup	Internet Explorer
Web page, move forward to previous in history list	WEB 2.13	Click the Forward button	Internet Explorer
Web page, refresh	WEB 2.13	Click the Refresh button	Internet Explorer
Web page, return to previous in history list	WEB 2.13	Click the Back button	Internet Explorer
Web page, print	WEB 2.30	See Reference Window: Printing the Current Web Page	Internet Explorer
Web page, save to disk	WEB 2.34	See Reference Window: Saving a Web Page to a Disk	Internet Explorer
Web page, stop loading	WEB 2.13	Click the Stop button	Internet Explorer
Web page graphic, save	WEB 2.38	See Reference Window: Saving an Image from a Web Page to a Disk	Internet Explorer
Web page text, save	WEB 2.35	See Reference Window: Copying Text from a Web Page to a WordPad Document	Internet Explorer
Web pages, move between using hyperlinks and the mouse	WEB 2.25	See Reference Window: Navigating Between Web Pages Using Hyperlinks and the Mouse	Internet Explorer

NETSCAPE NAVIGATOR TASKS

TASK	PAGE #	RECOMMENDED METHOD	WHERE USED
Attached file, save	WEB 3.41	See Reference Window: Viewing and Saving an Attached File Using Mail	Mail
Attached file, view	WEB 3.41	See Reference Window: Viewing and Saving an Attached File Using Mail	Mail
Bookmark, create	WEB 2.46	Click Bookmarks, click File Bookmark, type a name for the bookmark, click OK	Navigator
Bookmark, save in a folder	WEB 2.46	See Reference Window, Saving a Bookmark in a Bookmarks Folder	Navigator
Bookmark file, save to a disk	WEB 2.47	See Reference Window: Saving a Bookmark to a Disk	Navigator
Bookmark folder, create	WEB 2.45	See Reference Window: Creating a Bookmarks Folder	Navigator
Bookmarks window, open	WEB 2.46	Click the Bookmarks button, click Manage Bookmarks	Navigator
Cookies, manage	WEB 2.55	See Reference Window: Managing Cookies with the Navigator Cookie Manager	Navigator

TASK REFERENCE

TASK	PAGE #	RECOMMENDED METHOD	WHERE USED
File, attach to message	WEB 3.38	Click the Attach button, click File, locate the file, click Open	Mail
Help, get	WEB 2.57	See Reference Window: Opening Navigator Help	Navigator
History list, open	WEB 2.51	Click Tasks, click Tools, click History	Navigator
Home page, change default	WEB 2.52	See Reference Window: Changing the Default Home Page in Netscape	Navigator
Home page, return to	WEB 2.11	Click the Home button	Navigator
Mail, compose	WEB 3.38	Click the New Msg button	Mail
Mail, delete	WEB 3.47	See Reference Window: Deleting an E-Mail Message or a Folder Using Mail	Mail
Mail, delete permanently	WEB 3.47	Right-click the Trash folder in the Mail Folders pane, click Empty Trash Can	Mail
Mail, forward	WEB 3.45	See Reference Window: Forwarding an E-Mail Message Using Mail	Mail
Mail, print	WEB 3.46	Select the message, click the Print button, click OK	Mail
Mail, read	WEB 3.40	Click the Inbox folder, click the message in the message list	Mail
Mail, receive messages	WEB 3.40	See Reference Window: Using Mail to Receive Messages	Mail
Mail, reply to all recipients	WEB 3.44	See Reference Window: Replying to a Message Using Mail	Mail
Mail, reply to sender	WEB 3.44	See Reference Window: Replying to a Message Using Mail	Mail
Mail, send	WEB 3.38	See Reference Window: Sending a Message Using Mail	Mail
Mail, spell check	WEB 3.39	Click the Spell button	Mail
Mail, start	WEB 3.36	Click the Start button, point to Programs, point to Netscape 6, click Mail	
Mail account, change settings	WEB 3.36	Click Edit, click Mail & Newsgroup Account Settings	Mail
Mail account, set up	WEB 3.36	Click Edit, click Mail & Newsgroup Account Settings, click Local Folders, click the New Account button, complete Account Wizard	Mail
Mail Address Book, add a card	WEB 3.48	See Reference Window: Adding a Card to the Mail Address Book	Mail
Mail folder, create	WEB 3.45	Right-click Inbox in the Mail Folders pane, click New Folder, type the name of the folder, click OK	Mail

TASK	PAGE #	RECOMMENDED METHOD	WHERE USED
Mail folder, delete	WEB 3.47	See Reference Window: Deleting an E-Mail Message or a Folder Using Mail	Mail
Mailing list, create	WEB 3.50	See Reference Window: Creating a Mailing List In Netscape Mail	Mail
Navigator, close	WEB 2.10	Click the Close button	Navigator
Navigator, start	WEB 2.39	Click the Start button, point to Programs, point to Netscape Navigator (or Netscape), click Netscape 6	
Navigator window, maximize	WEB 2.10	Click the Maximize button	Navigator
Navigator window, minimize	WEB 2.10	Click the Minimize button	Navigator
Navigator window, restore maximized	WEB 2.10	Click the Restore button	Navigator
Netscape Netcenter, open	WEB 2.44	Click the My Netscape button on the Personal toolbar	Navigator
Start page, return to	WEB 2.11	Click the Home button	Navigator
Toolbar, hide	WEB 2.41	See Reference Window: Hiding or Showing a Toolbar in Navigator	Navigator
Toolbar, show	WEB 2.41	See Reference Window: Hiding or Showing a Toolbar in Navigator	Navigator
URL, enter and go to	WEB 2.42	See Reference Window: Entering a URL in the Location Bar	Navigator
Web page, move forward to previous in history list	WEB 2.13	Click the Forward button	Navigator
Web page, print	WEB 2.53	See Reference Window: Printing the Current Web Page	Navigator
Web page, reload	WEB 2.13	Click the Reload button	Navigator
Web page, return to previous in history list	WEB 2.59	Click the Back button	Navigator
Web page, save to disk	WEB 2.35	See Reference Window: Saving a Web Page to a Disk	Navigator
Web page, stop loading	WEB 2.13	Click the Stop button	Navigator
Web page graphic, save	WEB 2.62	See Reference Window: Saving an Image from a Web Page to a Disk	Navigator
Web pages, move between using hyperlinks and the mouse	WEB 2.48	See Reference Window: Navigating Between Web Pages Using Hyperlinks and the Mouse	Navigator

TASK REFERENCE

TASK	PAGE #	RECOMMENDED METHOD	WHERE USED
Web page text, save	WEB 2.60	See Reference Window: Copying Text from a Web Page to a WordPad Document	Navigator

FTP AND WINDOWS TASKS

TASK	PAGE #	RECOMMENDED METHOD	WHERE USED
Anonymous login using command-line FTP	WEB 6.04	Type anonymous, press Enter	FTP
Download file using command-line FTP	WEB 6.06	See Reference Window: Downloading a File Using Command-Line FTP	FTP
Downloading a file	WEB 6.10	See Reference Window: Downloading a File Using an FTP Client Program"	FTP
End session using command-line FTP	WEB 6.06	Type quit, press Enter	FTP
Internet route, trace	WEB 6.36	Click the Start button, click Run, type command, click OK, type the URL to trace	Windows
List files and folders using command-line FTP	WEB 6.06	Type ls or type dir, press Enter	FTP
Linked message, send	WEB 6.51	See Reference Window: Sending an E-mail Message Linked to a File in Briefcase	Yahoo!
Open a connection using command-line FTP	WEB 6.06	Type open followed by connection URL, press Enter	FTP
Uploading a file	WEB 6.14	See Reference Window: Uploading a File Using FTP	FTP
Yahoo! Briefcase, delete file from	WEB 6.54	See Reference Window: Deleting a File from Briefcase	Yahoo!
Yahoo! Briefcase, upload a file to	WEB 6.47	See Reference Window: Uploading a File to Yahoo! Briefcase	Yahoo!

The Internet Level I File Finder

Tutorial	Location in Tutorial	Name and Location of Data File	Files the Student Creates from Scratch
Tutorial 1		*There are no Data Files for this tutorial.*	
Tutorial 2			
	Session 2.1		
	Session 2.2		Wind Quintet Information\MiamiWind Quintet.htm Tutorial.02\WindQuintetBookmarks.html Tutorial.02\GRAM-Address.txt Tutorial.02\GRAM-Map.jpg
	Session 2.3		Wind Quintet Information\MiamiWind Quintet.htm Tutorial.02\MiamiWindQuintet.htm Tutorial.02\GRAM-Address.txt Tutorial.02\GRAM-Map.jpg
	Review Assignments		
	Case Problem 1		
	Case Problem 2		
	Case Problem 3		
	Case Problem 4		
	Case Problem 5		
Tutorial 3			
	Session 3.1		
	Session 3.2	Tutorial.03\Physicals.wri	
	Session 3.3	Tutorial.03\Physicals.wri	
	Session 3.4	Tutorial.03\Physicals.wri	
	Review Assignments	Tutorial.03\KAir.gif	
	Case Problem 1		Tutorial.03\signature.txt (if using Netscape Mail)
	Case Problem 2		Tutorial.03\Testing new BECO e-mail system.html (if using Outlook Express or Netscape Mail)
	Case Problem 3	Tutorial.03\Recycle.wri	Tutorial.03\signature.txt (if using Netscape Mail)
	Case Problem 4		
	Case Problem 5		Tutorial.03\Survey.* Tutorial.03\Completed Survey.*

*The file extension will reflect the default file extension of the word processor used.

The Internet Level II File Finder

Tutorial	Location in Tutorial	Name and Location of Data File	Files the Student Creates from Scratch
Tutorial 4		*There are no Data Files for Tutorial 4.*	
Tutorial 5		*There are no Data Files for Tutorial 5.*	

The Internet Level II File Finder

Tutorial	Location in Tutorial	Name and Location of Data File	Files the Student Creates from Scratch
Tutorial 6			

Note: Due to large file sizes, students must download files marked with an asterisk to a hard drive, Zip disk, or network drive. Downloaded file sizes and filenames are subject to change.

	Session 6.1		
	Session 6.2		Tutorial.06\ws_ftple.exe *ar500enu.exe *winzip80.exe
	Session 6.3	Tutorial.06\Memorandum.doc	Tutorial.06\Memorandum1.doc
	Review Assignments		Tutorial.06\eul3manl.pdf
	Case Problem 1		*Students will download a ping program of their choice to the Tutorial.06 folder or hard drive (depending on file size) if they have permission to do so.
	Case Problem 2		*Students will download a bookmark converter program of their choice to the Tutorial.06 folder or hard drive (depending on file size) if they have permission to do so.
	Case Problem 3		Tutorial.06\lusetup.txt
	Case Problem 4		Tutorial.06\f940.pdf Tutorial.06\f940ez.pdf Tutorial.06\f940pr.pdf
	Case Problem 5		